NUCLEAR STRATEGY
and
NATIONAL STYLE

Colin S. Gray

Hamilton Press
Abt Books

Hamilton Press
4720 Boston Way
Lanham, MD 20706

3 Henrietta Street
London WC2E 8LU England

Library of Congress Cataloging in Publication Data

Gray, Colin S.
   Nuclear strategy and national style.

   Bibliography: p.
   Includes index.
   1. Nuclear warfare.   2. United States—Military
policy.   3. Soviet Union—Military policy.   4. Nuclear
arms control.   I. Title.
U263.G73   1986   355'.0217   86-4665
ISBN 0-8191-5333-8 (alk. paper)
ISBN 0-8191-5334-6 (pbk. : alk. paper)

All Hamilton Press books are produced on acid-free
paper which exceeds the minimum standards set by the National
Historical Publications and Records Commission.

For my friends
and colleagues at the
National Institute for Public Policy

Contents

Acknowledgments

This book has been many years in the writing and rewriting. I would like to thank the following publishers for granting me permission to use in this book much revised versions of material that first appeared under their imprints:

The American Academy of Arts and Sciences for allowing me to use my article, "Strategic Stability Reconsidered," *Daedalus* 109, no. 4 (Fall 1980): 135-54; the MIT Press for "National Style in Strategy: The American Example," *International Security* 6, no. 2(Fall 1981): 21-47; the U.S. Army Command and General Staff College for "Reflections on Empire: The Soviet Connection," *Military Review* 62, no. 1(January 1982): 2-13; and the Foreign Policy Research Institute for *Nuclear Strategy and Strategic Planning*, Philadelphia Policy Papers (Philadelphia: Foreign Policy Research Institute, 1984).

Preface

This book explores the merit in the propositions that there are distinctive U.S. and Soviet national styles in nuclear strategy, that those styles are comprehensible on the basis of historical and anthropological understanding, and that they may interact in actual armed conflict with possibly fatal consequences for the United States.

The centerpiece of the book is a critical analysis in chapter 9 of five classes of options for U.S. nuclear posture and doctrine: (1) mutual assured vulnerability; (2) mutual assured vulnerability with (targeting) flexibility; (3) counterforce and countercontrol preeminence; (4) damage limitation for deterrence and coercion; and (5) damage limitation with defense dominant. The pros and cons of each class of options are analyzed in detail. I favor U.S. adoption of a strategic nuclear policy that is genuinely balanced between offensive and defensive capabilities. In short, I prefer option 4—damage limitation for deterrence and coercion.

The strongest single policy argument in this book is that U.S. strategic nuclear planning should be as attentive to the protection of the U.S. homeland as it is to the potential destruction of Soviet assets.

I believe that U.S. incomprehension of its own and Soviet strategic culture and national style has misled U.S. policymakers and, as a consequence, has led to the making of poor policy. This book documents how the United States developed a strategic force posture, endorsed strategic doctrinal concepts, and pursued strategic arms control agreements vis-à-vis a substantially fictional Soviet Union. It is demonstrated here how the Soviet Union, for reasons of its own, did not (and does not) share the U.S. approach to deterrence; has no vision of strategic stability that is even remotely congruent with that dominant in the United States; is dismissive of our traditional, doctrinally authoritative theory of escalation control and crisis management; and views arms control negotiations as an instrument for the waging of political struggle. These claims are debated and supported in detail.

Contrary to a widespread general assumption, the permanent advent of nuclear weapons has *not* effected a revolution in statecraft. Commentators on statecraft from Periclean Athens, Renaissance Italy, or "Concert

Europe" would have no difficulty comprehending statecraft today. The principal historical discontinuity of recent times has been not technological, but political, and it dates from 1917 rather than from 1945. Since that time, the USSR has rejected the legitimacy of the imperia of the other major states. This is a revolutionary change.

This book offers a detailed contrasting analysis of Soviet and U.S. national styles in nuclear strategy. Although the major part of this analysis focuses on the roots and the detail of discernible nuclear policy thinking in the two superpowers, one political fact dominates the enterprise: the USSR, by self-definition, is a true revolutionary actor in world politics (no matter how conservative it may often appear in its diplomatic activity). Pending fundamental political change at home, the USSR must be viewed as a permanent adversary. For the calculable future, the need to compete with the USSR is permanent. However, the cumulative improvement on the Soviet end of "the correlation of forces" has changed greatly—to the U.S. disadvantage—the basis on which foreign policy engagement can be designed. The central problem for the United States is not so much to understand Soviet power as to contain it. Although Soviet leaders are acknowledged to be cautious and pragmatic (and not "gangsters in a hurry" à la the Third Reich), Russian history and culture is found to weigh heavily in the Soviet worldview. Notwithstanding propagandistic denunciation of the possibility of the achievement of strategic superiority, the Soviet Union has an intensely traditional professional-military view of war, including nuclear war.[1] The Soviet Union has waged war on its own territory (a critical distinction vis-à-vis the United States) against a first-class adversary within living memory—and it very nearly lost.[2] This recent experience, added to the continental land-power tradition, produces a genuine seriousness about the actual conduct of war that is notably lacking in an insular power such as the United States. The Soviet attitude toward military power stems from Russian tradition combined with a creed that has universal pretensions and that is the very rationale for the legitimacy of Soviet rule in the Great Russian empire that is the USSR. Above all, the Soviet Union should be thought of as an insecure empire that defines its security in terms of the insecurity of others.[3] The conservative Western view of Soviet strategic doctrine, stressing its war-waging/war-survival aspects, is now, belatedly, the conventional wisdom.

U.S. thinking on nuclear-weapons policy is analyzed and contrasted with Soviet thinking (and actions) systematically, in chapters that address major concepts in Western nuclear-doctrinal thought (deterrence, strategic stability, escalation control and crisis management, arms competition and arms control, and strategic superiority). Because of its traditional geostrategic insularity and the military history that has flowed therefrom, the United States is not well equipped culturally to cope with the probable damage that would be suffered in a nuclear war, even one of relatively modest dimensions.

U.S. policymaking and influencing elites tend to be dominated by skill groups (lawyers/elected politicians) whose real expertise, the manipulation of U.S. domestic democratic procedures, does not equip them well to deal appropriately with the survivors of Stalin's Great Purge and their successors.

Traditionally, Americans have tended to believe:

- that "good" causes triumph;

- that the United States can succeed in anything it pursues energetically;

- that Americans cannot fail (as God's chosen people);

- that the United States can outproduce any enemy in the material needed for victory.

The world of the 1980s is more complex than this. This book explores the reasons behind the progressive diminution in U.S. self-confidence with respect to nuclear strategy in the 1960s and 1970s. The following American beliefs were important considerations:

- that nuclear war cannot be "won";

- that other cultures will soon come to share U.S. ideas;

- that strategic defenses are likely to be not merely ineffective, but also dangerous;
- that Soviet leaders can be educated into more constructive modes of thought and policy;

- that the U.S. defense establishment is as much the enemy as the Soviet defense establishment;

- that, for structural-societal reasons, the United States is, and will remain, superior in defense ideas and in defense technology.

This analysis finds that much of the content of our received wisdom on deterrence, stability, escalation, arms control, and so forth, reflects little more than the character (strengths and weaknesses) of our own culture. To take but one critical example, Western officials and theorists envisage "a process of escalation" (itself a highly culture-bound Western concept) essentially as a process of political "bargaining."[4] On the evidence of culture and style, the Soviets would most likely approach nuclear war simply as *war*—not as a bargaining process.

In areas of central importance to Western policy thinking, the United States has been driven by a vision of systemic stability, even meta-stability, which has not been shared by the Soviet adversary. Stated directly,

U.S. strategic doctrine and policy have been wrong, or at best dangerously imprudent, with reference to provisions for deterrent adequacy, stability, escalation control, and management of the strategic arms competition. Among other deficiencies, the bedrock of NATO strategy (as in MC-14/3 of 1967) and of U.S. strategic-warfare thinking—if not necessarily of potential practice—continues to assume a favorable U.S.-Soviet strategic nuclear balance of a kind that has not existed since the early 1970s at the latest.[5]

Most fundamentally of all, for the better part of 20 years (the 1960s and 1970s), the United States neglected to consider the USSR adequately on its own terms. Basically, deterrence is a psychological phenomenon, and deterrent effect must be active in Soviet minds and, no less obviously, according to Soviet criteria. This book stresses the imperative need for U.S. nuclear-weapons policy to be relevant to the Soviet worldview. Strategic-policy truth is not abstract; it is culture-specific—what do Soviet leaders fear? It is judged here that Soviet leaders fear most for the survival of the essential assets of the Soviet state, rather than for the survival of the Soviet citizenry at large.

This book concludes that although the United States must be true to its own unique culture in its defense preparation, many policy errors can be avoided if the cultural-stylistic engines of U.S. and Soviet strategic nuclear preparations are understood on their own terms.

The study of strategic culture and national style is in a rudimentary, or pretheory, stage today. Scholars of strategic behavior know that national style is important, but they are not sure *how* important. Moreover, those of us who have ventured into the relatively uncharted region of cultural and stylistic analysis are aware of the pitfalls to which we may be susceptible. If and when we err, there is no shortage of critics in the "republic of social science" who are ready and able to demonstrate the sins of commission and omission that have been perpetrated. A useful "shot across the bows" of cultural-stylistic analyses of strategic behavior has been fired by Scott Sagan of Harvard University. In the course of reviewing Robert Dallek's book, *The American Style of Foreign Policy: Cultural Politics and Foreign Policy*, Sagan judged:

> A focus on the impact of domestic political culture can be a healthy supplement to more traditional foreign policy analysis. *But only if taken in moderate doses.*[6] (emphasis added)

Further on, having appropriately criticized a particularly unconvincing argument offered by Dallek concerning Lyndon Johnson's policy motives over Vietnam, Sagan fired a full broadside against the perils of cultural-stylistic analysis:

Indeed, this points to a danger in many efforts to explain foreign policy or military strategy through a focus on "national style," psychological processes" or "strategic culture": such explanations often debase political debate. They can easily degenerate into *ad hominem* arguments; one does not have to demonstrate that any particular policy was wrong, only that it stemmed from "irrational causes," "misperceptions," or "cultural biases."[7]

Of more direct relevance to this book, Sagan proceeded to argue:

Analysts of "American strategic culture," for example, often argue that liberal ideology—lingering "Wilsonian" assumptions about foreign affairs—led American nuclear strategists to focus exclusively on deterrence and ignore operational planning for war. Yet, few would disagree that there is a need to plan for what to do if deterrence fails. The previous lack of emphasis on operational plans for war-fighting was not due to cultural biases. Indeed, there is a sound political reason, besides its prime importance as a national goal, for emphasizing deterrence in strategic writing. In a democracy, the making of nuclear operational plans are often easier done than said: excessive rhetoric about war-fighting can frighten the public as much as a potential adversary.[8]

Although he did not say so explicitly, there is a very distinct possibility that Sagan had me in mind in his criticism. An earlier version of chapter 2 of this book was published in *International Security* in the fall of 1981.[9] The major flaw in Sagan's argument is that the "sound political reason . . . for emphasizing deterrence in strategic writing"—the fears of the general public—lends itself to explanation in terms of culture and style. Sagan's argument, if extended very far, could altogether rule out consideration of culture and its derivative, style. On his own admission, Sagan does not wish to do that. Plainly, theories of strategic behavior that have the concepts of culture and style as their centerpieces have an explanatory power that is limited. Strategic culture and style can be misapplied so as to explain, even rationalize, anything and everything. The theory becomes tautological, and in seeking to explain everything, in fact it explains nothing.

This book rests on the premise that culture and style are useful keys for helping to improve our understanding of why particular security communities behave as they do. Moreover, it is claimed that these concepts have been unduly neglected by scholars and policymakers over the past several decades. I do not intend to suggest that national style should be treated as the monocausal explanation for strategic behavior, nor that better understanding of it, alone, would allow U.S. policymakers to move out boldly and with confidence to resolve their strategy dilemmas.

The origins of this book lie in a very long-standing conviction that the perspectives of history and cultural anthropology, are notably lacking in contemporary strategic studies. The influence of these "skill biases" on my part was heightened by the evidence that I saw, throughout the 1970s, of U.S. strategic policy, in all its aspects, addressing a substantially imaginary Soviet adversary. In an article published in 1979, I wrote, perhaps too generously:

> Most American strategic thinkers have always *known* that there was a uniquely "Soviet way" in military affairs, but somehow that realization was never translated from insight into constituting a serious and enduring factor influencing analysis, policy recommendation, and war planning.[10]

My intellectual debts are diffuse, but I would mention in particular my late colleague Herman Kahn, whose sensitivity to the cultural roots of strategic behavior was second to none. In addition, the writings of Ken Booth, Bernard Brodie, Fritz Ermath, Benjamin Lambeth, Richard Pipes, and Jack Snyder have played their several parts in encouraging me to persist to book length with a study of nuclear strategy and national style. Also, I am very grateful to Don Marshall, who was directly instrumental in launching the research that became a book, and to Clark Abt, whose belief in the manuscript proved to be all-important.

Michael Ennis of the National Institute for Public Policy merits special notice for his meticulous efforts on the bibliography. Also, I wish to thank my cheerful and hard-working typists at the National Institute—Beth Miller, Sue Munn, Candace Dickerson, and Diana Bennett—who triumphed over what amounted to a labor of Hercules. The burden of final proofreading was incurred cheerfully by my wife, Valerie, who now knows far more than she wants to about nuclear strategy. I am deeply grateful to her for her support during the years that this book was in the making.

Colin S. Gray

NOTES

1. This judgment is offered against the background of the ongoing debate among Western Soviet-watchers concerning what the Soviets (which Soviets?) *really* think about the use of nuclear force as an instrument of policy. Since the mid-1970s, Soviet political and military spokesmen at the highest levels have denied that nuclear war could be won or that strategic nuclear superiority is attainable or meaningful. However, declarations comprise only one part of the "policy triad"; the other elements are capabilities and actions. Particularly thoughtful recent contributions to our understanding of Soviet strategic policy are Jonathan S. Lockwood, *The Soviet View of U.S. Strategic Doctrine: Implications for Decision Making* (New Brunswick, N.J.: Transaction, 1983); Joseph D. Douglass, Jr., "What Happens If Deterrence Fails?" *Defense Science 2001+* 2, no. 5(October 1983):

29-43; and William E. Odom, "The Soviet Approach to Nuclear Weapons: A Historical Review," *Annals* 469 (September 1983): 117-35.

2.   Just how nearly the Soviet Union came to losing has been documented superbly in John Erickson, *The Road to Stalingrad* (Boulder, Colo.: Westview Press 1983; first pub. 1975).

3.   A provocative treatment of Soviet statecraft in the context of imperial behavior is Edward N. Luttwak, *The Grand Strategy of the Soviet Union* (London: Weidenfeld and Nicolson, 1983).

4.   This theme is assailed very effectively in Stephen Peter Rosen, "Vietnam and the American Theory of Limited War," *International Security* 7, no. 2(Fall 1982): 83-113.

5.   Notwithstanding the highly questionable nature of his preferred solution (a very heavy conventional emphasis), former Secretary of Defense Robert S. McNamara has outlined with brutal clarity some of the strategic problems that face the United States and NATO in "The Military Role of Nuclear Weapons: Perceptions and Misperceptions," *Foreign Affairs* 62, no. 1(Fall 1983): 59-80.

6.   Scott Sagan, "Review of Robert Dallek, *The American Style of Foreign Policy: Cultural Politics and Foreign Affairs*," *Survival* 25, no. 4(July–August 1983): 191.

7.   Ibid., p. 192.

8.   Ibid.

9.   Colin S. Gray, "National Style in Strategy: The American Example," *International Security* 6, no. 2(Fall 1981): 21-47.

10.   Colin S. Gray, "Nuclear Strategy: The Case for a Theory of Victory," *International Security* 4, no. 1(Summer 1979): 60, n. 13.

CHAPTER 1

Nuclear Weapons and World Politics

NUCLEAR POLICY TODAY

It is almost a cliché to claim that this is a period of transition. Every period is one of transition: today always hovers uncomfortably between yesterday (history) and tomorrow (the future—in which hopes and dreams may be assumed to be made manifest). However, with respect to strategic policy at least, today happens to have an unusually strong claim to be a period of transition. The early 1980s have seen the consolidation of an evolution of strategic policy toward what is widely termed a war-fighting theory of deterrence. The Reagan administration's issuance of the policy guidance document NSDD-13 in October 1981 was an endorsement and refinement of the ideas outlined in President Carter's PD-59 of July 1980, while PD-59 plainly was a linear descendent of NSDM-242, signed by President Nixon in January 1974.[1] The shifts of emphasis from NSDM-242 to PD-59 and to NSDD-13 have been important—although it should be noted that these are presidential-level policy guidance documents and that "policy" comprises capabilities and implementing actions as well as declarations, no matter how authoritative the declarations—but the trend has been as unambiguous as the policy motives. The most direct statement of the central theme in recent U.S. strategic policy has appeared in the report written in 1983 by President Reagan's Commission on Strategic Forces (known as the Scowcroft Commission, after its chairman, retired Air Force Lt. General Brent Scowcroft). The Scowcroft Commission report said:

Deterrence is not, and cannot be, bluff. In order for deterrence to be effective we must not merely have weapons, we must be perceived to be able, and prepared, if necessary, to use them effectively against the key elements of Soviet power. Deterrence is not an abstract notion amenable to simple quantification. Still less is it a mirror image of what would deter ourselves. Deterrence is the set of beliefs in the minds of the Soviet leaders, given their own values and attitudes, about our capabilities and our will.[2]

The report also offered the maxim that "deterrence . . . requires military effectiveness."[3]

Before the end of the century, however, the United States may face a true turning point on the road of strategic policy with respect to the possibility that it will shift from the currently authoritative war-fighting theory of deterrence to full endorsement of what would amount to a "classical strategy."[4] The key choice is whether the United States will proceed vigorously to seek to implement President Reagan's Strategic Defense Initiative of March 23, 1983.[5] It is possible, of course, that the 1980s and 1990s will constitute a turning point at which history (in the form of U.S. policy determination) does not turn. (By way of analogy, Russian history from the accession of Czar Alexander II, in 1855, until the eve of World War I saw several potential turning points at which turns were not made.[6])

With respect to both the political setting for and the military factors contributing directly to U.S. nuclear strategy and posture, it is reasonably well understood by opinion on the left, the center, and the right that the strategic ideas, the doctrines, and the postures that were deemed adequate for the 1970s may not serve at all well for the 1980s and beyond.

By the late 1970s, the feeling was widespread that all was not well with U.S. strategic policy. Prominent among the signs of the times was a statement by then Secretary of Defense Harold Brown:

Though we made some significant advances in the 1970s, especially in MIRVed warheads, our investment in strategic programs in that decade was less than one-third of what the Soviets spent on their strategic programs. If we had let that trend continue, we would have faced, by the mid-1980's, at best a perception of inferiority, at worst a real possibility of nuclear coercion.[7]

This statement implied that the danger was real but that appropriate corrective action had been taken. It is useful to augment that August 20, 1980, statement with Dr. Brown's words of January 1980:

Critical turning points in the histories of nations are difficult to recognize at the time. Usually they become clear only in retrospect. Nonetheless, the United States may well be at such a turning point today. We face a decision that we have been deferring for too long; we can defer it no longer. We must decide now whether we intend to remain the strongest nation in the world. The alternative is to let ourselves slip into inferiority.[8]

This was a remarkable admission from an administration that already had held office for three years at the time the statement was issued.

Scarcely less startling than Harold Brown's acknowledgment of the seriousness of U.S. military competitive problems were statements from the heartland of the U.S. arms control community to the very plain effect that all was not well with their cause. For example, Leslie Gelb, one of the principal official architects of SALT II (and the major author of the Protocol to the Salt II Treaty) wrote:

> Arms control has essentially failed. Three decades of U.S.-Soviet negotiations to limit arms competition have done little more than to codify the arms race.[9]

In addition, the director of the Arms Control Association, William Kincade, felt moved to write a careful analysis with the title, "A Farewell to Arms Control?"[10] Similar sentiments abounded among strong proponents of negotiated arms control. For example, Deborah Shapley argued: "Clearly, at many levels, some crisis of arms control is upon us."[11]

Moving from the general to the fairly specific, changing times were well heralded by the national security affairs correspondent of the *New York Times* when he told his readers: "After Almost a Decade, the ABM Dispute Resumes."[12] The ABM is not "just another weapon system." It was, and to some extent remains, a symbolic issue to rival schools of thought on strategy and defense policy. Because of significant evolution in the technologies of both offense and defense, the concept of a strategic stability resting vitally on the mutual vulnerability of superpower societies as the leitmotiv for U.S. defense planning has come increasingly under critical scrutiny.[13] The 1980s and 1990s should see not only the maturing of effective ballistic missile defense technologies for missions short of comprehensive defense of the American people,[14] but also the emergence of the age of "absolute accuracy,"[15] figuratively speaking. Zero circular error probable (CEP) is impractical with all-inertial missile guidance,[16] but for all intents and purposes, one should assume that all fixed facilities of precisely known locations will be fatally vulnerable. Even silo superhardening to a level in the 50,000-100,000 psi range would be vulnerable to maneuvering reentry vehicles (MARVs) that employ terminal homing technologies for guidance.[17]

This book attempts a near zero-base critical review both of the theories that have underpinned U.S. nuclear weapons policy and doctrine and of the policies that have given expression to those theories. This review is undertaken not in an attempt to indict particular individuals or administrations for error, but rather to help the U.S. defense community learn from past errors. Many of the apparent mistakes committed over the past twenty years were committed for entirely commendable reasons when judged in U.S. terms—and indeed in general Western terms.

The book seeks to identify a U.S. nuclear weapons policy, for both strategy and posture, that is compatible with U.S. cultural values and political interests and is prospectively responsive to putative U.S. prewar deterrent and war-fighting (for deterrence) requirements vis-à-vis a culturally distinctive Soviet Union. Although this analysis identifies a preferred policy (strategy and matching posture),[18] it is organized in such a way that readers should find value in the analysis whether or not they endorse the policy preferences of the author. A somewhat unusual feature of the U.S. defense debate of the past several years has been the gradual emergence of a great deal of common ground among policy protagonists with respect to identification of many important features of the nuclear weapons policy problem—even though the protagonists have proceeded from problem diagnosis to conflicting theories for effective treatment.

Today, U.S. nuclear weapons policy reflects a partial recognition of the new (partial) consensus that has emerged over the threat. Declaratory policy, as always, is more easily changed than action (or operational) policy, which, in turn, is more easily manipulable than capabilities. In the summer of 1980, three Presidential Directives (PDs)—PD-53, PD-58, and PD-59—provided much of the basis for Harold Brown's claims that "in our analysis and planning, we are necessarily giving greater attention to how a nuclear war would actually be fought by both sides if deterrence fails."[19] This was quite a startling statement from an administration long known to harbor the belief that a nuclear war would mean an uncontrollable catastrophe for both sides.[20] However, not content with announcing a near-revolution in official U.S. thinking on the possible character of nuclear war, the secretary proceeded to bury the better part of fifteen years' worth of "mainstream" American doctrine on strategic deterrence:

> There is no contradiction between this focus on how a war would be fought and what its results would be, *and* our purpose of insuring continued peace through mutual deterrence. Indeed, this focus helps us achieve deterrence and peace, by ensuring that an ability to retaliate is fully credible.[21]

Official disclaimers notwithstanding, those sentences constituted a significant change in U.S. doctrine. For many years in the late 1960s and early 1970s, Western commentators nurtured the forlorn hope that the

Soviet defense community would come to converge in its strategic thinking upon the orthodox Western theory of strategic stability.[22] Instead,
though with some notable exceptions in the realm of performance, the
United States has now converged its official strategic thinking upon that
of the Soviet Union. Both superpowers profess to believe that deterrent
effect is a function of anticipated war-waging prowess.

The aforementioned notable exceptions include the continuing disre-
gard in practice for the physical protection of homeland assets that charac-
terizes U.S. policy.[23] This may be judged to be an unfair characterization,
given the Strategic Defense Initiative (SDI) of the Reagan administration.
Secretary of Defense Weinberger has written as follows:

> Nevertheless, we would not want to let our efforts toward a transition-
> al defense exhaust our energies or dilute our efforts to secure a thor-
> oughly reliable, layered defense that would destroy incoming Soviet
> missiles at all phases of their flight. Such a system would destroy
> weapons, not people. It would not raise the question of whether we
> were trying to defend missiles or cities. We would be attempting to
> destroy Soviet missiles by nonnuclear means before Soviet missiles
> could approach any targets in the United States or the territory of
> our allies. The choice, therefore, is not one of defending people or
> weapons.[24]

Necessarily, the analysis and conclusions in this book are strictly
personal to the author. However, there is a large area of consensus among
defense and arms control professionals about the nature of U.S. nuclear
policy problems and even about much of the character of desirable solutions. The report of the Scowcroft Commission in April 1983 both helped
to forge and discovered a consensus on the essentials of strategic nuclear
policy.[25] A necessary qualification for entering into debate is an ability to
state the position of the other side to the satisfaction of that side. Unfortunately, a hardy perennial feature of U.S. debate over nuclear weapons
policy has been the erection, by all the contending parties, of straw targets—which have been duly demolished. In practice, a good fraction of the
time and energy of competent strategists of all doctrinal persuasions has
been spent attacking positions that no one has sought to defend. This
study, in the first instance, is a theoretical exploration, leading, in the
second instance, to policy exploration and recommendation. Readers will
find no villainous MADvocates (advocates of a doctrine of mutual assured
destruction in a reasonably pure form[26]) in these pages, nor will they find
functionally treasonable SALTaholics.[27] Such creatures may exist, but they
are not of great policy significance today.

Notwithstanding the earlier reference to a substantial amount of common ground among strategic analysts today, it is sensible to categorize the
elements driving this study into *facts* and *opinions* (termed *propositions*—to

be discussed, tested insofar as possible, and accepted as fact or plausibly candidate fact, or to be discarded as probably false). What follows is a terse summary of the facts and propositions that underlie this discussion.

Fact: The Soviet Union outspent the United States on strategic forces in the ratio of 3:1 during the SALT decade of 1969-79 (averaged over a decade).[28] At the time of this writing (1985), the momentum in Soviet development, test, and deployment of new and improved strategic weapons is undiminished. There is firm evidence available today that the Soviet Union has positioned itself technically and in terms of production facilities for truly comprehensive modernization of its strategic forces—offensive and defensive—over the next decade, should it so choose.[29]

Fact: To the present day, the superpowers have had noticeably distinctive strategic doctrines, with the United States, alone, distinguishing between the functions of deterrence and defense.[30]

Fact: Although the superpowers have competed with a degree of reciprocated "enemy" identification that has to qualify for arms race status, neither has reacted to the initiatives of the other as would be predictable if they were waging an arms race with a dominant view to preserving the putative "stability" of mutual assured destruction capabilities.[31]

Fact: Arms control agreements between the superpowers have proved to be negotiable solely on the basis of the registration of "a photograph of the existing balance."[32]

Fact: Because of its democratic political structure and the fearfulness of its political opinion leaders, the United States has been unable to confront squarely the problem of nuclear war.[33]

Fact: Because of its democratic political structure and, consequently, the fear of electoral punishment as the bearer of unwelcome tidings, the United States has yet to see elected an administration that would "come clean" to the general public and "stay clean" on the subject of its nuclear weapons policy.[34]

Proposition: Soviet pursuit of an efficient war-waging strategic posture for war survival does not reflect only hawkish military and Party opinion.[35] Such pursuit is mandated by the Marxist-Leninist theoretical basis for the legitimacy of Soviet rule in the USSR as well as by a Soviet-Russian strategic culture that is reflected in and fed by ideas prominent in Leo Tolstoy's *War and Peace*.[36] However, the USSR though committed to believing in victory over the capitalist West, is not committed to the achievement of military victory. Whether or not victory will come by direct military means that are acknowledged to be very painful is said to be a function of Western policy.

Proposition: Both the United States and the Soviet Union have distinctive "strategic cultures" that reflect their separate political cultures.[37] These cultures give evidence both of the unique histories of the countries in question and of the ways in which U.S. and Soviet citizens perceive their unique histories.[38]

Proposition: In addition to the contemporary issues that divide them, conflict between the superpowers has been greatly exacerbated by the mutual miscomprehension of two very different strategic (and political) cultures. Mutual cultural empathy would not have precluded what has been mistermed "the cold war,"[39] any more than it would have precluded the arms competition that flowed inevitably from political conflict, but it might have obviated gross and dangerous misassessments of intent. Soviet-U.S. antagonism is not so much about anything in particular as it is about the threat that each side perceives in the capability of the other to cause it harm. The destruction of German and Japanese military power in World War II, and the relegation of Britain and France to the second rank of states, left only the United States and the Soviet Union as powers of the first order of magnitude. Aside from the malign influences of Soviet-Russian strategic culture and Soviet state ideology, the reduction in the ranks of the first order of great powers to two guaranteed their mutual suspicion and antipathy.[40]

Proposition: Some critically important U.S. nuclear policy decisions rested on either a plain misreading of Soviet strategic culture or, perhaps more likely, a naive unawareness of the distinctions between the Soviet and U.S. "ways" of defense preparation.[41]

Central to every major element in this book is the idea that both the United States and the Soviet Union have a distinctive national style, reflecting a strategic culture, that has a significant impact on their separate ways of strategic deliberation and defense preparation. The idea of cultural distinctiveness has come to be familiar in recent years,[42] but it has yet to be applied systematically to nuclear policy issues. This book does not seek to argue either that one particular culture is inherently superior to another[43] or that the United States should seek to emulate a strategic culture that it finds fundamentally alien. Rather, the analysis here is grounded in the beliefs that the United States (1) can improve its nuclear policy performance as a consequence of more accurate appreciation of Soviet strategic culture; (2) might be able to alter its nuclear weapons policy so as to thwart more directly critical elements in Soviet policy; (3) may be willing to consider different lines of strategic reasoning to see whether they might have potential value for inclusion in U.S. policy; (4) might be better placed to convey convincing deterrent messages if it were able to divine more accurately those threats that Soviet leaders tend to view with particular abhorrence; and finally (5) would serve its national security better if it could close the large gap that exists between the war-fighting theory of deterrence that is official policy and the military means that are available for policy execution.

The remainder of this chapter steps back somewhat from contemporary strategic ideas and nuclear policy issues to discuss the framework of international political life to which nuclear weapons must relate. One often finds that contending strategic theorists and policy commentators have very different premises concerning the structure of world politics and the role of force, including nuclear force, therein. My analysis of nuclear strategy is influenced decisively by my perspective on the prudent "rules of the road" for contemporary statecraft.

NUCLEAR STRATEGY AND HISTORY

In the minds of many people, there is a deep uncertainty about the validity of the concept of *nuclear strategy*. If strategy is intended, in some purposeful way, to translate military power (latent force) into an instrument for the prospectively efficient accomplishment of political ends, does not the very destructiveness of nuclear weapons negate their operational value?[44] Together with Bernard Brodie, one may endorse the idea of "utility in non-use,"[45] but can one identify any likely utility in actual use? And how might "utility in non-use" relate to "utility in use"? In other words, can one design a plausible strategy of (prewar) deterrence if one cannot also design a plausible operational strategy? These are important questions, and they continue to lurk behind the more specific debating issues of the day (particular weapon systems, targeting schemes, and arms control proposals).

This book is written from the following perspective:

- Even the best-laid schemes of officials and strategic theorists may fail "on the night." There is an absence of reality testing about any and all nuclear strategies.[46]

- However, nuclear weapons exist. There is no way in which the United States can effect their total and permanent abolition, and any unilateral move by the United States down the path of nuclear disarmament would virtually invite attempts at coercion by other powers.

- The decision for or against the initiation of nuclear war may not always be exclusively in the hands of a U.S. president. Nuclear use may be initiated by another power, or the United States may find itself in a situation where vital foreign policy interests can be defended only through the opening of nuclear operations.

- Clearly, for the reasons just cited, the United States must have a nuclear strategy—the question is which one. This is not to imply a necessity for a rigid, rigorously exclusive choice of strategy. Flexibility, options, and a capability for adaptive planning are strongly desirable, just as a focus on operational strategy (as, on occasion, in this book) should not cause readers to forget that the principal purpose of nuclear-armed forces is deterrence (pre- and intrawar), not the efficient conduct of military operations. (As noted earlier, the U.S. defense community remains somewhat uncertain about the prudent relationship between deterrence and defense.[47])

As a general rule, strategists do not spend their days debating moral issues. With reference to the alternative postures and doctrines discussed in this book, I cannot identify any operational nuclear strategy that would not, in its implications for casualties inflicted in war, shock the moral sensibilities of any thinking person. All that a strategist can say is, first, that the debate over nuclear strategy is really about the prevention of war; second, that debate over efficient ways to fight a war rests on the belief that prospective prowess in war waging will contribute vitally to success in deterrence; and third, that nuclear war may happen for reasons quite beyond our control—that is, that the real choice may lie between fighting the war that we did not or could not deter either well, thereby preserving U.S. lives and vital interests, or badly.[48] Finally, contrary to the apparent meaning of some of the rhetoric of the ongoing nuclear arms debate, the United States (and the Soviet Union) does not have the prevention or avoidance of nuclear war as an absolute goal of policy. If that were the case, the U.S. nuclear deterrent would soon lose all foreign policy utility. Barring some dramatic restructuring of world politics, U.S. nuclear power, as generally latent threat, is essential to the maintenance of what passes for international peace and security.[49]

Most of this book is devoted to discussion of the key concepts pertaining to nuclear strategy and to a range of strategies (and postures) that are, or should be, candidates for U.S. official consideration. Although I strongly believe both that the concept of nuclear strategy has integrity and that some strategies are preferable to others—beliefs that pervade this text—I see this study as an exploration in which, for many readers, the journey may be of more value than the attainment of the specific ("preferred policy") destination. Critically important to the assessment of alternative doctrines and postures is an understanding of the roles of force—latent force and, above all, *nuclear* force—in the world politics of the last quarter of the twentieth century. Expressed in the simplest and crudest of terms: What use are nuclear weapons? The discussion here attempts to provide a political context for discussion of what McGeorge Bundy has termed, pejoratively, "the refined calculations of the nuclear gamesmen."[50]

Whatever sense one may make of his policy advice,[51] McGeorge Bundy's strictures against "nuclear gamesmen" do contain a distressingly substantial grain of truth. A great deal of what passes for strategic analysis of nuclear weapons issues is really nothing of the kind. In truth, the U.S. defense community tends to be both apolitical and astrategic in orientation. All too often, the hypothetical central (U.S.-USSR homeland-to-homeland) wars of the "nuclear gamesmen" begin with such words as "Let us assume a large-scale red attack upon the blue silo-housed ICBM force." Such a war has no political context; indeed, innocent of context, it has no political meaning.[52] Debate over major weapon systems—such as the B-1, the MX/Peacekeeper ICBM, and antisatellite (ASAT) weapons—tends to be impoverished because the debaters, on all sides of the argument, often are not equipped or even motivated to think strategically. This thesis will recur many times in the argument that follows.[53]

One of the most intriguing questions that can be posed by a strategist looking backward, or by an international historian attuned to contemporary policy debate, is the following: What difference have nuclear weapons, and their means of delivery, made to world politics? To rephrase, of all the differences that may be detected between the world politics of the mid-1980s and the world politics of 1939, 1900, or 1850, how many—and to what degree—can one attribute to nuclear weapons technology and to the means of long-range delivery of that technology?

This question is of more than academic interest alone. It inquires into the scope of the historical domain of the evidential base behind policy advice.[54] For example, can the U.S. government learn anything of value from Munich in 1938, the July crisis of 1914, or the imperial statecraft of Rome[55] or Athens? Argument by historical analogy is endemic; but which, if any, analogies have integrity as a part of the relevant evidential base? Above all, bypassing the potential pitfalls of focusing on one rather than another preferred analogy (e.g., do policymakers in the 1980s have more to learn from 1914 than from 1938-39?[56]) is there a general body of knowledge about statecraft, deriving from appreciation of all recorded history, that can be understood at a suitably nonspecific level (since particular conditions change)? This apparently academic question is designed to direct readers to an understanding of what may be called "the rules of the road" of world politics today[57]—with a particular view to helping prepare U.S. officials to consider nuclear policy problems in the light of a comprehension of statecraft that transcends U.S. political culture. Much of the U.S. understanding of world politics in the nuclear age is parochial and ahistorical to the point where judicious nuclear weapons policy deliberation is unlikely. For example, only in very recent years has the U.S. defense community considered its principal overseas adversary in the light of the distinctive history and, hence, culture that must pervade Soviet policy determination.[58]

An acute problem of historical evidence besets this discussion: There is but a single stream of world political activity since 1945. In essence, one is asking: "How could world politics from 1945 to the present have been different had nuclear weapons not been invented?" No case or argument can be proved.

It is useful to begin at the level of the structure of world politics. The familiar prenuclear concept of a "great power"—a power essential to the functioning of the international order of the day—has retained some fraction of its meaning.[59] Through most of modern (i.e., post-Renaissance) history, it has been well understood that a handful of (dynastic—later national) states had extraordinary duties and responsibilities for the maintenance of "international order."[60] From time to time one or more states joined or left the exclusive company of great (or "first-rate") powers, and from time to time one or more of these states pursued foreign policy objectives that were incompatible with the very idea of a society of states, or a *community* of great powers, but the concept of a great power endured.

Probably the most important elements in the great power catechism were that every great power had a right to exist, was essential to the system of international security of the day, and had legitimate interests. Each great power would and was expected to seek unilateral advantage where it could. However, the requirements of the balance-of-power system, considered as a whole, were expected ultimately to take precedence over individual parochial interests, while the hidden hand of a nearly automatically operating balancing system would soon restrain any power that neglected its obligations to the integrity of the system as a whole.[61] After all, the great power that is humiliated today may be the great power whose "balancing" assistance is needed tomorrow.

It may be objected that the foregoing thumbnail description of the great power balance-of-power system has been overly attentive to some nineteenth-century practices while ignoring a great deal of contrary evidence, and that it presents what may be characterized as a historical anomaly as the norm. A European balance-of-power system, which effectively was synonymous with a global system for most of the period, was recognized to exist and was valued for its contribution to order and security (though not always peace)—from the Peace of Westphalia in 1648, marking the end of the Thirty Years' War, until 1939.[62] That system, notwithstanding periodic hiccups, did operate, at its best, according to a code of behavior intended to preserve not peace, but order (that is, the system itself) and general security. It was destroyed by a malign combination of rampant nationalism, rigid countervailing alliance structures, the rise of a Germany too powerful to be contained, and a new technology of war and a new feasibility of economic mobilization for war, which ensured that quick victory would evade the clutches of both sides.

Behaving sensibly, which was not always the case by any means, the great powers of the nineteenth century (Great Britain, France, Prussia/ Germany [after 1866], Austria-Hungary, and Russia) recognized a community of concern for international security, embraced no ambitions for a universal territorial or hegemonic imperium, and—as may be surmised— shared a common code of statecraft, just as they shared a common language of diplomacy (French). I am acutely aware of the exceptions that should be noted to the generalizations just offered. The Imperial Russia of the Romanovs was viewed, particularly in liberal Britain, as something of an international outcast because of the "barbarism" of its domestic autocratic structure;[63] Germany's foreign policy after the fall of Bismarck in 1890 was as inept as it was often erratic; and so forth. Nonetheless, at the time of the Boer War (1899–1902), Great Britain was willing to consider seriously a limited colonial settlement with Germany, which might have blossomed into a deeper political relationship;[64] and in 1907, Great Britain and Russia did achieve a reconciliation of their respective and formerly antagonistic interests with reference to South Asia.[65] In short, this European balance-of-power system, though vulnerable to incompetent statecraft (witness the Crimean War), was sufficiently flexible that very few alliance or entente combinations were wholly impractical.

What is of particular interest to this study is the fact that the international system as it emerged out of the ashes (in Europe and Asia) and prosperous industries (in the United States) in 1945 was essentially set on its course, in its structure, and perhaps even substantially in its civilities and incivilities before the nuclear age had any noteworthy physical military reality. The old order of the European balance-of-power system lingered on in the machinations of European diplomats in the 1920s and 1930s, but the world had already changed.

Nuclear weapons were developed in the 1940s by what came to be termed the "superpowers," but the superpowers were considered superpowers before the world had assimilated the fact of weaponized nuclear fission. Quite unaware of the existence of the Manhattan Project, William T. R. Fox wrote his book, *The Super Powers*, during the course of World War II.[66] Even if the atom had never been split, the United States and the Soviet Union would have emerged from World War II as they did, preeminent (if heavily damaged, in the Soviet case) and eventually condemned to an enduring antagonism—even though the Soviet Union threatened no very specific long-standing U.S. interests in a direct fashion. Soviet-U.S. hostility was a geopolitical inevitability. The United States was compelled to assume the role of principal defender of the Eurasian "Rimland" against the outward pressure of the Heartland power, the USSR.[67]

The two world wars, born most immediately out of the inability of the old European balance-of-power system to contain the ambitions of an overly powerful and recently united Germany, effectively destroyed the international system, as one might depict it, as of about 1900. World War

I totally eliminated one of the five "essential" actors in the system, Austria-Hungary; pushed another actor (Russia) virtually out of European politics for more than ten years; fatally weakened the two democratic actors (Britain and France); and left the remaining actor (Germany) first a victim of one of the victors' (France) ill-judged determination to achieve revenge and recompense, and later a pariah state directed by criminal, if not psychopathic, adventurers who could recognize no concept of "international order" save that imposed by the jackboot.

The near-total, though nonlethal, hostility between East and West that is implied by the concept of cold war has to be traced to causes far more substantial than the cycle of mutual misperception that one can detect in the 1940s. This book is not interested in the question of "who started the cold war," not merely because that hoary issue has absorbed considerable historical research talent for too long already, but also—and particularly—because the mere posing of that question shows a profound misunderstanding both of the character of the Soviet Union and of the enduring nature of world politics.

Although the European balance-of-power system limped on through the 1920s and 1930s (as France sought with increasing desperation to contain a resurgent Germany through alliance connections with Czechoslovakia and Poland, inter alia), the largely excluded semi-European factor of the *new* Russia/Soviet Union posed a part-traditional, part-novel threat to the integrity of the international system of the day. By political definition, the new Soviet Republic, in what had been Imperial Russia, from the day of its birth has been at war with the political and imperial system of capitalism. There is a rigidity in the structure of world politics flowing from this fact that has no close analogue in modern history (though some scholars of Bonapartist imperialism may disagree). As U.S. nuclear strategists discovered belatedly, in the 1970s, the character of the USSR was not solely a matter of scholarly interest. Indeed, as some strategic theorists were to acknowledge, again belatedly, a signal weakness in U.S. strategic nuclear doctrine as it was developed in the 1950s and 1960s was that it was virtually innocent of any recognition of Soviet, *qua* Soviet, reality.[68]

The period 1917-45 not only saw the emergence of three states whose political, and hence strategic, cultures were fundamentally challenging to the previously established rules of the Europe-oriented balance-of-power system (the Soviet Union, the German Third Reich, and the United States), it also saw the demise, pro tem, of the relevance of the theory of limited war. As Clausewitz explained, with some overstatement, limited war was a rational product of a states' system wherein only limited political objectives were sought.[69] The idea of nationality inevitably was erosive of the practice of waging war for limited territorial objectives. For example, the loss of Alsace-Lorraine in 1870-71 functioned as a canker in the French body politic for a generation—nurturing an enduring demand for *revanche.* In the fifteenth, sixteenth, and even seventeenth and eighteenth centuries, such an idea would have been ridiculous. However, what the idea and even the fact of mass national identification implied for the freedom of action of statesmen, the military technology of the late nineteenth and early twentieth centuries made inevitable.[70]

For reasons of popular national identification (and the social cohesion that occurs in war—for a time, at least[71]), industrial strength, political ineptitude, and technical developments in weaponry, the military regulator of the European balance-of-power system could not function effectively in 1914.[72] A protracted military struggle, engaging all of the assets of the participants, was an eventuality that none, save for a handful of unheeded theorists, had anticipated.[73] The brutality implicit in the scenarios of the "nuclear gamesmen" of the nuclear age has already been practiced in the total wars of this century.

Without seeking to downplay the potential harm of nuclear war, I would remind American readers that "unthinkable" casualty lists were a fact of life in 1914-18 and 1939-45 for many countries in continental Europe.[74] Although every individual war casualty is a tragedy, it is a fact of history that only in the Civil War, more than a century ago, did the United States/Confederate States of America take casualties at all close, in percentage terms, to those suffered by France, Germany, Russia, Serbia, and Great Britain in World War I. The purpose of this line of argument is not to suggest that large casualty lists are commonplace in the twentieth century (though they are), only that some of the features of "the nuclear age" that have struck U.S. officials and theorists as unique may benefit from a little historical perspective. It is unfortunate, perhaps, that the only power after 1945 able to counterbalance Soviet influence around the periphery of Eurasia—the United States—should be a power unused to waging war "at home" or to paying a major price for military victory.

In short, some of the novel features of the nuclear age were novel only in the U.S. context among important state actors. The nuclear age, which came to mean both very high potential casualty lists and the total vulnerability of civilian society, was an extension, though admittedly a significant extension, of the twentieth-century experience of the European powers. The idea of one warhead killing hundreds of thousands of people was novel—but the Royal Air Force and the USAAF already had effected its functional equivalent in single air raids on Hamburg, Dresden, and Tokyo.[75]

Brutality in war, alas, tends to be a simple function of military utility. The nuclear age, one may argue, has seen new heights of planned barbarism, perhaps made all the more repulsive for the pseudoscientific strategic jargon with which prospective mass murder is explained.[76] However, it is not obvious that nuclear weapons constitute, in moral terms at least, a step-level jump in man's potential inhumanity to man.[77] The world wars of this century have seen the use of poison gas, the resort to unrestricted submarine warfare, the attempted starvation of whole populations through economic blockade, the attempted genocide of the Jewish (and Gypsy) people, and indiscriminate aerial bombardment of civilian "targets." Nuclear employment could be worse, but it is well to contemplate all aspects of military practice in the first half of the twentieth century.[78] Clearly, the international system of the twentieth century, because of national sentiment (and, hence, association with the goals of government in war), the economic resilience of states, and the sheer convenience of military usage, accepted the waging of total war among societies.

NUCLEAR STATECRAFT

It is difficult to draw a meaningful distinction, in ethical terms, between a United States willing to create firestorms in Japanese cities in 1945 and a United States willing to employ nuclear weapons on Soviet cities in the 1980s. Lest there be any misunderstanding, I believe both that the air war against Japan was conducted properly (up to and including the atomic weapon attacks on Hiroshima and Nagasaki) and that a nuclear threat that cannot preclude menacing Soviet civilians is justifiable.[79] The point of this argument is not to justify either event/hypothetical event or atrocity; rather, is it to point to the kind of countercivilian action that was effected (not merely threatened) prior to the nuclear age.

For many years the U.S. public seemed to be blasé about events that had long been contemplated yet had failed to occur. Nuclear war is no more "acceptable" or less horrible because U.S. society has lived in its shadow for all of forty years. Until the 1980s, at least, the cliché of "the nuclear age" seemed to have dulled what otherwise might have been perceptive commentary stemming from public concern. The failure of the formal arms control process to produce acceptable agreements, and media misrepresentation of the policy attitudes of Reagan administration officials,[80] combined in the early 1980s to trigger genuine grass-roots concern that not enough was being done about a danger of nuclear war that allegedly was increasing. This concern has been both expressed in and formed by such activities as the "nuclear freeze now" movement, the consciousness-raising venture of the Ground Zero group, and the drafting of the Pastoral Letter of the National Conference of Catholic Bishops.

What has the nuclear age meant for world politics? Prior to the nuclear age great powers competed for influence, engaged in arms competition (reflecting their competing political aspirations), signed up allies, and generally avowed their faith in a somewhat locally oriented definition of the good life. Also, from time to time—though with increasingly catastrophic results—the great powers had resort to war. Germany, defeated in World War I, suffered only a very limited occupation and the imposition of an indemnity—albeit a crushing one—whereas defeat in World War II resulted in total military occupation and a division of the national territory that may or may not prove to be permanent.

The principal fact of post-1945 international politics, the countervailing alliance or satellite/client-state structures organized by the United States and the Soviet Union, would have occurred even if nuclear weapons had not been invented. The superpower qualities of the United States and the Soviet Union have been enhanced by their unevenly evolving military nuclear capabilities, but their preeminent stature in the league table of international authority was preordained by reason of economic strength (in the U.S. case) and the way in which economic assets ruthlessly were applied to military problems (in the Soviet case).

It is tempting to suggest that neither World War I nor World War II would have occurred had the crisis-principals of 1914 and 1939 been armed with nuclear weapons and, ab extensio, that one of the post-1945 crises would have exploded into a general East-West war had nuclear weapons not been invented; but I remain unconvinced. Nuclear weapons should, indeed, promote an unusual measure of caution in statecraft, but it is difficult to see how a military invention could, for long, have damped the fires that were burning in the Balkans of 1914 or, again for long, have impressed a cautionary wisdom on a desperate Vienna, a frivolous Berlin, and a vacillating, divinely inspired St. Petersburg.[81] Similarly, one cannot resist the thought that a nuclear-armed Germany in the late 1930s would have been a Germany even more boldly bent on conquest through blackmail and bluff than was in fact the case.[82]

With respect to the United States after 1945, it is easy to see why an unduly expansive understanding of the roles of nuclear weapons was accepted in support of U.S. diplomacy. In a major speech in 1979, commenting on the foreign policy implications of strategic nuclear parity, Henry Kissinger said that "our strategic doctrine has relied extraordinarily, perhaps exclusively, on our superior strategic nuclear power."[83] There is much to recommend Dr. Kissinger's view, as later chapters explain, but his thesis encourages a narrowly military view of the sources of U.S. authority in support of world order, which certainly is alien to what is known about the Soviet perspective.[84]

The Soviet concept of "the correlation of forces" is far broader than the Western idea of the "strategic balance."[85] Indeed, as Keith Payne has suggested, "the correlation of forces" bears a marked resemblance to Hans Morgenthau's concept of national power.[86] Although nuclear weapons are acknowledged to be the "primary" element in the correlation, other significant elements include national will or morale, economic strength, and technological prowess. The concept of the correlation of forces is really as obvious as it tends to be alien to a U.S. defense community, which is all too prone to think in unduly narrow military ways.

The structure of countervailing alliances and client-state systems in Eurasia has not been the product of changes in military technology. NATO came to depend very heavily on a contingent U.S nuclear guarantee after "the Lisbon goals" of 1952 for conventional rearmament lost their authority—very rapidly indeed—and nuclear policy issues repeatedly have engaged the attention of intra-NATO diplomacy. However, the basic structure of the alliance, and particularly the leading role of the United States, has been the result of the overall strength of the United States and the relative weakness of a politically fractionated Western Europe.

East-West relations since 1945, as I have explained in detail elsewhere,[87] are but the latest phase in a continuing struggle for control of what geopoliticians have called the World-Island of Eurasia—Africa (and "Who rules the World-Island commands the World"[88]). Nuclear weapons almost certainly have encouraged the major alliance-leading protagonists in world politics to take only the minimum risks of a direct military clash between themselves and may well have rendered the defense of forward positions easier than would have been the case in a world where there was no potential audit trail from frontier clash to nuclear holocaust. However, one can make geopolitical sense of East-West conflict (and limited cooperation) either with or without reference to nuclear weapons. In addition, one should recognize that the impact of nuclear weapons technology on U.S. political consciousness and strategic planning was particularly severe because of the near-simultaneous development of the means of long-range, particularly trans-Arctic, weapons delivery. Any country wishing to pose a credible nuclear threat to the United States in, say, 1900 would have had a very serious (though not insuperable) delivery problem.

Since 1945, notwithstanding the nuclear fact, world politics has been conducted very much on the basis of "business as usual." The rigidities in the major alliance pattern have flowed not from the evolution of military, let alone military-nuclear, technology, but rather from the basic characters of the two principal alliance organizers and the historically extraordinary, though not unprecedented, degree of their international preponderance in terms of the factors that make for national power. Consider, in summary form, the major changes that distinguish late twentieth-century from, say, late nineteenth-century world politics.

1. The international political system is truly global for the first time in history.

2. Although Europe remains the principal "prize" in East-West competition, one superpower is totally non-European in its geography, and the other has most of its territory outside of Europe.

3. The only empire remaining in the world is the Great Russian/Soviet one.[89]

4. The "coming" great powers, each of which will have a military mobilization potential of, or close to, the first rank, are all non-European: Japan, the Chinese People's Republic, and Brazil.

5. The global character of the international political system is both matched and fueled by a global economic system and, effectively, a global system of very rapid communications.

Where do nuclear weapons fit in the global political structure today? It is unclear whether or not the possession of an overt nuclear weapon capability conveys, ipso facto, the contemporary equivalent of great power status (bearing in mind that there are very few precedents for the superpower phenomenon, particularly in modern European history—perhaps Spain for most of the sixteenth century and the France of Louis XIV, for a while, and of Napoleon Bonaparte—though even in these cases the precedents are very imperfect). As Soviet writers are fond of saying, "it is no accident" (probably—for an un-Soviet qualification) that the Permanent Members of the United Nations Security Council are all nuclear weapons states. To have any very serious pretensions to perform an international "ordering" function, a state today must possess nuclear weapons. The reason is as obvious as the logic is inescapable. Major challenges to international order are likely to stem from and be encouraged by other great power "guardians"—and those states are nuclear-armed. A state cannot seek to cut a significant and independent figure in the guarding of international order if it has no like answer of its own to nuclear threats. However, it does not follow that every nuclear weapon state aspires to contribute in a noticeable way to international order on the global stage. Today—and to be expected increasingly in the future—the international order to be guarded by national nuclear weapons capabilities will largely be local and parochial. For example, Israel and South Africa, two states that are probably in possession of nuclear weapons today, have little interest in accomplishing anything more than keeping regional enemies at bay.

Notwithstanding the French theory of proportional nuclear deterrence,[90] the fact of the enduring Western alliance structure illustrates the truth that the traditional definition of a great power is no longer valid. That definition held that a great power was a power capable, alone, of standing up to any of the other great powers. The emergence of two superstates has meant the demise of that definition. A nuclear weapons capability per se, regardless of quantity and quality, does not serve as an effective equalizer in "the correlation of forces"—save, just possibly, with respect to a very narrow range of extaordinarily vital, indeed survival interests.[91]

In good part, perhaps, because of the historical facts of an initial U.S. nuclear weapons monopoly (1945-49), a long period of unquestionable U.S nuclear superiority (1950-69), and then a decade and a half of an increasingly rough parity (1970-85), one should hesitate before offering any confident-sounding, broad-brush characterizations either of the rules of nuclear statecraft or, perhaps of greater relevance, of the rules of statecraft conducted in the shadow of nuclear weapons. Scant evidence is available regarding how the Soviet Union will in fact choose to conduct its foreign relations in an era of marginal or perhaps clear nuclear advantage, in a context where other elements in the correlation of forces may be so unsatisfactory as to incline Soviet leaders toward the path of caution. Through the late 1940s, the 1950s and the 1960s, Soviet forward diplomacy, actual and potential, was checked by the fact of U.S. nuclear superiority, while Soviet advantages in nonnuclear projection forces in Europe were offset convincingly by the escalation dominance implicit in the healthy (for the West) imbalance in so-called strategic forces.[92] The 1970s should be seen as a decade of transition, as the Soviet Union sought to lay the basis for a potential across-the-board military advantage in the 1980s.[93] Relative Western relaxation in defense efforts in that decade provided the Soviet Union with a unique historical opportunity to engage in a forward diplomacy with sound military backing. Whether or not Soviet leaders will feel moved to leap through a window of military opportunity, or even will perceive it, remains very much a matter of speculation. It can be and has been argued that such window leaping, historically, has been characteristic only of the British and the Japanese.[94] To date, Soviet foreign policy in the 1980s has not been particularly assertive and certainly has not been as assertive as the military balance at all levels should have permitted. The succession process, from Brezhnev and then from Andropov and Chernenko to Gorbachev, must explain a good deal of the lack of boldness in recent Soviet policy.

Whether or not the Soviet Union will seek to reap some very tangible rewards for its still unmatched and fairly steady defense effort has to be a subject of some uncertainty. However, there are grounds for believing that Soviet statecraft in the years ahead could have some features that will surprise those Western commentators who adhere to the view that there are some reasonably fixed "rules of the road" for the guidance of prudent superpower behavior. The point is not that the Soviet Union may be more likely to adopt risky or dangerous policies than it has been in the past (that might constitute the sin of adventurism); rather, it is that Soviet assessment of risk and danger should be expected to change as the correlation of forces, in Soviet estimation, moves further to the Soviet advantage. In other words, the problem probably is a question not so much of the willingness of a particular group of Soviet leaders to take risks, but rather of the substance to the risks they calculate.

The Soviet Union is not committed to a guardianship role vis-à-vis the current international order. On the contrary, it is committed, for excellent

Russian and Soviet reasons, to guarding the process of transition from the present order to a future wherein socialism (i.e., the Soviet imperium) will be triumphant. The external role of the Soviet armed forces, as stated quite unambiguously by Soviet authorities, is to protect and forward the transition to Soviet-led socialism. Whether one ascribes this viewpoint to Great Russian imperialism, to Marxist-Leninist ideology, or to a malign combination of the two is quite unimportant in the context of this book.[95]

Soviet nuclear weapons, unlike U.S. nuclear weapons, are not developed and deployed for the purpose of defending an existing international order that is deemed legitimate. Looking to the second half of the 1980s, one cannot affirm the following without qualification:

- Neither superpower will seek to change the allegiance of a country long understood either to be within the sphere of influence of the other or to have a neutral, perhaps "buffer," status.[96]

- Neither superpower will risk direct military action in cases where there is a strong probability that the other superpower also will commit forces.

- Very generally, neither superpower will take actions long understood to carry the risk of igniting an escalation chain to massive central nuclear use.

The qualification, as already suggested, is that the great cumulative improvement in the Soviet end of the correlation of forces almost certainly has changed the basis on which the rules of foreign policy engagement are designed and enforced. Western commentators, in the hubris of the period, indulged in the definition and promotion of a set of so-called rules of crisis management in the aftermath of the Cuban missile crisis of October 1962.[97] What those commentators neglected to observe, was that—in Soviet eyes, at least—rules of the road, up to and including the question of who concedes the most, are matters for objective determination. Soviet intervention policy in the 1970s in Angola, Ethiopia, South Yemen, and Afghanistan should warn us that the rules of the road for nuclear-backed statecraft are deemed by Soviet leaders to change with the correlation of forces.[98] In the words of a Soviet observer:

> The nuclear and missile potential of the Soviet Union and of the entire socialist community cancels out imperialism's opportunity to use its war machine to obtain any political advantages, thus explaining the apparent paradox that imperialism's military arsenal grows by the year, while the power factor of its foreign policy is increasingly depreciated. In fact, the imperialist powers have not succeeded in employing the threat or use of arms to achieve any of their aims, whether in

Vietnam, in Cuba, or Angola or in scores of other "flashpoints" over the last few decades. Moreover, the power conflicts of modern times end more and more often in the aggressor's defeat with respect to the overall balance of power between reaction and progress.[99]

CONFLICT AND COOPERATION IN WORLD POLITICS

Unlike the state-system that was reconfirmed at the Congress of Vienna in 1814-15, the international system today contains an actor that, since its birth in revolution and civil war, has been committed to the destruction of the Western idea and practice of international order. Nuclear weapons, as accommodated in "the [Soviet] revolution in military affairs,"[100] do not pose a challenge to the historical necessity of the transformation of world politics. On the contrary, Soviet nuclear weapons serve, at the least , as an effective counterdeterrent, "holding the ring square" for the support or even direct conduct of "just" wars in the Third World;[101] whereas, if need be, the proper employment of nuclear weapons in war could bring decisive results. Western officials, in their conduct of statecraft, should never forget that in the Soviet Union they have an adversary who holds essentially to a battlefield philosophy of nuclear planning.[102] From time to time, Western policy may be paralyzed by the effect of the belief that nuclear weapons are really only weapons of threat (i.e., bluff), that they are not weapons that could be used for the achievement of political goals; whereas Soviet policy—though not adventurous in any Soviet sense—is informed by the apparent belief that nuclear weapons are the heavy artillery of this age. Nuclear weapons are self-evidently more destructive than other weapons, and certainly they are not to be employed casually, but their very destructiveness is held by Soviet officials to hold the promise of truly decisive, rapid military results.

The weighting of the correlation of forces in favor of the West through most of the nuclear era has helped, thus far, to render moot the foreign policy implications of Soviet strategic doctrine. The transition from the rough strategic parity of the late 1970s to marginal and then perhaps to less marginal superiority as the 1980s proceed could mean that Soviet strategic doctrine will have considerable influence on Soviet foreign policy behavior. In years past, when the United States believed that Soviet leaders shrank from the brink of catastrophe, those leaders may have shrunk not from the idea of a generalized nuclear catastrophe but, rather, from the uncomplicated conviction that the Soviet Union would lose a war. Should Soviet leaders come to believe not only that victory is possible, which is an ideological requirement (as well as being sensible for sustaining morale) but also that victory is likely, then Soviet foreign policy, quite responsibly (from the Soviet perspective), could assume a course fundamentally challenging of those rules of the road for nuclear peace that Americans typically believe to be hallowed by their longevity.

Perhaps the single most distressing fact of contemporary world politics for a country traditionally as optimistic in its outlook as the United States is the idea of permanence of competition with the Soviet Union. People do not like to be told that the Soviet Union is obliged because of its very raison d'être to define the United States objectively as an enemy. However slow the present transition to a fully socialist (and Soviet-dominated) world, the formal Soviet commitment to conflict and struggle with the West is inalienable. The USSR is a state based on a highly dubious interpretation of an extremely fragile theory of inevitable historical change. The USSR, in its own terms, only makes sense as a way station en route to worldwide socialism. This does not mean that the Soviet Union is committed to waging eventual (military) war with the West; Marxism-Leninism, as interpreted, offers several alternative paths to socialism. It does mean, however, that the Soviet Union, of necessity, is fully committed to the prospect of war with the West.

Western governments persist in believing that policies of cooperation are as important as, if not more important than, policies of conflict. At most, Western governments appear to believe that a permanent modus vivendi, based on mutually tolerable rules of the diplomatic road, can be encouraged to emerge. Given the basic character and sense of legitimacy of the Soviet state, these beliefs are simply wrong. Tactical cooperation with the Soviet Union is both desirable and, from time to time, essential. For the long term, however, the predominant theme in East-West relations must be one of conflict. The West has an elementary choice: to compete effectively or ineffectively. If one declines to endorse the proposition that a permanent struggle is mandated by the source of authority for the Communist party of the Soviet Union, one is not necessarily in much calmer waters. Somewhat abstract systemic analysis of the character of relations between two predominant powers or analysis of Soviet-U.S. relations that emphasizes the Russian nature of Soviet behavior both produce the same advice as does a more ideologically sensitive perspective. The struggle for prestige and influence between the superpowers prospectively is of such a long-term character that it has to be judged to be permanent for the purpose of statecraft today.

It has become commonplace for scholars to observe that the nuclear age differs from all previous recorded history in that the functional equivalents of the great powers of yesterday cannot have resort to force à outrance to solve problems that cannot be resolved by other means. Until the nuclear age, this argument proceeds, great powers could "go to war"— even to what amounted to total war—with some plausible prospect that victory was achievable and that the distinction between victory and defeat would be unmistakable and very important.

The foregoing argument contains a large kernel of truth, but the qualifications that must be noted are almost as important. One is not seeking to "conventionalize" nuclear weapons[103] or pretend that they comprise "just another weapon" if one takes due note of the following facts:

- Nuclear war, small-scale or very large, could occur. It may not be a profitable venture for any of the protagonists, but it is distinctly possible.

- Both superpowers, in their different ways, have labored to render nuclear war a prospectively survivable event and, therefore, a credible option for national initiative.

- The proposition that nuclear war cannot be won, that political objectives cannot be secured by nuclear force, is not a demonstrated fact—it is speculative theory. Both superpowers plan as if nuclear war could be waged and survived. Moreover, when one considers the possible fragility of early-warning and command-and-control assets, contemplates the dynamism of the weapon technology of offense *and defense*, and thinks about the policy choices that may be available over weapon employment, it is far from self-evident that the very nature of the nuclear age precludes resort to force on a large scale among alliance principals of the state-system.

Without seeking to downgrade the weapon revolution of nuclear technology, the path of realism suggests that one should pay due attention to the facts that general war could occur and that the superpowers plan to wage war as efficiently as they are able (as great and less great powers have done for centuries past). Moreover, it is possible that nuclear force could be employed operationally, as well as brandished diplomatically, actually to solve political problems through military success. Many people may believe that nuclear force is too dangerous to be usable operationally, but that belief is not and cannot be politically authoritative in Moscow and Washington given the extant structure of strategic relations.

NOTES

1.   NSDD—National Security Decision Directive; PD—Presidential Directive; NSDM—National Security Decision Memorandum. See Desmond Ball, *Targeting for Strategic Deterrence*, Adelphi Papers No. 185 (London IISS, Summer 1983); and Jeffrey Richelson, "PD-59, NSDD-13 and the Reagan Strategic Modernization Program," *Journal of Strategic Studies* 6, no. 2 (June 1983): 125–46.

2.   President's Commission on Strategic Forces, *Report* (Washington, D.C.: The White House, April 1983), pp. 2–3.

3.   Ibid., p. 7.

4.   See Keith B. Payne, *Nuclear Deterrence in U.S.-Soviet Relations* (Boulder, Colo.: Westview, 1982), chap. 8.

5.   "President's Speech on Military Spending and a New Defense," *New York Times*, March 24, 1983, p. 20.

6.   This theme runs through Edward Crankshaw, *The Shadow of the Winter Palace: The Drift to Revolution, 1825–1917* (London: Macmillan, 1976). Also useful is Marc Raeff, *Understanding Imperial Russia: State and Society in the Old Regime* (New York: Columbia University Press, 1984).

7.   Harold Brown, Speech at the U.S. Naval War College, Newport, R.I., August 20, 1980, p. 2.

8.   Harold Brown, *Department of Defense Annual Report, Fiscal Year 1981* (Washington, D.C.: USGPO, January 29, 1980), p. 14.

9.   Leslie Gelb, "A Glass Half Full," *Foreign Policy*, no. 36(Fall 1979): 21.

10.   William Kincade, "A Farewell to Arms Control?" *Arms Control Today* 10, no. 1(January 1980): 1–5.

11.   Deborah Shapley, "Arms Control as a Regulator of Military Technology," *Daedalus* 109, no. 1(Winter 1980): 145.

12.   Richard Burt, "After Almost a Decade, the ABM Dispute Resumes," *New York Times*, August 30, 1980, p. 5.

13.   See chapter 5.

14.   On the problems and opportunities of this predictable trend, see the contrasting views in Keith B. Payne and Colin S. Gray, "Nuclear Policy and the Defensive Transition," *Foreign Affairs* 62, no. 4(Spring 1984): 820–42; and McGeorge Bundy, George F. Kennan, Robert S. McNamara, and Gerard Smith, "The President's Choice: Star Wars or Arms Control", *Foreign Affairs* 63, no. 2(Winter 1984/85): 264–78.

15.   See Deborah Shapley, "Technology Creep and the Arms Race: A World of Absolute Accuracy," *Science* 19(September 1978): 1192–96.

16.   The asymptotic range probably is reached in the vicinity of 300-400 feet.

17.   See James B. Schultz, "En Route to End Game Strategic Missile Guidance", *Defense Electronics*, September 1984, pp. 57–63. For a useful discussion of recent developments in silo superhardening, see Edgar Ulsamer, "The Prospect for Superhard Silos," *Air Force Magazine* 67, no. 1(January 1984): 76–77. If terminally guided MARVs were to be prohibited by arms control, both superpowers could achieve important accuracy improvements by placing GPS (Global Positioning System—U.S.) or GLONASS (Global Navigation Satellite System—USSR) receivers on maneuverable reentry vehicles. Reliance on GPS/GLONASS would not be risk-free, of course. There would be a small possibility that precursor antisatellite (ASAT) action would have degraded or destroyed the GPS/GLONASS satellite constellations.

18.   See chapter 9.

19.   Brown, Speech at the U.S. Naval War College, p. 6.

20.   See Desmond Ball, *Developments in U.S. Strategic Nuclear Policy Under the Carter Administration*, ACIS Working Paper No. 21 (Los Angeles: Center for International and Strategic Affairs, UCLA, February 1980).

21.   Brown, Speech at the U.S. Naval War College, p. 6.

22.   See Thomas Wolfe, "The Convergence Issue and Soviet Strategic Policy," in *Rand 25th Anniversary Volume* (Santa Monica, Calif.: Rand Corporation, 1973), particularly p. 24.

23.   On the significance of this exception, see Colin S. Gray and Keith B. Payne, "Victory Is Possible," *Foreign Policy*, no. 39(Summer 1980): 14–27.

24.   Caspar W. Weinberger, *Annual Report to the Congress, Fiscal Year 1986* (Washington, D.C.: USGPO, February 4, 1985), p. 55. An apparent absence of enthusiasm for the ultimate goal of population defense has been a feature of some Department of Defense assessments of the rationales for the SDI. See Caspar W. Weinberger, Secretary of Defense, *Annual Report to the Congress, Fiscal Year 1985* (Washington, D.C.: USGPO, February 1, 1984), pp. 57–59. Also see Department of Defense, *Defense Against Ballistic Missiles: An Assessment of Technologies and Policy Implications* (Washington, D.C.: Department of Defense, March 6, 1984); and the prepared statements on the president's Strategic Defense Initiative by Fred C. Iklé, under secretary of defense for policy and Richard D. DeLauer in U.S. Congress, Senate, Committee Services, *Department of Defense Authorization for Appropriations for Fiscal Year 1985, Hearings*, Part 6, *Strategic Defense Initiative*, 98th Cong., 2nd sess. (Washington, D.C.: USGPO, 1984), pp. 7907–10, and 7912–1.

25.   The strength of this consensus is uncertain. There is a possibility that officials will cling to the Scowcroft formula, which argued a close linkage among MX/Peacekeeper, a new small ICBM, and arms control, even as political circumstances move on and require a revised architecture of policy arguments. See Colin S. Gray, *Nuclear Strategy and Strategic Planning*, Philadelphia Policy Papers (Philadelphia: Foreign Policy Research Institute, April 1984), chap. 5.

26.   This refers to analysts who contend that deterrence is assured if some "magic fraction" of the enemy's population and industrial base can be destroyed under all circumstances.

27.   This refers to people who are addicted to the SALT process.

28.   This was the official figure issued by the Carter administration and, to the best of my knowledge, was not controversial.

29.   A reliable summary description of the breadth and depth of Soviet strategic modernization options is provided in Caspar W. Weinberger, Secretary of Defense, *Soviet Military Power, 1985*, (Washington D.C.: USGPO, 1985). Also see Weinberger, *Annual Report to the Congress, Fiscal Year 1985*, pp. 21–23.

30.   This "fact" is explained in chapter 4. A persuasive brief sketch of the Soviet perspective is John Erickson, "Toward 1984: Four Decades of Soviet Military Policy," *Air University Review* 35, no. 2(January-February 1984): 30–34. Also very useful is Jonathan S. Lockwood, *The Soviet View of U.S. Strategic Doctrine: Implications for Decision Making* (New Brunswick, N.J.: Transaction, 1983).

31.   See chapter 7.

32.   Prepared statement of Henry Kissinger in U.S. Congress, Senate, Committee on Foreign Relations, *The Salt II Treaty, Hearings*, Part 3, 96th Cong., 1st sess. (Washington, D.C.: USGPO, 1979), p. 166.

33.   Every competently conducted study of U.S. civil defense problems has shown that a major shelter plus evacuation program would make a dramatic difference to U.S. societal survival and recovery. A particularly useful collection of views is U.S. Congress, Senate, Committee on Banking, Housing and Urban Affairs, *Civil Defense, Hearing*, 95th Cong., 2nd sess. (Washington, D.C.: USGPO, January 8, 1979).

34.   The Reagan administration appears to have learned that frank discussion of nuclear policy is politically damaging. The Secretary of Defense and his senior officials take every available opportunity to say that "we believe that neither side could win such a [nuclear] war." Weinberger, *Annual Report to the Congress, Fiscal Year 1985*, p. 29. In fact, there is ample reason for believing that a nuclear war *could* be won—meaning that political objectives could be secured at tolerable cost—although there is also good reason to doubt whether is *would* be. On the strategic nonsense that has been generated over the question of whether a nuclear war is or is not winnable, see Colin S. Gray, "War-Fighting for Deterrence," *Journal of Strategic Studies* 7 no. 1(March 1984): 5–28.

35.   However, for a careful analysis of the proposition that the past several years may have seen some genuine changes in Soviet attitudes toward nuclear war as an instrument of policy, see Dan L. Strode and Rebecca V. Strode, "Diplomacy and Defense in Soviet National Security Policy," *International Security* 8, no. 2(Fall 1983): 91–116; and the correspondence triggered by this article, George G. Weickhardt, "The World According to Ogarkov." *International Security* 8, no. 4(Spring 1984): 182–85.

36.   See Freeman Dyson, *Weapons and Hope* (New York: Harper & Row, 1984), pp. 188–89, 231.

37.   See Ken Booth, *Strategy and Ethnocentrism* (London: Croom, Helm, 1979). This book is severely flawed by its often perverse judgments on U.S. strategic policy, but "warts and all," it is one of the most important works to appear over the past twenty years.

38.   The U.S. and Soviet strategic cultures are explored in detail in chapters 2 and 3.

39.   In my opinion, the Soviet Union has been at "war" with the West since its birth. Political protagonists tend to mix competition and cooperation in their statecraft in pursuit of net advantage. To periodize post-1945 history in terms of "cold war," "détente," and so forth, is to do violence to the very nature of international politics.

40.   Thomas Powers, "What Is It About?" *Atlantic* 253, no. 1(January 1984): 35–55.

41.   The American public in 1972 may have hoped for an era of peace, but it was certainly willing to be persuaded concerning the possibility of inimical Soviet program actions. United States strategic nuclear weapons policies in the early and mid-1970s simply did not take proper account of the Soviet commitment

to achievement of a credible war-fighting capability. The cumulative impact of a growing appreciation of Soviet strategic realities on U.S. nuclear policy is discussed in Leon Sloss and Marc Dean Millot, "U.S. Nuclear Strategy in Evolution," *Strategic Review* 12, no. 1(Winter 1984): 19–28.

42. For example, see Jack L. Snyder, *The Soviet Strategic Culture: Implications for Limited Nuclear Operations*, R-2154-AF (Santa Monica, Calif.: Rand Corporation, September 1977).

43. However, I do believe that the Soviet way in strategic policy is more responsible than the U.S. way. For a strongly dissenting view, see Donald W. Hanson, "Is Soviet Strategic Doctrine Superior?" *International Security* 7, no. 3(Winter 1982/83): 61–83.

44. This case is argued strongly in George W. Ball, "The Cosmic Bluff," *New York Review of Books* 30, no. 12(July 21, 1983): 37–41.

45. This is the subtitle of chapter 9 in Bernard Brodie, *War and Politics* (New York: Macmillan, 1973).

46. This contemporary fact does not excuse policymakers from taking prudent and timely corrective measures to attend to threats that are demonstrable only in theory. Also, military history has demonstrated that more often than not, peacetime war planning has proved to be monumentally inappropriate to the circumstances of action.

47. See Weinberger, *Annual Report to the Congress, Fiscal Year 1985*, p. 30, where the authors erroneously contrast deterrence and defense.

48. This assumes that one is willing to grant the concept of a "well-fought" nuclear war.

49. It has long been charged by radical critics of nuclear strategy that debates over nuclear strategy tend to embrace only people who have establishment values (e.g., a question such as "Should the United States have a nuclear strategy?" is deemed by the nuclear strategy cognoscenti to be inadmissible, or irrelevant). See Philip Green, "Method and Substance in the Arms Debate, *World Politics* 16, no. 4(July 1964): 642–67; and Philip Green, "Science, Government and the Case of RAND: A Singular Pluralism," *World Politics* 20, no. 2(January 1968): 301–26.

50. McGeorge Bundy, "To Cap the Volcano," *Foreign Affairs* 48, no. 1(October 1969): 13.

51. See, for example, McGeorge Bundy, "Maintaining Stable Deterrence," *International Security* 3, no. 3(Winter 1978/79): 5–16.

52. Whatever sins one may attribute to the Soviet Union, a willingness to wage war without political meaning is not among them. See General-Major S. N. Kozlov, ed., *The Officer's Handbook (A Soviet View)*, Soviet Military Thought Series of the U.S. Air Force, No. 13 (Washington, D.C.: USGPO, 1977; Moscow, 1971), chap. 3.

53. Harry Summers, in by far the most persuasive analysis of the reasons for U.S. failure in Vietnam to appear to date, has written that "the problem in Vietnam, as in the early days of the Civil War, was not evil leaders or faulty arithmetic as much as it was a lack of strategic thinking." *On Strategy: A Critical Analysis of the Vietnam War* (Novato, Calif.: Presidio Press, 1982), p. 182.

54. See Martin van Creveld, "Caesar's Ghost: Military History and the Wars of the Future," *Washington Quarterly* 3, no. 1(Winter 1980): 76–83; and Colin S. Gray, "Across the Nuclear Divide: Strategic Studies, Past and Present," *International Security* 2, no. 1(Summer 1977): 24–46.

55. Skeptics could do a great deal worse than to read Edward N. Luttwak, *The Grand Strategy of the Roman Empire: From the First Century A.D., to the Third* (Baltimore: Johns Hopkins University Press, 1976). Luttwak has the rare distinction of being both a strategist of nuclear issues and a historian.

56. See Miles Kahler, "Rumors of War: The 1914 Analogy," *Foreign Affairs* 58, no. 2(Winter 1979/80): 374–96.

57. An excellent—indeed, outstanding—analysis of "the rules of the road" is Robert Gilpin, *War and Change in World Politics* (Cambridge: Cambridge University Press, 1981).

58. Some persuasive reasons for this signal deficiency are advanced in Booth, *Strategy and Ethnocentrism*.

59. A particularly enlightening discussion of the meaning of "great power" status is in George Modelski, *Principles of World Politics* (New York: Free Press, 1972), chap. 8. See also Martin Wight, *Power Politics* (New York: Holmes and Meier, 1978), chap. 3.

60. See Hedley Bull, *The Anarchical Society—A Study of Order in World Politics* (New York: Columbia University Press, 1977). The concept of a great power was not institutionalized until the Congress of Vienna in 1815.

61. The literature on Europe's "classical" balance of power system is vast indeed. Useful commentaries include Arnold Wolfers, *Discord and Collaboration: Essays on International Politics* (Baltimore: Johns Hopkins University Press, 1962), chap. 8; Wight, *Power Politics*, chap. 16; Ludwig Dehio, *The Precarious Balance: Four Centuries of the European Power Struggle* (New York: Vintage, 1962; first pub. 1948); P. M. Wright, ed., *Theory and Practice of the Balance of Power, 1486–1914: Selected European Writings* (London: Dent, 1975); F. Parkinson, *The Philosophy of International Relations: A Study in the History of Thought* (Beverly Hills, Calif.: Sage, 1977), chap. 3; and F. R. Bridge and Roger Bullen, *The Great Powers and the European States System, 1815–1914* (London: Longman, 1980). For a historical perspective on the nineteenth-century states system, see Martin Wight, *Systems of States* (Leicester: Leicester University Press, 1977).

62. Or until 1914 or 1919, as alternative defensible dates. Certainly, the ethos of the Versailles Conference of 1919 and the idea (though not the reality) of collective security that was popular in the 1920s and 1930s were not those of the classical balance-of-power system. See Arno J. Mayer, "The Problems of Peacemaking," in Hans W. Gatzke, ed., *European Diplomacy Between Two Wars, 1919–1939* (Chicago: Quadrangle, 1972), pp. 14–39.

63. And because of the ferocity with which revolting Poles were disciplined in 1830–31 and 1863.

64. See Gordon A. Craig, *Germany, 1866–1945* (New York: Oxford University Press, 1978), particularly pp. 310–14. For the full context, see Paul M. Kennedy, *The Rise of the Anglo-German Antagonism, 1860–1914* (London: Allen and Unwin, 1982; first pub. 1980).

65. Technically, the Anglo-Russian Convention of 1907 was simply an agreement delineating spheres of interest in Persia, Afghanistan, and Tibet.

66. William T. R. Fox, *The Super Powers* (New York: Harcourt, Brace, 1944).

67. See Nicholas J. Spykman, *America's Strategy in World Politics: The United States and the Balance of Power* (Hamden, Conn.: Archon, 1970; first pub. 1942); and Nicholas J. Spykman, *The Geography of the Peace* (New York: Harcourt, Brace, 1944).

68. Even if one disagrees with his conclusions vis-à-vis contemporary Soviet nuclear weapons policy (which I do not), Richard Pipes performed a major service by seeking to connect strategic policy debate to the historical reality of the country of most concern to U.S. defense planners. See Pipes, "Why the Soviet Union Thinks It Could Fight and Win a Nuclear War," *Commentary* 64, no. 1(July 1977): 21–34.

69. See Carl von Clausewitz, *On War* (Michael Howard and Peter Paret, eds.) (Princeton, N.J.: Princeton University Press, 1976; first pub. 1832), particularly book 1, chap. 2.

70. An outstanding study is William McElwee, *The Art of War: Waterloo to Mons* (London: Weidenfeld and Nicolson, 1974). Also useful is Hew Strachan, *European Armies and the Conduct of War* (London: Allen and Unwin, 1983).

71. See Robert Wohl, *The Generation of 1914* (London: Wiedenfeld and Nicolson, 1980).

72. When the balance-of-power system was functioning, war was a means of testing the balance and solving problems.

73. As Paddy Griffith has argued, there were seemingly good reasons why the theorists of stalemate were unheeded: "Behind the tactical assumptions carried into the First World War there lay a great deal of sound reasoning, based upon both concrete examples and abstract principles." *Forward Into Battle: Fighting Tactics from Waterloo to Vietnam* (Chichester [U.K.]: Antony Bird, 1981), p. 71.

74. This is not to deny the vastly accelerated pace that most likely would characterize the duration of a nuclear conflict. Similarly, there is no doubt that the speed with which mass devastation could be inflicted must have a major impact on the ability of states to recover. Whether or not a nuclear war would have unprecedented effects on the global climate is both unknown and unknowable. The nuclear winter thesis is unproven and unprovable. On the novelty of the nuclear age, see Michael Mandelbaum, *The Nuclear Revolution: International Politics Before and After Hiroshima* (Cambridge: Cambridge University Press, 1981); Gilpin, *War and Change in World Politics*, particularly chap. 6; and the Harvard Nuclear Study Group, *Living with Nuclear Weapons* (New York: Bantam, 1983), chap. 2.

75. For example, in World War II the Soviet Union suffered 13.7 million dead in its armed forces plus approximately 11 million dead civilians.

76. See Fred C. Iklé, "Can Nuclear Deterrence Last Out the Century?" *Foreign Affairs* 51, no. 2(January 1973): 267–85.

77. For interesting discussions with which I do not agree, see Michael Walzer, *Just and Unjust Wars: A Moral Argument with Historical Illustrations* (New

York: Basic Books, 1977), chap. 17; and Ian Clark, *Limited Nuclear War: Political Theory and War Conventions* (Princeton, N.J.: Princeton University Press, 1982). A superior study is Geoffrey Best, *Humanity in War* (New York: Columbia University Press, 1983). The Pastoral Letter on War and Peace of the (American) National Conference of Catholic Bishops is reproduced and discussed in Philip J. Murnion, ed., *Catholics and Nuclear War: A Commentary on "The Challenge of Peace," the U.S. Catholic Bishops' Pastoral Letter on War and Peace* (New York: Crossroad, 1983). Analysis critical of the Pastoral Letter is provided in Albert Wohlstetter, "Bishops, Statesmen, and Other Strategists on the Bombing of Innocents," *Commentary* 5, no. 6(June 1983): 15–35.

78. Enlightening commentaries can be found in Michael Howard, *War and the Liberal Conscience* (New Brunswick, N.J.: Rutgers University Press, 1978); and Michael Howard, ed., *Restraints on War: Studies in the Limitation of Armed Conflict* (Oxford: Oxford University Press, 1979).

79. In fact, I have argued strongly against the "city" targeting of nuclear weapons. See Colin S. Gray, "Nuclear Strategy: The Case for a Theory of Victory," *International Security* 4, no. 1(Summer 1979): 54–87; Colin S. Gray, "Targeting Problems for Central War," *Naval War College Review* 33, no. 1(January-February 1980): 3–21; and Gray and Payne, "Victory Is Possible." The United States does not target cities or civilian population per se. In fact, great care is taken in nuclear target planning to minimize the harm that would be done to civilians. The Joint Strategic Target Planning Staff (JSPS) has explicit criteria regarding how much calculated collateral damage is permissible. For a good general treatment of the mechanics of nuclear targeting, see Richard L. Walker, *Strategic Target Planning: Bridging the Gap Between Theory and Practice*, National Security Affairs Monograph Series 83–9 (Washington, D.C.: National Defense University Press, 1983).

80. The worst example of misrepresentation was Robert Scheer, *With Enough Shovels: Reagan, Bush and Nuclear War*, 2d ed. (New York: Vintage, 1983). For a suitably critical review of Scheer's book, see Keith Payne, "Commentary on Robert Scheer's *With Enough Shovels*," *Comparative Strategy* 4, no. 3(1984): 315-18.

81. My late colleague, Herman Kahn, liked to argue that the details of the July 1914 European crisis were so bizarre that no scenario writer today who was attentive to his reputation could possibly write such a fanciful sequence of events and expect to be taken seriously. Kahn was correct, but it is well to remember that the diplomatic maneuverings behind the 1908 Bosnian crisis were at least as idiosyncratic as were the details of July 1914, and Europe survived that crisis in peace. The moral of this story may be that the crisis-management skills of each historical international system, though considerable, are finite. Few, if any, international systems can long be proof against near-determinedly frivolous and incompetent policymaking in several capitals. This interpretation sidesteps the thesis that imperial Germany wanted war in the summer of 1914.

82. Nuclear weapons, far from having a sobering effect, almost certainly would have encouraged Adolf Hitler to bolder and bolder diplomatic démarches. A classic treatment of "the manipulation of risk" is Thomas C. Schelling, *Arms and Influence* (New Haven: Yale University Press, 1966), chap. 3.

83. Henry Kissinger, "The Future of NATO," *Washington Quarterly* 2, no.

4(Autumn 1979): 6. His argument, though a good one, does suffer from overstatement.

84. Most statesmen function in pursuit of a particular vision of "world order;" this concept tends to be implicit and to evade close critical scrutiny. See Bull, *The Anarchical Society*.

85. See S. Tyushkevich, "The Methodology for the Correlation of Forces," *Voyennaya Mysl*, FPD 0008/70, no. 6(June 1969): 26–39, reproduced in Joseph D. Douglass and Amoretta M. Hoeber, eds., *Selected Readings from Soviet Military Thought (1963–1973)*, SPC Report 584 (Arlington, Va.: System Planning Corporation, April 1980), pp. 415–70. Also see Michael Deane, "The Soviet Assessment of the 'Correlation of Forces': Implications for American Foreign Policy," *Orbis* 20, no. 3(Fall 1976): 625–36.

86. See Keith Payne, *Soviet and American Approaches to Escalation*, HI-3208-DP (Croton-on-Hudson, N.Y.: Hudson Institute, July 30, 1980), p. 14; and Hans J. Morgenthau, *Politics Among Nations: The Struggle for Power and Peace* (New York: Knopf, 1948), part 3.

87. Colin S. Gray, *The Geopolitics of the Nuclear Era: Heartland, Rimlands, and the Technological Revolution* (New York: Crane, Russak [for the National Strategy Information Center], 1977).

88. Halford Mackinder, *Democratic Ideals and Reality* (New York: Norton, 1962), p. 150. A superb biographical treatment of Mackinder and his ideas is W. H. Parker, *Mackinder: Geography as an Aid to Statecraft* (Oxford: Clarendon, 1982).

89. See Helene C. d'Encausse, *Decline of an Empire: The Soviet Socialist Republics in Revolt* (New York: Newsweek Books, 1979).

90. See André Beaufre, *Deterrence and Strategy* (London: Faber and Faber, 1965).

91. This narrow range, encompassing issues strictly of national survival, is of course the range believed by French theorists to be covered by the threat of the employment of the *force de frappe*. On national interests, see the excellent analysis in Donald E. Nuechterlein, "National Interests and National Strategy: The Need for Priority," in Terry L. Heyns, ed., *Understanding U.S. Strategy: A Reader* (Washington, D.C.: National Defense University Press, 1983), pp. 35–63.

92. See Arnold Horelick and Myron Rush, *Strategic Power and Soviet Foreign Policy* (Chicago: University of Chicago Press, 1965).

93. See the careful factual presentations and analysis in John M. Collins, *U.S.-Soviet Military Balance: Concepts and Capabilities, 1960–1980* (New York: McGraw-Hill, 1980). Also see Weinberger, *Soviet Military Power, 1985*.

94. See John P. Roche, "Moscow and the 'Window of Opportunity': A Cautionary Brief," unpublished manuscript, 1980.

95. Nonetheless, this is an issue of great historical interest. For the view that Marxism-Leninism is a disease afflicting (Holy) Russia, see Aleksandr Solzhenitsyn, "Misconceptions About Russia Are a Threat to America," *Foreign Affairs* 58, no. 4(Spring 1980): 797–834. For the view that Soviet Marxism-Leninism has been substantially a Russian phenomenon, see Richard Pipes, "A Reply" (to Wladislaw G. Krasnow, "Anti-Soviet or Anti-Russian"), *Encounter* 54, no. 4(April 1980): 72–75.

(The Krasnow article is on pp. 67–72 of the same issue.) Also see Richard Pipes: *Russia Under the Old Regime* (New York: Scribner's, 1974); "Soviet Political Dynamics," in *Soviet Dynamics—Political, Economic, Military*, (Pittsburgh: World Affairs Council of Pittsburgh, 1978), pp. 19–29; and "Soviet Global Strategy," *Commentary* 69, no. 4(April 1980): 31–39.

96. It is ironic that Afghanistan was long held up as a textbook example of a "buffer" state.

97. See the discussion of this theoretical development in Colin S. Gray, *Strategic Studies and Public Policy: The American Experience* (Lexington: University Press of Kentucky, 1982), chap. 9. For extended treatment, see Phil Williams, *Crisis Management: Confrontation and Diplomacy in the Nuclear Age* (London: Croom, Helm, 1976).

98. The thesis that political change (perhaps through the road test of war) follows dysfunctions between the distribution of power and established relations of relative influence and the rules that express those relations is developed persuasively in Gilpin, *War and Change in World Politics*.

99. V. Kortunov, "Socialism and International Relations," *International Affairs* (Moscow), no. 10(October 1979): 45.

100. For example, see Colonel-General N. A. Lomov, ed., *Scientific-Technical Progress and the Revolution in Military Affairs (A Soviet View)*, Soviet Military Thought Series of the U.S. Air Force, No. 3 (Washington, D.C.: USGPO, 1975; first pub. Moscow, 1973).

101. For an authoritative Soviet view of "just war", see Colonel N. I. Basov et al., *The Philosophical Heritage of V. I. Lenin and Problems of Contemporary War (A Soviet View)*, Soviet Military Thought Series of the U.S. Air Force, No. 5 (Washington, D.C.: USGPO, 1975; Moscow, 1972), chap. 2.

102. John Erickson, "The Soviet Military System: Doctrine, Technology and 'Style'," in John Erickson and E. J. Feuchtwanger, eds., *Soviet Military Power and Performance* (Hamden, Conn.: Archon, 1979), particularly pp. 24–35.

103. See Robert Jervis, *The Illogic of American Nuclear Strategy* (Ithaca, N.Y.: Cornell University Press, 1984), particularly chap. 2.

CHAPTER 2

National Style in Strategy I: The United States

THE IDEA OF NATIONAL STYLE

Discovery of the obvious can be important. Thanks to the rise of the idea and political organization of "the nation," it has long been appreciated that the French, the English, and Americans (and so forth) have important qualities as French, English and Americans (and so forth). Notwithstanding its multinational and certainly multiethnic foundations, the United States has a very clear sense of national identity—a sense that there exists a distinct "us" and that all others are "them," more or less carefully differentiated. Nonetheless, U.S. strategic thinkers have been curiously insensitive to possible national differences in modes of strategic thought and behavior.[1]

These U.S. strategists have always known, deep down, that Soviet, French, and British approaches to security issues differ from their own in good part because Soviet, French, and British policymakers are heirs to distinctive perspectives that are, at root, comprehensible through an appropriate combination of historical, geographical, anthropological, psychological, and sociological study. However, the recognition of national differences has only very rarely moved the U.S. government to take explicit account of the impact of those differences on policy goals and methods in its conduct of affairs.

In the late 1970s, U.S. defense commentators discovered what they really had known all along—that the Soviet Union did not appear to share many of the more important beliefs and practices beneficial to the U.S. idea of international order. This should not have come as a surprise, but it did. Although the Western strategic literature of the past quarter-century is replete with warnings against the practice of mirror-imaging and projecting U.S. desires and perspectives uncritically upon Moscow, those warnings by and large proceeded unheeded until the late 1970s. At present, in the mid-1980s, the U.S. defense community is at a point where it acknowledges the apparent facts of national cultural and stylistic differences—a great advance—but it has yet to determine what those differences should mean for U.S. policy.

Two works in particular merit identification as path-breaking studies in this field: Jack Snyder's Rand Report, *The Soviet Strategic Culture: Implications for Limited Nuclear Operations*, in 1977,[2] and Ken Booth's outstanding book, *Strategy and Ethnocentrism*, in 1979.[3] As Alfred Thayer Mahan had done in 1890,[4] they dignified and elevated insight to the level of principle.

The concept of strategic culture is a direct descendant of the concept of political culture—which has been debated, developed, variously employed, and even more variously defined by political scientists since the early 1950s.[5] The idea of national style is logically derived from the concept of political culture: a particular culture should encourage a particular style in thought and action. However, it is worth noting that this book, notwithstanding its culture/style theme, is fundamentally inductive-empirical. I have observed, for example, that the Soviet Union intellectually frames its defense tasks in ways that are generally unfamiliar to the United States and behaves in defense-related matters in a fashion that is inexplicable in standard U.S. terms.

The differences in observable thought and practice have so enduring a character that, even when idiosyncratic decision possibilities are factored out, it is plausible to hypothesize that the Soviet Union has approached, and continues to approach, defense issues in a fairly distinctive Soviet manner—comprehensible only in those terms. To understand why the Soviet Union thinks and behaves as it does, it should be useful to trace that thought and behavior to influencing factors of a fundamental kind. Even fully accepting the possible dangers of crude reductionism (if one or more allegedly "determining" factors are identified),[6] of insensitivity to change (even culture and style will alter over time), and of finding undue cultural distinctiveness (if one looks for the culturally bizarre, in U.S. terms, one is very likely to find it), their potential benefit for the quality of defense prediction and understanding of extant performance seems to be very considerable.

The discovery of cultural distinctiveness in strategic thought and practice has been attended, probably inevitably, by an unduly simple appreciation of this dimension of strategic affairs. As preliminary caveats, the following should be noted:

- Some strategic-cultural traits are common to many supposedly and even truly distinct cultures.

- A strategic culture may accommodate several very distinctive strategic subcultures (which may have more in common with some foreign strategic cultures than they have with their dominant national culture).

- Many, and probably most, alleged strategic cultural traits are fully rational, in strict realpolitik terms, given the self-perceived historical experience of the nations in question. The strategic cultural thought processes and behavior of interest to this book do not noticeably rest on individual psychocultural phenomena (e.g., the child-rearing practice of Great Russian mothers).

- From time to time, a state may act in ways that represent, in toto, a break from the traditional, dominant strategic culture.

The strategic-cultural theme of this book has its roots in a concern flagged informatively by Jack Snyder:

> It is useful to look at the Soviet approach to strategic thinking as a unique "strategic culture." Individuals are socialized into a distinctively Soviet mode of strategic thinking. As a result of this socialization process, a set of general beliefs, attitudes and behavioral patterns with regard to nuclear strategy has achieved a state of semipermanence that places them on the level of "culture" rather than mere "policy." Of course, attitudes may change as a result of changes in technology and the international environment. However, new problems are not assessed objectively. Rather, they are seen through the perceptual lens provided by the strategic culture.[7]

As often as not, the intriguing and potentially enlightening idea of strategic culture becomes a distorting idea when defense commentators search too assiduously, and too uncritically, for the cultural roots of contemporary defense practice. Hence, although one can compare and contrast Soviet and U.S. cultures, the comparison and contrast would often be a lot less stark if the full range of U.S. and Soviet attitudes were to be assessed, as opposed to only the policy-dominant ones. As with sound geopolitical analysis, with strategic-cultural analysis, one is discerning tendencies, not rigid determinants. Nevertheless, contemporary U.S., Soviet, and other strategic commentators have to be very much the products of their particular, unique cultural milieux.

It is hypothesized here that there is a discernible U.S. strategic culture—that culture, referring to modes of thought and action with respect to force, derives from perception of the national historical experience, from aspirations for responsible behavior in national terms, and from all of the many distinctively American experiences (which stem from geography, political philosophy, and practice—i.e., civic culture—and way of life) that determine a U.S. citizen. The idea of a U.S. national style derives from the idea of a U.S. strategic culture, suggesting that there is a distinctively American way in strategic matters.

Notwithstanding the necessary indeterminacy of some of the evidence, this chapter presents a complex hypothesis. First, it is suggested that there is a U.S. (and, ab extensio, other) strategic culture that flows from geopolitical, historical, economic, and other unique influences. Second, it is suggested that U.S. strategic culture provides the milieu within which strategic ideas and defense policy decisions are debated and decided. Third, it is suggested here that an understanding of U.S. strategic culture and style can help explain why U.S. policymakers have made the decisions they have. Moreover, if some light can thus be thrown on the past and the present, it may be possible to employ the concepts of strategic culture and style to predict decision tendencies in the future.

Admittedly, it is, unclear just how helpful studies of strategic culture may prove to be. However, it does not seem unduly optimistic to assert at least the following potential benefits:

- An improved understanding of our own and other cultures on our/ their own terms;

- An improved ability to discern enduring policy motivations and to predict;

- An improved ability to communicate what we wish to communicate (whatever that may be);[8]

- An improved ability to comprehend the meaning of events in the assessment of others.

A rather obvious danger in this theme lies in the realm of cultural relativism. Soviet drives for further influence abroad need be no less menacing because Americans think they understand much better what lies behind them. The central problem is not so much to understand Soviet power as it is to contain it (which is not to demean the virtue of understanding). Moreover, it is not argued here, implicitly or explicitly, that U.S. policy necessarily should be changed solely because its frame of conceptual reference fits poorly with that identified for the USSR. However, it cannot be denied that definitive judgment regarding the adequacy of U.S.

defense preparations for deterrence is rendered in Moscow, not in Washington.

Virtually by definition, strategic culture and national style have very deep roots within a particular stream of historical experience, as locally interpreted. Although it is not assumed here that culture and style are immutable (such would be absurd), it is assumed that national patterns of thought and action—the preferred ways of coping with problems and opportunities—are likely to alter only very gradually, short of a new historical experience that undeniably warrants a historically discontinuous response. Clearly, the Soviet Union of the mid-1980s is different from the Soviet Union of the late 1930s. However, pending some major system shocks, the weight of the past, and the way the past is interpreted as a (largely implicit) guide to the present, far outweighs in enduring importance the marginal changes in culture that are discernible year by year.

It is my contention that major streams of policy decisions in the United States and the Soviet Union cannot simply be explained in terms of the characteristics of particular people, their unique assessment of policy options, and the bureaucratic-political milieux in which they find themselves—though very often these factors could (and did) help shape the mix of contending bureaucratic-political forces. In addition, it is necessary to consider the strategic culture of the policymakers. Although aberrant, culturally innovative, or just plain eccentric decision making is always possible, there is a tendency for policymakers of a particular strategic culture to make policy in ways and substance that are congruent with the parameters of that culture. A national style, to endure and attain that status, is a style that "works" well enough for a particular nation. A national style is not the random product of imaginative thinking by policymakers; rather, it is a pattern of national response to challenge that has worked adequately in the past.

Although, as stated earlier, strategic-cultural analysis should not incline one to judge, almost reflexively, that identified U.S. proclivities are necessarily inappropriate simply because they are incongruent with the known proclivities of probable adversaries, neither should one be content to assert, complacently, that each party simply is what it is. Strategy is largely a matter of adaptation to perceived reality, and some societies have adapted more effectively than others. It is not enough just to note the details of "the American way" and "the Soviet way"; more important is the question of how those ways would likely fare if they were ever tested in direct conflict. To date, at least, the very few studies of comparative strategic culture and style that have appeared have not ventured into the realm of the implications for U.S. policy. The inherent merit of U.S. strategic thinking is not the issue—this is not a contest in intellectual aesthetics; the real issue is how appropriate U.S. ideas are as sources of policy guidance for a conflict process with a particular adversary.

Much that a country does, or attempts to do, is done because of force of circumstance. A central problem with cultural-stylistic explanations of U.S. and other national thought and behavior is that alternative hypotheses may also explain the phenomena in question. But, it is true that, as John Shy has argued, "the idea that there are national patterns of international behavior retains an impressive degree of plausibility."[9]

Nonetheless, the determined deductivist usually can find impressive ex post facto empirical support for his deductions. Fortunately, the plausibility of this book does not rest on the prior establishment of unambiguous evidence concerning the historical reality of what Shy has termed "national peculiarities."[10] Instead, this book notes, with reference to the key concepts pertinent to nuclear strategy, the differences between the United States and the Soviet Union, and it is content to proceed inductively, and cautiously, back to possible cultural influences.

It is worth noting that this book takes a broad view of "national peculiarities." By "peculiarities," I refer not so much to ethnocentrically perceived eccentricities or colorfully bizarre "foreign" habits, but rather to different mind sets and behavior patterns that flow, as responses, from a very distinctive historical-geographical and, hence, cultural context. The potential problem of multiple causation may easily be overstressed. Assessed in isolation, quite a wide range of theories may be invoked to explain U.S. and Soviet defense behavior. To sift these theories for their plausibility and then their explanatory power, one needs to engage in cross-cultural analysis. For example, if one has a structural theory of U.S. defense policy behavior that identifies some mix of a military-industrial complex and bureaucratic politics as the collective determinant, or villian, of defense policy outputs, how does one account for the fact that a Soviet military-industrial complex, and Soviet bureaucratic politics, produces a very different policy output. The answer, presumably, has to be that the industrial-bureaucratic-political forces in the two superpowers are configured differently. Even if this is true, however, one still has to ask why those forces are configured differently. In short, even the structural-determinist cannot evade the issue of possible cultural impact on the analysis.

It is important to restate, at this juncture, that this book rests on a basically agnostic stance vis-à-vis national differences in approaches to national security. While one has no difficulty identifying apparent U.S., Soviet, British, approaches to national security, it is less obvious that those different approaches reflect anything more peculiar than a uniqueness of historical circumstance. In other words, Americans and Russians may be different as individuals in psychocultural "thoughtways,"[11] but such putative differences are not important here. What is of interest is state, not individual, behavior, and what is required is an open mind to the possibility that very different national experiences tend to produce different policy responses.

In asserting, as a hypothesis, that Great Russians think differently about national security issues than Americans do, one need not imply anything about the "curious" psychology of individual Great Russians or Americans. Instead, one may simply imply that the geopolitical inheritance of the two people is very different and that that inheritance has very natural local consequences for contemporary assessment of security problems.

It is important that the cultural-stylistic theme not be muddied in appraisal by views on the merits of national character analysis. I will confine myself to asserting that each society has a unique, distinctive history; that each society learns (or mislearns) from its assessment of that unique, distinctive history; and that each society with a unique, distinctive history is likely to learn and mislearn à wisdom for statecraft that is different from that of other societies.

It is not too difficult to find in the history of each state experiences that are closely analogous (at least superficially) to those of many other states. For example, as Ken Booth has done, one can show that the U.S. military experience is sufficiently rich and varied to cast doubt on all simple assertions concerning "the American way in war."[12] Booth's successful foray into the realm of myth destruction, though quite impressive as a scholarly exercise, is reminiscent of the old conundrum of deciding whether a tumbler of water is half-empty or half-full. Many, if not most, allegedly U.S. cultural traits in warfare and approaches to warfare can be found elsewhere. Booth is correct; however, in his worthy determination to slay the dragon of myths concerning the convenient metaphor of "American strategic man," he neglects to address a still-valid question: What, if any, are the implications for defense and international security of the unique U.S. geopolitical experience? To be truly useful, the exercise of destruction requires a follow-up, constructive phase. Nonetheless, essentially nihilistic or not, Booth's assault on the concept of the uniqueness of "American strategic man" should serve as a very useful corrective to those who are anxious to offer simple cultural-determinant or "essentialist" explanations of state behavior.

It is almost as easy to debunk theories of "national peculiarities" as it is to advance them. The most that may be accomplished is the acquisition of new insights or the rediscovery of forgotten insights into apparent U.S., Soviet, and so forth, tendencies that may warrant identification as national styles in strategy. As with many potentially enlightening concepts, national strategic culture and style is useful so long as it is approached with a healthily skeptical eye. One should be prepared for discovery but should not assume that recognition of the concept alone constitutes genuine discovery. The concept of strategic culture and national style is as easily understood as the concept of strategic superiority, but does historical reality, actual or potential, match the concept?

UNITED STATES EXPERIENCE, PRACTICE,
AND STYLE

Notwithstanding Ken Booth's assault on the myth of the "American strategic man," I agree with John Shy:

> Whenever Americans before the end of the nineteenth century thought
> about questions of war or military force, their perception of those
> questions was strongly affected by certain peculiar attitudes and be-
> liefs that, through the conditioning effect of long historical experience,
> had become almost reflexive. [They had a] dichotomous idea of na-
> tional security, an unthinking optimism about the national American
> aptitude for warfare, and an ambivalent attitude toward those Ameri-
> cans who specialized in the use of force.[13]

It would be an elementary exercise to demonstrate why Americans
should be different—how their attitudes and behavior should betray unique
tendencies. The U.S. military experience, as John Shy illustrated,[14] has
indeed been extraordinary (a succession of victories from the Seven Years'
War of 1756–1763 through to 1945). Similarly, one could, and perhaps
should, dwell on the strategic-cultural legacy of continental insularity and
isolation from truly serious security dangers, on the conditioning effect of
living with weak, nonthreatening neighbors on one's frontiers, on the
experience of taming a frontier of continental dimensions, on the enduring
impact of fundamentalist religious beliefs, and on the strategic meaning
of constituting a nation of immigrants—and so on. Although Bernard
Brodie was correct in his assertion that "good strategy presumes good
anthropology and sociology,"[15] the starting point for the professional strategist should be with the subject that he understands best—strategy—not
with cultural anthropology. It is important to begin with the facts. What
are the facts? Since facts tend to be historically bounded, the historical
mandate adopted here is the facts of the period from 1960 to 1985.

First, the United States acquiesced in a style of defense leadership that
was "managerial" rather than "strategic."[16] The McNamara revolution in
the Pentagon effected, for the first time, genuine central civilian domination, in detail, of the military establishment, and a domination of quanti-
tively expressible analysis over "mere military judgment."

Second, the United States has been unable, to date, to come to grips
with the prospect of viewing, and planning for, nuclear war *as war*. American and, more generally, Western democratic values are deemed to be so
incompatible with the actual conduct and consequences of nuclear war
that the vast bulk of U.S. nuclear-age strategic thinking has been confined
to the problems of prewar deterrence.

Third, though not positively intending to surrender a condition of strategic nuclear superiority, the United States nonetheless acquiesced in the loss of that condition by virtue of program inaction and even welcomed the loss because of its anticipated reassuring effect on Soviet leaders, and was willing to register the loss publicly through the mechanism of arguably equitable strategic arms limitation agreements.

Fourth, the United States endorsed theories of strategic stability that rationalized the loss of strategic superiority.

Fifth, the United States pursued an arms control process that, by its very nature and structure, was erosive of the foreign policy reasoning that underpinned the U.S. strategic nuclear force posture.[17] United States overseas security commitments generally require the backing of a U.S. strategic forces posture that is superior to that of the Soviet Union, not in a state of parity or essential equivalence.

Sixth, the United States failed to recognize the character (motives are another matter) of the Soviet strategic forces program until the prudentially required U.S. response time had elapsed (the condition today).

Finally, the United States did not recognize the Soviet Union as a culturally and historically unique adversary that was unlikely to prove reponsive to U.S. political-military desiderata—no matter how eloquently or persistently expressed.

STRATEGY AND MANAGEMENT

As Edward Luttwak has argued,[18] until very recently, the United States really had scant need of strategy beyond the often highly technical functions associated with "war planning." War planning and strategy are different concepts. War planning for the efficient allocation of scarce defense capabilities may or may not be guided by close attention to the achievement of judiciously selected political goals. Essentially, war planning is a technical exercise conducted by uniformed staff officers who are guided by agreed strategy. There is a case to be made, of course, for the point of view that in the absence of explicit strategy formulation, war planners will make strategy by default. However, in principle at least, the distinction is clear between strategy and contingency planning for its implementation.

It is the U.S. style to devote more attention to the management of large defense programs than to operational issues. Indeed, there is a startling historical contrast between the selection processes and subsequent courses of study of German and U.S. staff officers prior to World War II.[19] As a generalization, whereas U.S. officers were taught how to be good at the management of men and the provision of material, German officers were taught, almost exclusively, how to handle military assets in combat. The management bias in U.S. higher military education has survived to the present—with predictable results.[20] The United States in the twentieth century has been a resource-rich country. Questions pertaining to the actual employment of force, particularly limited force, have been deemed secondary to the marshalling of muscle. In terms of its mobilized and mobilizable assets, Germany was grossly inferior to her enemies in World Wars I and II. Eventually, this inferiority produced the predictable out-come—defeat. However, the German army in those two wars, although ultimately defeated for reasons of deficiencies of substance, outperformed its adversaries to a noteworthy degree. The political fact of victory for the United States, achieved through brute force or sheer quantity of assets, tended to subsume issues of strategy.

Until the mid-1960s, issues of so-called strategy strictly required that scant U.S. attention be paid to political objectives. Traditionally, war plan-ning was informed by an elementary, and eminently defensible, desire to win. Military experience from the Seven Years' War to 1945 yielded some dominant national beliefs.

First, it was believed that good causes tend to triumph and that Ameri-cans wage war only in good causes. The United States, as the modern pioneer in democracy and religious liberty (the "city upon a hill,"[21] the light from Plymouth Rock, and so forth), is an extraordinary country. In some broad essentials, U.S. ideology on participation in war is notably congruent with that of the Soviet Union. Just as the Soviet Union, by Soviet doctrinal definition, cannot wage an unjust war,[22] so U.S. political culture cannot accommodate the idea that the United States can, and occasionally should, wage a war for goals that are even controversial in terms of enduring American ideas of justice. The U.S. antiwar movement of the Vietnam era was a thoroughly American phenomenon. The United States of Lyndon Johnson and Richard Nixon was judged and found wanting in terms of traditional American values.

Second, it was believed that Americans could achieve anything to which they set their hands in earnest. The United States, until 1966-67 at least, was, by very popular consensus (by and large acknowledged, though not untinged by jealousy, abroad) one of history's nearly unquestionable success stories—Horatio Alger at the national level. The U.S. national experience provides ample evidence for an optimistic ideology. Americans survived and triumphed in the seventeenth and eighteenth centuries against the might of intermittently hostile and numerically vastly superior Indian tribes, against the might of France and Great Britain, and, perhaps most impressive, against a very challenging physical geography. By 1814, as John Shy has argued, the infant United States had registered a historically very unusual achievement:[23] complete victory, in all essentials, against enemies of the Republic and consolidation of a secure base for repetition of the same, if need be. Admittedly, as Ken Booth points out, contempo-rary Americans, reasoning prudentially, did not view their defense condi-tion in quite so optimistic a light.[24] However, assessed historically (i.e., with the virtue of hindsight), the United States after 1814, and really even earlier, was unassailable, save by domestic fission.

Third, in Sir Denis Brogan's phrase, there was an "illusion of [American] omnipotence," which was fed and justified by reference to the national success story.[25] American wars in the nineteenth century had been waged against third-class opponents—Mexico, Spain, and the series of Indian Wars—whereas the drawn war against Great Britain in 1812-14 was waged against a first-class adversary that was able and motivated to commit only a small fraction of its defense capability. The only truly hard-fought war of the nineteenth century, the Civil War, did not dent the American ideology of guaranteed success for the simple reason that it was waged between Americans. Americans of all persuasions could—and did—take pride in the *American* resilience of the Confederacy. Robert E. Lee is a genuinely national hero, North and South.

Although the United States waged war against a first-class adversary in World Wars I and II, Americans have tended to downplay the contribution of others to Germany's successive defeats. The United States may well have saved the Allies (co-belligerents, in American terms) from defeat in 1918, but the Germany of 1918 was not the Germany of 1914-17, and U.S. forces played a relatively minor battlefield role.[26] Similarly, the Germany defeated to a very significant degree by U.S. arms in 1943-45 was a Germany already bled white by America's Russian ally. This is not to argue that the United States could not have triumphed over an enemy at the peak of its power; it is only to note the historical fact that—until 1945, at least—Americans, save for their Civil War, waged war against enemies that were severely disadvantaged by geography, in relative strength of political will for the struggle, or by massive attrition effected by others. Imperial Japan was very much a first-class adversary in some local situations, but not strategically (after 1942, at least). As its own leaders recognized, Japan had no hope of ultimate victory over a fully mobilized United States.

As Edward Luttwak has argued, in the nineteenth century Great Britain effectively conducted U.S. strategic thinking,[27] since the offshore insular diplomacy of British "balance of power" machinations served U.S. interests as well as British. In the twentieth century, as an economic and potentially military superpower, protected until the mid-1950s by oceanic distance from theaters of major threat of conflict, the United States was permitted the luxury of intervening in wars that were already very well underway. It is true that U.S. entry into both world wars was precipitated by events created by others, but the scale and character of U.S. military intervention was uniquely, among the major belligerent powers, at the national discretion.

Fourth, in their industrial resource hubris, Americans believed that, if so moved, they could mobilize sufficient military muscle to overwhelm any enemy. Since Americans had first scented world power in the 1890s, they tended to have faith in the ability of U.S. technology, pragmatic know-how, and managerial skills of all kinds to overwhelm any evil cause. This faith generally has not been ill-grounded. In their individual ways of war, countries naturally stress their comparative advantages and reflect their societal values. In the twentieth century, whenever possible, the United States has waged technological war rather than wars of human (American) attrition. Very sensibly, U.S. governments have been sensitive to potential U.S. casualties, as befits a country that is heir to the idea that government is a necessary evil charged with facilitating the "life, liberty, and pursuit of happiness" of its citizens.

The long historical experience of a condition of nearly total security (perhaps as near as makes no difference), thanks to transoceanic distance from potential enemies and industrial preeminence, was erosive of what pressure there might otherwise have been for strategic thought. The U.S. experience from the Napoleonic era to 1945 was characterized by an absence of year-in and year-out external menace and—in the twentieth century—a once-in-each-generation need to surge actual military capability to overwhelm an enemy.[28] The idea of devising long-term political-military strategy, or grand strategy, to help control the U.S. external security condition, although defensible in terms of objective factors, could not be retailed successfully against the weight of the U.S. popular security culture. The United States was far removed from danger geographically and had nearly limitless potential to mobilize for defense, if need be. In addition, most Americans, as more or less recent immigrants, were not at all eager to see their new country and themselves involved intimately in the conflicts of a world that they thought they had left behind. By and large, Central and Eastern Europeans, Jews, Germans, Italians, Swedes, Irish, and so forth, did not—as new Americans—feel an indissoluble nexus to the "old country." Aside from the very important fact that no single immigrant group, relative to the total size of the U.S. electorate, (or even by virtue of geographical concentration), could affect U.S. foreign policy in decisive ways prior to 1945, it seems that immigrants to the United States were eager to cast off their European memories and possible residual loyalties.

To summarize, prior to 1945 it was unusual to find Americans endorsing the idea that the United States should be a permanent guardian of international order. In the popular American conception, the United States was a haven for the disadvantaged (though very restrictive immigration legislation had effectively negated the practical force of that thesis); was an example to the rest of mankind (the "city upon a hill"[29]); and would and could intervene decisively on the side of good when disorder in the Old World so required. The reality of material abundance, married to a historic engineering-pragmatic national style,[30] was not a fertile soil for strategic seeding. Skill in the tactical-operational handling of forces tends to be encouraged by a shortage of material means. In the popular phrase, necessity is the mother of invention. A United States rich in machines, men, and logistic support of all kinds is not obviously in need of clever strategems or of a careful balancing of likely political benefit against probable cost in material and human assets. In contrast, German tactical skills in the two world wars of this century were the product of military necessity; the side that is inferior in material and human assets needs to seek compensation in the quality of its tactics and strategy.

THE TWENTIETH CENTURY

Although there have always been individual exceptions, it is valid to argue that strategic thinking has been, and remains, alien to the mainstream of U.S. thought on defense questions.[31] Prior to 1945, wars were waged, intermittently, for the purpose of defeating a particular enemy (representing an evil cause), and the only admissible goal was victory. In World War I, Woodrow Wilson endorsed the goal of a decisive military victory as an essential prelude to establishment of a just and lasting peace. The means for total victory were outlined in the plan approved by the president in July 1918 to contribute 4,165,119 U.S. soldiers to France for a summer campaign in 1919.[32] U.S. military power was not applied in World War I in a manner sufficiently timely as to give the United States even a modest prospect of achieving its more important political objectives (absurdly idealistic though those objectives seemed to the leaders of the U.S.' co-belligerents). General Douglas MacArthur was correct when he asserted that "there is no substitute for victory." If one wishes to dominate the process of designing the postwar political order, one first has to win that right on the battlefield. From time to time, countries are unable to translate military victory into political success (witness France vis-à-vis the war in Algeria), but it is a general truth that in the absence of clear military success, only extraordinary incompetence on the part of the enemy permits one to have a decisive voice in the design of the postwar order.

World War II is a less complex case than World War I, in that the goal of defeating Nazi Germany, unlike the Allied goal of beating the Kaiser's Germany, clearly was politically valid in and of itself. It is a relatively elementary matter to defend U.S. military conduct in World War II against the charge that considerations of the postwar balance of power in Europe were unduly discounted. It may be argued that U.S. politicians were sensibly reluctant to expend American lives in pursuit of (distant) political goals unrelated to, and possibly even subversive of, the immediate needs of the conflict; that they believed that the Soviet Union was owed a preponderant voice in the design of the security order of postwar East-Central

Europe, by virtue of both the magnitude of its wartime contribution and the behavior of Poland, Rumania, and Hungary in the late 1930s (and beyond); that they believed that there was little or nothing the United States could do to prevent Stalin from having his way in East-Central Europe and that the only practical policy option open to the Western Allies was to be unambiguously accommodating to reasonable Soviet wishes, thereby helping to diminish Stalin's possible sense of need for an extensive glaçis.

In retrospect, Roosevelt's policy of nearly unconditional cooperation with the Soviet Union plainly was unwise and even naive, but it was understandable, given the "national peculiarities" of U.S. political culture, and was and is easy to defend in the light of contemporary U.S. policy assessment. One should not forget, from the vantage point of the mid-1980s, that the Western Allies of 1943–44 (when the critical decisions were taken concerning zones of occupation in postwar Germany) felt profoundly guilty about the massive inequality of effort, between the Soviet Union and themselves, devoted to the actual engagement of the German armed forces. When an ally is doing most of the fighting and dying, one is not in a strong position, or even likely to feel very motivated, to design strategies intended to deprive him of most of the potential fruits of a victory to which he has made a disproportionately large contribution.

Nonetheless, with the excuses admitted, the fact remains that competent war leaders are supposed to have vision and to pursue long-term as well as short-term security measures. Once the Grand Coalition was fully assembled and had weathered the crises of 1942 (i.e., after Midway, Alamein, and Stalingrad), strategic genius was not required to discern that Germany's and Japan's defeat was inevitable (barring the improbability of German production of atomic weapons), and that the most important issues of Anglo-American statecraft pertained to the character of the postwar world. For good though insufficient reasons, U.S. statecraft proved unequal to the historic challenge. Western allied forces could, and should, have liberated Prague, Berlin, and much of what is now East Germany—and should have remained in place pending a postwar peace settlement. Greater vision in 1944–45, admittedly at the risk of incurring a nontrivial cost in military casualties, could have denied the Soviet Union many of the geostrategic advantages it obtained vis-à-vis Western Europe. Certainly, the Soviet Union could have been denied control of Czechoslovakia.

American military performance in World War II was effective and successful, but it was effective and successful in a context where—overall, though perhaps arguably—it was difficult to fare very badly. As already noted, U.S. staff training prior to the war stressed management rather than tactical-operational skills and lacked a firm commitment to true excellence in the candidates selected for higher command. With a few exceptions, as always, U.S. (and British) military professionals in World War II (referring to the army only) were virtually amateurs compared with their German counterparts, save in the admittedly important realm of management skills.[33] The German Army that American soldiers met in combat in Normandy was in decline, devoid of air cover, and mishandled in good part because of Hitler's ill-timed interventions, but it remained a formidable combat force.[34] Military resource superiority,[35] not to mention the debilitating requirements of coalition management, led the Western Allies, in effect, to pursue a strategy of attrition instead of annihilation through maneuver (except for Patton's "right hook," which seemed to come close to capturing the German forces in Normandy in the Falaise Pocket). Attrition, of course, is the risk-minimizing option, since the larger side must win (provided that the adversary does not have available any annihilation options of his own).[36]

However unimaginative and deficient in strategic vision the general U.S. conduct of its campaigns in World War II, at least it had the virtue of pursuing the unambiguous, attainable, popular, and necessary (though not sufficient) goal of *victory*.

The astrategic U.S. tradition—the product of continental insularity and abundant defense mobilization potential—continued into the nuclear age, although it took different forms. The U.S. national military experience prior to 1945 was characterized by relatively short, relatively cheap, and unambiguously successful campaigning against enemies plausibly portrayable in demonological terms. In practice, if not in general public recognition, the United States waged two balance-of-power wars in 1917–18 and 1941–45 to prevent the domination of Eurasia by a single country or coalition. However, as Henry Kissinger came to lament, Americans do not think geopolitically[37] and they tend to be unwilling to sacrifice their nearest and dearest for the balance of power or for international equilibrium— even if U.S. security rests on the preservation, or restoration, of such a balance or equilibrium. This is not acceptable language in the U.S. political culture.

The New Strategy[38]

The period from the mid-1950s until the early 1960s saw the evolution and development, largely by civilian theorists, of ideas on—or supposedly on—strategy that, superficially at least, were fundamentally challenging to the traditional U.S. way of war. The three central pillars of "the new strategy"—deterrence theory, limited war theory, and arms control theory—appeared to represent a sharp break with traditional American style:

1. *Deterrence theory* came to require a condition of nearly wartime readiness in peacetime, year after year. (The traditional U.S. pattern was

unpreparedness during peacetime "normalcy"—initial setbacks, mobilization, and eventual triumph.)

2. *Limited war theory* required a readiness to apply a limited quantity and quality of force for limited political goals (thereby requiring circumstantial redefinition of the meaning of victory).[39]

3. *Arms control theory* explained the merit in "some kind of collaboration with the countries that are potential enemies."[40] (This involved conducting business with those presumed to be evilly disposed.)

These theories could have been developed in a way, and with policy implications, compatible with prudent strategic thinking. By and large, however, they were not. In 1957, Henry Kissinger, in the first popular work published on nuclear strategy, castigated the traditional absence of strategic thinking in the United States—the inability to relate power to political purpose.[41] For the better part of a decade, in 1955–65, U.S. theorists elaborated schemes for the fine-tuning of military power—in threat and, if need be, in execution—for securing limited political objectives.[42] The era of U.S. strategic thinking appeared to have arrived. Indeed, as Ken Booth reminds us, many commentators in the United States and abroad were distressed by what they discerned as an overintellectualized U.S. approach to military-diplomatic problems.[43] This book has no quarrel with the endeavor to think strategically; rather, its quarrel is with the content of much of that thought and with the eventual consequences of that thought as it came to dominate U.S. policymaking in the 1960s and 1970s.

Because of the effective preponderance of uniformed military opinion within the U.S defense establishment prior to 1961[44]—in a context of massive, if unplanned, U.S. military superiority over the Soviet Union (by virtue of the relative strength and dynamics of U.S. high-technology industry)—U.S. war planning in the 1950s, if ever tested in combat, should have led to the military, political, and economic annihilation of the Soviet Union (and China).[45] However, as early as August 18, 1948, official U.S. thinking rejected the idea of unconditional surrender, or total victory, as a prudent and feasible war aim.[46] This novel departure from the U.S. tradition reflected both lessons learned from the recent experience with Germany and, above all else, an appreciation of the scale of effort required to elicit such an outcome in a war with the Soviet Union. After 1954–55, however, the deployment of thermonuclear weapons—with a Strategic Air Command and naval aviation expanded and reequipped as a consequence of the more than threefold increase in defense funds triggered by the Korean mobilization—meant that the U.S. defense community was back in the victory-effecting business.

Notwithstanding the contemporary (mid-1950s) civilian theorizing on the subject of deterrence, with its highly critical (of official policy) tone and content,[47] SAC did have a war plan that made strategic sense.[48] A U.S. president could back his foreign policy, if need be, with threats of central nuclear employment and expect to be believed. American political objectives could be forwarded by nuclear action, because the United States should have won such a war in classic fashion. Soviet military power could have been defeated, and most Western—certainly most American—assets could have been protected.

By and large (though there were exceptions), leading defense intellectuals in the United States preferred to focus on prewar deterrence and to abstain from investigation of putative operational strategy. More to the point, they neglected the logical and practical political connections between likely net prowess in war and the quality of prewar deterrent effect. For much of the postwar period this neglect was a matter of relatively little importance, because Soviet leaders had no difficulty appreciating that, whatever the deficiencies in U.S. strategic thought might be, the Soviet Union assurededly would lose a war. This is a fairly generous interpretation, because if the Soviet Union anticipated being able to compel the United States to take the lead in a process of escalation, then the phenomenon of self-deterrence might have paralyzed U.S. will, rather than Soviet will. The United States would have been the first country to face the decision whether or not to initiate action that could result, by way of Soviet retaliation, in catastrophic damage.

The quantity and quality of weaponry available, and the professional inclinations of SAC, produced a robust theory of victory in the 1950s, albeit one that was dramatically short of flexibility in the war plan that gave it authoritative expression.[49] The next decade began in a promising fashion, as the Kennedy administration hastened to effect a very large buildup in ballistic missiles and, overall, to ensure the invulnerability of U.S. strategic forces. However, the 1960s saw, for the first time, the domination of defense planning by civilian defense intellectuals who, by and large, had a managerial, or defense-analytical, rather than a strategic orientation.[50]

Even with historical hindsight, it is not obvious whether the poverty of U.S. strategic thought and practice in the 1960s and 1970s reflected the reassertion of longstanding traditional patterns or whether those two decades, instead, saw the temporary dominance of a strategic subculture. The facts of the past twenty-five years are clear, even if the relations among all of the responsible driving forces are not. In 1960–61, the United States almost certainly could have won a war against the Soviet Union under *most* probable conditions—not a war of attrition, with both sides taking comparable damage and the more resilient side staying the course longer, but a war of annihilation. By the mid-1980s, the Soviet Union had achieved a position of marginal strategic superiority—meaning that with good luck and judgment, it would win at modest cost; with less good luck and less good judgment, it should still win, though very possibly at a level so catastrophic as to call into question the meaning of victory.[51] Overall, it is a condition wherein the United States should be deterred from pressing political conflicts to the point of direct Soviet-U.S. military action. The absence of a margin of military advantage in strategic nuclear power could inhibit the United States from resisting Soviet conventional intrusions or attacks.[52]

AMERICAN ATTITUDES

The dominant strain in the U.S. defense community for more than twenty years, though not generally demeaning the theoretical value of strategic superiority,[53] came to believe the following:

1. Meaningful superiority could not be regained or, if regained, sustained. Moreover, such superiority was not necessary to meet the goals set by national security policy.

2. The evolution of technology was imposing an impasse, a strategic deadlock.

3. Continued doctrinal commitment to strategic superiority would merely license the armed services to request larger forces from which little, if any, net political or military benefit could be anticipated.

4. Little benefit could be expected because the Soviet Union would react to any efforts to secure superiority in such a fashion as to nullify those efforts. The quest for damage limitation came to be seen as the primary dynamic of the arms race.

As a plausible generalization, the U.S. defense community came to fear the arms race more than it did the Soviet Union. After a brief flurry of interest in strategic operational issues, Robert McNamara declined to press for major revisions in targeting strategy.[54] Although the targeting professionals in Omaha continued to do their best to match available weapons to an expanding target list, minimal high-level civilian, or military, guidance was offered for the shaping of war plans that would provide for flexibility in execution in support of particular war aims.[55] (This is not to deny that in time of acute crisis, in principle at least, very selective attack options could have been designed ad hoc in a process of adaptive planning.)

Overall, however, it can be claimed that the defense community, at the high policymaking level, came to be profoundly disinterested in nuclear (operational) strategy. Nuclear weapons had "Utility [only] in Nonuse";[56]

they came to be considered more and more explicitly through the 1960s in terms of a particular theory of strategic stability.[57]

What American, and in some cases *uniquely American*, attitudes, have contributed to the cumulative relative decline in U.S. deployed strategic nuclear power over the past twenty years? First, there has been, and remains, a belief that nuclear war of any kind and scale cannot be won. The United States, except in the Civil War, has always taken relatively modest casualties in war. (In World War I, for example, the United States suffered 100,000 deaths, compared to 950,000 for Great Britain and 1,350,000 for France.) High casualties, actual or easily comprehended, are a sad fact of European military experience. In 1945 and after, the United States could not—and still cannot—come to terms culturally with the probable fact that war against a first-class enemy is a very expensive enterprise. The traditional American definition of victory appears to have excluded any outcome other than one that entailed only very modest American casualties. This definition reflected American historical experience (apart from the Civil war) and a value system that accords great importance to the well-being of individuals. However, it is worth noting that there is some friction between this devotion to low American casualties and the facts, throughout most of U.S. history, both of an abundance of U.S. manpower and of a relative indifference on the part of U.S. military commanders to local material and civilian loss (not to mention enemy combat loss). General Van Fleet, commander of the Eighth Army in Korea, said in May 1951: "We must expend steel and fire, not men. I want so many artillery holes that a man can step from one to the other."[58]

As the instrument of a materially rich country, the United States Army in World War II often attempted to clear minefields with a profligate artillery barrage. The Soviet Army expended men (and women) on the same duty.

Second, U.S. defense intellectuals have tended to believe that other cultures either share, or will come to share, American values and strategic ideas. An important example of this phenomenon has been the fact that although U.S. (and NATO) defense policy envisages the conduct of nuclear war, if need be, for the better part of twenty years that policy has been contradicted by the reality that nuclear war has not been approached operationally as an instrument of policy—even with reference to cases of true desperation. A United States serious about its declared, contingent intention to use nuclear weapons would not be totally naked of homeland defense. Because very reliable defense against all forms of nuclear attack is exceedingly difficult to construct, it has been assumed (and even argued explicitly) that defenses are without value; indeed, they should serve simply to stimulate the adversary to deploy larger and more sophisticated offensive forces.[59]

It has been widely believed in the United States that evidence of

Soviet preparation for the conduct of nuclear war, by way of homeland defenses, reflects morale-boosting programs, domestic political control concerns, atavistic though attenuating traditional attitudes, or plain folly. The possibility that Soviet leaders view the American eschewal of homeland defense as reflecting low morale and an imprudent faith in prewar deterrence has not been a popular position in the United States.

Third, there has been an optimism that Soviet thought and behavior, if encouraged by cooperative American policies, can evolve in a constructive direction. This reflects a belief that the two superpowers can stabilize their strategic relationship in tandem with a stabilization of their political relationship. Further, it has been hoped that a process of tentative détente can move, thanks to a growing mutual respect, to the complex institutionalization of a relationship characterized by a determination on each side not to infringe on the legitimate interests of the other. The optimism that has underpinned the thought of many U.S. arms controllers may be traced to a combination of idealism, classical liberalism, and rationalism. In this American view, war is an aberration in the natural order. Humankind can pursue its productive pursuits and maximize its values only in the absence of war. Since war cannot serve the best interests of any community, the possibility of war must reflect some malfunction in relations. In this argument, the Soviet Union is not "the focus of evil in the modern world" or even genuinely threatening; rather it is fearful of U.S. capabilities, from which it judges intentions. It should follow that if only— or, rather, when—Soviet leaders can be brought to understand the rationality of and mutual benefit that would flow from general acceptance of U.S. stable deterrence and arms control reasoning, much of the fuel would be removed from the engine of the arms race.

Fourth, it has been believed that the U.S. military establishment, in all its manifold ramifications, poses as great a threat—if not greater—to traditional U.S. values than do Soviet ambitions (which almost certainly have been misassessed on the hostile side by official assessors with vested interests).[60] The decline in U.S. willingness to compete in strategic weapons began prior to the depredations caused by popular (or, at least, vocal and undeniably politically significant) reactions to the Vietnam War. That decline flowed from the already noted honest, if astrategic, convictions of defense intellectuals: that strategic superiority could not be maintained; that attempts to maintain it would simply spur the Soviet Union to compete more energetically (and ultimately successfully—that is, towards the attainment of a rough parity); and that strategic stability achieved in substantial part through a broadly conceived commitment to arms control processes would constitute a realistic recognition of technological necessity.

However, the adverse trend in the strategic balance that became unmistakably evident in the early 1980s, though traceable to the posturally debilitating long-term impact of highly questionable (and very distinctly un-Soviet) stability theory, is no less easily traceable to the several political-budgetary effects of the Vietnam War. The mere fact of the war reduced the financial resources available for strategic force modernization (particularly in the context of an ongoing Great Society program which President Johnson would neither abandon pro tem nor finance soundly through tax increases), while the unpopularity of the war spilled over to political opposition to all military programs, including the strategic forces.

Fifth, there has been a widespread belief in the superiority of U.S. technology and strategic ideas. The Soviet Union was viewed as an unsophisticated, fundamentally peasant country, capable of challenging in quantity but not in quality—in short, technological and intellectual *hubris*. Americans could find convenient scapegoats for defeat in Vietnam: military incompetence, political incompetence, a deviation from true American values in the waging of an unjust war—the range of choice is considerable.[61] But Americans could not, and possibly still cannot, seriously anticipate the Soviet Union's achieving a condition of strategic nuclear advantage. After all, strategic weapons—for all the ambivalence as to their political utility—were close to home. They spoke almost to the nature of the United States: of all the elements in the defense posture, they are high technology, and high technology is the United States.

The belief in U.S. defense (and other) high technology was not ill-founded, but it took all too little account, in practice, of the difference between actual defense capability and defense mobilization potential. For example, U.S. ICBMs almost certainly are more accurate and reliable than Soviet ICBMs, and it is at least plausible to argue that U.S. nuclear weapons design permits a more efficient yield-to-weight ratio than Soviet nuclear weapons design. Unfortunately, the size and number of Soviet ICBM launchers, married to a reliability, accuracy, and warhead design that is not very far behind those of the United States, results in a gross operational imbalance to the U.S. disadvantage in hard-target counterforce comparison. The size of Soviet ballistic missiles used to be cited in the United States as clear evidence of Soviet technological backwardness. Today, that size is recognized, and even envied by some, as providing the flexibility allowing for an impressive measure of future payload fractionation; relatively low-risk warhead design; and safe-siding with high yields (to compensate for anticipated operational degradation in CEP). Defense scientists in the United States may be on the technological frontier, but it has been the Soviet rather than the U.S. defense establishment that has worked steadily to translate technical accomplishment into weapons deployed. At the time SALT I was signed in 1972, it was nearly axiomatic for many to assert that neither side—and certainly not the United States—would or should permit the other to achieve a politically or militarily meaningful lead in strategic weaponry.[62] Since 1972, the Soviet Union may have accomplished just that.

In their hubris, or arrogance, U.S. defense intellectuals in the 1960s and the early to mid-1970s had difficulty even conceiving of the possibility that there could be more than one strategic theoretical enlightenment. The distinctive strategic-cultural doctrine of France, the idea of proportional deterrence, could be dismissed from the vantage point of superpower logic yet accepted as representing the particular circumstances of an inherently minor nuclear weapons power. It was widely believed that Soviet thinking on strategic nuclear weapons lagged behind that of the United States by perhaps five years. Therefore, the contemporary absence of plain evidence suggesting Soviet endorsement of U.S. concepts of strategic stability did not occasion much alarm.[63] The Soviet Union would be elevated to the U.S. level of understanding as Soviet defense technology and weapon procurement allowed; as more Soviet policymakers came to appreciate the merit in American ideas; and as a result of the educational benefits of the SALT process. It was popular to assert that the SALT process would result in the politicization of many strategic weapon decisions, bringing them to the urgent attention of Politburo-level policymakers and very senior civilian foreign affairs officials for the first time, thereby producing a healthy (for stability) dilution of erstwhile unduly professional military perspectives on major defense programs.[64]

The politicization of some major strategic weapons decisions in the Soviet Union may well have occurred, but—as Richard Pipes has argued[65]—there is no evidence to suggest that civilian political views of the value of those weapons differ notably from the view of the professional military. Moreover, the long course of SALT, from November 1969 until June 1979, produced no discernible shift in Soviet military science.[66] If anything, the decade of the 1970s was characterized by a marked convergence of U.S. strategic ideas upon those that were popular, and evidently authoritative, in the Soviet Union.

Sixth, the United States effectively substituted a well-meaning endeavor to manage the strategic balance and relationship in place of defense planning geared to its unique foreign policy responsibilities. The whole collection of shapeless and indefinable strategic concepts that have muddied the waters of U.S. strategic thought since 1969—sufficiency, rough parity, essential equivalence[67]—was bereft of reference to the unique geostrategic context of U.S. and U.S. allied military and, hence, political security needs. The enterprise of controlling—or, more accurately, of appearing to control—the nuclear arms competition tended to take precedence in practice over genuinely strategic planning. The United States was not developing and deploying weapons to ensure U.S. freedom of action in crisis and war and, hence, to ensure (insofar as possible) a high quality of pre- and intrawar deterrence. Instead, the United States was developing and deploying weapons above all else for their negotiability or utility as bargaining tools for the better management of a U.S.-style stable strategic balance.

Deep in the psyche of the U.S. policy elite of the 1970s—as one would expect of a subculture dominated by lawyers (and politicians who were trained in law), expert only in U.S. domestic phenomena—was the belief that all peoples are fundamentally reasonable. Force, latent or applied, is anathema to this subculture.

Seventh, moving from beliefs to the rhythm of defense behavior, it is the American way for the country to mobilize in response to "evil" behavior by foreigners (assessed accurately, or otherwise, in retrospect), to overwhelm the enemy with the products of U.S. industry, or to enjoy the underappreciated blessings of military superiority, and then gradually to sink back into a condition of greater or lesser defense ill-preparedness pending the next security shock. This political phenomenon has obvious and historically traceable effects on defense preparation in general and on major weapon procurement cycles in particular.

The admirable and historically accurate (for the United States) American belief that peace is normal, married to the associated optimistic cultural conviction that progress can be and is being achieved in the quality of interstate relations, means that the United States has inordinate difficulty in sustaining an adequate domestic political constituency for a high level of peacetime defense expenditure. To assert that the United States should maintain a preponderance of military power over the Soviet Union, prospectively forever, is to attract the counterassertion that one has fallen victim to "an ideology of international conflict" or is in the pay of "the warfare state." Because of U.S. history and geography, it is not perceived as normal for the United States to remain semimobilized for war, year in and year out. Unlike Soviet political culture, major social costs are associated in the United States with a high level of defense preparation.

"Feast and famine" is the American way of defense preparation. During the years of diminished political alarm over security dangers the country has coasted, gradually downhill, on the hardware legacy of the most recent procurement surge. For example, the United States deployed the 3-MIRVed Minuteman III ICBM in the early 1970s and spent the next decade and a half debating the proper technical character of successor systems.[68] Minuteman III, the fourth-generation U.S. ICBM, entered service in 1970; the fifth generation, the MX/Peacekeeper ICBM, is not scheduled to become operational (Congress permitting) until the end of 1986. Although improvements have been made in the NS-20 guidance system for Minuteman III, the U.S. defense community is locked into a true "generational jump" system. Unlike the situation in the Soviet Union, the U.S. Department of Defense has to justify and rejustify every major (and many minor) weapons program at virtually every stage of its development-procurement cycle. Underlying this continual controversy over weapons is a deficiency of consensus on strategic doctrine.[69] In the Soviet Union, strategic force modernization, year by year, is expected and is justifiable by reference to a composite of beliefs that probably scarcely needs explicit presentation at all.

CONCLUSIONS

The U.S. strategic culture and national style in strategy, the product of the significantly unique U.S. historical experience, contains some apparently opposed tendencies—which is why it is so easy to locate historical exceptions to any sweeping generalizations that flow from "essentialist" premises. The U.S. style encompasses oscillations between extremes, and both extremes are quintessentially American.

The U.S. national experience produced a nuclear-strategic and nuclear-strategy-related policy in the 1970s that had the following characteristics:

1. A theory of strategic stability was endorsed that rested on the belief that the superpowers shared a tolerably congruent perspective on a desirable status quo.
2. A confidence was placed in reason and (U.S.-style) rational decision making to the extent that the physical protection of Americans came to reside solely in anticipated pre- or intrawar deterrent effect.
3. The policy was simply not serious at the operational level. U.S. policymakers endorsed flexibility as a desideratum, but U.S. strategic forces continued to be postured for a short-spasm war.
4. Inchoate, optimistic notions of progress in international cooperation were invested in an arms control process whose evident failure was rationalized by reference to ever more minimalist criteria.

One can trace these specific items to "the American way." However, one could reverse the policy logic in these items and still trace them to "the American way." It must be stressed that the analysis here is time-specific. This chapter refers to a United States that is still reconsidering the merits of the path it has pursued for the past twenty years. Although national political culture and its derivatives—strategic culture and national style in strategy—evolve over time, American oscillation between under- and over-preparedness, between wishful thinking and Manichaeanism, seem to be endemic to "the American way" for the predictable future. It is instructive to speculate on the reasons for this.

First, the United States is an insular political culture. There is an expectation of safety as the norm, which flows from the geographical fact of insularity. For an insular power to be stirred to take expensive and allegedly highly risk-prone actions, foreign threat has to be believed to be, rightly or wrongly, immediate. Drawing a sharp distinction between peace and war is natural to Americans and the British; traditionally, they have not lived in constant fear of loss of life or liberty. Geographical isolation from proximate danger, however illusory, encourages one to discount apparently distant dangers. However, the cultural proclivity to assume that peace is normal, when turned around by apparently unambiguous evidence of foreign threat, produces a possibly disproportionate military response.

Second, with few exceptions, U.S. policymaking in the national security area (foreign policy, defense policy, arms control policy) tends to be dominated by people who have a poor sense of the value of history. In the inimitable words of one U.S. policymaker: "All this history business! We've got to make policy decisions."[70]

To the average U.S. maker of "high" policy, international events must occur as if by constant revelation, and, they have meaning, if any, solely with reference to his or her personal historical experience. It is commonplace to observe that U.S. decision-making style tends to bear, preeminently, the hallmark of policymakers who judge each event on its merits, in isolation, because they know no better. Pragmatism without principle produces a reactive, "muddling through" style. Since history provides the only possible basis, or data base, for prediction, lawyers and engineers do not and cannot ignore it; they simply employ it, by and large, in unacknowledged and uncritical fashion and very crudely. The U.S. government is vulnerable to almost any professor-turned-policymaker who has a historically grounded (or apparently grounded) theory of statecraft.

Third, in part thanks to the ahistorical or even antihistorical training of U.S. policymakers, U.S. national security policy typically tends to be dominated by people who truly are expert only in inappropriate U.S. domestic matters. A few individuals excepted, as always, Harvard Law School, Wall Street, or a state house generally do not prepare one well for coping with the surviving graduates of Stalin's "Great Purge" of the 1930s (or with their younger protégés).

In practice, "the best and the brightest" of the U.S. educational process tend to be almost heroically ill-equipped to cope with the Soviet Union. It is unreasonable to expect prudent and judicious foreign policy assessments from an official who has essentially no historical knowledge of the Soviet Union/Russia and no personal life experience that is likely to facilitate his or her rapid on-the-job education. It is a tentative contention of this chapter that the perilous defense condition in which the United States finds itself today stems, in part, from the fact that most U.S. policymakers of fifteen to twenty years ago had no accurate sense of history and essentially had no understanding of the enduring Great Russian character of the USSR.

The study of strategic culture and the associated concept of national style should enable Americans to understand themselves better, to understand others better, and (scarcely less important) to understand better how others interpret Americans. Although, as illustrated earlier, many elements of U.S. defense policy in the 1960s and 1970s are traceable, inter alia, to cultural traits, the concept of strategic culture is policy-neutral. Americans are what their interpretation of their history and their contemporary roles has made them. If the United States has a recurring security problem that flows from a relatively unchanging national strategic culture, that is altogether a more serious and intractable condition than the typical subjects of U.S. defense policy contention. For example, American strategists may debate the merit in near-term strategic defensive systems, but what can one suggest, sensibly, to encourage a level of prudence in threat estimation in a strategic culture that swings almost rhythmically between under- and overpreparation? It would be fatuous to urge that Americans be other than what they are. All that can be achieved here is in the nature of an inductive exercise in policy science—that is, an analysis of the structure of the problem that rests on the evidence of expressed beliefs and actual behavior. A Western security dilemma is that both Russians and Americans have a distressing, though predictable, proclivity for behaving "in (national) character" and that by the 1980s, these two cultures and styles have produced, in competition, a shortfall in sustained defense effort on the U.S. side that could prove to be dangerous.

NOTES

1.   See Ken Booth, *Strategy and Ethnocentrism*, (London: Croom, Helm, 1979), particularly chap. 1.

2.   Jack L. Snyder, *The Soviet Strategic Culture: Implications for Limited Nuclear Operations*, R-2154-AF (Santa Monica, Calif.: RAND Corporation, September 1977).

3.   See the review by Adda Bozeman in *Survival* 22, no. 4(July/August 1980): 187–88. Bozeman points, quite rightly, to the biased judgments that Booth tends to level in criticism of U.S. policymakers; but—that granted—the book merits landmark status.

4.   Alfred Thayer Mahan, *The Influence of Sea Power Upon History, 1660–1783* (London: Methuen, 1975; first pub. 1890). Mahan "discovered" what the Royal Navy had actually been practicing for two and half centuries.

5.   See Stephen White, *Political Culture and Soviet Politics* (London: Macmillan, 1979), chap. 1; Dennis Kavanaugh, *Political Culture* (London: Macmillan, 1972); and A. H. Brown, *Soviet Politics and Political Science* (London: Macmillan, 1974), chap. 4.

6.   As David Holloway observes (in the context of changes in Soviet military doctrine): "One should not take an 'essentialist' view of Soviet policy, seeing it as springing from some innate characteristic of Russian culture or the Soviet

system, impervious to phenomena in the real world." "Military Power and Political Purpose in Soviet Policy," *Daedalus* 109, no. 4(Fall 1980): 28.

7. Snyder, *Soviet Strategic Culture*, p. v.

8. Some commentators have harbored the idea that, with much better understanding, the United States could orchestrate an "interdiction" campaign vis-à-vis Soviet policymaking. The idea is attractive but almost certainly infeasible. David Holloway, for example, has noted that "these elements [Soviet conceptions of security and attitudes to military power, strongly influenced by Russian and Soviet history and state structure] do make it difficult for Western governments to exert remote and precise pressure on Soviet military decisions: the policy-making process is largely closed to outside influence." "Military Power and Political Purpose in Soviet Policy," p. 28. A somewhat more optimistic view is presented in Franklyn Griffiths, "The Sources of American Conduct: Soviet Perspectives and Their Policy Implications," *International Security* 9, no. 2(Fall 1984): 3–50.

9. John Shy, "The American Military Experience: History and Learning," *Journal of Interdisciplinary History* 1(1971): 207.

10. Ibid., p. 205.

11. Booth, *Strategy and Ethnocentrism*, p. 14.

12. Ken Booth, "American Strategy: The Myths Revisited," in Ken Booth and Moorhead Wright, eds., *American Thinking about Peace and War* (Hassocks, Sussex [U.K.]: Harvester, 1978), pp.1–35.

13. Shy, "American Military Experience," p. 220.

14. Ibid.

15. Bernard Brodie, *War and Politics* (New York: Macmillan, 1973), p. 332.

16. See James M. Roherty, *Decisions of Robert S. McNamara: A Study of The Role of the Secretary of Defense* (Coral Gables, Fla.: University of Miami Press, 1970), pp. 105–106. Powerful extended treatment of this issue is provided in Harry G. Summers, Jr., *On Strategy: A Critical Analysis of the Vietnam War* (Novato, Calif.: Presidio Press, 1982); and Edward N. Luttwak, *The Pentagon and the Art of War* (New York: Simon and Schuster, 1985). Also very much to the point is Robert W. Komer, "The Neglect of Strategy," *Air Force Magazine* 67, no. 3(March 1984): 51–56.

17. See Richard Burt, "The Relevance of Arms Control in the 1980s,"*Daedalus* 110, no. 1(Winter 1981): 159–77; and Colin S. Gray, "Arms Control: Problems," in R. James Woolsey, ed., *Nuclear Arms: Ethics, Strategy, Politics* (San Francisco: Institute for Contemporary Studies, 1984), pp. 153–69.

18. Edward N. Luttwak, "On the Meaning of Strategy . . . for the United States in the 1980s," in W. Scott Thompson, ed., *National Security in the 1980s: From Weakness to Strength* (San Francisco: Institute for Contemporary Studies, 1980), pp. 260–63.

19. See Martin van Creveld, *Fighting Power: German and U.S. Army Performance, 1939–1945* (Westport, Conn.: Greenwood Press, 1982), pp. 146–51. But see the perceptive review in David Schoenbaum, "The Wehrmacht and G.I. Joe: Learning *What* from History? A Review Essay," *International Security* 8, no. 1(Summer 1983): 201–7.

20.   See Jeffrey Record, "Why Our High-Priced Military Can't Win Battles," *Washington Post*, January 29, 1984, p. D-1.

21.   See Daniel J. Boorstein, *The Americans: The Colonial Experience* (New York: Vintage, 1958), Part 1.

22.   See General-Major A. S. Milovidov and Colonel V. G. Kozlov, *The Philosophical Heritage of V. I. Lenin and Problems of Contemporary War (A Soviet View)*, Soviet Military Thought Series of the U.S. Air Force, No. 5 (Washington, D.C.: USGPO, 1975; Moscow, 1972), pp. 28–34; and Colonel M. P. Skirdo, *The People, the Army, the Commander (A Soviet View)*, Soviet Military Thought Series of the U.S. Air Force, No. 14 (Washington, D.C.: USGPO, n.d.; Moscow, 1970), chap. 1.

23.   Shy, "American Military Experience," particularly pp. 211–16.

24.   Booth, "American Strategy," pp. 7–8.

25.   Sir Dennis Brogan, *American Aspects* (New York: Harper & Row, 1966), chap. 2.

26.   The terms of the Treaty of Versailles reflected the reality of the respective weight of allied contributions to the defeat of Germany.

27.   Luttwak, "On the Meaning of Strategy," pp. 260–63.

28.   The best single work on the subject is Russell F. Weigley, *The American Way of War* (New York: Macmillan, 1973).

29.   This thesis has enduring drawing power in relation to U.S. political self-perception. Ronald Reagan made repeated explicit reference to the "city upon a hill" idea in his presidential campaigns in 1980 and 1984. This thesis of U.S. uniqueness has been challenged in Richard Rosecrance, ed., *America as an Ordinary Country: U.S. Foreign Policy and the Future* (Ithaca, N.Y.: Cornell University Press, 1976). There is a good idea underlying this book, but it becomes a much less good idea when it is elevated to the rank of a major thesis, as opposed, more appropriately, to a healthy corrective.

30.   See Stanley Hoffmann, *Gulliver's Troubles: Or the Setting of American Foreign Policy* (New York: McGraw-Hill, 1968), part II, "America's Style."

31.   This is not to deny the force of Ken Booth's argument that genuinely strategic thinking is a rare phenomenon in any country. See Booth, "American Strategy," pp. 13–18.

32.   This was the Eighty Division Program (for a division "slice" of 52,000 men, excluding replacements). See U.S. Department of the Army, Historical Division, *United States Army in the World War, 1917–1919: Policy-Forming Documents, American Expeditionary Forces* (Washington, D.C.: USGPO, 1948), pp. 544, 614–15. Actual AEF strength on December 4, 1918, was 1,932,154.

33.   Although I am stressing the relative (to Germans) absence of operational-tactical skill on the part of U.S. officers, I do not at all dismiss the significance of logistic management. Readers are strongly recommended to see Martin van Creveld, *Supplying War: Logistics from Wallenstein to Patton* (Cambridge: Cambridge University Press, 1977). If a general cannot feed, move, or reequip his men, he will lose, whatever his measure of operational skill may be.

34.   See Russell F. Weigley, *Eisenhower's Lieutenants: The Campaigns of France and Germany, 1944-1945* (Bloomington: Indiana University Press, 1981); John Keegan, *Six Armies in Normandy:* (New York: Viking, 1982); and Carlo D'Este, *Decision in Normandy* (New York: Dutton, 1983).

35.   This refers to superiority relative to the Germans—though too much can be made of this. It should be recalled that after Normandy Allied supply lines to the front lengthened, while German supply lines shortened. See van Creveld, *Supplying War,* chap. 7.

36.   Critics of NATO strategy have noted that NATO's military thinking and planning more closely approximates attrition than it does visions of annihilation through maneuver. Germany could not win a war of attrition in 1944-45; the Soviet Union in the late 1980s could. See Edward N. Luttwak, "The Operational Level of War," *International Security* 5, no. 3(Winter 1980/81): 61-79.

37.   Henry Kissinger, *White House Years* (Boston: Little, Brown, 1979), p. 914.

38.   *The New Strategy* is the title of James King's nearly definitive, but still unpublished, study of U.S. strategic thinking in the so-called golden era of 1955–65. I have been fortunate enough to read and comment on King's manuscript. For reviews of nuclear age strategic thinking and policy, see Lawrence Freedman, *The Evolution of Nuclear Strategy* ((London: Macmillan, 1981); and Colin S. Gray, *Strategic Studies and Public Policy: The American Experience* (Lexington: University Press of Kentucky, 1982).

39.   See Robert E. Osgood, *Limited War Revisited* (Boulder, Colo.: Westview Press, 1979).

40.   Thomas C. Schelling and Morton H. Halperin, *Strategy and Arms Control* (New York: Twentieth Century Fund, 1961), p. 142. An excellent recent review of the early (about 1960) literature on arms control theory is Robin Ranger, "The Four 'Bibles' of Arms Control," *Book Forum* 6, no. 4(1984): 416-32.

41.   Henry Kissinger, *Nuclear Weapons and Foreign Policy* (New York: Harper Brothers, 1957), chap. 1.

42.   See King, *The New Strategy;* Michael Mandelbaum, *The Nuclear Question: The United States and Nuclear Weapons, 1946-1976* (Cambridge: Cambridge University Press, 1979), chap. 3-5; and Stephen Peter Rosen, "Vietnam and the American Theory of Limited War," *International Security* 7, no. 2(Fall 1982): 83-113.

43.   Booth, "American Strategy," pp. 5-7.

44.   This is not to claim that U.S. statecraft was dominated by soldiers, still less that it was dominated by soldiers who approached political problems in a distinctively military way. It is a fact that until Robert McNamara became secretary of defense, the Office of the Secretary of Defense did not dominate the process of defense planning—though it did have a major influence via the fiscal guidance it provided. See Carl Borklund, *Men of the Pentagon, from Forrestal to McNamara* (New York: Praeger, 1966); Richard K. Betts, *Soldiers, Statesmen, and Cold War Crises* (Cambridge, Mass.: Harvard University Press, 1977).

45.   See David Alan Rosenberg, "The Origins of Overkill: Nuclear Weapons and American Strategy, 1945-1960," *International Security* 7, no. 4(Spring 1983): 3-71.

46.   See "U.S. Objectives with Respect to Russia, NSC 20/1, August 18, 1948 (Top Secret)," in Thomas H. Etzold and John L. Gaddis, eds., *Containment: Documents on American Policy and Strategy, 1945–1950,* (New York: Columbia University Press, 1978), pp. 173–203.

47.   See William W. Kaufmann, ed., *Military Policy and National Security* (London: Oxford University Press, 1956).

48.   This is not to deny the validity of many of the criticisms that pervade Rosenberg, "The Origins of Overkill."

49.   Ibid., particulary pp. 27–71; and Desmond Ball, *Targeting for Strategic Deterrence,* Adelphi Papers No. 185 (London: IISS, Summer 1983), pp. 6–10.

50.   An early statement of the proposition that defense may be approached as an economic problem (or an exercise in the efficient allocation of scarce resources) was Bernard Brodie, "Strategy as a Science," *World Politics* 1, no. 4(July 1949): 476–88. The proposition is valid, provided that it is qualified. Defense is an economic problem, but it is not only, and should not be approached largely, as an economic problem. "The art of war" is not synonymous with defense management and cannot be approached solely via defense analysis.

51.   By "win," I mean achieve its political objectives at tolerable cost.

52.   This argument is advanced in Samuel P. Huntington, "The Renewal of Strategy," in Huntington, ed., *The Strategic Imperative: New Policies for American Security* (Cambridge, Mass.: Ballinger, 1982), p. 34.

53.   On strategic superiority, see chap. 8.

54.   See Henry S. Rowen, "Formulating Strategic Doctrine," in Commission on the Organization of the Government for the Conduct of Foreign Policy, Vol. 4, Appendix K, *Adequacy of Current Organization: Defense and Arms Control* (Washington, D.C.: USGPO, June 1975), pp. 231–32; and Ball, *Targeting for Strategic Deterrence,* pp. 10–15.

55.   Rowen, "Formulating Strategic Doctrine," p. 233.

56.   Brodie, *War and Politics,* chap. 9.

57.   See chap. 5.

58.   Quoted in James H. Toner, "American Society and the American Way of War: Korea and Beyond," *Parameters* 11, no. 1(March 1981): 84.

59.   Times may be changing, however. See Fred S. Hoffman, *Ballistic Missile Defenses and U.S. National Security,* Summary Report of the Future Security Strategy Study (Washington, D.C.: Department of Defense, October 1983); and Keith B. Payne and Colin S. Gray, "Nuclear Policy and the Defensive Transition," *Foreign Affairs* 62, no. 4(Spring 1984): 820–42.

60.   The 1970s saw the full-blown reemergence of a popular, generically antidefense literature in the United States. Even supposed scholars, with proper scholarly credentials, felt comfortable with such a concept as "the national security state"—as if there could be a state that was disinterested in national security. (What would constitute the reverse phenomenon of "the national security state"?) See Edward Luttwak's appropriately merciless review of Daniel Yergin's book, *Shattered Peace: The Origins of the Cold War and the National Security State* (Boston:

Houghton Mifflin, 1977), in Luttwak, *Strategy and Politics: Collected Essays* (New Brunswick, N.J.: Transaction, 1980), pp. 271–74.

61. See Peter Braestrup, ed., *Vietnam as History: Ten Years After the Paris Peace Accords* (Washington, D.C.: University Press of America, January 1984); Bruce Palmer, Jr., *The 25-Year War: America's Military Role in Vietnam* (Lexington: University Press of Kentucky, 1984); and Summers, *On Strategy.* Summers faults the military professionals as well as the politicians, while Luttwak faults the military professionals more than he does the politicians in *The Pentagon and the Art of War,* chaps. 1–2.

62. Henry Kissinger made such a claim in a press conference on May 26, 1972. See U.S. Congress, Senate, Committee on Armed Services, *Military Implications of the Treaty on Limitation of Anti-Ballistic Missile Systems and the Interim Agreement on Limitation of Strategic Offensive Arms, Hearings,* 92nd Cong., 2d sess. (Washington, D.C.: USGPO, 1972), p. 98.

63. See Lawrence Freedman, *U.S. Intelligence and the Soviet Strategic Threat* (London: Macmillan, 1977), particularly chap. 6.

64. See Thomas W. Wolfe, *The SALT Experience* (Cambridge, Mass.: Ballinger, 1979), p. 61.

65. Richard Pipes, "Militarism and the Soviet State," *Daedalus* 109, no. 4(Fall 1980): 11–12, n. 21.

66. On the Soviet meaning of these terms, see John J. Dziak, *Soviet Perceptions of Military Power: The Interaction of Theory and Practice* (New York: Crane, Russak [for the National Strategy Information Center], 1981), chap. 3; and Harriet Fast Scott and William F. Scott, *The Armed Forces of the U.S.S.R.* (Boulder, Colo.: Westview Press, 1979), chap. 3.

67. See Warner R. Schilling, "U.S. Strategic Nuclear Concepts in the 1970s: The Search for Sufficiently Equivalent Countervailing Parity," *International Security* 6, no. 2(Fall 1981): 48–79.

68. See R. James Woolsey, "The Politics of Vulnerability: 1980–83," *Foreign Affairs* 62, no. 4(Spring 1984): 805–19.

69. On the extent of political consensus on strategic matters, see Colin S. Gray, *Nuclear Strategy and Strategic Planning,* Philadelphia Policy Papers (Philadelphia: Foreign Policy Research Institute, 1984), chap. 5.

70. Richard Quandt, in J. B. Kelly, "Interview with Richard Quandt," *Near East Report* 25, no. 4(January 23, 1981): 15.

CHAPTER 3

National Style in Strategy II: The Soviet Union

This study is interested in the Soviet Union as the Soviet Union, not—as are so many academic texts on comparative governments—as an example of totalitarianism, mature authoritarianism, or whatever the latest fashion in political modeling may be.[1] The Soviet Union is of interest here as the principal recipient of U.S. strategy messages and as the principal candidate-adversary for any bilateral nuclear combat in which the United States is likely to be compelled to engage. The United States is obliged, *faute de mieux*, to compete for international influence with the USSR, to be prepared to seek to dissuade the USSR from taking undesired (by the United States) actions, and, if need be, to endeavor to thwart Soviet policy by means of applied military power. Given these elementary and enduring policy facts, it is important that the Soviet Union be as well comprehended in the West as possible.[2] Soviet strategic policy cannot be likened to a loose gun carriage on a rolling deck (indeed, that simile more nearly approximates the enduring U.S. policy condition); it is not eccentric, irrational (either in local Soviet or in classic Clausewitzian terms), or even particularly mysterious in its driving motivations and its goals. However, it is different from U.S. policy; it cannot usefully be approached in familiar American terms; and many of the Western policy errors of the past forty years could have been avoided, or reduced in scope, if a proper respect had been paid both to Soviet cultural uniqueness and simply to the plain facts of local Soviet conditions.[3]

It is relatively easy both to acknowledge, in a formal way, the trivially obvious fact that the Soviet Union is very different from the United States and then to engage in policy analysis that focuses far more heavily on the apparently familiar, rather than the unfamiliar, elements in the Soviet system.[4] Except for the intrusion of the democratic (Western-style) political process,[5] strategic policy analysts may easily locate comfortingly familiar elements in the Soviet policymaking and policy-executing process. They find a familiar set of technologies (a ballistic missile is comprehensible as a ballistic missile, regardless of the politics of the pertinent decision maker); a powerful military establishment (though one that, like that of the United States, has no "Bonapartist" tradition) riven with interservice rivalries; a massive defense-industrial complex that is, perhaps, both servant and master of the military user organizations;[6] and a monitorable defense policymaking/influencing elite, military and civilian, that appears to encompass a range of views that, although more restricted than in the American case, covers quite a broad spectrum even of American-analogous opinion.[7] The point is that it is almost too easy to seek the familiar in the Soviet Union with respect to features on the defense landscape. One may not seek to emulate Richard Rosecrance's project and edit a book entitled *The Soviet Union as an Ordinary Country*,[8] but in practice one may discern relatively little about contemporary Soviet policymaking circumstance that would incline one to seek to stress the alien or even the distinctive character of Soviet political-strategic culture. Moreover, one may be tempted to dismiss discordant elements by making reference to the fact that the Soviet Union, like other states and societies, is dynamic. The Soviet Union may not be a fun-loving democracy in the American sense, but neither is it the grim *festung Russland* of Stalin's day.[9]

This study has no difficulty in steering a prudent middle course between the absurd extremes of asserting either that the USSR is a "worker's paradise" or that it is little better than a prison (which is not to say that truth necessarily will lie in the middle). However, I am concerned about the common phenomenon of Western scholars so immersing themselves in the apparent detail of Soviet affairs that they neglect to examine, or reexamine, the character of the overall system they are studying. In the words of Robert Conquest:

> If one skips the fact that the Soviet leaders are the product of a political history alien to ours, and are exemplars of a deep-set political psychology unlike—and consciously hostile to—our own, no amount of erudition about formal detail is worth a wooden kopek.[10]

As David Holloway has argued, following Alexander Dallin, one must beware of "essentialist" explanations.[11] A large and necessarily heavily bureaucratized state, ruling over a vastly numerous and culturally very diverse multinational society, must be a highly complex entity. The well-springs of Soviet official thought and behavior may be sought in geopolitics (the response of the Great Russian people to a very hostile physical-economic and political-military environment),[12] in ideology (Holy Russia and Pan-Slav Russia assuming the mantle of vanguard of the international proletariat in execution of the "historic mission" of spreading socialism worldwide, and so on), or in a somewhat vulgar realpolitik.[13] These are only the most prevalent of the "essentialist" approaches to Soviet phenomena.

This study acknowledges the dangers that lurk close to an "essentialist" explanation: a disinclination to examine possibly discordant details (since one has to hand already "the essential truth"); a closed-mindedness toward competing theories; and, in general, an undue ease of explanation. Scholars tend to seek intellectual order in what, in practice, may well fairly be described as disorder. Not infrequently, book reviewers criticize authors for failing to impose order on their material. History may unfold as "one damn thing after another," but historians are charged (at least by reviewers who categorize themselves as political scientists) with "making sense of events."[14] Although I discern a Soviet style with respect to nuclear strategy, I am attentive to the charge of undue determinism. "Essentialist" explanations are dangerous, but to register that fact is akin to observing that babies should not be thrown out with bathwater. Most of the more promising propositions regarding the strategic behavior of particular states have the potential for gross distortion if they are taken beyond their proper perimeter.

SOVIET STRATEGIC STYLE: OBSERVABLE CHARACTERISTICS

Respected students of Russian and Soviet history differ almost as much in the conclusions that they offer as do economists endeavoring to offer authoritative advice on the causes of and cures for inflation. The ultimate focus of this study (in chapter 9) is the choice of an appropriate U.S. nuclear strategy for the remainder of the 1980s and for the 1990s. That choice should be grounded in the best attainable understanding of Soviet motives and capabilities. In my opinion, the links between current and recent Soviet nuclear policy and nuclear-policy-related behavior and the Soviet/Russian past are extensive, enlightening, and of considerable potential value for prediction. However, given that it is open season on offering explanations of the Great Russian legacy of the Soviet leadership,[15] it is essential to provide some fixed and relatively noncontroversial features for the analytical landscape. One cannot know, with absolute certainty, what strategic nuclear posture and doctrine the Soviet Union will choose to endorse for the late 1990s.[16] Also, although there is no shortage of theories on the subject, the Romanov and pre-Romanov indebtedness of the contemporary Soviet state remains a matter of scholarly conjecture. This book, though no less willing than others to indulge in the creation of possibly dubious transhistorical patterns, at least seeks to begin with a firm factual foundation. Although judgment cannot be totally precluded, the discussion that follows constitutes a presentation of the facts concerning some of the more important elements in strategic style.

The "Revolution in Military Affairs"

In a self-proclaimed "revolution in military affairs," the Soviet General Staff of the mid to late 1950s achieved the accommodation of nuclear weapons in the Soviet science of war.[17] Soviet theorists of the highest caliber did not seek to deny the unique qualities of nuclear weapons, but they did deny that nuclear weapons had effected a historical discontinuity in the utility, in extremis, of the resort to force. V. M. Bondarenko, for example, offered the following thought:

> We are able to define *the contemporary revolution in military affairs as a radical upheaval in its development, which is characterized by new capabilities of attaining political goals in war, resulting from the availability of nuclear missile weapons to the troops.* (emphasis in the original)[18]

Notwithstanding Malenkov's aberrational view, in 1954, that nuclear war would mean the end of civilization,[19] and notwithstanding Khrushchev's aberrational view, in January 1960, that nuclear weapons in and of themselves would be decisive,[20] the Soviet General Staff—and the new collective leadership that assumed authority in October 1964—endorsed the policy line that nuclear war, as other kinds of war, would be an experience that a robust, prepared society would endure and survive, if need be. The historically unique features of nuclear weapons, the quality of energy released, and the very brief time span for destruction were folded into military thought and preparations that envisaged decisive results from military action. Far from rendering war "unthinkable," nuclear weapons held out the promise of prompt, decisive results.[21]

Prevention of War and Preparation for War

Soviet theorists and officials have always seen the prevention of war as a political task, essentially unrelated to the day-by-day activities of the military establishment. In the Soviet perspective, it is the duty of the statesman and the diplomat to manage the political environment for potential armed conflict; it is the duty of the soldier to prepare as well as he is able to wage war if the threat of the reality of war should emerge.[22] This Soviet view, and its defense-programmatic implications, stands in dramatic contrast to U.S. thought and practice. In the United States since World War II, there has been a near fusion of foreign policy and strategic thought. Several generations of senior U.S. policymakers have been educated, or miseducated, by Barbara Tuchman[23] and Thomas Schelling[24] into believing that military posture and doctrine, in peacetime and in crisis time, may have a decisive negative or positive effect on the course of political events. In the Soviet view, war has deep political causes—it cannot be triggered by "mechanistic instabilities"[25] in the superpower strategic balance. Soviet military professionals appear to take very seriously Clausewitz's dictum: "Its [war's] grammar, indeed, may be its own, but not its logic."[26]

To a degree perhaps culturally unattainable by most U.S. policymakers, it should be appreciated that Soviet strategic preparation for the effective conduct of war bears relatively little relation to authoritative Soviet expectations of the occurrence of war. In the Soviet universe, preparation for war and prevention of war, though logically linked, are quite distinctive endeavors.

Threat Perceptions

In 1956, Nikita Khrushchev may have delivered a serious body blow to the thesis that war was "fatalistically inevitable," but any Soviet military officer who has studied Lenin carefully may believe that he knows better.[27] Whether from the Leninist doctrinal (ideological) or the Russian/Soviet geopolitical (realpolitik) perspective, the Soviet defense establishment knows that war can happen. The Soviet regime was born out of quasi-military action, was established in the period of war communism, and eventually achieved such legitimacy as it could in large part, though of course not entirely, through the military defense of Mother Russia in the Great Patriotic War.[28] If Soviet theorists have a vision analogous to that of the American self-perception of a "city upon a hill," they anticipated that city to be closely invested by hostile tribes. The Great Russian historical experience in the taiga, and in tentative steps taken outside, is of a very hostile external world.[29] The Soviet Union/Russia does not expect to live in peace and harmony with its neighbors. Instead, it hopes to be permitted sufficient time to consolidate the latest territorial or hegemonic acquisitions so that it will be able to withstand the inevitable hostile reaction.

Russian colonial experience on the open steppes bred the same anticipation of military threat that the process of Soviet imperial expansion since 1945 has fostered.[30] The insecurity of empire has been an enduring Russian/Soviet theme, which is developed in detail later in this chapter.

Victory in Nuclear War

Soviet military science has never endorsed any outcome to war, at any level, short of victory. Soviet military and political theorists have never had any notable difficulty understanding what victory meant, and they have been and remain unable to cope with any concept of a less ambitious kind. This does not mean that Soviet leaders anticipate victory in any and every war that they wage, only that they can envisage the possibility of victory and deem themselves obliged to seek such an outcome. This endorsement of victory does not have connotations of a mindless pursuit of military solutions to political problems. Instead, it means a determination to achieve political objectives, modest or otherwise. Soviet style in the exercise of military force, to intimidate and if need be to overwhelm, has been well exemplified in the operations against Hungary in 1956 and Czechoslovakia in 1968. Afghanistan does not represent aberrant behavior; rather, it may show evidence of Soviet miscalculation of the scope and depth of its local political-military problems.

In contrast to the U.S. practice of limited war, from Korea through Vietnam,[31] it has been the Soviet way to have a high threshold for the taking of military action and—when action is taken—to attempt to apply overwhelming force in pursuit of rapid political results. In recent decades, Americans have sought to minimize the risks and potential costs of armed conflict by sharply graduating applied violence (or never doing by halves what might be accomplished by quarters). In Vietnam, for example, the United States was always behind the (necessary) "power curve." Consistently, the Johnson administration applied too little force too late (not to mention the many sins of military malexecution that were committed, against the policy background of inchoate and unpersuasive political objectives).[32] The Soviet Union has favored a reverse strategy. Following the old dictum that no general ever lost a battle because he was too strong, Soviet leaders have sought to minimize risk and costs by threatening and applying military force on such a scale as, hopefully, to guarantee prompt success. Whether or not this historical pattern would be reflected in the Soviet conduct of central nuclear war is a question of more than tangential interest to this study.

The U.S. proclivity in recent decades for easing its way into combat with symbolic quarter- and half-measures—for the excellent purpose of dampening the pace of conflict expansion and maximizing the prospects for political control of military events—extends into the realm of central war planning. The popularity of the ideas of flexible response (or initiative), graduated deterrence, escalation control, and crisis management and crisis bargaining, and the planning facts of limited nuclear options in partial implementation of some of the recommendations of NSDM-242,[33] all attest to the dominant U.S. approach to risk management in the nuclear age. That approach appears to be eminently prudent. However, U.S. defense planners should be concerned lest their preferred style of operations be overtaken and rendered valueless or even counterproductive by a contrasting Soviet style. The possibility of strategic miscalculation in Washington is nontrivial when one considers that U.S. leaders may have to wage war against a country that is far more determined upon winning than it is upon early war termination on *mutually* acceptable terms.

The Conduct of War

American officials and scholars do not and cannot know with high confidence just how Soviet leaders would choose to wage a central nuclear war. Indeed, it may not even be prudent to assume that Soviet leaders would perceive that they enjoyed the luxury of strategic choice.[34] There is no alternative for Western policymakers other than to speculate on this subject. To the limited degree that there is Western expertise on the subject of Soviet strategic-nuclear operational intentions, the story is a grim one for American hopes for escalation control. The Western experts on probable Soviet style in the conduct of central nuclear war—preeminently John Erickson, William T. Lee,[35] Joseph Douglass, and Amoretta Hoeber[36]—all agree (which does not, of course, mean that they are correct). John Erickson has argued as follows:

> The Soviet strategic missile forces are organized into armies, brigades, and regiments, geared to salvo firing—in short it is a battlefield deployment of strategic weapons, "nuclear guns," if you like, aimed at the enemy in order to fight a "counternuclear battle," knocking out the enemy nuclear guns and exploiting at the same time accepted military principles of surprise, deception, and maneuver. . . . It is worth noting in passing that the founders of the Soviet strategic missile force were not strategic theoreticians but experienced and distinguished artillery commanders. . . . In the sequence of strikes, the maximum number should be allocated to the first launch, in order to maximize survivability.[37]

Such evidence as there is suggests that if the politicians fail to prevent war, the Soviet military establishment would do its duty and endeavor to conduct it in efficient pursuit of a clear, favorable military outcome. The consistency of evidence (from writings, from behavior in other military-diplomatic respects, from the technical details of Soviet military deployment, from exercises, and from Soviet/Russian strategic-political culture) is remarkable and probably should be viewed as persuasive—if only for reasons of prudence. In practice, Soviet political leaders may prove to be interested in attempting to retain political control of military events through flexibility in military execution, as their predecessors were in July 1914. The partial mobilization option against Austria-Hungary only, which attracted the Russian Foreign Minister, Sazonov (a man heroically ignorant of military and many diplomatic realities), was absurd because it would have been certain to trigger an Austro-Hungarian general mobilization that would have triggered German general mobilization—and so on to the Marne.[38] Although one cannot be certain, it is only prudent to assume that, in the event, Soviet political leaders will be unable—assuming, perhaps overoptimistically, that they would try—to cope with the apparently sound military arguments of the General Staff (and its political allies) for waging the war according to plan.[39]

If they are obliged to fight a nuclear war for truly compelling political reasons, Soviet soldiers should be expected to seek to achieve a prompt military decision, all the while anticipating the strong possibility that even a sequence of very heavy early blows against U.S. strategic forces, C^3I, logistic chokepoints, and war-supporting industries would not suffice to win the war. The United States may be too large, too powerful, and too cohesive a society to be neutralized promptly. Expressing what he discerns as the dominant Soviet military opinion, John Erickson has written:

> A battle, or an operation or a war cannot be reduced to one act of destruction of the enemy; all must be considered in terms of a series of consecutive strikes, each of which is different in nature.[40]

Attitudes Toward Military Power

The Soviet state, like the Czarist state before it, was founded on and sustained by military power. To a greater or lesser degree, this is a necessary and, hence, rather trivial truth about all countries, not excluding the United States. The United States was born by force, from 1775–83, and perpetuated by force, from 1861–65. Furthermore, the continental interior between the Alleghenies and the Rockies, notwithstanding the legal niceties of treaties, was occupied effectively by force. The acquisition of Texas and the Southwest could provide Mexico with as much, if not more, cause to complain about "unequal treaties" as China has in its continuing territorial disputes with the Soviet Union. Notwithstanding the general historical fact of the military basis for political territorial organization,[41] there are important differences of degree of military dependence between countries. It is not true to assert of the USSR as was said of the Prussia of the Great Elector, that it is "an army with a country," but such a judgment does err on the correct side.

Territorial aggrandizement has always been "the Russian way." As Richard Pipes has argued:

Russia's traditional expansionism and the militarism to which it gave
rise were primarily caused by economic factors. . . . There is a tragedy
in the vicious circle that permeates Russian history: poverty calls for
conquests; conquests demand a large military establishment; a large
military establishment saps the productive forces of the country, per-
petuating poverty.[42]

The Slavs who founded what was to become Russia occupied the least
desirable territory in Europe, the taiga—the infertile northern forest. For
several centuries, the history of Russia was a history of the colonization
of more fertile lands and of military protection of that colonization. The
military power of the Kievan, Muscovite, and then Imperial Russian state
was not an occasional necessity when foreign threat appeared to loom.
Rather, Russians could survive—geographically vulnerable from East and
West once they advanced to the open black-earth steppe from the relative
safety of the inhospitable taiga—only if "the national economy was mainly
geared to warfare."[43]

The Muscovite and Czarist states did, indeed, abut genuine enemies,
and the price of defeat was terrible. Warfare for Russia, as a centrally
placed continental power lacking natural defenses other than sheer distance and "general winter," was always, at least potentially, a total experience. (The destruction of Riazan, and the grisly fate of its inhabitants at
the hands of the Mongols in the winter of 1237, makes grim reading even
today.)[44] As the heirs to a Russian, distinctively *continental* experience,
Soviet leaders and officials have a cultural legacy of attitudes that disin-
clines them to place much trust in the possibility of limited conflict against
first-class enemies.

Russian and Soviet history is dominated by its military experience.
Quite aside from the important Petrine legacy (Peter the Great instituted
the first standing army based on conscription in Europe), not to mention
the scarring effect of the Mongol conquest and preponderance—from 1237
until (formally, at least) 1480—Soviet power and military power are really
inseparable facts. The Soviet regime owes its foundation, its continued
existence, and its international reputation to its ability to generate and
sustain a level of military power that commands awe and respect (not least
at home).

In a very important sense, the CPSU draws its domestic political
legitimacy from its military assets. The Bolsheviks seized power and sustained themselves through the frequently critical period of war communism (until the winter of 1920–21)[45] because they had higher quality or
more military assets than their many, divided and frequently indecisive
adversaries. The revolution should not, of course, have occurred in Imperial Russia (according to Marx and Engels). Russia may have been the
"weakest link of capitalism," but contrary to self-serving and some genu-

inely misinformed commentary, the Russia seized by Lenin and his band of adventurers in 1917 was not a moribund feudal structure (at least not in some critical respects). The Russia of 1914–17 was racing into the twentieth century (or perhaps the late nineteenth century) at a pace that exceeded its ability to manage. It is no exaggeration to say that the domestic crises of Imperial Russia in World War I were not so much the crises of a hopelessly backward country as the crises of a country that was modernizing too rapidly.[46] It may be possible to claim that, because of catastrophic inflation and general economic paralysis, "the Bolshevik Revolution was a fact before it happened,"[47] but having once happened, it was sustained by the bayonets of the Red Army.

Commentators who are impressed by the apparent novelty of the Soviet military modernization drive of the past twenty years should be reminded of the fact that the Soviet army and air forces of 1935 were probably the most modern, as well as the largest, in the world.[48] Furthermore, to cast back further, ever since Peter the Great defeated Sweden at Poltava in 1709, Russia has almost always been, or has been believed to be, a first-class military land power.[49] Soviet leaders, like Russian leaders before them, know that although military power is far short of everything,[50] it does offer essential compensation for some other deficiencies.

Soviet strategic culture is acutely aware of the consequences of military weakness: two and a half centuries of Tatar domination (1237–1480); near-permanent insecurity for Russian colonists in the face of militarily well-organized nomadic tribesmen; humiliation by Poles, Lithuanians, and Swedes; catastrophic invasion by the French; defeat in the Crimea in 1854–56; defeat in Manchuria in 1905 (and revolution at home); humiliation at Brest-Litovsk in December 1917 (armistice) and March 1918 (peace treaty); intervention by the Allies on behalf of the Whites (and their keeping an eye on each other); near-defeat by the Poles in 1920; near-defeat by Nazi Germany in 1941–42; and humiliation by the United States in October 1962—to select only a few of the high (or low) points in the potential recital.

The Slav tribesmen, Russians, and Soviets have been obliged to live very dangerously by virtue of their geopolitical condition. This is not to deny the force of Richard Pipes's argument that "a country does not become the largest state in the world, as Russia has been since the seventeenth century, merely by absorbing or repelling foreign invasion."[51] However, Russian and Soviet history, up to and including living memory, is not of a kind that is likely to encourage Soviet leaders—any Soviet leaders—to choose to neglect their military power. To summarize, from the Soviet perspective, one cannot be too strong militarily. Soviet policymakers demonstrate no observable sensitivity to what Western commentators term "the security dilemma." Specifically, the security of one country can easily become the insecurity of others (which tends to trigger security-enhancing responses on the part of those others, which feed new or augmented insecurity feelings and assessments on the part of the first country, and so on).

The Value and Cost of Military Power

The Soviet Union, like Imperial Russia and Muscovy before it, is a heavily militarized society. The maintenance of a very large standing army requires no particular effort of justification in Moscow. As the legatee of a somewhat unstable multinational empire, surrounded by actual or potential enemies—not to mention the inalienable Soviet duty to prosecute the "historic mission" for which the USSR was nominally founded—the Soviet case for a very large military establishment virtually makes itself. No matter what the character of defense policies in NATO countries, Soviet military and paramilitary preparedness will remain massive.[52] When Western theorists of disarmament in the early 1960s sought to devise schemes for complete and general disarmament, they failed to find a way to cope with the awkward fact that the USSR (by today's count) maintains roughly 460,000 fairly heavily armed "internal security" troops (border guards under the KGB and MVD security forces). The USSR/Russia has long been obsessed with the fear of domestic disorder,[53] and internal security has always been a military or paramilitary duty.

The Soviet Union does not view its heavy economic-social burden of defense preparation in ways at all analogous to those familiar in U.S. terms. Although the separate Soviet armed services may, and do, squabble over relatively scarce industrial and human resources, there appears never to be a question of debating the legitimacy of the fundamental state drive for multilevel military preponderance over any and all potential enemies *combined.* This may mislead the unwary, since, clearly, the steady slowdown in the rate of growth of the Soviet economy must sharpen defense/nondefense allocation controversies. However, the Soviet weltanschauung does not admit of any controversy over the need for constant military vigilance. Without denying the growing need of Soviet high-technology industry for the Great Russian youth who currently must spend two or three years performing generally economically unproductive military tasks, Soviet leaders discern no alternative—for the following reasons (or cultural conditions):

- A very large armed force is "the Russian/Soviet way." The tradition of public service in the mass army is as solidly entrenched in the Soviet Union as it is in France.[54]

- The USSR knows, by ideological definition, that it has deadly enemies in the outside world.

- The military power of the Soviet state induces politically beneficial awe and respect among its citizens, untrustworthy Warsaw Pact allies, and those currently beyond direct Soviet control.

• Military and paramilitary organizations of all kinds, from units in schools and factories to elite guards regiments, are a source of national pride, an instrument of social cohesiveness, and a tool for nation building and national integration.[55] Almost regardless of its actual military functions, DOSAAF (*Dobrovol'noye Obshchestvo Sodeystviya Armii, Aviastsii i Flotu*—the Volunteer Society for Cooperation with the Army, Aviation, and the Fleet) has in excess of 80 million members (nominally) and is charged, de facto, with the militarization of Soviet youth and working people (at the school and factory-floor levels).[56]

The Rhythm of Defense Preparation

There is a steady rhythm to Soviet military preparation that lends itself all too easily to misassessment in the West. Whereas the United States stumbles, or lurches, from feast to famine in its allocation of resources to defense, the Soviet Union—for enduring reasons of style and structure—adheres to a tolerably even course, year after year. This well-attested fact is subject to the phenomenon of redundant causation. In other words, several quite distinct, and plausible, theories serve to explain the steady pace of Soviet defense preparation. Western misassessment flows from the alien character of this Soviet rhythm of preparedness. In some Western eyes, it seems virtually self-evident that the unrelenting social and economic costs of Soviet defense preparation must have political meaning in terms of "a day of reckoning." The familiar phrase, "the Soviet military build-up," suggests a purposefully directed activity—and what purpose can a military buildup have other than to intimidate and coerce enemies? Consideration of buildup leads easily enough to the Soviet window of opportunity/Western window of vulnerability thesis that was popular in the United States in 1980–81. I do not wish to risk propagating spurious reassurance, but I believe that the Soviet military "buildup" should be viewed, first, in Soviet perspective.

The steadiness in Soviet defense allocation, year by year, is what one should expect of a state that enjoys a stable, long-term appreciation of the character of its security problems and opportunities. Soviet statecraft, a malign mixture of Great Russian imperialism, Leninist opportunism and millenialism, and vulgar realpolitik, is capable of almost any tactical diplomatic maneuver (or terroristic act—recall the abortive "Bulgarian" plot to kill the Pope), but it does not lurch from one characterization of external and internal threat assessment to another that is radically different. Soviet leaders, like other leaders, may miscalculate in detail, but they have a grand strategy (or doctrine, in the Soviet term)[57] that is not subject to peurile Manichaeanism or to juvenile détente euphoria.[58] No matter what

Pravda, Tass, or itinerant Soviet "scholars" may say, day-by-day Soviet statecraft is dominated, at a high level, by an enduring comprehension of the essential rules of the game of world politics and of the proper Soviet role as a player in that game.

In addition, a country with a centrally planned economy, with respect to the priorities within which major decisions are made at quinquennial intervals, is not a country that can easily adjust its kinds and levels of defense production on a flexible, year-by-year basis. Every serious Western student of the Soviet defense industry of recent years has stressed the inertia in that system[59] and the difficulty there would be in attempting to shift resources on a large scale as threat estimates varied.

Unlike the situation in the United States, the Soviet defense industry (in alliance with its particular military users) maintains a fairly steady work flow, year after year, on the products that it knows how to build. Although major innovation is possible, the system disproportionately rewards formally satisfactory performance and discourages risk taking. Regular patterns of defense industrial activity can be and have been upset by policy decisions taken in Moscow;[60] witness the creation of the defense-industrial base for what was to become the Strategic Rocket Forces. However, the tendency, generically, is for relatively low-risk improvement of existing products and for very conservative testing programs for higher risk technologies. In addition, there is good reason to believe that certain programs are continued long after there is excellent reason to doubt their prospective military utility. As with all styles in defense preparation, the Soviet style has the vices of its virtues.

Nonetheless, however one elects to explain it, there is no significant dispute concerning the character of Soviet style in defense-industrial activity. The U.S. defense community is able to predict, with high confidence, the level and kind of Soviet defense product output through the 1980s and much of the 1990s (barring some traumatic system shock) in a way that simply is not feasible for Soviet intelligence analysts contemplating the United States. The U.S. cycle of defense-industrial feast and famine is not a regular one. By 1995, the United States may have deployed the MX/ Peacekeeper ICBM, Trident II, "Stealth" bomber, a new small ICBM, and some very limited initial ABM weapons, or it may not.

THE SOVIET UNION AS AN EMPIRE

Although the subject of this study is nuclear strategy and national style, it is imperative that political drives and temptations not be subsumed in, for example, technical consideration of nuclear war planning and approaches to arms control. Above all, this chapter seeks to provide the reader with a clear sense of the character of the Soviet Union as a strategic actor—with particular reference to strategic-nuclear concerns. The preceding section detailed certain prominent facts about Soviet thought and behavior, and this section advances a somewhat sweeping hypothesis concerning the political engine that may summon forth Soviet nuclear posture and strategy to action. To be specific, it is contended here that the Soviet Union may usefully—indeed, most usefully—be approached as an empire, moved in its thought and behavior by distinctively *imperial* considerations. As will be made evident, this hypothesis is advanced not as a preclusive explanation and basis for prediction, but simply as a very useful one. There have been many empires, each of them unique in important respects. However, the purpose here is not to uncover general truths about empire; rather, it is, much more modestly, to contribute to improved understanding of the Soviet Union. In this context, it is proposed that some frequent and enduring (if not necessarily universal) themes of empire are very useful for comprehending Soviet reality.

The Meaning of Empire

In looking for the essence of empire, one is compelled, *faute de mieux*, to have recourse to common sense. What are the characteristics of empire—properly understood? Typically, they include the following:

- Rule by one nation over many nations.[61] (Virtually by definition, a uninational state cannot be an empire.) Contemporary China (Beijing), for example, is not an empire because the Han people constitute more than 90 percent of the total population. Traditionally, the Chinese (Han) response to ethnically alien intrusion has been absorption.

- A sense of mission or duty—properly authorized by some "mandate of heaven"—to exercise authority over ethnically different (inherently lesser or temporarily backward) peoples.[62]

- A profound sense of insecurity, since the domination of "others" carries with it the implication that they have loyalties other than to the empire.

Fundamentally, imperial rule implies a relationship of authority founded on the power to coerce. Imperial rulers, even in the heyday of their authority—and notwithstanding the possible reality of their actually believing in some form of a *mission civilisatrice*—are often wont to recognize that there is an abnormality (a permanent crisis of legitimacy) in their relationship with many of their subjects, such that coercion must underlie all ruler-ruled connections. This argument can easily be overstated. The relations between rulers and ruled in most empires, at most times, have not been characterized by overt coercion. Nonetheless, the judgement that putative national separatism is unlikely to succeed because of the power of the coercive instruments of central imperial rule is essential to the authority of empire.

Very often, the idea of empire is confused with the idea of "colonial empire." A colonial empire, by definition, is an empire of colonies, with colonists. More often than not, imperial reality has had no colonial referents worthy of note. For a prominent example, the British Empire in India never extended, in personnel, beyond administrators, the army, and traders; there was never any question of bringing native British people out to "colonize" the Indian Empire. It should be noted that colonization, as an adjunct to empire, may have several distinct motives. In the Soviet case, one can observe Great Russian colonization both as responsive to population pressure and as intended to dilute, and eventually overwhelm, local nationalisms that otherwise might become politically troublesome.

Even though the nation-state is a comparatively modern invention—after 1500—the sentiments that make for nationhood are anything but modern. Empires have always had to contend against the local particularisms of group, tribe, clan, city, and nation. It would appear to be a universal and historically ancient preference for people to favor rule, and even misrule, by one (or some) of their own kind to rule by foreigners. Any nation that rules another nation in the absence of freely given consent (an unlikely condition) assumes a permanent insecurity burden. The price of multinational empire is high, and the essential dynamics of imperial expansion have been notably constant over the centuries. The thesis presented here is but one of those concerning the security perimeter of empires. It is possible, and indeed probable, that different theses have explanatory value concerning other empires.

The Russian/Soviet empire—like, for example, the Roman, the British, and the Austro-Hungarian empires—has chosen to seek enhanced security through expansion. At root, the motive has been defensive in character (though far from exclusively). The Romans invaded Britain not in quest of gold and glory, but rather to deny rebellious tribes in Gaul a sanctuary (and to provide a victory that the domestic politics of the moment in Rome required).[63] Similarly, Rome expanded to the Rhine and the Danube in a search for natural, defensible frontiers but found that the security of those river lines required a forward policy with client-states beyond them.[64]

Until the 1880s, the British Empire was relatively unpopular at home,[65] and much of it had been acquired to protect the two routes to India (around the Cape and, later, via Egypt)—a classic example of unplanned imperial expansion. The Honorable East India Company came to acquire an Indian empire as a direct and generally undesired (because of the expense) consequence of the need to protect trade. Anglo-Russian hostility throughout the nineteenth century was fed, above all—on the British side at least—by largely unwarranted fears concerning Russian designs on

India. The British policy of "bolstering Turkey" was driven in good part by a determination to deny St. Petersburg easy access to the Eastern Mediterranean (thereby threatening the route to India); while British paranoia concerning Soviet designs drove generations of British diplomats-spies-soldiers to play the "Great Game" in Central Asia. In toto, Great Britain waged three unprofitable Afghan wars (the third one in 1919).[66] The northwest frontier of India offers a near-perfect example of how an empire, basically satisfied with its extant holdings, feels compelled to seek some measure of control beyond the existing frontier—by and large through a system of subsidized "clients"—in order to safeguard that which is already held.

Austria-Hungary, with its ethnic smorgasbord, offers potentially the most compelling, and alarming, analogy with the Soviet Union today. Vienna and Budapest prior to 1914, confronting a domestic multinational time bomb, decided that their best strategy for coping with Slav separatism was to restrict the growth of Slav states on the borders. The formal annexation of Bosnia and Herzegovina in 1908 led directly to the events of 1914.

The Drive for Empire

Almost as important as what is claimed here is what is not claimed here. I am not arguing that there is only one model of imperial statecraft; that empires can never be satisfied with their frontiers; nor that empires are created with only a single motive in mind. Instead, I am arguing that there is a model—a historically dominant model—of imperial statecraft that is characterized by a largely defensively motivated urge to expand, and that the Soviet Union (following Imperial Russia) behaves true to this particular tradition. Moreover, expansion need not mean the geographic absorption of troublesome neighbors. It is more efficient, as a general rule, to expand hegemonically via a growing structure of bribed and intimidated client states. Also, although it is contended here that a key to comprehending Soviet foreign policy should be sought in this dominant model of an imperial need to expand for essentially defensive security reasons, many other factors play their part. Naturally, the mix of motivating factors will differ from case to case and from time to time; nonetheless, it is worth mentioning the following reasons for empire:

- *Profit:* For example, in the fifteenth and sixteenth centuries, at least until the defeat at Lepanto in 1571, imperial expansion—besides being seen as a religious duty—was highly profitable for the Ottoman Empire.[67]

- *Glory and self-esteem:* The French acquired much of their empire in Africa as psychological compensation for their shame at defeat by Germany in 1870.[68]

- *Land hunger:* This was a particularly strong motive in the Russian case. Backward methods of farming, a very adverse climate, and poor soil in the heart of Great Russian territory—the taiga—motivated persistent colonization onto the open steppes.[69]

- *Balance of power:* The British saw their overseas empire after 1890 in part as redressing the adverse British diplomatic condition in Europe.[70] Also, empires can expand for preemptive political reasons—for example, "If we do not take it, someone else will."

- *Personal careerism:* Poor communications and great distances meant, for example, that Russian and British proconsuls of distinction could create empires in Central Asia and the Far East and in India, respectively, with scant reference to policy in St. Petersburg and London. Able individual adventurers often were of greater historical consequence than distant policymakers. There was scope for talent on the frontier. As Great Britain had its Cecil Rhodes, so the Russia of the Czars had Count Muraviev-Amursky; both were in the business of building empire. Calculated ambiguity in the credentials of bold empire builders meant that the metropolitan authority could disavow their more rapacious activity if need be.

- *Civilizing (or other) mission:* Essential to the mental hygiene of most imperialists has been the provision of legitimacy. Empire has to be not merely fun and profitable but somehow beneficial to those acquired as subjects. Cultural differences usually suffice to provide the pretext for imposing "civilization." The determined imperialist is not often at a loss to find some local practices sufficiently obnoxious to require the benefits of imperial discipline. The right to good government (Westminister or Paris style) of native peoples tended to be placed above the right of those peoples to self-government (even if only autocratically and perhaps inefficiently by one of their own).

- *Lust for and enjoyment of power:* Individuals and states enjoy exercising authority over others.

After 1917, the Soviet Republic, following a brief, insincere experiment with the right of peoples to secede, unsurprisingly came to function as the vehicle for the Great Russian imperialism long embraced by "the Czar of all the Russias." Out of the turmoil of World War I and the civil war that followed, only Finland, Poland, and the Baltic peoples of Lithuania, Latvia, and Estonia managed to sustain a new-founded, Versailles-decreed, and blessed independence. Independence did not, of course, come free— both Poland and Finland had to affirm their independence in blood.

It would probably be an error to look for a general theory of empire and imperialism.[71] One of the leading authorities on the idea of empire has offered the following cautionary words:

Politics and semantics make uneasy bedfellows, and anyway "Empire" has always appealed more to oratory than to analysis. . . . For what is imperialism anyway? It is the predictable expression of a will to power, which in turn is something that manifests itself in unpredictable ways.[72]

One can find several compelling partial historical analogies to the situation and policies pursued by the Soviet Union as an imperial power. However, the insecurity of empire, which is a general condition flowing from the inherent tension between local particularism and central imperial authority, is unusually acute in the Soviet case. In addition, the phenomenon of empire, with the necessary strength of that "will to power" cited by Professor Thornton, almost invariably excites suspicion and hostility abroad. For example, the British Foreign Office in the 1830s (and well beyond) could make little sense of the Russian drive into Central Asia and the trans-Caucasus region save in terms of a hypothesized Russian ambition eventually to exercise authority (imperium) over India and Persia. Russia, it was believed (with good reason) in London, already had more territory than it could exploit, control, or people (colonize) effectively—what need had it to extend its dominion? Moreover, the Khanates of Central Asia posed no threat of significance to extant Russian "holdings," so any defensive-security rationale was weak.

The Insecurity of the Soviet Empire

The Soviet empire today is unusually insecure in terms of historical imperial phenomena, because the authority of the Communist Party of the Soviet Union (CPSU) is fragile even in its core (Great Russia) domestic area. Historically, many groups of imperial statesmen have feared, appropriately, that trouble on the frontier could easily spread, and that their individual political fortunes required at least the appearance of policy success. It is a little unusual, however, for the character of the state itself to be potentially at risk in every crisis on the marches—unusual, but not unprecedented. For recent examples, the Portuguese revolution of the early 1970s was a fairly direct consequence of policy failure in Angola and Mozambique; and the Fourth French Republic fell in 1958 over the issue of policy in Algeria. Thus, Soviet domestic political stability, though unusually sensitive to imperial failure of policy, is by no means unique in this condition.

The Soviet government has a problem of legitimacy even among Great Russians. Because of its particular history, Russia/ the USSR produced a fragile relationship between rulers and ruled. The state in Russia/the USSR has always functioned essentially for purposes apart from the interests of individual subjects (though interests may coincide). Since the Mongol conquest of 1237–40 (probably the single most important event in

Russian/Soviet history),[73] Russian leaders have represented interests that have borne no necessary relationship to the interests of their subjects, which is not to deny that the passion for order evidenced by all Muscovite Grand Princes, Czars, and Soviet leaders benefited the populace as well as the courtiers who were its immediate beneficiaries. Raison d'état, in practice, reached (and reaches) heights of patrimonial hubris undreamed of even by Louis XIV. Russians, and other peoples within the Russian or Soviet Empire, have acquiesced in imperial rule fundamentally because of their awe of the power of the state and because of their perennial fear of chaos. Russians fear disorder almost to a pathological degree, accept the need for firm government, and respect a leadership that demonstrates an inflexible will to power.

The legitimacy of the Czars rested on two essential pillars: a "mandate of heaven," endorsed by the Orthodox Church and—as noted earlier— respect for the power of the state. The Czar was held to be God's representative:

> To the Emperor of all the Russias belongs the supreme and unlimited power. Notably fear, but also conscience commanded by God Himself, is the basis of obedience to this power. (*Article 1 of the Fundamental Laws of Imperial Russia*)

With regard to the awe in which Russian subjects held the power of the state, and on the character of the connection between the ruler and ruled, the following observations by Edward Crankshaw are noteworthy:

> The Russian autocracy in its most positive manifestations has always been so spectacular in its absolutism that it has compelled the myth of omnipotence with almost hypnotic force.[74]
>
> The obedience of the Russian people was . . . negative, or passive, obedience. It was an abdication of responsibility. In only the most limited sense could the Russian autocrats command: except in moments of extreme national peril they could only repress. . . . The central government of Russia with its tightly organized provincial apparatus extending over unimaginable distances was, insofar as it affected the governed, less the administrative nexus of a unified nation than the colonial service of an occupying power, having no organic connection with the subject people. . . . One person and one person alone, in the eyes of the subject people, stood above the detested government and was at the same time its victim; and he, whose supreme office did indeed reflect the people's need, was the very man who believed that he was the government: the Tsar.[75]

The alleged omnipotence of the Czar and, earlier, of the Grand Prince of Muscovy was a carefully constructed legal-mystical myth designed to combat disorder. The myth of omnipotence was invented in the mid-fifteenth century, following nearly fifty years of appalling domestic disorder. The actual practice of Grand Princely, Czarist, and (save for most of the truly exceptional Stalinist era) Soviet power has tended more to the oligarchical than to the individual-absolutist.[76]

The bureaucrats who comprise the innermost circle of the CPSU leadership today typically provide no human focus for Soviet loyalty, and the contemporary Soviet version of the "mandate of heaven" is the claim by the party to be the vanguard in prosecuting a "historic mission." If, as virtually every apparently authoritative report attests, Soviet society is suffused with cynicism concerning the "historic mission," what is left save respect for the power of the state and, for Great Russians at least, identification of Soviet power with a Great Russian power in which pride is felt?

Soviet leaders obviously are aware of the fact that popular—indeed, well-nigh universal—doubts and cynicism regarding socialism and the self-asserted Soviet role as vanguard of the international proletariat pose a potentially deadly threat to the legitimacy of CPSU authority. If the doctrine is wrong, the CPSU has no claim to authority—in which case the domestic crimes committed in the name of raison d'état since 1917 will require some skilled explaining.[77] Aside from the distressing realization that both they and their general public appreciate the tenuousness of Marxist-Leninist ideology, Soviet leaders also have to be aware that lurking not far beneath the surface of society in their Great Russian core area is a vision of the Russian future that is notably different in key aspects from the tenets of state socialism. The crass materialism and doctrinal internationalism of the state ideology has few roots worthy of mention in Russian soil. There is reason to believe that the mysticism of the Orthodox Church and Great Russian nationalism (or chauvinism) go far deeper than any of the doctrines taught officially since 1917.[78] Nonetheless, the style of contemporary Soviet government—its oligarchical court politics, the presumption that the state is all-powerful, and the absence of contractual nexi between rulers and ruled—are all quintessentially Russian. The contemporary leadership style would have been familiar to Ivan III in the fifteenth century.

In short, even the heart of the Soviet empire contains potentially politically combustible material. The British could divest themselves of empire, sometimes even in humiliating circumstances, without political revolution occurring at home. However fairly, or otherwise, Britain treated the inhabitants of its imperial holdings, there was always a contractual nexus binding the British government and the British people. Defeat abroad was not seen by British radicals as clear evidence that "they"—the authorities—were not invincible (since there was no myth of invincibility), and therefore was not taken as encouragement to seek systemic political change at home.[79] The contrast with the USSR could hardly be more stark.

Within living memory, suggestive evidence is available concerning the essential fragility of the Soviet empire. In much of the southern area of the European USSR, and in the former Baltic states, the German Army was welcomed in 1941 as a liberator. That welcome did not last long, but it suggests what might have been had the Third Reich been other than it was. Crude comparison cannot be made, or course between the USSR today and the USSR of 1941. Victory in the Great Patriotic War for the CPSU in defense of the Russian Motherland bequeathed a legitimacy it had lacked previously; the passage of forty more years of CPSU rule is significant in and of itself; conditions of everyday life are much easier today than they were then; and the days of arbitrary terror are long past.[80]

Nonetheless, the domestic political stability of the USSR is fragile in ways well appreciated by Soviet leaders. Their empire comprises the following:

- A core area attracted by Russian nationalism, not by state-socialist ideology.

- Other domestic holdings, such as the Ukraine, Moldavia, Kazakhstan, Georgia, and so forth, which are in the USSR because the inhabitants perceive no realistic alternative at present.

- An Eastern European glacis with enomous potential for the promotion of domestic instability, yet from which Moscow believes it cannot afford to be seen to retreat.

The Soviet Union is rigid on territorial issues (such as vis-à-vis China) because it believes that it dare not appear to show weakness—for fear of who might be tempted to test Moscow's will next. Similarly, the Soviet Union is rigid on the essentials of political control, though the local form may vary, in Eastern Europe—for fear of the risk of domestic contagion.

It is not suggested here that the Soviet government lacks domestic support. Soviet subjects, like people everywhere, take a natural pride in the success of their country. Also, it is not suggested that the Soviet empire is a house of cards that is likely to collapse at the first push or setback. There is a ruthless will to power about Soviet leaders that both warrants and receives respect. Whether or not they were convinced that they could win a nuclear war, it is safe to assume that Soviet leaders would take any military risk if they could discern no alternative path to save their patrimony (albeit at the risk of having to absorb a catastrophic level of damage).

Soviet foreign policy behavior may be explained with reference to the dynamics of insecure empire.[81] Because I am suspicious of monocausal explanation, I elect not to place weight exclusively on this factor. However, I do believe that such a theory would not lead the student too far astray. The "dynamics of insecure empire" thesis holds that power centers independent of Moscow must be defined as a threat. In particular, the empire in Eastern Europe can never really be secure as long as Western Europe is free to attract, functionally propagandize (however inoffensive the motive), and provide a peninsular beachhead for U.S. power and influence. The Soviet Union certainly does not want to fight a war in Europe, but, to be much more secure, it does need at least to neutralize currently non-Soviet-controlled Europe as a generic threat to the extant empire. Beyond Europe, the USSR to be secure in Eurasia, needs to deny the United States access of all kinds and to isolate it in the Western hemisphere. Such an accomplishment would dramatically change the terms of the long-range Soviet-U.S. competition to the Soviet advantage.

The theory of the ever-expanding (hegemonic) empire is very similar to the geopolitical explanations of Soviet behavior that I have advanced elsewhere.[82] It is important to recognize that the argument advanced here on behalf of an insecure imperial model of Soviet political structure and behavior is compatible with other explanatory themes. For example, ignoring all aspects of imperial statecraft, a geopolitical/realpolitik explanation of Soviet foreign policy must come to very much the same conclusions as those advanced here. That explanation is not incorrect; it is simply enriched by the addition of the imperial theory. Also, unfashionable though it remains (by and large for good and sufficient reasons), ideological interpretations of Soviet foreign policy behavior need not mislead the careful observer very much.

The conclusions and implications of this section are disturbing because they point to structural as opposed to transient, individual-human influences on Soviet foreign policy behavior. In short, this discussion identifies enduring features in Soviet thought and practice. First, the USSR may usefully be thought of as an empire. Although scholars disagree on definitions of empire—as scholars will—the essential qualities of empire are not much in dispute, Second, a general theory of empire is a chimera, or Holy Grail, that may absorb years of wasted effort on the part of scholars. However, though admitting of the strong possibility that, historically, empires have emerged, evolved, and died in different ways, the evidence suggests a tentative hypothesis to the effect that there is a nonexclusive dominant theory of empire to which contemporary Soviet phenomena relate fairly directly. Third, like France in the 1920s—though for different reasons—empires in the Soviet mold are compelled to seek an impossible *securité totale*. The price of greatness is eternal vigilance—or, in the Soviet case, paranoia. Fourth, the imperial theory of Soviet foreign policy permits one, usefully, to sidestep the issue of aggressiveness. The Soviet empire is insecure in all its geographical layers, from the Great Russian heartland, through the non-Great Russian Republics of the USSR, to the Eastern European glacis. As with the Romans, the British, and the Austro-Hungarians, enhanced security is perceived in expansion (of influence, rather than territory). Fifth, because of Soviet insecurity, even in the heartland, it is difficult to discern any reasonable path for imperial divestiture.

Sixth, in essence, the legitimacy of the Soviet state reposes in the awe in which its power, its will to succeed, is held by its subjects. A military or political defeat on the frontiers of the empire could shake the worldview of many formerly acquiescent subjects who simply could not envisage the possibility of Soviet defeat. A healthy political system can survive the shock of foreign defeat, although it may choose to punish the current officeholders. Soviet state ideology is an ideology of long-term success, of inevitable victory in the "historic mission" of spreading socialism world-wide. Defeats for Soviet arms or diplomacy strike both at the credibility of the omnipotence of the state and at the robustness of the myth that the CPSU rules by right of being the correct interpreter of the authoritative doctrine. Finally, given the very obvious insecurity of its extant, multilayer imperium, the USSR discerns no option other than to seek to expand its control of the outside world. Geopolitics/realpolitik, ideology, Great Russian national hubris, and the dynamics of empire all impel the USSR to an expansive foreign policy.

SOVIET STYLE AND NUCLEAR STRATEGY

The image of the Soviet Union as an insecure empire bent upon achieving the impossible dream of total security will be unwelcome to many readers. From the left, I will no doubt be accused of inventing a permanent Soviet military danger, one that flows directly from the very structure of the Soviet imperial polity. From the right, I will be accused of inventing an essentially defensive rationale for the Soviet propensity to commit aggression. To return to a theme already introduced en passant several times in this chapter, I am not convinced that there is a single "essential" drive behind Soviet foreign policy in support of which Soviet strategic nuclear posture and strategy is designed (or maldesigned). However, the insecure empire proposition, for all its simplicity (or desirable parsimony—from the point of view of elegant theory design), seems to offer little prospect of misleading the reader, it fits the historical facts persuasively. In short, a superior proposition may be waiting to be discovered, but I judge this one to be good enough for the limited purposes of this study. It is against the background of appreciation of Soviet imperial statecraft that U.S. defense planners should design their conflict scenarios for the remainder of the 1980s and the 1990s. If World War III should occur in this period, it will most likely not occur because adventurous Soviet leaders are willing to leap through a perceived "window of opportunity" in pursuit of gains, nor because mechanistic technical instabilities in the strategic balance produce a condition characterized by "the reciprocal fear of surprise attack"[83] (which I view as constituting largely a U.S. "engineering" fantasy), but rather because a Soviet leadership, accurately or otherwise, fears for the political integrity of its empire.

The detailed strategic implications of differences in the national styles of the superpowers are presented in chapters 4 through 8. By way of scene-setting for those detailed discussions, the following are some terse pointers to the impact of Soviet national style on Soviet nuclear posture and strategy.

First, Soviet state ideology, married malignly to Soviet historical memories, identifies certain foreign powers as enemies, by definition. Limited tactical accommodation, as in SALT, is always possible, but there can be no fundamental and lasting accommodation of interests. War with these enemies is an ever-present possibility. Second, as students of some very painful historical lessons, and as the principal banner carriers for the "historic mission" of spreading socialism worldwide, Soviet leaders know that there is no adequate substitute for victory in war. Third, in the Soviet view, wars of all kinds can be won (or lost). The prevention of war is the duty of politicians; the duty of soldiers is to prepare for the efficient conduct of war. Fortunately, deterrence and defense are believed to be fully compatible.[84]

Fourth, it is the Soviet belief that war of any kind should be a survivable experience.[85] Damage limitation is a nonnegotiable concept. For temporary tactical reasons, a Soviet leadership may sign on for an arms control regime that appears to limit Soviet freedom of national action in this regard (for example, the ABM Treaty of 1972), but careful net assessment of putative combat prowess demonstrates the undiminished primacy of damage limitation considerations—appearances to the contrary notwithstanding.[86] Fifth, born of repeated and catastrophic-level national experience, Russia/the Soviet Union does not approach the possibility of nuclear war with a facile expectation of cheap and easy success. The dominant Soviet idea of victory in an undesired World War III encompasses expectations of human and economic loss that the United States tends to deem incompatible with a meaningful concept of victory.

Finally, the Soviet Union has only one authoritative body of military science. All Soviet publications are subject to rigorous censorship. Although Soviet political and military leaders undoubtedly would like to be able, permanently, to prevent the outbreak of nuclear war—a political task—the somewhat traditional battlefield, war-waging themes that one can easily discern in the official General Staff organ, *Voyennaya Mysl* *(Military Thought)*, should be taken at very close to face value. The Soviet General Staff's view of nuclear war is not one of a violent bargaining process; rather it is one of nuclear battle—and as John Erickson has observed, "battles have winners and losers."[87]

American politicians, officials, and commentators may make of this what they will. At the very least, I hope readers will take full account of the apparent facts of Soviet strategic cultural-stylistic distinctiveness. The issue here is not one of abstract truth or desirability—which superpower national style is more correct or preferred; rather, it is the possible or probable consequences for Western security when two very different cultures and styles are engaged in conflict.

NOTES

1.   Otherwise excellent scholarly studies often forget that the Soviet Union for example is real, whereas political *science* is an invention that as often as not—to be generous—comes between author and subject. This is the case with Seweryn Bialer, *Stalin's Successors: Leadership, Stability, and Change in the Soviet Union* (Cambridge: Cambridge University Press, 1980). For a perceptive review, see Robert Conquest, "Worse to Come?" *New Republic*, January 17, 1980, pp. 29–33.

2.   It is fairly commonplace to assert a need to understand Soviet attitudes and opinions on their own terms. Somewhat less commonplace is the scarcely less valid assertion that there is a need for a U.S. understanding of the attitudes and opinions that Soviet policymakers believe Americans to hold (rightly or wrongly). In that regard, see Jonathan S. Lockwood, *The Soviet View of U.S. Doctrine: Implications for Decision Making* (New Brunswick, N.J.: Transaction, 1983).

3.   This is a sweeping judgment. In very general terms, however, the judgment is well-nigh an obvious truth. To be specific, I believe that much of East-Central Europe need not have been conceded to Stalin in 1944–48; that the Korean War could have been prevented; that major political-military disengagement opportunities may have been lost in 1953 and 1954; that the Soviet Union could and should have been prevented from reconquering Hungary in 1956; that a United States less obsessed with Southeast Asia might have deterred Soviet intervention in Czechoslovakia in 1968; and that U.S. foreign policy from Nixon through Carter, in its Soviet dimension, was a cumulative disaster for U.S. national security and for international order.

4.   This is analogous to the scholar who notes in an introduction to a book that there are many ways of examining the subject matter and then, having paid brief, formal obeisance to theoretical ecumenism, proceeds for the entire length of the book to employ only the preferred theory—without explaining why that theory should be preferred.

5.   Unfortunately, democracy is a concept that is not patented; perversions abound—as in "people's democracy" or "democratic centralism."

6.   A useful introduction to this subject is Harriet Fast Scott and William F. Scott, *The Armed Forces of the U.S.S.R.* (Boulder, Colo.: Westview Press, 1979), chap. 9.

7.   For example, see Robert Arnett, "Soviet Attitudes Toward Nuclear War: Do They Really Think They Can Win?" *The Journal of Strategic Studies* 2, no. 2(September 1979): 172–91.

8.   Richard Rosecrance, ed., *America as an Ordinary Country: U.S. Foreign Policy and the Future* (Ithaca, N.Y.: Cornell University Press, 1976).

9.   Commentators are addicted to the assertion that their subject is "in transition." This wise-seeming observation often refers, in practice, to little more than the necessary fact that today is placed between yesterday and tomorrow.

10.   Conquest, "Worse to Come?" p. 31.

11.   David Holloway, "Military Power and Political Purpose in Soviet Policy," *Daedalus* 109, no. 4(Fall 1980): 28.

12.   This, fundamentally, is Richard Pipes's thesis. For the fullest presentation of his ideas, see Pipes, *Russia Under the Old Regime* (New York: Scribner's, 1974).

13.   "Vulgar realpolitik" does not suffice to explain Soviet foreign policy behavior. Commentators who are attracted to the idea that Soviet leaders are just crass opportunists have yet to explain to my satisfaction why Finland (an ally of Nazi Germany) escaped occupation in 1945.

14.   Though often very competent and informative, fundamentally historical Ph.D. dissertations in international relations are trivialized, if not ruined, by the professional requirement that some political science theoretical architecture be added. Prominent among my favorite comments on the state of international relations theory are the following by James Rosenau:

> Thus these are hard times for those who theorize about world affairs and foreign policy. No sooner had we successfully come through several decades of enormous theoretical progress than the world which we began to comprehend manifested unmistakable signs of profound change, rendering our hard-won theoretical sophistication increasingly obsolete. . . . In short, nothing seems to fit. Our great strides in theory and research during the 1950s, 1960s, and 1970s, no longer correspond well to the world they were intended to describe.

"Muddling, Meddling and Modelling: Alternative Approaches to the Study of World Politics in an Era of Rapid Change," *Millenium* 8, no. 2(Autumn 1979): 130.

15.   For example, see Richard Pipes, "Soviet Global Strategy," *Commentary* 69, no. 4(April 1980): 31–39; and Aleksandr Solzhenitsyn, "Misconceptions About Russia Are a Threat to America," *Foreign Affairs* 58, no. 4(Spring 1980): 797–834.

16.   However, it takes many years to change a strategic posture in fundamental ways—which means that the Soviet strategic posture observable today has to be the posture dominant in many major features through the 1980s and even the 1990s. Similarly, Soviet doctrine and military science are not the casual invention of transient political elites. Although innovation is always possible, it is sensible to anticipate continuity rather than radical change. See Scott and Scott, *Armed Forces of the U.S.S.R.*, part 1; and the Soviet Military Thought Series of Soviet military texts translated and published under the auspices of the U.S. Air Force. The basic Soviet text remains V. D. Sokolovskiy, *Soviet Military Strategy*, 3d ed. (Harriet F. Scott, ed.) (New York: Crane, Russak, 1975). Soviet scholars have been claiming, at least for Western ears, that the Sokolovskiy text (first edition, 1963) is obsolete and is going to be replaced.

17.   See Colonel General N. A. Lomov, ed., *Scientific-Technical Progress and the Revolution in Military Affairs (A Soviet View)*, Soviet Military Thought Series of the U.S. Air Force, No. 3 (Washington, D.C.: USGPO, 1975; Moscow, 1973). Also see William R. Kintner and Harriet F. Scott, eds., *The Nuclear Revolution in Soviet Military Affairs* (Norman: University of Oklahoma Press, 1968).

18.   V. M. Bondarenko, "The Modern Revolution in Military Affairs and the Combat Readiness of the Armed Forces," *Communist of the Armed Forces*, December 1968, p. 29.

19.   See Herbert Dinerstein, *War and the Soviet Union* (New York: Praeger, 1962).

20.   For a summary and discussion of Khrushchev's speech of January 14, 1960, see Scott and Scott, *Armed Forces of the U.S.S.R.*, pp. 41–46.

21.   See John Erickson, "The Soviet Military System: Doctrine, Technology, and 'Style,' " in John Erickson and E.J. Feuchtwanger, eds., *Soviet Military Power and Performance* (Hamden, Conn.: Archon, 1979), p. 25.

22.   This is well explained in Holloway, "Military Power and Political Purpose in Soviet Policy," pp. 19–21.

23.   Barbara Tuchman, *The Guns of August—August 1914* (London: Constable, 1962).

24.   Thomas C. Schelling, *Arms and Influence* (New Haven, Conn.: Yale University Press, 1966), chap. 6.

25.   Richard Burt, "Arms Control and Soviet Strategic Forces: The Risks of Asking SALT to Do Too Much," *Washington Review* 1, no. 1(January 1978): 22. See also the discussion in chapter 7 of this book.

26.   Carl von Clausewitz, *On War* (Michael Howard and Peter Paret, eds.) (Princeton, N.J.: Princeton University Press 1976; first pub. 1832), p. 605. For a thought-provoking discussion of the relevance of Clausewitz to the nuclear age, see Raymond Aron, *Clausewitz: Philosopher of War* (London: Routledge and Kegan Paul, 1983; first pub. 1976).

27.   See Richard Pipes, "Militarism and the Soviet State," *Daedalus* 109, no. 4(Fall 1980): 5–6.

28.   See Bialer, *Stalin's Successors*, chap. 9.

29.   On this and related points, see the stimulating paper by Edward L. Keenan, "Russian Political Culture," Unpublished manuscript (Cambridge, Mass.: Harvard University, Russian Research Center, July 1976).

30.   See Pipes, *Russia Under the Old Regime*, particularly chap. 1.

31.   For a detailed critique of the U.S. style of limited war see Colin S. Gray, *Strategic Studies and Public Policy: The American Experience* (Lexington: University Press of Kentucky, 1982), pp. 61–64, 119–26, 134–66. Also see Robert E. Osgood *Limited War Revisited* (Boulder, Colo.: Westview Press, 1979); Robert E. Osgood, "The Post-War Strategy of Limited War: Before, During and After Vietnam," in Laurence Martin, ed., *Strategic Thought in the Nuclear Age* (Baltimore: Johns Hopkins University Press, 1979), pp. 93–130; and Stephen Peter Rosen, "Vietnam and the American Theory of Limited War," *International Security* 7, no. 2(Fall 1982): 83–113.

32.   See Harry G. Summers, Jr., *On Strategy: A Critical Analysis of the Viet-nam War* (Novato, Calif.: Presidio Press, 1982). U.S. policymakers ignored the "lesson of history": "When victory is essential, it is safer to use a sledgehammer than a nutcracker." Paul Kennedy, "Japanese Strategic Decisions, 1939–1945," in Kennedy, *Strategy and Diplomacy, 1870–1945: Eight Studies* (London: Allen and Unwin, 1983), p. 187. It is perhaps more accurate to say that those policymakers did not recognize the necessity for a concept of victory.

33.   See Henry Rowen, "The Evolution of Strategic Nuclear Doctrine," in Martin, ed., *Strategic Thought in the Nuclear Age*, pp. 151–56.

34.   Careful speculation on this subject pervades Benjamin S. Lambeth, *Selective Nuclear Options in American and Soviet Strategic Policy*, R-2034-DDRE (Santa Monica, Calif.: RAND Corporation, December 1976).

35.   William Lee's studies of Soviet targeting policy are classified.

36.   Joseph D. Douglass, Jr., and Amoretta M. Hoeber, *Soviet Strategy for Nuclear War*, (Stanford, Calif.: Hoover Institution Press, 1979). Also of interest is Joseph D. Douglass, Jr., *A Soviet Selective Targeting Strategy Toward Europe* (Arlington, Va.: System Planning Corporation, August 1977).

37.   John Erickson, "The Soviet View of Nuclear War," Transcript of broadcast on BBC Radio 3, June 19, 1980, p. 8. Also see Erickson, "The Soviet View of Deterrence: A General Survey," *Survival* 24, no. 6(November-December 1982): 242–51.

38.   Instructive detail may be found in L. C. F. Turner, "The Russian Mobilization in 1914," in Paul M. Kennedy, ed., *The War Plans of the Great Powers, 1880–1914* (London: Allen and Unwin, 1979), pp. 252–68. For a contrasting view, see D. C. B. Levine, *Russia and the Origins of the First World War* (London: Macmillan, 1983), chap. 5.

39.   Although a great measure of flexibility in military execution may have apparent political merit to rightly terrified statesmen, the military arguments for "going large" and preemptively, rather than "going small," are likely to be very pressing. Strategic forces that are deliberately withheld in time of war are liable to destruction; their C^3I will be a very high priority target set; and—in general—it may be next to impossible to execute a series of strikes in an efficient manner in accordance with anything that resembles a war plan if one suffers a great deal of prelaunch damage. I have discussed this problem in some detail in my *Nuclear Strategy and Strategic Planning*, Philadelphia Policy Papers (Philadelphia: Foreign Policy Research Institute, 1984), chap. 2.

40.   Erickson, "The Soviet View of Nuclear War," pp. 9–10. Also see Douglass and Hoeber, *Soviet Strategy for Nuclear War*, pp. 12–13.

41.   Above all, a state is a security community, and its first duty—and certainly its sine qua non—is the physical protection of its citizens.

42.   Pipes, "Militarism and the Soviet State," pp. 2, 3.

43.   Ibid., p. 3.

44.   See James Chambers, *The Devil's Horsemen: The Mongol Invasion of Europe* (New York: Atheneum, 1979). p. 73.

45. The protracted military crisis of the Republic ended in late 1920. An armistice was signed with the Poles in October (the Treaty of Riga), and the Whites evacuated the Crimea in November. (It should be noted that the Japanese did not evacuate Vladivostok until 1922.)

46. This argument is advanced and defended persuasively in Norman Stone, *The Eastern Front, 1914–1917* (London: Hodder and Stoughton, 1975). Stone goes so far as to argue:

> There was, in other words, a burst of economic activity between 1914 and 1917 that brought as much change to Russia as the whole of the previous generation. It was, indeed, the economic 'takeoff' that men had been predicting for Russia; that had, in a sense, caused the First World War, since German apprehensions of it had led Germany's leaders into provoking a preventive war. The First World War provoked a crisis of economic modernization, and Bolshevik revolution was the outcome. (p. 285–86)

A sharply contrasting picture is painted in Edward Crankshaw, *The Shadow of The Winter Palace: The Drift to Revolution, 1825–1917* (London: Macmillan, 1976); see particularly the summary judgment on p. 460.

47. Stone, *The Eastern Front,* p. 301.

48. See John Erickson, *The Soviet High Command, 1918–1941* (London: St. Martin's, 1962), p. 326. But see Ronald R. Rader, "Anglo-French Estimates of the Red Army, 1936–1937," in David R. Jones, ed., *Soviet Armed Forces Review Annual, Vol. 3, 1979* (Gulf Breeze, Fla.: Academic International Press, 1979), pp. 265–80.

49. Practice and performance have often been ill-matched, but dreams or nightmares (depending on the pertinent political relationship) of "the Russian steamroller" long predated the birth of the Red Army on January 28, 1918. See Norman Stone, "The Historical Background of the Red Army," in Erickson and Feuchtwanger, eds., *Soviet Military Power and Performance,* pp. 3–17. Useful historical perspective is provided in Christopher Duffy, *Russia's Military Way to the West: Origins and Nature of Russian Military Power, 1700–1800* (London: Routledge and Kegan Paul, 1981).

50. This fact is affirmed in the breadth of the Soviet concept of "the correlation of forces." See S. Tyushkevich, "The Methodology for the Correlation of Forces," *Voyennaya Mysl,* FPD 0008/70, no. 6(June 1969): 26–39.

51. Pipes, "Militarism and the Soviet State," p. 2.

52. Although the argument can be overstated, the fact remains that the more Western scholars and officials have come to understand about the dynamics of Soviet military preparation, the less detailed responsiveness they have discerned in that process of preparation to exogamous factors (a decrease or increase in Western defense preparation, arms control treaty provisions, the state of East-West political relations).

53. This has been a chronic, enduring Russian fear. See Keenan, "Russian Political Culture."

54. However, in the days of Czarist authority, up to and even during World War I, an extravagant system of "exemptions" operated. As Stone has noted:

"Russia called up just over 14 million men between 1914 and 1917, from a population of almost 180 million. This was barely more than France, with a population
of 40 million, and less than Germany, with one of 65 million." *The Eastern Front,
1914–1917*, p. 213. The Russian military manpower problem in World War I was
a direct result of administrative incompetence.

    55. See Teresa Rakowska-Harmstone, "The Soviet Army as an Instrument
of National Integration," in Erickson and Feuchtwanger, eds., *Soviet Military Power
and Performance*, pp. 129–54; and Herbert Goldhamer, *The Soviet Soldier: Soviet
Military Management at the Troop Level* (New York: Crane, Russak, 1975).

    56. See William E. Odom, "The 'Militarization' of Soviet Society," *Problems
of Communism* 25, no. 5(September-October 1976): 34–51.

    57. See Benjamin S. Lambeth, "The Sources of Soviet Military Doctrine,"
in Frank B. Horton III, et al., eds., *Comparative Defense Policy* (Baltimore: Johns
Hopkins University Press, 1974), pp. 200–216.

    58. For one interpretation that is usefully all-embracing, see Edward N.
Luttwak, *The Grand Strategy of the Soviet Union* (London: Weidenfeld and Nicolson, 1983).

    59. See, for example, Arthur J. Alexander, *Decision-Making in Soviet Weap-
ons Procurement*, Adelphi Papers Nos. 147–48 (London: IISS, Winter 1978–79);
David Holloway, "Technology and Political Decision in Soviet Armaments Policy," *Journal of Peace Research* 4(1974): 257–79; and David Holloway, *The Soviet
Union and the Arms Race* (New Haven: Yale University Press, 1983), particularly
chaps. 6–7.

    60. See Alexander, *Decision-Making in Soviet Weapons Procurement*, p. 27.

    61. See Helene Carriere d'Encausse, *Decline of an Empire: The Soviet Social-
ist Republics in Revolt* (New York: Newsweek Books, 1979), p. 11; and Luttwak,
Grand Strategy of the Soviet Union, p. 11.

    62. One can do no better than to refer to William T. Stead, "The White
Man's Burden," *Review of Reviews*, February 15, 1900, pp. 107ff.

    63. In retrospect, it is fairly obvious that the occupation of most of Britain
imposed a strategically unjustifiable burden on the slender military assets of the
Roman Empire.

    64. On the evolution of Roman imperial strategy, see Edward N. Luttwak,
The Grand Strategy of the Roman Empire: From the First Century A.D. to the Third
(Baltimore: Johns Hopkins University Press, 1976).

    65. See A. P. Thornton, *The Imperial Idea and Its Enemies* (London: Macmil-
lan, 1963).

    66. See T. Heathcote, *The Afghan Wars: 1839–1919* (London: Osprey, 1980).

    67. A lively discussion can be found in Jack Beeching, *The Galleys at Lepanto*
(New York: Scribner's, 1983).

    68. Imperial Germany encouraged French expansion in Africa in the hope
of diverting Gallic energies and ambitions in a direction of little relevance to the
European balance of power. National pride that otherwise might insist on revanche (regaining Alsace and Lorraine) might be satisfied by an expanding extra-
European empire.

69.   See Pipes, *Russia Under the Old Regime*, chap. 1. Also of value is Roy E. H. Mellor, *The Soviet Union and Its Geographical Problems* (London: Macmillan, 1982).

70.   From London, "splendid isolation" appeared more dangerous than splendid in the late 1890s and early 1900s. See Kennedy, *Strategy and Diplomacy*, pp. 127–60.

71.   A useful treatment is Charles Reynolds, *Modes of Imperialism* (Oxford: Martin Robertson, 1981).

72.   A. P. Thornton, *For the File on Empire: Essays and Reviews* (London: Macmillan, 1968), pp. 290, 299.

73.   See Tibor Szamuely, *The Russian Tradition* (New York: McGraw-Hill, 1974), chap. 2; Pipes, *Russia Under the Old Regime*, chap. 3; and James Chambers, *The Devil's Horsemen*, chap. 6. The "Tatar yoke" ceased formally with the ending of the payment of tribute in 1480, on the crowning of Ivan III. Although the Mongol inheritance can be seen in the relationships between the Grand Princes of Muscovy, the Czars, and Soviet leaders and their people, it remains a matter of some historical contention whether or not Muscovy borrowed much of note in political organization, method, and attitude from the Tatars. Muscovite political structure, at the level of the village (*mir*) and the court, was almost entirely its own—given the need to respond to unique geographic-economic and political problems—whereas Mongol state organization fundamentally reflected the military power of nomadic clans. See Keenan, "Russian Political Culture."

74.   Crankshaw, *The Shadow of the Winter Palace*, p. 43.

75.   Ibid., pp. 45–46. The Czar owed duties to God and to the Orthodox Church, but not to the Russian people. In a decree of December 22, 1697, Peter the Great made an uncomplicated assertion of the divine right behind his throne: "We, by the grace of God, most radiant and powerful great Lord." Quoted in Marc Raeff, *Understanding Imperial Russia: State and Society in the Old Regime* (New York: Columbia University Press, 1984), p. 6.

76.   Keenan, "Russian Political Culture." However, the thesis or myth of absolutism continues to be believed widely. See, for example, Ronald Hingley, *The Russian Mind* (New York: Scribner's, 1977), chap. 4.

77.   See Robert Conquest, *The Great Terror: Stalin's Purge of the Thirties* (New York: Collier, 1973; first pub. 1968).

78.   Aleksandr Solzhenitsyn is an eloquent, if misleadingly pacific, spokesman for this submerged Great Russian yearning. See Solzhenitsyn, "Misconceptions about Russia Are a Threat to America."

79.   The British Empire was at least as popular an idea among the British working class as it was among the upper classes who benefited more directly from it.

80.   Stalin's reign of terror was historically unusual because of its arbitrariness. In most totalitarian or aspiring-totalitarian countries, people can play reasonably safe by giving to Caesar that which Caesar demands (provided that they are not unfortunate enough to be inherently guilty by some ethnic accident); the qualification "reasonably" is needed, because any system neglectful of "due process"

lends itself to personal exploitation (by individuals secretly eager to denounce personal enemies and rivals). In Stalin's day, innocence provided no assurance whatsoever of personal safety.

81.   See Vernon V. Aspaturian, "The Anatomy of the Soviet Empire: Vulnerabilities and Strengths," in Keith A. Dunn and William O. Staudenmaier, eds., *Military Strategy in Transition: Defense and Deterrence in the 1980s* (Carlisle Barracks, Pa.: U.S. Army War College, 1984), pp. 97–146.

82.   Colin S. Gray, *The Geopolitics of the Nuclear Era: Heartland, Rimlands, and the Technological Revolution* (New York: Crane, Russak [for the National Strategy Information Center], 1977), particularly chap. 3.

83.   Thomas C. Schelling, *The Strategy of Conflict* (Cambridge, Mass.: Harvard University Press, 1960), chap. 9. A refreshingly innovative deflation of the significance of what Western analysts mean by strategic stability is Stephen Peter Rosen, "Foreign Policy and Nuclear Weapons: The Case for Strategic Defenses," in Samuel P. Huntington, ed., *The Strategic Imperative: New Policies for American Security* (Cambridge, Mass.: Ballinger, 1982), pp. 141–61.

84.   This is a subject on which Western officials and commentators continue to be confused. For an attempt to clarify the confusion, see Colin S. Gray, "War Fighting for Deterrence," *Journal of Strategic Studies* 7, no. 1(March 1984): 5–28.

85.   Soviet leaders over the past decade have been very sensitive to the political damage that can be wrought by honest Soviet military theorists. A valuable discussion of trends in Soviet declaratory policy can be found in Dan L. Strode and Rebecca V. Strode, "Diplomacy and Defense in Soviet National Security Policy," *International Security* 8, no. 2(Fall 1983): 91–116.

86.   To date, at least, the Soviet Union has not endorsed any arms control regime that would have a net negative impact on its ability to wage war in a militarily effective manner. See Thomas W. Wolfe, *The SALT Experience* (Cambridge, Mass.: Ballinger, 1979), pp. 247–50.

87.   Erickson, "Soviet View of Nuclear War," p. 3.

CHAPTER 4

Deterrence:
The Western Paradigm

From the dawn of the nuclear age in 1945 until the present, the concept of deterrence has been the master leitmotiv for Western policymakers and strategic theorists. However, deterrence as an unchallengeable, very general concept has often been confused with one or another particular theory of "what deters."[1] As the next chapter will demonstrate, a nearly identical fate has overcome the closely related concept of stability and the hybrid idea of stable deterrence.[2]

A serious intellectual (or policy) historical survey of the concept of deterrence and its executive doctrines would be of interest but is not the purpose of this chapter. I have traced Western, largely American, thinking on deterrence in considerable detail elsewhere;[3] here, I am far more concerned with advancing understanding than with presenting the historical record yet again.

Deterrence is not a controversial concept; everyone is for it, just as everyone is for peace and security. Nonetheless, notwithstanding the non-controversial status of the concept, it is a fact that rival theories of deterrence (what deters whom, and from doing what) underlie contemporary debate over targeting doctrine and over individual weapon systems. Outside a very small community of strategic policy debaters, the U.S. body politic is generally ignorant of the interface between theories of deterrence and strategic doctrine as reflected, however imperfectly, in plans and forces. Nuclear weapons employment policy and targeting strategy is a subject that rarely sullies the university lecture halls wherein deterrence theory is presented and discussed (and they are none too numerous).

Students introduced to the mysteries of deterrence theory all too rarely are told that the language of policymakers may find only a pale reflection in the war plan design actions of the Joint Strategic Target Planning Staff (JSTPS) in Omaha.[4] Strangely, perhaps, the peacetime, prewar deterrence focus of university teaching reflects all too accurately the nonoperational orientation of many U.S. defense professionals, in and out of uniform.[5] For many years U.S. and other Western defense intellectuals were proud of their accomplishments in bringing the military aspects of nuclear energy under firm theoretical control. For example, as contemporary commentaries attest, the U.S. defense and arms control community entered the SALT I negotiations very confident that it knew what it was about, and no less confident that what it was about was right.[6] (Later chapters will probe in detail the intellectual context for U.S. SALT/START policies.)

Although an ocean of ink has been expended on the subject of deterrence theory, Bernard Brodie could write in 1978 that civilian scholars have "almost totally neglected" the question of "for what objectives" should we fight a nuclear war if deterrence fails.[7] It has always been understood that deterrent effect may be as much a matter of will and credibility of use as it is of weapons per se,[8] and that will and credibility of use should be related to anticipated events in war. However, nuclear war has not been approached as war—that is, as a struggle that one would seek to win for the achievement of political goals.[9] Instead, U.S. defense intellectuals, and even U.S. governments, have appeared to approach nuclear war as though it could be conceived of in terms of a game of violent diplomatic bargaining, or a particularly painful exercise in coercive diplomacy. Strategic ideas of considerable subtlety and cleverness were designed and refined by Western strategists; the familiar litany includes graduated deterrence,[10] city avoidance/controlled counterforce,[11] limited nuclear options,[12] and more.[13] The issue here is not whether those ideas were interesting and relevant to the problem as Western scholars see it; rather, it is whether such ideas, and their late 1970s and early 1980s facsimiles, help promote sensible strategic programs and an intelligent targeting doctrine vis-à-vis a Soviet Union whose force posture and war plans have been designed by somewhat traditionally minded Soviet general staff officers—in short, by Soviet officers who appear to view nuclear war as war, not as a "diplomacy of violence."[14]

THEORIES, PLANS, AND CAPABILITIES

The actual details of how the United States would "go to war"—to employ the old-fashioned term—and of how it would conduct a central nuclear war are necessarily among the most classified of all government information. Indeed, few people, even within the Department of Defense, have access to very much of that information. The United States, *faute de mieux*, is in the business of deterring a range of inimical Soviet actions by threat of resort to nuclear violence, ultimately effected by so-called central systems. That threat reposes in military organizations that are prepared and able to conduct warlike operations, but it is expressed for public consumption, at home and abroad, in words. (It is also expressed, of course, in noticeable changes in the alert status of forces, and such "mobilization/readiness signals" can be manipulated to transmit political messages.[15]) Although each side very carefully monitors the words uttered by the other, by far the more reliable indicators are programs and actions. To date, the actions in question with regard to nuclear forces have been confined to exercises and crisis-time precautionary moves.

The language of deterrence policy is formulated and reformulated with predictable regularity as administrations come and go in Washington, and the choice of words can indeed be important. However, in the past, the reality of U.S. war planning often has diverged noticeably from contemporary fashion in official declaratory deterrence policy.[16] Much, though far from all, of the scholarly and public political debate over nuclear weapons policy has focused far too heavily on the words of senior officials and far too little on the plans and programs required to carry those words into effect. It appears that a president can shift policy merely by speaking or by endorsing a document, some details of which may then be leaked.

Whatever the merits of the Carter administration's policy guidance document, PD-59, and its November 1981 Reagan administration successor, NSDD-13—and they are substantial[17]—the following considerations apply:

- The Soviet Union is unlikely to be impressed by a strategy that lacks the necessary means of implementation. Some of the military requirements of the strategy can be satisfied by existing forces and command and control arrangements, but by no means all.[18]

- Post-PD-59 and NSDD-13 nuclear strategy, with its "war-fighting" view of an adequate deterrent, requires an implementing force posture that is able to take out hard and elusive Soviet military and political targets.[19] The United States must have strategic forces with the appropriate survivability, warhead yields, and accuracy, and those forces must be supported by intelligence gathering, transmitting, and assessment facilities that are capable of finding targets and assessing damage. The United States today, and for many years in the future, cannot strike *effectively and promptly*, with great reliability, at the complex of Soviet deep underground political command bunkers or at most Soviet missile silos and nuclear weapons storage sites.[20] This is an easily demonstrable fact; it is not a matter of opinion.[21]

• U.S. nuclear strategy under the Reagan administration is not really new. The United States has always targeted Soviet military forces and has long planned to attempt to strike at key political targets.[22] Policy has evolved; it has not been marked by sharp discontinuities.

• Cities per se have not been targeted for many years. Indeed, even in the years when the official rhetoric in praise of mutual assured destruction was fairly undiluted by acknowledgement of "war-fighting" considerations (say, in 1967–69), actual force allocation in SIOP planning was weighted overwhelmingly toward countermilitary targeting.[23]

• The countervailing strategy and its refinement by the Reagan administration, as reported, envisages the possibility, though not the probability, of prolonged central, and other, war.[24] To be able to wage such a war, the United States would need to ensure the physical survival *and endurance* of (1) a substantial fraction of the strategic forces; (2) the National Command Authorities (NCA); and (3) the C^3I essential as a basis for adaptive planning. At the present time none of the three are very close to prospective reality. The reason is that the U.S. strategic force posture has been designed, essentially, for a spasm war.[25] This is not to deny that improvements are in train, particularly in the realm of C^3I able to ensure a prompt strike-back, but the United States is a very long way indeed from possessing the physical assets necessary for the conduct of protracted nuclear operations (whatever one's view of the desirability of such a capability).

The debates that leaks (planned and unplanned) of the content of, PD-59, NSDD-13 and the "Defense Guidance" for FYs 1984–1988 predictably catalyzed are but the latest in a long series of public contentions over nuclear strategy that was far removed from being policy, in terms of actual capabilities, at the time it was announced. On February 18, 1970, for example, President Richard Nixon (actually, Henry Kissinger) wrote in his first "state of the world" message:

> Should a President in the event of a nuclear attack be left with the single option of ordering the mass destruction of enemy civilians, in the face of the certainty that it would be followed by the mass slaughter of Americans?[26]

Aside from the facts that, even in 1970, a president did have a range (though admittedly a small range) of preplanned SIOP-level strike options and that special-purpose strike options could be designed rapidly, President Nixon's call for greater flexibility in targeting strategy was not given planning effect until SIOP 5 was approved in December 1975 and implemented in 1976.[27] Much earlier, in 1962, Robert McNamara had called for a considerable measure of flexibility in U.S. targeting. At Ann Arbor, in June 1962, he said:

> The U.S. has come to the conclusion that to the extent feasible basic military strategy in a possible general war should be approached in much the same way that more conventional military operations have been regarded in the past. That is to say, principal military objectives, in the event of a nuclear war stemming from a major attack on the Alliance, should be the destruction of the enemy's military forces, not of his civilian population.[28]

As Henry Rowen has explained, although McNamara did succeed in revising the "optimum mix" targeting scheme that he inherited, which did not provide for discrete strikes only against military targets, he presided over a targeting community that assigned first priority to placing Soviet urban-industrial assets at risk.[29] This is not to say that the United States would have struck first at Soviet cities in the 1960s, only that the threat to Soviet cities was seen as being the most important, indeed the "ultimate" threat.[30] Much of the debate over a counterforce strategy that surfaced in 1962–63 in response to McNamara's publicly declared position[31] rapidly lost its relevance as the Soviet Union increased, hardened, and dispersed its strategic nuclear assets.[32] After 1966, the United States had rapidly deteriorating prospects of effecting major counterforce success, even though the lion's share of the strategic force allocation was directed to countermilitary tasks.

Many commentators in the late 1960s mistook McNamara's declaratory shift in favor of the assured destruction of the urban-industrial Soviet Union for a shift in targeting strategy. In practice, there were no major changes in SIOP design from the early 1960s until the mid-1970s;[33] what did change was the ability of the strategic forces to effect the forcible disarmament of the prospective enemy (that is, the Soviet military target structure changed in a cumulatively dramatic fashion, insufficiently matched by advances in U.S. counterforce—countersilo and antisubmarine warfare—prowess). Although, as observed earlier, many commentators simply assumed McNamara's doctrinal shift from damage limitation to assured destruction to be reflected in SIOP design—which it was not—they were correct in assuming that the administration of the day accurately saw nuclear threat, and even nuclear war, very largely in terms of urban-industrial destruction. Henry Rowen has sought to defend McNamara by arguing:

> The primary purpose of the Assured Destruction capabilities doctrine was to provide a metric for deciding how much force was enough: it provided a basis for denying service and Congressional claims for

more money for strategic forces. It also served the purpose of drama-tizing for the Congress and the public the awful consequences of large-scale nuclear war and its inappropriateness as an instrument of policy. (However, it was never proposed by McNamara or his staff that nuclear weapons actually be *used* in this way.)[34] (Emphasis in the original)

The worth of these excuses admitted, the facts remain that McNamara chose not to fight the Joint Chiefs of Staff on SIOP design—he did not press for changes that stressed flexibility and selectivity; that he accepted the increasing invulnerability of Soviet strategic forces as a desirable fact of life—he did not press research and development programs intended to offset at least some of the survivability features of new Soviet programs; and finally, that he blessed the evolving technological trend with the concept of mutual assured destruction, which was really the idea of an apolitical bookkeeper or engineer, not of a strategist.[35]

Robert McNamara, considered overall, as the strongest of all the secre-taries of defense to date (though James Forrestal, the first defense secre-tary, might have been just as strong had he enjoyed the backing of a well-manned office and had the domestic political context been very different)[36]—appears, in judicious retrospect, to have had an enduring and unfortunate impact on U.S. nuclear weapons policy. McNamara had a powerful mind, had undoubted leadership qualities, was hard-working, and so forth. Unfortunately, he had a powerful bookkeeper's, managerial mind; he did not have the mind of a strategist or even an understanding of the need for strategy.[37] On the evidence available, which includes his policies (declarations and programs) in the strategic nuclear area and the U.S. conduct of the most crucial years of the Vietnam War, McNamara simply did not understand that a defense establishment has to be ready to fight wars; that if wars are not won, they tend to be lost;[38] and that expectations of military success for status quo powers are beneficial for deterrence. Perhaps this discussion is becoming unduly personalized, but the facts remain that Robert McNamara set a tone of *defense management* rather than *strategic leadership;*[39] that through his strengthening of the secretary's office, he virtually required the services to follow analytical suit and neglect strategy in favor of systems analysis;[40] that he presided, appar-ently contentedly, over the evolution of the central nuclear balance from a condition of very healthy, clear U.S. superiority to near parity; and that when tested as a strategist in a real war (that is, in Vietnam), he failed lamentably.[41]

Although it can be claimed that Robert McNamara played a critically important role in helping to shift U.S. nuclear weapons policy from an operational focus on "winning" toward the support of far less heroic theories of strategic stability, it cannot be denied that his contribution to the impoverishment of strategic thought and debate was matched fully by an increasingly management-minded Joint Chiefs of Staff. I have felt somewhat uncomfortable in criticizing Robert McNamara, when really he merely represented U.S. strategic culture, albeit in an unhealthily faithful way.[42] If Americans feel moved to criticize Robert McNamara, they should realize that they are also criticizing themselves. McNamara was an outstandingly worthy and competent example of the American way in peacetime defense thinking.[43]

THE U.S. APPROACH TO DETERRENCE

Although U.S. strategic forces were targeted overwhelmingly against Soviet military targets throughout the 1960s, the essence of official U.S. deterrence thinking after 1963 was that strategic stability (and peace, insofar as peace was believed to be forwarded by strategic stability) flowed from a situation in which neither superpower could protect its civil society. By implication, this meant that neither superpower should be able to threaten the prelaunch or penetration survivability of a major fraction of the strategic forces of the other. Almost needless to say, this was (and remains) a prescription for stalemate, or paralysis, in U.S. statecraft.[44]

By historical accident, the United States happened to enjoy the underappreciated benefits of clear strategic nuclear superiority from the late 1940s until the 1960s. By "superiority" I am not referring to some astrategic bookkeeper's metric of relative force levels; rather, I am referring to the certainty, or near certainty, that had the United States waged war against the Soviet Union in the period in question, it would have won in a quite unmistakeable manner (and in a manner whereby the American survivors would not have envied the dead[45]). Unfortunately, the kind of diplomatic leverage that should have flowed as a consequence of strategic superiority was diluted by the early U.S. attraction to the idea of mutual deterrence. Civilian U.S. policymakers, even in the Eisenhower years, did not think in operational terms about strategic nuclear weapons.[46] It probably is no exaggeration to assert that the U.S. Air Force's Strategic Air Command (SAC) could have won a World War III at any time from the early 1950s until the mid-1960s, at very little cost in direct nuclear damage to U.S. society. Because of their very cumbersome and time-consuming alert-status-enhancement procedures and their very poor communications security, Soviet strategic forces in the 1950s should have been a relatively easy target for SAC. This fact was well known among defense professionals in the 1950s, yet it somehow never percolated up to opinion leaders and, thence, out to the general public.

In terms of the "objective facts" of the strategic nuclear weapons balance (the most important element in "the correlation of forces"), the

United States should have enjoyed virtually a free hand in the 1950s. The critics of "rollback" in the 1952 election were wrong, as were the critics of John Foster Dulles's carefully hedged theory of "a capacity for massive retaliation" in January 1954.[47] In addition, there was no obvious *military* reason why the United States and NATO-Europe could not have embraced Imre Nagy's Hungary in the fall of 1956 and dared the USSR to do its worst. It is true that the Soviet political stake in Hungary was far greater than that of NATO, but the strategic balance in 1956 should have permitted the West to begin to undo some of the damage in which it had acquiesced pusillanimously in 1945–48.[48] Because of its absence of war aims worthy of the name, the United States won the war and proceeded with indecent speed to lose the peace. Stalin's gains in East-Central Europe in 1944–48 far exceeded his prior expectations.

American and NATO-European strategic cultures simply could not accommodate the idea of using nuclear threats for forward, compellent political purposes—for the very congruent, if unheroic, reason that Western political cultures did not harbor any forward political ambitions (if only for contemporarily misassessed strategic prudential reasons).[49] As should be obvious by now, I believe that the Soviet imperium in Eastern Europe both could and probably should have been "rolled back" during the period of clear U.S. strategic nuclear superiority.

There have been fashions in the preferred popular details of U.S. deterrence theory, but notwithstanding shifts of emphasis, a leitmotiv skeptical of operational utility has persisted. The nonoperational—indeed, almost antioperational—theme was set very early in the nuclear age. Writing in 1946, Bernard Brodie offered the following thoughts:

> The first and most vital steps in any American security program for the age of atomic weapons is to take measures to guarantee to ourselves in case of attack the possibility of retaliation in kind. The writer in making that statement is not for the moment concerned with who will win the next war in which atomic bombs are used. *Thus far, the chief purpose of our military establishment has been to win wars. From now on, its chief purpose must be to avert them. It can have almost no other useful purpose.*[50] (emphasis added)

For reasons that are understandable in U.S. cultural terms and are indeed praiseworthy by reference to humane values, U.S. politicians, U.S. civilian defense officials, and—increasingly—even U.S. military professionals have accepted the view that nuclear weapons are not usable, that they are fundamentally different from other kinds of weapons.[51] As already argued in this book, Soviet defense professionals, civilian and military, have also accepted the different quality of nuclear weapons; indeed, they have endorsed the idea that such weapons, together with new means of delivery and new technologies of communication, computation, and control, have produced a multistage "revolution in military affairs." However, this revolution is not the revolution signaled by Brodie in his quoted 1946 judgment.

The Soviet Union recognizes the potentially decisive role of nuclear missile weapons, albeit in the context of a "combined arms" doctrine.[52] Soviet civilian and military leaders have rejected the fatal inevitability of war, but they have not denied the possibility of war, nor—more to the point—have they provided very convincing evidence for the proposition that they endorse the idea that a nuclear war could not be won.[53] Although it can be argued that a Soviet commitment to the idea of victory in nuclear war is mandated by ideological necessity and is useful for the sustaining of morale (just as the Soviet general public and, particularly, the Soviet conscript soldier were not subjected to very much agitation and propaganda in the 1970s in praise of East-West détente), there is good reason to believe that Soviet leaders view the prospect of nuclear war as an experience to be survived if it cannot be avoided and as a contest that it is their duty to try to win.[54]

Brodie's statement is not totally alien from the Soviet perspective. Soviet doctrine probably could accommodate Brodie's thought that the principal purpose of a military establishment is to avert war, though it would not accept the emphasis in the succeeding sentence: "It can have almost no other useful purpose." Latent military force can be "employed" for intimidation. Strategic nuclear weapons, as one component in the military and nonmilitary arsenal of weapons available to support a country's statecraft, may be thought of, at the very least, as a "counterdeterrent."[55]

In the mid-1950s, the burgeoning debate over nuclear strategy—and strategy in the nuclear age more generally—again produced the idea that if there were "stability" at the level of the central strategic nuclear balance, there could logically be instability at lower levels of possible conflict.[56] This idea was not new; an early variant of it may be found in NSC-68, the key State–Defense planning document of spring 1950, which, inter alia, foresaw the need for general-purpose force rearmament once the Soviet Union succeeded in canceling out the temporary U.S. atomic advantage.[57]

Stability in the central balance—meaning, in this context (reflecting the intellectual history of the 1950s), low or nonexistent incentives to initiate central nuclear war—should mean a more permissive environment for local conflict. Trigger fingers on strategic forces should not be itchy if there is no military advantage to be gained from escalation to central war. Although Western theorists labored ingeniously in the 1950s to find military-strategic compensation for the emergence of a condition of mutual strategic deterrence, it seems, in retrospect, that they misassessed the nature of the deterrent threat as perceived in Moscow. Mutual deterrence was a political reality after 1954 because President Eisenhower and other U.S. opinion leaders said that it was. The military reality of the 1950s and beyond, as already noted, was that the Soviet Union would or should have been defeated in war. Some contemporary RAND studies showed, or purported to show, how first-generation Soviet ICBMs, with follow-on attacks by long-range aviation (LRA), could have disarmed SAC. Those studies make frightening reading, even today.[58] However, operational realities on both sides, particularly pertaining to timely strategic intelligence, were such that SAC would have had to try very hard indeed to lose a war.[59]

In 1955–57, when the U.S. civilian defense intellectual establishment first flowered, having been catalyzed into being and into action by the evolution of the RAND Corporation[60] and by the trend in public policy events,[61] understanding was widespread that the strategic stability of a mutuality of deterrence posed major problems for the security of geographically forward-located friends and allies. A great debate over limited war ensued,[62] to be terminated effectively in 1958 as a consequence of intellectual exhaustion and new doubts about the stability of the central balance (occasioned by speculation over the possible strategic meaning of ballistic missiles).[63]

Out of the lively strategic debates of the late 1950s and early 1960s came the concept of escalation—controlled or uncontrolled.[64] Even if one does not believe that nuclear war can be won in any meaningful sense, and even if one has grave difficulty believing that credible nuclear threats can be issued, one might perhaps concede the possibility that nuclear-armed states would be able to threaten to behave in so dangerous a fashion that the obvious risk of an unintended escalation explosion or eruption would promote sober policy reassessment on the other side. The dangers of accidental war almost certainly have been much exaggerated by some commentators over the years,[65] but a U.S. strategic force posture in a very high alert status—say, Defense Condition 2—or NATO in a state of General Alert, would be more war-prone than they are in normal peacetime operations.[66] As Thomas Schelling expressed it in a noteworthy theoretical essay written in the late 1950s, one may pose a "threat that leaves something to chance."[67]

This theme still pervades U.S. thinking about nuclear weapons policy. In trying to explain PD-59 before a congressional committee in 1980, then Secretary of State Edmund Muskie asserted that the contervailing strategy was not a war-fighting strategy and that the Carter administration did not believe that a central nuclear war could be won.[68] In short, the secretary affirmed the "rationality of irrationality" thesis or paradox. The Reagan administration has not said that nuclear war would escape control, but it has stated, repeatedly, that it does not believe that such a war could be won.[69] The tension between this stated belief and the declared intention to "terminate the conflict on terms favorable to the forces of freedom"[70] remains unresolved at the time of this writing. If nuclear war cannot be won—meaning that nuclear weapons cannot be used to secure political goals—how could one support foreign policy interests by the threat of nuclear employment?[71] Various answers have been provided.

First, it may be argued that it is rational for the United States to threaten to behave irrationally (that is, to invoke societal suicide or mutual holocaust, or a high risk thereof) if such a threat of irrational behavior is not totally incredible in some circumstances and with some politicians.[72] Second, even if, with Secretary Muskie, one does not believe that nuclear war can be limited, one may yet believe that by posing particularly fearsome threats to those assets valued most highly by the Soviet Union, adequate compensation may be provided for the self-deterrent logic implicit in one's view of the probable explosive dynamism of nuclear war. By this argument, a threat to the survival of the Soviet state is so deterring a prospect that the credibility of its execution probably need only be very modest indeed. One may argue that the credibility of U.S. execution of such a threat lies in the "fog of crisis" or—should the conflict proceed that far—in the "fog of war" itself. As Clausewitz affirmed, there is a degree of "friction" in war,[73] a military logic to armed conflict,[74] such that the actual course òf combat may surprise policymakers on both sides. In other words, Soviet General Staff officers, if they reasoned aprés Paul Nitze in his article "Deterring Our Deterrent," may logically anticipate a paralysis of nuclear policy will in Washington for reasons of self-deterrence. However, as students of the history of war, they may well believe that people in moments of extreme stress do not always do or refrain from doing what strategic logic should command. Moreover, the military dynamics of thermonuclear war may, in practice, escape careful central political supervision.[75] Deterrence may succeed as a consequence of the uncertainty of victory as well as of the certainty of defeat.

Third, and finally, one may seek to argue that through a reciprocated flexibility and selectivity in nuclear execution, intrawar deterrence may function in a central war so as to interdict the slide to mutual holocaust. Even if one affirms a belief in ultimate mutual holocaust, one may also affirm, without self-contradiction, a belief in a putative process of combat escalation, with thresholds (some of which may be discovered in the event).[76] Indeed, by this logic, it would be reasonable to argue that it is the clear and increasingly present perceived danger of the ultimate threat of holocaust that would provide the major incentive for both sides to find, in real time, some prominent solution for their common need to settle on some basis for prompt war termination.[77]

Since the mid-1960s, the U.S. defense community has not merely acknowledged the prospect of mutual holocaust as a (debatable) technological fact of life,[78] it has positively embraced such an eventuality as constituting a desirable reciprocated threat—truly the foundation of stability.[79] From the early 1960s to the present, the United States, intermittently and with various degrees of high-level policy persistence, has sought to diversify the range of threats posed in its strategic nuclear war plans; but at the end of the threat corridor lies, and has always lain, the specter of society-wide destruction. In January 1980, when he was fully conversant with the details of the strategic nuclear targeting review (the "Sloss Report"),[80] Harold Brown went on very public record as follows:

> We need, *first of all*, a survivable and enduring retaliatory capability to devastate the industry and cities of the Soviet Union.[81] (emphasis added)

Dr. Brown proceeded to stress the limited policy relevance of such a threat, but as the words quoted make clear, he did see a massive countervalue threat as being the "bottom line" of the range of U.S. strategic threats. Indeed, he asserted:

> What has come to be known as assured destruction is the bedrock of nuclear deterrence, and we will retain such a capacity in the future.[82]

What had happened over the decade of the 1970's was that the U.S. defense community had come more than half-way, particularly at the rhetorical, declaratory level of policy, toward adopting the logic of a warfighting strategy, but major elements of an alternative stream of logic persisted. Although official deterrent reasoning publicly endorses countermilitary and even hard-target counterforce targeting, and although it is officially fashionable today to talk of victory denial or success denial as comprising the heart of the U.S. deterrent requirement, the element of deterrence through the threat of punishment endures. Indeed, it is possible that the advertised emphasis in PD-59 on posing threats to Soviet political and military assets[83] is really thought of as constituting a threat to punish the Soviet state rather than a threat to deny military success to Soviet arms and statecraft.

It is true that President Reagan—with his speech on March 23, 1983, and the policy document NSDD-119 of January 6, 1984—has called for and authorized research on strategic defense whose ultimate goal is to render nuclear weapons "impotent and obsolete,"[84] but the depth of government-wide commitment to the president's goal is uncertain. I believe the case for a war-fighting theory of deterrence is a very powerful one (see the discussion of Option 4 in chapter 9), but it can be overstated.[85] Civilian workers and a great deal of the economy may not strictly warrant definition as belonging to the essential assets of the Soviet state, but beyond an uncertain point, quantitative effects become qualitative effects. Some defense theorists, in pouring scorn on assured destruction threats, have come very close to slipping into the absurd position of saying that U.S. nuclear threats to a large fraction of Soviet civil society and its means of livelihood have little, if any, deterrent value. That is not the position taken in this book.

Much of the recently revived academic theorizing about deterrence has signally failed to understand the variegated character of the political problems that deterrence must address.[86] Although the design of an effective deterrence policy is a quest for persuasive negative sanctions, those sanctions do not have to and probably should not be viewed in terms of punishment. In attacking what he has termed the "managerial models of conflict and deterrence elaborated in the United States," John Erickson pointed to "the sort of semantic nonsense which hid 'war' behind a phrase like 'violent bargaining.' "[87] Official U.S. prose in the era of PD-59 and NSDD-13 has recognized that for deterrence to succeed, enemies must be convinced that "they would be frustrated in their effort to achieve their objective *or suffer so much damage that they would gain nothing by their action*".[88] (emphasis added).

Some U.S. officials and many extra-official theorists, not without some ambivalence, continue to view the probable dynamics of nuclear war as a very painful exercise in "violent bargaining"—really as a psychological process wherein the side most willing to bear pain—or apparently most willing[89]—should win. This is a reasonable vision of conflict, except, alas, that it is noticeably at odds with what the available evidence suggests to be the dominant Soviet view of nuclear conflict. It is not obvious that the Soviet Union can be, or ever has been, deterred by the prospect, even the very credible prospect, of suffering pain. When the anticipation of pain may be effective as a deterrent almost certainly has been, and is, when pain and military and political effectiveness are believed to be synonymous. This is not to argue that Soviet leaders are indifferent to the prospect of societal punishment. Many aspects of the Soviet civil defense program attest to a substantially instrumental concern for the fate of the Soviet general public.[90] However, that concern is heavily qualified, as should be expected of a state that remains essentially patrimonial.[91]

Official deterrence theory, as declared and as reflected in actions and capabilities, has been roundly criticized by scholars for such failings as overemphasizing negative sanctions at the expense of positive sanctions;[92] assuming an undue potency to the concept of *rational* decision making;[93] assuming an unambiguous scope to the policy relevance of strategic deterrence; and assuming too often that the adversary comprises a unitary actor with fixed values. These and similar charges have permeated the literature for more than fifteen years. The recent scholarly literature on deterrence, notwithstanding some of its ingenuity and inherent interest,[94] has been disappointing. Although many deficiencies in official thought and practice have been exposed, the most important questions have tended to escape close scholarly attention. It is encouraging, however, to see Robert Jervis addressing the subject of "ethnocentrism and status quo biases," albeit very briefly.[95]

With reference to the needs of U.S. policy makers for improving the U.S. theory of deterrence with a view to incorporating it in policy, five questions stand out as needing particularly urgent attention. First, what do Soviet leaders find deterring? Second, should deterrence "fail," what employment policy would it be in the U.S. interest actually to execute? Third, when is deterrence policy relevant? Fourth, how should nuclear weapons employment policy enhance deterrence? Fifth, what is the relationship between the U.S. ability (or perceived ability) to limit damage at home and the credibility and efficacy of nuclear threats?

It should never be forgotten that the credibility and the efficacy of a threat may not—indeed, need not—be synonymous. The Soviet Politburo may believe a U.S. president who issues a threat, but it may judge that threat to be insufficiently fearsome. Credibility is important, but it is not all-important.

REVISING THE THEORY

Before turning to detailed answers to the foregoing five questions, several points of logical and factual reference need to be registered. First, I do not believe that the U.S. government should be satisfied with its nuclear weapons policy unless that policy is guided by and reflects a theory of victory.[96] In other words, any policy is unsatisfactory if it envisages as the final or "ultimate" threat the imposition of massive urban-industrial destruction upon the Soviet Union, or the destruction of the major political assets of the Soviet state *in a context where a no less destructive Soviet retaliatory response cannot physically be thwarted*. In terms of deterrence logic, the public emphasis placed by senior U.S. officials on countermilitary and counterpolitical control targeting, considered in isolation from homeland defense, is as flawed as its declaratory predecessors. It, and they, betray the absence of strategic thinking and the absence of campaign analysis of nuclear conflict. This is not to criticize the content of the new emphases in targeting, registered in PD-59 and refined somewhat in NSDD-13, although those emphases do warrant careful investigation.[97] Rather, it is that the United States cannot prudently enter a process of competitive escalation if it anticipates holocaust as the final rung of the ladder.

Second, and in partial explanation of the reasoning behind the first point, official strategic thinking in the United States would appear to have been, and to continue to be, remarkably casual over the vital question of which side will be the deterrer and which the deterred. I am framing my argument in frank recognition of the fact that I cannot predict the answer to that question with any assurance. Official, contemporary U.S. indifference to damage limitation as a major policy objective—save for the hope that the SDI, *one distant day*, may mature to the point where it can place a "leaky astrodome" over the United States—reflects, indeed logically has to reflect, one of two things. Either it is assumed that the United States will be the deterrer at critical times, or it is calculated (or just assumed, to be less generous) that a noteworthy measure of damage limitation is not technically attainable (for the next twenty years, at least). Damage limitation, to the extent that it is anticipated officially, is deemed to be a result only of deliberate targeting restraint—the consequence of an intrawar deterrence process that is disciplined by reciprocated fears of punishment of various kinds.

If—as seems most probable, given the continuing deficiencies in Western conventional and theater-nuclear stopping power around the periphery of Eurasia—it is the United States that would feel compelled to initiate a resort to the employment of central systems, the burden of escalation logically must fall on U.S. shoulders. If, as this book argues, the United States needs to be able to enjoy the benefits of escalation dominance,[98] it is incumbent upon the United States to be able to deter, thwart, or absorb the Soviet response that escalatory initiatives may license. An undefended United States can promise to effect revenge in the event of Soviet strikes of different kinds, but it is far more difficult to threaten, credibly, to impose great damage on the Soviet state by way of an initiative (thereby inviting a Soviet response).

The foregoing logic chain is fatal (theoretically) to extant official U.S. policy reasoning, but it also contains a major possible flaw, which is destructive vis-à-vis virtually all schools of Western intrawar deterrence theory. To be specific, Western theorists of all shades of doctrinal persuasion appear to have been captured by the metaphor of the escalation ladder.[99] In practice, it is entirely possible that the course of a central war will not reflect a recognizable sequence of escalation and counterescalation. Western aspirations for the functioning of an intrawar deterrence mechanism may be dashed by an unanticipated Soviet style in strategic warfare or by Clausewitz's "grammar" of war, short-circuiting the schemes of theorists.[100] If the Soviet Politburo approaches a Soviet-U.S. central war as a war—not as a violent bargaining game—then Western theories of controlled escalation and intrawar deterrence are most unlikely to be applicable.

Third, and finally, it is worth recalling that deterrence was the first and the most important of the three major pillars of contemporary Western strategic theory; the other two were limited war and arms control theory.[101] Limited war theory, insofar as it was reflected in U.S. conduct in Vietnam, was fatally flawed in conception (as well as in execution).[102] Thanks to ten years of rather intensive SALT experience, we know that arms control theory was substantially misconceived.[103] The only element in the strategic theory triad that has yet avoided a rigorous real-world field test is deterrence theory. No matter how grave one's reservations about U.S. strategic policy, one cannot point to unambiguous evidence proving that the theory is incorrect. To date, one cannot point to strategic threats that have failed to deter, any more than one can point to a strategic exchange that did not proceed as theory predicted and as prewar plans prescribed. There is a major problem of evidence. Nonetheless, when it has been field tested, the U.S. (and, more generally, Western) strategic theory that was invented and refined in the "Golden Age" of 1955–65 has proved unable to withstand the traffic of stressful events. Pertinent events have included real-world Soviet diplomatic démarches and arms programs and real-world North Vietnamese political and military style. On the basis of the historical record, one should at least be alert to the possibility that U.S. doctrinal preferences in the region of nuclear deterrence similarly might fail if they were ever applied in the heat, fog, and electromagnetic pulse of genuinely acute crisis.

When reliable data on the putative adversary are missing, officials (and extra-official theorists) tend to resort to the supply of U.S. data. We do not know what will deter Soviet leaders, but we do know what *we* find deterring; therefore, the United States designs a nuclear deterrent posture that is comfortably adequate to deter an American-style adversary. In the United States strategic nuclear deterrent issues are framed and judged by Americans, who cannot help but frame and judge in American terms. We are all prisoners of our political-strategic culture.[104]

In revising its nuclear deterrence theory, the United States has to be vigilant and self-critical in assessing the answers provided to the most vital question: "What do Soviet leaders find deterring?" U.S. officials and theorists need to be constantly mindful of the facts that strategic nuclear weapons comprise only one, albeit the single most important, element in "the correlation of forces" as appraised in Moscow and that the full force of nuclear deterrent effect is likely to be needed diplomatically only once in twenty or thirty years. As my late colleague Herman Kahn liked to argue, our problems of nuclear weapons policy design are analogous to the problems of planning to survive a major earthquake. We know that a major earthquake is very likely or even certain once in, say forty or fifty years, but we do not know when. This means that we have to be constantly prepared for an event that is exceedingly unlikely on a day-to-day basis.[105] However, if the United States cannot cope with such a once-in-a-lifetime event, its policy planning has been inadequate. Nuclear deterrence policy, day-by-day, is almost irrelevant to U.S. foreign policy. The problem is that there is no way to predict when it might suddenly become the most relevant aspect of official U.S. activity.

This chapter, and indeed this book as a whole, does not assume that nuclear deterrence design, if properly conceived, will always work. Indeed, it is only prudent to consider the possibility that there may occur a political context for which there is no "proper conception" of nuclear deterrence.[106] A major reason why this discussion seeks to explore the overall design of U.S. strategic preparation is that I suspect that U.S. policies of deterrence, no matter how cleverly and intelligently designed, might fail on the night—that is, on the one night in twenty or thirty years when they are desperately needed. In principle, there should be a scale of plausible threats that would deter even the most desperate and determined Soviet leaders from seeking military solutions to political problems. In practice, however, because of cultural blindness, war-planning rigidity, the "fog of crisis," or plain incompetence, a situation could arise wherein a Soviet leadership group would be effectively beyond deterrent influence by a U.S. government. This situation could arise either because the Soviet leaders were unable to discern any politically acceptable alternative to taking military action or because they had become convinced that war was inevitable.

Careful study of Soviet phenomena suggests very strongly that the most deterring prospect in Soviet eyes is the anticipation of military defeat. As former Secretary of Defense Harold Brown appears to have suggested, deterrence and defense are really identical.[107] Soviet leaders fear military defeat because such an outcome would threaten their ability to sustain political control at home. Since the late 1970s, it has become fashionable to argue that the ultimate threat to Soviet leaders is the threat to damage or destroy the ability of the centralized political apparat in Moscow to control the country.[108] Intellectually, the threat to Soviet political control assets is certainly powerful. But a basic question remains unanswered: Is a threat to the Soviet political control structure seen as a possible (early) war-fighting option intended to paralyze or at least to degrade the quality of performance of the Soviet war machine, or is such a threat seen as the ultimate penalty that could be imposed by a United States that had exhausted all lesser options—the functional equivalent of the 1960s threat to destroy Soviet cities?

In support of nuclear deterrence policy, U.S. targeteers should seek to target what may be termed the essential assets of the Soviet state, rather than undifferentiated sets of major political-control or political-leadership aim points. It seems likely that no matter how hard the United States tries, the Soviet central political (and military) control structure is most unlikely to be totally vulnerable to U.S. offensive attention. Moreover, even if central political control assets could be isolated for a while or severely degraded, their eventual fate must rest on the course and ramifications of military operations. It follows that the essence of an intelligent U.S. nuclear deterrent policy should comprise a credible threat to deny victory to

Soviet arms. The ultimate threat that can be posed to Soviet leaders is not the massive punishment of Soviet society but rather the defeat of Soviet arms and the political implications of that eventuality. Russian imperial history, which has major elements of continuity with the contemporary scene, suggests that military defeat in foreign wars can translate into political defeat at home.[109]

To summarize, the most deterring prospect for Soviet leaders is the thought that political control at home might be attenuated or destroyed. That control can and should be targeted directly in the U.S. strategic war plan, insofar as this is feasible. Plausibly, however, that control would also be damaged or destroyed if the coercive authority of Moscow were to be challenged persuasively. The defeat of Soviet arms at all levels should transmit potentially fatal ripples of political encouragement for revolt throughout the Soviet empire. An ability to defeat Soviet military power, from the U.S. perspective, has the joint virtues of blunting and thwarting the Soviet ability to hurt the West and threatening to emasculate the principal asset supportive of the Soviet regime.

I am concerned lest U.S. officials, persuaded that the Soviet political control structure is "the target of last resort," neglect to recognize that a United States that could not decide the military conflict on favorable terms probably could not do permanent damage to the Soviet state. I am, and remain, an advocate of countercontrol targeting (or "political-leadership targeting" in the long-preferred official jargon), but I would warn of the following:

- The United States may not be able to find enough of the vital targets.

- The United States may not know who is dispersed where, and with what residual responsibilities.

- The United States does not understand very well how the USSR would be likely to function in time of war; thus, it is very difficult to calculate just how much political control damage would be inflicted by particular strikes.[110]

- The United States has less than perfect information on the quantity and quality of Soviet internal communications and on the vulnerabilities of those communications.

- By executing a truly major countercontrol strike, the United States probably would leave the surviving Soviet government believing that it had little or nothing left to lose. In short, actual execution of an "ultimate threat" would free the Soviets from any consideration of intrawar deterrent effect in their conduct of further strategic operations.

- The United States might want to negotiate war termination with a Soviet government—a task that could be exceedingly difficult if the United States has just sent a thousand or more nuclear warheads in search of the Soviet political control structure.[111]

It is difficult to deny the logic in the position that holds that if Soviet military power should be defeated or even just stalemated, the entire Soviet political control structure might (indeed, should) come unraveled. To a large though uncertain degree, Soviet authority rests on the respect for Soviet power that is felt by subject nationalities. If Soviet military power is seen to be defeated, the awe in which Moscow is held must diminish.[112]

Next, following directly from the foregoing discussion of the deterrent threats most likely to induce fear in Soviet official minds, U.S. nuclear weapons employment policy should be directed in the first instance to the defeat of Soviet military power projection and strategic nuclear forces. Second, U.S. nuclear weapons employment policy should be directed both to the destruction of the overcentralized apparat of the Soviet state and—in the course of a central war that may be protracted—to the destruction of the entire Soviet state-system at all levels. This is a case in which the best is likely to be the enemy of the "good enough." The United States cannot plausibly threaten to hit every target essential to the functioning of the Soviet state. U.S. defense analysts cannot be sure that they understand what would be truly essential to the survival and recovery of the Soviet state. However, the United States can plausibly threaten to do very great damage to the command network that is the Soviet state. It should not be forgotten that just as U.S. officials cannot be certain that fatal damage would be inflicted on the central Soviet control apparat, so Soviet officials cannot be certain that fatal damage would *not* be inflicted. At the very least, one can assert with high confidence that this is the kind of threat that Soviet officials would be most unlikely to take lightly.[113]

Third, nuclear deterrence policy is relevant—in eyeball-to-eyeball, war-threshold terms—probably only once in twenty or thirty years. However, as best may be judged, the Soviet Union has not seen its strategic posture primarily as an instrument for the direct coercion of the United States and others. Instead, the Soviets have invested in a strategic nuclear posture intended (1) to deter (or, more accurately, to *counterdeter*) or negate the relevance of U.S. strategic nuclear power in local crises around the Rimlands of Eurasia and (2) to defend the Soviet homeland, "the citadel of socialism," as competently as possible if central war should occur. These somewhat negative classically deterrent/defensive goals, bereft of explicit compellent context, should not blind us to the possible diplomatic use of strategic nuclear forces for intimidation in a context of direct or indirect aggression at lower levels of violence. It is possible, given the continuum of potential force that everybody fears, that Samuel Huntington is correct in warning that the Soviet Union may hope to "use" its nuclear forces to deter even Western conventional responses to aggression.[114]

Given the continuing adverse trends in major elements of the East-West military balance, it is evident that the mainstream of post-1965 U.S. deterrent reasoning simply has been imprudent. Because of the enduring insufficiency in Western military provision for Eurasian theater defense, U.S. strategic forces cannot sensibly be designed solely to deter a Soviet assault against the U.S. homeland. The United States needs a strategic force posture capable of seizing the initiative in the event of some galloping theater disaster in Eurasia and imposing an enduring and enforceable condition of escalation dominance in central war.

Largely for cultural reasons, the U.S. defense community has tended to see overwhelming value in a strategic nuclear posture clearly compatible with a somewhat narrow and American-centric (and distinctly un-Soviet) interpretation of the requirements of stability.[115] Criteria for strategic force adequacy have tended to relate to putative day-to-day needs and to presumed crisis-time needs that reflect lessons learned in the nuclear age thus far. To date, the quality of U.S. strategic nuclear deterrence policy probably has not been tested. The fact that there has been no general war in Europe and no central nuclear war does not necessarily prove the massive stability of the strategic balance; instead, it probably attests to the relatively low level of political incentive to take action felt by Soviet leaders. In short, U.S. and NATO deterrence policies have yet to be tested severely.

Many officials and commentators who are intensely skeptical of or hostile toward the Reagan Strategic Defense Initiative (SDI) argue that there is today a benign condition of strategic deadlock that enforces stable mutual deterrence. The SDI, it is alleged, threatens this healthy deadlock by promoting U.S. hopes and Soviet fears of major military advantage. The conservative case against the SDI contrasts the long-proven reality of an offensive-dominant deterrent that we know works (witness the absence of war) with the theoretical benefits of a deterrence relationship transformed by the presence of strategic defenses. Needless to say, perhaps, I believe that the United States is inviting catastrophe if it enshrines "the Word" on stable deterrence by looking backward to a temporary technological condition (of the late 1960s and early 1970s) while neglecting the *strategic* roles of nuclear forces and ignoring Soviet perspectives. By the time defense theorists can demonstrate beyond all doubt the inefficacy of an offense-only strategic force posture, it would be too late for the United States (if it still existed) to take corrective action on its posture.

A close reading of Soviet history suggests that U.S. policymakers should consider the strong probability that the Soviet Union is fairly easy to deter up to a certain point—beyond which it may be almost impossible to deter. In other words, there may well not be a broad region wherein deterrence policy, in varying intensity, can function.

Because of their antipathy to risk taking (really to anything that might be characterized as adventurism), Soviet leaders probably do not need deterring in the terms most familiar in Western strategic discourse. The nuclear deterrence equation may well be relevant only once in twenty or thirty years, when the Soviet military proposes to solve a major and dire political problem in a military way. In that event, the first question in Soviet minds will be: "Can the West (the United States) deny us victory?" The second question will be: "Will the United States seek to deny us victory, given the strategic nuclear deterrence relationship?"

Finally, readers should recall the fourth and fifth questions asked in the preceding section of this chapter: "How should nuclear weapons employment policy enhance deterrence?" and "What is the relationship between the U.S. ability to limit damage at home and the credibility and efficacy of deterrent threats?" There is much to recommend the view that deterrent effect flows from Soviet perceptions of U.S. acquisition and declaratory policies rather than from weapons employment policy. Assuming proper security, the Soviet defense establishment has to speculate on the real details of U.S. nuclear weapons employment policy. However, that speculation can be influenced substantially by the clues offered in the U.S. defense debates that they monitor and in the strategic logic of particular weapons and C^3I assets.

The United States should be able to enhance a healthy deterrent effect in Soviet minds by talking about the kinds of nuclear weapons employment options believed to be most worrisome to Soviet officials—given the known, unique strengths and vulnerabilities of the Soviet system. Essentially, as already outlined, U.S. deterrent policy should place emphasis on the threat posed to the likely efficacy of Soviet military power at all levels and to the ability of the centralized Soviet political command structure (1) to control its instruments of domestic and external coercion, (2) to survive physically, and (3) to be able to organize postwar recovery. This formulation recognizes that the first duty of the armed forces of the United States and of NATO is to deny victory to Soviet arms (that is, to defend Western society). If the Soviet Union can win a war militarily, it will very likely be able to pick up the somewhat radioactive pieces at home.[116] Moreover, Americans should be more interested in avoiding defeat than they are in defeating the USSR, let alone in posing extremely severe problems of postwar recovery for the enemy.[117] However, victory denial, when examined rigorously as a goal, translates with little difficulty into the requirement for a theory of victory. Victory denial rests on the idea that the Soviet state and/or society can be so punished that Soviet policy goals either cannot be achieved or can be achieved only at prohibitive and presumably deterring cost. In practice, I believe that to deny the Soviet Union victory, the United States would have to defeat Soviet arms—which, given the very probable political disintegration this would promote at home, could and should mean victory for the West.

Whether victory for the West is attainable and—more to the point, given the deterrence focus of this chapter—whether the prewar and perhaps intrawar beneficial deterrent effect of Soviet anticipation of such a conflict outcome is attainable has to rest critically on the ability of Western countries to limit damage to their homelands.[118] The most important revision needed in official U.S. thinking on nuclear deterrence prior to the signing of NSDD-119 on the Strategic Defense Initiative was the accommodation of the very obvious point that a country cannot prudently take nuclear action if it has every reason to expect an intolerably damaging retaliatory response. Much—probably most—of the potential deterrent benefit of a generally praiseworthy document such as PD-59 is negated when an administration balances the presentation of militarily and politically intelligent targeting ideas with statements to the effect that it really does not believe that nuclear war can be limited or won.

At the time of this writing, it is not plain beyond doubt that the SDI is viewed by the Reagan administration as a strategic imperative for damage limitation. If by "win" one means that political objectives will be secured, it is easy to understand why the U.S. government has difficulty advancing a coherent nuclear strategy story when it denies that nuclear war could be won. If a war can only be lost, it should never be fought (and from a deterrence perspective, who will believe that nuclear weapons ever would be used?).

Mainstream U.S. thinking on damage limitation—PD-59, NSDD-13, and NSDD-119 notwithstanding—probably has not advanced much since Harold Brown offered the following judgment in January 1978:

> I am not persuaded that the right way to deal with a major Soviet damage limiting program would be by imitating it. Our efforts would almost certainly be self-defeating, as would theirs. We can make certain that we have enough warheads—including those held in reserve— targeted in such a way that the Soviets could have no expectation of escaping unacceptable damage.[119]

In 1973-75, Secretary of Defense James Schlesinger at least recognized the crucial role of civil defense vis-à-vis his theme of flexibility of initiative and response. Such recognition is far from general in Washington today, even in the context of an SDI launched and blessed from the highest level of government. There are, of course, major practical questions in need of answers. Can damage be limited in the context of a nuclear campaign waged by an adversary not noted for great sensitivity to the issue of unwanted collateral damage? What would be the probable cost of purchasing worthwhile domestic damage limitation? And what is meant by "worthwhile"? Could the Soviet Union offset U.S. damage-limitation endeavors with relative ease? These are serious questions indeed. But the strategic value, really necessity, of a major ability to limit damage is also serious and should not be ignored simply because it would be very difficult and expensive to effect.

A defense community that fails to recognize the relevance of damage limitation for the quality of its deterrence policy is a defense community that is failing to think strategically. Because of the extended-deterrent duties placed on U.S. strategic forces, nuclear weapons policy, in the last resort, has to be about freedom of action (not, as in the Soviet case by and large, about "holding the ring square"—checking the strategic nuclear posture of the adversary). If he cannot hold damage to the U.S. homeland down to the level of a survivable catastrophe, a U.S. president could not responsibly initiate a process of escalation into the realm of central nuclear war. In other words, the United States would prudently have to acquiesce in defeat in the theater.

Unfortunately, this problem cannot be finessed cleverly by an attempt to slice it into many parts. More or less elaborate schemes for targeting flexibility and restraint do not address the point that, at every potential threshold, it would most likely be the United States that would have to contemplate the probable consequences of its next escalatory move—knowledge of which contemplation might trigger Soviet preemptive action. In practice, I have grave doubts about the realism in Western escalation thinking—the idea that a nuclear war might comprise a series of fairly discrete moves and countermoves.[120] Nonetheless, the discussion here has been cast in terms of the familiar framework of Western escalation theory, to show that U.S. nuclear policy would be unlikely to function as intended, even on its own terms (assuming, unrealistically, a USSR willing and able to play the escalation game Western style).

Without damage limitation capability, the United States does not have an adequate policy of nuclear deterrence; instead, there is a condition of nuclear self-deterrence.

NOTES

1.   The history of strategic ideas after 1945 has been traced in James King, *The New Strategy*, Unpublished manuscript; Colin S. Gray, *Strategic Studies and Public Policy: The American Experience* (Lexington: University Press of Kentucky, 1982); Michael Mandelbaum, *The Nuclear Question: The United States and Nuclear Weapons, 1946–1976* (Cambridge: Cambridge University Press 1979); and Lawrence Freedman, *The Evolution of Nuclear Strategy* (London: Macmillan, 1981).

2. "Stability," for all its importance as a policy-relevant concept, has attracted remarkably little discussion. See John Steinbruner, "National Security and the Concept of Strategic Stability," *Journal of Conflict Resolution* 22, no. 3(September 1978): 411-28. Writing in the spring of 1983, the Scowcroft Commission advised: "Whether the Soviets prove willing or not, stability should be the primary objective both of the modernization of our strategic forces and of our arms control proposals." President's Commission on Strategic Forces, *Report* (Washington, D.C.: The White House, April 1983) [hereafter cited as Scowcroft *Report*].

3. See Gray, *Strategic Studies and Public Policy.*

4. I have lectured on defense questions in universities and war colleges, and I have been attentive to the problem of the implementation of doctrine. Surprisingly few of the university students who are introduced to the mysteries of contemporary strategic theory are also introduced to the problem of the interface between ideas and policy execution.

5. This thesis, in somewhat exaggerated form, was advanced admirably in Edward N. Luttwak, "A New Arms Race?" *Commentary* 70, no. 3(September 1980): 27-34.

6. A classic reflection of this confidence is John Newhouse, *Cold Dawn: The Story of SALT* (New York: Holt, Rinehart and Winston, 1973).

7. Bernard Brodie, "The Development of Nuclear Strategy," *International Security* 2, no. 4(Spring 1978): 66.

8. For example, see William W. Kaufmann, "The Requirements of Deterrence," in Kaufmann, ed., *Military Power and National Security* (Princeton, N.J.: Princeton University Press, 1956), pp. 12–38; Glenn Snyder, *Deterrence and Defense: Toward a Theory of National Security* (Princeton, N.J.: Princeton University Press, 1961); and, for an overly strong statement of the case for will as opposed to weapons, Richard Ned Lebow, "Misconceptions in American Strategic Assessment," *Political Science Quarterly* 97, no. 2(Summer 1982): 187-206.

9. I have criticized this approach in "War-Fighting for Deterrence," *Journal of Strategic Studies* 7, no. 1(March 1984): 5-28. A nearly diametrically opposed view of the proper way to approach the roles of nuclear weapons is advanced with great sophistication in Robert Jervis, *The Illogic of American Nuclear Strategy* (Ithaca, N.Y.: Cornell University Press, 1984).

10. See Anthony Buzzard, "Massive Retaliation and Graduated Deterrence," *World Politics* 8, no. 2(January 1956): 228-37; and Anthony Buzzard et al., *On Limiting Atomic War* (London: Royal Institute of International Affairs, 1956).

11. See Thomas C. Schelling, *Controlled Response and Strategic Warfare,* Adelphi Papers No. 19 (London: ISS, June 1965).

12. See Lynn Etheridge Davis, *Limited Nuclear Options: Deterrence and the New American Doctrine,* Adelphi Papers No. 121 (London: IISS, Winter 1975-1976); and Benjamin S. Lambeth, *Selective Nuclear Options in American and Soviet Strategic Policy,* R-2034-DDRE (Santa Monica, Calif.: RAND Corporation, December 1976).

13. The "more" include such ideas as controlled city exchange schemes. See Klaus Knorr and Thornton Read, eds., *Limited Strategic War: Essays on Nuclear*

Strategy (New York: Praeger, 1962); and Thomas C. Schelling, *Arms and Influence* (New Haven, Conn.: Yale University Press, 1960), chap. 5.

14.   Very much to the point is Benjamin S. Lambeth, "On Thresholds in Soviet Military Thought," *Washington Quarterly* 7, no. 2(Spring 1984): 69-76.

15.   The intelligence communities of East and West constantly monitor the alert status of one another's forces. So numerous are the indicators of enhanced military preparation for combat that it should be impossible for either party to achieve surprise. However, many enhanced readiness signals may be covered by exercise activity. See John Gooch and Amos Perlmutter, eds., *Military Deception and Strategic Surprise* (London: Frank Cass, 1982). The pre-1914 axiom that mobilization means war is not true today, any more than it was a universal, invariable truth then. For some useful historical perspective, see Paul Kennedy, ed., *The War Plans of the Great Powers, 1880-1914* (London: Allen and Unwin, 1979). Some powers could mobilize to bluff.

16.   See Henry S. Rowen, "Formulating Strategic Doctrine," in Commission on the Organization of the Government for the Conduct of Foreign Policy, Vol. 4, Appendix K, *Adequacy of Current Organization: Defense and Arms Control* (Washington, D.C.: USGPO, June 1975), pp. 219-34. The trend since the early 1970s has been toward a closer match between declaratory policy and operational policy. See Leon Sloss and Marc Dean Millot, "U.S. Nuclear Strategy in Evolution", *Strategic Review* 12, no. 1(Winter 1984): 26.

17.   See my discussion of PD-59 in "Presidential Directive 59: Flawed but Useful," *Parameters* 11, no. 1(March 1981): 29-37. For a contrasting view, see Jervis, *Illogic of American Nuclear Strategy*, chap. 3-4.

18.   See Jeffrey Richelson, "PD-59, NSDD-13 and the Reagan Strategic Modernization Program," *Journal of Strategic Studies* 6, no. 2(June 1983): 125-46.

19.   See Scowcroft *Report*, p. 6.

20.   This judgment may need modification, depending on the ultimate political fate of the MX/Peacekeeper ICBM program. The Scowcroft Commission stated bluntly that the MX program "demonstrates the United States' willingness to do whatever is necessary to offset Soviet counterforce advantages." President's Commission on Strategic Forces, *Final Report* (Letter Report to the President), March 21, 1984, p. 9. The strategic significance of the very prompt hard target strike-back potential of the Peacekeeper is well argued in Blair Stewart, "Peacekeeper," *Defense Systems Reveiw and Military Communications*, June 1984, pp. 46-52.

21.   SIOP targeteers on the JSTPS in Omaha can cover most of the target set, but after 1976-77, they were unable to cover the target set with appropriate weapons. The yield, accuracy, and reliability of U.S. strategic weapons are well known within an analytically acceptable range of doubt, and good guesses as to the psi resistance of Soviet hard and superhard targets are not difficult to make (which is not to deny that there is a range of uncertainty). There appears to have been a roughly threefold increase in the psi resistance level of Soviet silos over the past decade.

22.   See Desmond Ball: *Déja Vu: The Return to Counterforce in the Nixon Administration* (Santa Monica: California Seminar on Arms Control and Foreign

Policy, December 1974); and *Targeting for Strategic Deterrence*, Adelphi Papers, No. 185 (London: IISS, Summer 1983).

23.   The overwhelming problem in those years was that the United States was devoting more and more weapons in expectation of diminishing results—as Soviet strategic forces were hardened in silos or dispersed to sea in the Yankee-class SSBNs.

24.   See Richard Halloran, "Pentagon Draws Up First Strategy for Fighting a Long Nuclear War," *New York Times*, May 30, 1982, pp. 1, 12. Robert Scheer reports that "Reagan's NSDD 13 [of November 1981] is the first declaratory state-ment of a U.S. Administration to proclaim that U.S. strategic forces must be able to win a protracted nuclear war. This goes considerably beyond earlier tendencies toward nuclear-war-fighting strategies." *With Enough Shovels: Reagan, Bush and Nuclear War*, 2d ed. (New York: Vintage, 1983), p. 10.

25.   From a military perspective, it is neater and more manageable to have virtually a single "precanned" war plan that one executes promptly when so ordered. It is profoundly complicating to have to plan to withhold many of one's more competent force elements, to be prepared to effect major retargeting design in response to political orders in the course of a war, and to prepare attacks in near real time that are very heavily constrained by imposed, and probably shifting, political considerations. I have discussed this subject in *Nuclear Strategy and Strate-gic Planning*, Philadelphia Policy Papers (Philadelphia: Foreign Policy Research Institute, 1984), chap. 2. On the process of war planning, see Richard Lee Walker, *Strategic Target Planning: Bridging the Gap Between Theory and Practice*, National Security Affairs Monograph Series 83-9 (Washington, D.C.: National Defense Uni-versity Press, 1983).

26.   Richard Nixon, *U.S. Foreign Policy for the 1970s: A New Strategy for Peace* (Washington, D.C.: USGPO, February 1970), p. 122.

27.   See Peter Pringle and William Arkin, *SIOP* (London: Sphere, 1983), chap. 8.

28.   Robert McNamara, "Defense Arrangements of the North Atlantic Com-munity," *Department of State Bulletin* 47(July 9, 1962): 67-68.

29.   See Rowen, "Formulating Strategic Doctrine," particularly pp. 229–34. Also see Henry S. Rowen, "The Evolution of Strategic Nuclear Doctrine," in Laurence Martin, ed., *Strategic Thought in the Nuclear Age* (Baltimore: Johns Hop-kins University Press, 1979), pp. 131–56.

30.   A powerful critique is Albert Wohlstetter, "Bishops, Statesmen, and Other Strategists on the Bombing of Innocents," *Commentary* 75, no. 6(June 1983): 15-35.

31.   For example, see Michael Brower, "Controlled Thermonuclear War," *New Republic*, July 30, 1962, pp. 9-15; and Schelling, *Controlled Response and Strate-gic Warfare*.

32.   See Fred Kaplan, *The Wizards of Armageddon* (New York: Simon and Schuster, 1983), chap. 18, 22.

33.   Ball, *Targeting for Strategic Deterrence*, p. 15.

34. Rowen, "Formulating Strategic Doctrine," p. 227.

35. For an insiders', participants' explanation of the development of the criteria for assured destruction sufficiency, see Alain Enthoven and K. Wayne Smith, *How Much Is Enough? Shaping the Defense Program, 1961–1969* (New York: Harper & Row, 1971), chaps. 5–6.

36. See Arnold A Rogow, *James Forrestal: A Study of Personality, Politics, and Policy* (New York: Macmillan, 1963).

37. For a devastating critique, see James M. Roherty, *Decisions of Robert S. McNamara: A Study of the Role of the Secretary of Defense* (Coral Gables, Fla.: University of Miami Press, 1970), particularly chap. 3. Also useful is Gregory Palmer, *The McNamara Strategy and the Vietnam War: Program Budgeting in the Pentagon, 1960–1968* (Westport, Conn.: Greenwood Press, 1978).

38. See Harry G. Summers, Jr., *On Strategy: A Critical Analysis of the Vietnam War* (Novato, Calif.: Presidio Press, 1982), particularly pp. 182, 186.

39. On reflection, it is not obvious that Mr. McNamara had any conception of strategy. More to the point, perhaps, it is not obvious that many of Mr. McNamara's Rand-trained senior advisors had any conception of strategy. See Bernard Brodie, "The McNamara Phenomenon," *World Politics* 17, no. 4(July 1965): 672-86; and Bernard Brodie, *War and Politics* (New York: Macmillan, 1973), pp. 473-79. On strategy and management, see the contributions by Robert Komer and Richard Betts in Asa A. Clark IV, et al., eds., *The Defense Reform Debate: Issues and Analysis* (Balitmore: Johns Hopkins University Press, 1984), chaps. 1 and 5, respectively.

40. See Aaron Wildavsky, "Rescuing Policy Analysis from PPBS," in U.S. Congress, Senate, Committee on Government Operations, Subcommittee on National Security and International Operations, *Planning—Programming—Budgeting*, 91st Cong., 2d sess. (Washington, D.C.: USGPO, 1970), pp. 639-58; and Eliot Cohen, "Guessing Game: A Reappraisal of Systems Analysis," in Samuel P. Huntington, ed., *The Strategic Imperative: New Policies for American Security* (Cambridge, Mass.: Ballinger, 1982), pp. 163-91.

41. To be fair, however, the greater failure was that of the U.S. armed services, which neglected to approach Vietnam as though it were a real war. See Summers, *On Strategy*, p. 143.

42. This point is strongly supported by the argument in Mackubin Thomas Owens, "The Utility of Force," *Backgrounder* (The Heritage Foundation), No. 370 (August 1, 1984).

43. Robert McNamara's statements in the 1960s on the quality of American resolve concerning the possible use of nuclear weapons are difficult to reconcile with his partially retrospective views, expressed in his article, "The Military Role of Nuclear Weapons: Perspectives and Misperceptions," *Foreign Affairs* 62, no. 1(Fall 1983): 59-80.

44. This point was advanced forcefully—indeed, too forcefully—in Henry A. Kissinger, "The Future of NATO," *Washington Quarterly* 2, no. 4(Autumn 1979): 3-17.

45. This alludes to the famous question posed (and answered) by Herman Kahn, "Will the Survivors Envy the Dead?," in Kahn, *On Thermonuclear War* (Princeton, N.J.: Princeton University Press, 1960), pp. 60-95.

46.   See Colin S. Gray, *The Defense Policy of the Eisenhower Administrations, 1953-1961*, Unpublished doctoral dissertation (Oxford: Rhodes House Library, Oxford University, 1970), particularly chaps. 5–7; and David Alan Rosenberg, "The Origins of Overkill: Nuclear Weapons and American Strategy, 1945–1960," *International Security* 7, no. 4(Spring 1983): 3-71.

47.   I have analyzed the so-called massive retaliation doctrine in detail in *Strategic Studies and Public Policy*, chap. 5. Also see Paul Peeters, *Massive Retaliation: The Policy and its Critics* (Chicago: Regnery, 1959).

48.   Notwithstanding the popular belief in 1956 that the age of mutual deterrence had dawned, the military facts of that year carried a politically permissive message for Western foreign policy that is almost unimaginable by the standards of the mid-1980s. The text here does *not* imply that the United States and NATO should have defended free Hungary (though that is my personal belief), only that this option was a very real one, based on prudent military considerations.

49.   Decade after decade, the U.S. defense community has resolutely declined to think about the possible compellent merits of nuclear threats. Not only has it failed to consider the forward, or offensive, use of compellence, it has also failed to consider the compellent requirement that is built into the current architecture of NATO strategy. On compellence, see Schelling, *Arms and Influence*, particularly pp. 69–91. Strictly speaking, of course, Hungary in 1956 need not have been a case for nuclear compellence. Once the Soviet forces withdrew, the U.S. nuclear threat could have been posed to deter their further engagement.

50.   Bernard Brodie, "Implications for Military Policy," in Brodie, ed., *The Absolute Weapon: Atomic Power and World Order* (New York: Harcourt, Brace, 1946), p. 76.

51.   See Scowcroft *Report* p. 2; and the discussion in Jervis, *Illogic of American Nuclear Strategy*, chap. 2.

52.   See Joseph D. Douglass, Jr., and Amoretta H. Hoeber, *Soviet Strategy for Nuclear War* (Stanford, Calif.: Hoover Institution Press, 1979). Soviet combined arms doctrine emerged as the product of experience in Spain, the Far East, and Finland prior to the German invasion on June 22, 1941; also, in the early months of the Great Patriotic War, it was the product of necessity (the Soviet Union did not have the armored striking power that might have tempted it to copy seriously the German "model" of 1939–40 and of Fall Barbarossa). Both Russians and Germans learned in the encirclement battles waged by Army Group Center around Bialystok and, particularly, Smolensk, that combined arms was the superior military method. Blitzkreig could not work in Russia in 1941 because of the extent of Russian territory and the absence of mobility for the infantry approximating that of the armored fighting vehicles.

53.   See Dan L. Strode and Rebecca V. Strode, "Diplomacy and Defense in Soviet National Security Policy," *International Security* 8, no. 2(Fall 1983): 91-116. On approaches to divining real as opposed to pretended Soviet doctrine, see Douglas M. Hart, "The Hermeneutics of Soviet Military Doctrine," *Washington Quarterly* 7, no. 2(Spring 1984): 77-88.

54.   These ideas permeate the books in the Soviet Officer's Library series, published from 1965-75 (many of which have now been translated by the U.S. Air

Force); V. D. Sokolovskiy, *Soviet Military Strategy*, 3d ed. (Harriet F. Scott, ed.) (New York: Crane, Russak, 1975); and articles in the official journal of the Soviet General Staff, *Voyennaya Mysl*, in the 1960s and 1970s.

55.   This idea was developed in detail in Paul Nitze, "Deterring Our Deterrent," *Foreign Policy*, no. 25(Winter 1976/77): 195-210.

56.   This proposition underpinned much of Henry Kissinger's theorizing on the subject of limited nuclear war in *Nuclear Weapons and Foreign Policy* (New York: Harper Brothers, 1957).

57.   For the text of NSC-68, see "NSC-68: A Report to the National Security Council," *Naval War College Review* 27, no. 6(May/June 1975): 51-108. Also see Samuel F. Wells, Jr., "Sounding the Tocsin: NSC 68 and the Soviet Threat," *International Security* 4, no. 2(Fall 1979): 116-58; and John Lewis Gaddis, *Strategies of Containment: A Critical Appraisal of Postwar American National Security Policy* (New York: Oxford University Press, 1982), chap. 4.

58.   For example, see Albert Wohlstetter *et al.*, *Protecting U.S. Power to Strike Back in the 1950s and 1960s*, R-290 (Santa Monica, Calif.: RAND Corporation, April 1956).

59.   In the 1950s, Soviet LRA (1) did not exercise very far beyond its national territory (meaning that its pilots probably would have had severe problems finding the United States, let alone finding SAC bases) and (2) had only the most rudimentary notions of communications security (meaning that the USAF probably knew as much about LRA readiness and operations as Soviet military leaders did).

60.   See Bruce Smith, *The RAND Corporation: Case Study of a Non-Profit Advisory Corporation* (Cambridge, Mass.: Harvard University Press, 1966); and Kaplan, *Wizards of Armageddon*.

61.   I believe that strategic debate both has been and has to be catalyzed by official, public "events." The triggering event for the initial takeoff of civilian strategic analysis in the mid-1950s was John Foster Dulles's announcement of what came to be mistermed the "massive retaliation" doctrine on January 12, 1954.

62.   See Henry Kissinger, "Military Policy and Defense of the 'Gray Areas,' " *Foreign Affairs* 33, no. 3(April 1955): 416-28; Kaufmann, "Requirements of Deterrence;" and James King, "Nuclear Plenty and Limited War," *Foreign Affairs* 35, no. 2(January 1957): 238-56.

63.   A useful near-contemporary overview of the limited war debate of the mid to late 1950s is Morton H. Halperin, *Limited War in the Nuclear Age* (New York: Wiley, 1963).

64.   For the logic of Western thinking on escalation, see Herman Kahn, *On Escalation: Metaphors and Scenarios* (New York: Praeger, 1965).

65.   A useful discussion can be found in Daniel Frei, *Risks of Unintentional Nuclear War* (Totowa, N.J.: Allanheld, Osmun, 1983).

66.   See the wide-ranging discussion in Thomas C. Schelling, "Reciprocal Measures for Arms Stabilization," in Donald G. Brennan, ed., *Arms Control, Disarmament, and National Security* (New York: Braziller, 1961), pp. 167–86; and Paul Bracken, *The Command and Control of Nuclear Forces* (New Haven: Yale University Press, 1983).

67.   Thomas C. Schelling, *The Strategy of Conflict* (Cambridge, Mass.: Harvard University Press, 1960), chap. 8. Also see Schelling, *Arms and Influence*, chap. 3.

68.   Statement in U.S. Congress, Senate, Committee on Foreign Relations, *Nuclear War Strategy, Hearing*, 96th Cong., 2d sess. (Washington, D.C.: USGPO, September 16, 1980), pp 3-4.

69.   Caspar W. Weinberger, *Annual Report to the Congress, Fiscal Year 1985* (Washington, D.C.: USGPO, February 1, 1984), p. 29.

70.   Ibid.

71.   This and related questions have been explored rigorously in Stephen Maxwell, *Rationality in Deterrence*, Adelphi Papers No. 50 (London: IISS, August 1968). Also useful is Patrick M. Morgan, *Deterrence: A Conceptual Analysis* (Beverly Hills, Calif.: Sage, 1977), chap. 4.

72.   Credibility and rationality are not the same.

73.   Carl von Clausewitz, *On War* (Michael Howard and Peter Paret, eds.), (Princeton, N.J.: Princeton University Press, 1976; first pub. 1832), chap. 7.

74.   Ibid., p. 605.

75.   This might occur for reasons developed in detail in Desmond Ball, *Can Nuclear War Be Controlled?* Adelphi Papers No. 169 (London: IISS, Autumn 1981).

76.   However, see the arguments in Lambeth, "On Thresholds in Soviet Military Thought."

77.   One critic of so-called war-fighting doctrine has asserted that war fighters "have paid scant attention to organization, cognitive, and political impediments to war termination." He concludes by asserting: "Twenty years after Wohlstetter and Kahn proposed strategy for waging nuclear war, it is time to make war fighters think about terminating one." Leon V. Sigal, "Rethinking The Unthinkable," *Foreign Policy*, no. 34(Spring 1979): 51. Sigal was correct in stressing the importance of war termination but not correct in asserting that Kahn neglected the subject. See Herman Kahn, "Issues of Thermonuclear War Termination," 392(November 1970): 133-72. Nonetheless, the U.S. government could profit from a major renewal of interest in how nuclear war might be terminated ("on terms favorable to the forces of freedom"). Such interest should be encouraged by Clark C. Abt, *A Strategy for Terminating a Nuclear War* (Boulder, Colo.: Westview Press, 1985).

78.   Wolfgang K. H. Panofsky, "The Mutual Hostage Relationship Between America and Russia," *Foreign Affairs* 52, no. 1(October 1973): 109-18. Some scientists argue that the holocaust would be general to humankind and, indeed, to the ecosphere vital to human life, rather than mutual strictly to the direct participants; this is the "nuclear winter" claim. See Carl Sagan, "Nuclear War and Climatic Catastrophe," *Foreign Affairs* 62, no. 2(Winter 1983/84): 257-92; and Richard Turco *et al.*, "The Climatic Effects of Nuclear War," *Scientific American* 251, no. 2(August 1984): 33-43. A balanced judgment may be found in Freeman Dyson, *Weapons and Hope* (New York: Harper & Row, 1984):

> The science of climate-modelling has not yet progressed far enough to predict with certainty, in the absence of a nuclear war, whether next winter will be mild or severe; it is unreasonable to expect the same

science to give us reliable descriptions of the meteorology of a nuclear holocaust. The meteorological uncertainties of nuclear war will remain at least as great as the uncertainties of peacetime weather prediction. (p. 21)

79. For a very sympathetic study of this phenomenon, see Jerome H. Kahan, *Security in the Nuclear Age: Developing U.S. Strategic Arms Policy* (Washington, D.C.: Brookings Institution, 1975). Analysis in a very similar vein pervades both Jervis, *Illogic of American Nuclear Strategy,* and Freedman, *Evolution of Nuclear Strategy.* All three of these books, more and less explicitly, challenge the idea that there can be a nuclear *strategy* as strategy traditionally has been understood.

80. See Ball, *Targeting for Strategic Deterrence,* pp. 21-23.

81. Harold Brown, *Department of Defense Annual Report, Fiscal Year 1981* (Washington, D.C.: USGPO, January 29, 1980), p. 65. Also see Harold Brown, *Thinking About National Security: Defense and Foreign Policy in a Dangerous World* (Boulder, Colo.: Westview Press, 1983), chap. 5.

82. Brown, *Department of Defense Annual Report, Fiscal Year 1981,* p. 65.

83. See Harold Brown, Speech at the U.S. Naval War College, Newport, R.I., August 20, 1980; and U.S. Congress, Senate, Committee on Foreign Relations, *Nuclear War Strategy, Hearing.*

84. "President's Speech on Military Spending and New Defense," *New York Times,* March 24, 1983, p. 20.

85. I have argued this point in "War-Fighting for Deterrence," pp. 21-23.

86. See Robert Jervis: "Deterrence Theory Revisited," *World Politics* 31, no. 2(January 1979): 289-324; "Why Nuclear Superiority Doesn't Matter," *Political Science Quarterly* 94, no. 4(Winter 1979-80): 617-33; and *Illogic of American Nuclear Strategy.* Jervis defends a counter-city theory of deterrence, though not without ambivalence (see *Illogic . . . ,* p. 168). Other works of interest include Alexander George and Richard Smoke, *Deterrence in American Foreign Policy: Theory and Practice* (New York: Columbia University Press, 1974); Richard Rosecrance, *Strategic Deterrence Reconsidered,* Adelphi Papers No. 116 (London: IISS, Spring 1975); and Morgan, *Deterrence.* A useful survey of the evolution of American ideas on nuclear deterrence during the most fecund years is Michael W. Kanzelberger, *American Nuclear Strategy: A Selective Analytic Survey of Threat Concepts for Deterrence and Compellence,* R-1238-AF (Santa Monica, Calif.: RAND Corporation, September 1979).

87. John Erickson, "The Soviet View of Nuclear War," Transcript broadcast on BBC Radio 3, June 19, 1980, p. 5. Probably as perfect a recent example as one can find of the kind of American reasoning to which Erickson referred is Jervis, *Illogic of American Nuclear Strategy,* pp. 167-70.

88. Brown, *Department of Defense Annual Report, Fiscal Year 1981,* p. 65.

89. I am attracted to Herman Kahn's advice: "Usually the most convincing way to look willing is to be willing." *On Thermonuclear War* (Princeton, N.J.: Princeton University Press, 1960), p. 287.

90. See Leon Gouré, *War Survival in Soviet Strategy* (Coral Gables, Fla.: University of Miami, Center for Advanced International Studies, 1976). A Soviet

author tells us that "Soviet civil defense intensifies the peaceful actions taken by our state and strengthens international security as a whole." General-Major A. S. Milovidov and Colonel V. G. Kozlov, eds., *The Philosophical Heritage of V. I. Lenin and Problems of Contemporary War (A Soviet View)*, Soviet Military Thought Series of the U.S. Air Force, No. 5 (Washington, D.C.: USGPO, 1975; Moscow, 1972), p. 251.

91. In the words of Richard Pipes: "The essential quality of Russian politics derives from the identification of sovereignty and ownership." *Russia Under the Old Regime* (New York: Scribner's, 1974), p. 24. The CPSU reigns, rules, and *owns* the Soviet Union. For a complementary analysis, see Tibor Szamuely, *The Russian Tradition* (New York: McGraw-Hill, 1974), chap. 4.

92. See David A. Baldwin, "The Power of Positive Sanctions," *World Politics* 24, no. 1(October 1974): 19-38; and Jervis, "Deterrence Theory Revisited," pp. 294-96, 304-5.

93. This charge and those that follow immediately (comprising but a small sample of the focus of scholarly concern) are discussed in detail in my book *Strategic Studies: A Critical Assessment* (Westport, Conn.: Greenwood Press, 1982).

94. An intriguing empirical study is Paul Huth and Bruce Russett, "What Makes Deterrence Work? Cases from 1900 to 1980," *World Politics* 36, no. 4(July 1984): 496-526.

95. Jervis, "Deterrence Theory Revisited," pp. 296-99. Also see Ken Booth, *Strategy and Ethnocentrism* (London: Croom, Helm, 1979).

96. These remain unfashionable words. See Colin S. Gray: "Nuclear Strategy: The Case for a Theory of Victory," *International Security* 4, no. 1(Summer 1979): 54-87; and "War-Fighting for Deterrence," particularly pp. 5-9.

97. From the evidence available to me, it is not obvious that the U.S. government has thought through some of the more fundamental issues pertaining either to countercontrol or to countermilitary targeting, (silos, mobile strategic forces, projection forces). See Colin S. Gray, "Targeting Problems for Central War," *Naval War College Review* 33, no. 1(January-February, 1980): 3-21. Just as U.S. nuclear strategy in the mid to late 1960s would have foundered in operational reality on the rocks of Soviet hardening and mobility of missiles, so the war-fighting themes of NSDM-242, PD-59, and NSDD-13 face a similar major technical challenge in the 1980s and beyond.

98. Sensible comments on "escalation dominance" may be found in Kahn, *On Escalation*, pp. 23, 289–91. Particularly useful is Kahn's judgment that "mere military superiority will not necessarily assure 'escalation dominance.' Escalation dominance is a complex concept in which the military calculations are only one element. Other elements are the assurance, morale, commitment, resolve, internal discipline, and so on, of both the principals and the allies" (p. 23). However, as Kahn recognized, this does not mean that one can afford to be relaxed about military balance and imbalance.

99. For some historical case studies, see Richard Smoke, *War: Controlling Escalation* (Cambridge, Mass: Harvard University Press, 1977). Also useful is Ole R. Holsti, *Crisis, Escalation, War* (Montreal: McGill-Queen's University Press, 1972).

100.   It is worth noting that Kahn, in *On Escalation*, explicitly discusses "The Problem of the 'Fog of War' " (p. 211-13).

101.   See the discussion in Gray, *Strategic Studies and Public Policy*, chap. 4.

102.   This is true essentially because (1) the theory failed to take proper account of the inherent tension between "limited" and "war"—and the U.S. government neglected to notice that the restrictions it placed on military means by and large foreclosed on the possibility of achieving even limited political ends; (2) the U.S. armed forces conducted the war as best suited their short-term, peacetime bureaucratic interests (that is, "combat experience" rather than "war")—and it is not obvious that the United States could have behaved otherwise (given the domestic politics of the war); and (3) the authors of the theory seemed not to consider the fact that U.S. values and U.S. strategy have to be tolerably congruent—limited war theory, in major respects, was not and is not compatible with U.S. strategic culture. An excellent, judicious review of the limited war record, written by one of the founding fathers of U.S. limited war theory, is Robert E. Osgood, *Limited War Revisited* (Boulder, Colo.: Westview Press, 1979). Also see Summers, *On Strategy*; and Stephen Peter Rosen, "Vietnam and the American Theory of Limited War," *International Security* 7, no. 2(Fall 1982): 83-113.

103.   See Richard A. Burt, "The Relevance of Arms Control in the 1980s," *Daedalus* 110, no. 1(Winter 1981): 159-77; Robin Ranger, *Arms and Politics, 1958-1978: Arms Control in a Changing Political Context* (Toronto: Macmillan of Canada, 1979); and for a merciless review of flawed theory and undistinguished practice, William R. Van Cleave, "The Arms Control Record: Successes and Failures," in Richard F. Staar, ed., *Arms Control: Myth and Reality* (Stanford, Calif.: Hoover Institution Press, 1984), pp. 1-23.

104.   See Booth, *Strategy and Ethnocentrism*; and Jack L. Snyder, *The Soviet Strategic Culture: Implications for Limited Nuclear Operations*, R-2154-AF (Santa Monica, Calif.: Rand Corporation, September 1977).

105.   Kahn also argued that people take earthquake survival planning very seriously only because there is an unambiguous, fairly recent record of major earthquake activity. If there had never been a truly major earthquake, serious planning probably would not take place, regardless of the scientific predictions of expert seismologists.

106.   Fred Iklé's important question, "Can Nuclear Deterrence Last Out the Century?" may thus be inadequately pessimistic in its implications. *Foreign Affairs* 51, no. 2(January 1973): 267-85. Also see Iklé's more recent commentary, "Nuclear Strategy: Can There Be A Happy Ending? *Foreign Affairs* 63, no. 4(Spring 1985): 810-26.

107.   Brown, Speech at the U.S. Naval War College, Newport R.I., August 20, 1980 (mimeo), p. 6.

108.   Among a large number of analyses that support this point of view, see Richard B. Foster, *The Soviet Concept of National Entity Survival*, SSC-TN-7167-1 (Arlington, Va.: Strategic Studies Center, SRI International, March 1978). A detailed study of the Soviet control structure is Harriet Fast Scott and William F. Scott, *The Soviet Control Structure: Capabilities for Wartime Survival* (New York: Crane, Russak [for the National Strategy Information Center], 1983).

109.   The most prominent examples of this recurring phenomenon were the freeing of the serfs in 1861 following the humiliation of the Crimean War (though this example was a defeat for major landed and other ultraconservative interests, not a defeat for the new Czar, Alexander II); the granting of the First Duma (Parliament, of a pale kind) in 1906 following the defeat by Japan; and the revolution in 1917.

110.   See Steve F. Kime, "How the Soviet Union is Ruled," *Air Force Magazine* 63, no. 3(March 1980): 54-59; and Scott and Scott, *Soviet Control Structure*.

111.   The efficacy of leadership targeting is assailed in Bracken, *The Command and Control of Nuclear Forces*, chap. 3. Further skeptical commentary is offered in Ball, *Targeting for Strategic Deterrence*, pp. 31-34. A positive view of such targeting is taken in Samuel P. Huntington, "The Renewal of Strategy," in Huntington, ed., *The Strategic Imperative*, p. 33.

112.   Analyses supportive of this view include Peter H. Vigor, *Soviet Blitzkrieg Theory* (New York: St. Martin's, 1983), chap. 1; Edward N. Luttwak, *The Grand Strategy of the Soviet Union* (London: Weidenfeld and Nicolson, 1983); Richard Pipes, "How to Cope with the Soviet Threat: A Long-Term Strategy for the West," *Commentary* 78, no. 2(August 1984): 13-30; and Colin S. Gray, *Protracted War: The Lessons of History* (Fairfax, Va.: National Institute for Public Policy, 1984).

113.   See Colin S. Gray, "Soviet Strategic Vulnerabilities," *Air Force Magazine* 62, no. 3(March 1979): 60-64.

114.   Huntington, "The Renewal of Strategy," in Huntington, ed., *The Strategic Imperative*, pp. 33-36.

115.   See chapter 5.

116.   This point has authority provided that it is not taken too far. I have sought to emphasize in the text that the United States could inflict a quantity of damage on the Soviet populace and economy such that control structure survival should be of little value—given that little would be left to be controlled. Also, it is just possible that the following comments by Carl Sagan might catch the attention of Soviet leaders:

> But the decision to launch a first strike that is tantamount to national suicide for the aggressor—*even if the attacked nation does not lift a finger to retaliate*—is a different circumstance altogether [from a first strike scenario wherein the initiator hopes the attacked nation will be deterred from retaliation]. If a first strike gains no more than a pyrrhic victory of ten days' duration before the prevailing winds carry the nuclear winter to the aggressor nation, the "attractiveness" of the first strike would seem to be diminished significantly.

Sagan, "Nuclear War and Climatic Catastrophe," pp. 276-77 (emphasis in the original).

117.   On the rise and maturing of the U.S. interest in counterrecovery targeting, see Kurt R. Guthe, *MARS: America's Strategic Retaliatory Doctrine and Its Implications for Force Posture*, Honors thesis, Harvard College, Department of Government, March 1978.

118.   As usual, Robert Jervis is one of the very few liberal critics of the

countervailing strategy who understands the structure and practical implications of the nuclear strategy debate. Jervis states, correctly, that I require strategic defense for my call for a "theory of victory" to be other than rhetorical. See Jervis, *Illogic of American Nuclear Strategy*, p. 84. Jervis is right in noticing that defense was "not a part of the countervailing strategy," but he is not right in saying that "few analysts think it is possible." To be fair, however, it is correct to say that most of the analysts who talk and write for the public do not think defense is possible. However, I find that the overwhelming majority of the people who actually are working out the physics and the engineering of strategic defense are honestly convinced that defense of a strategically significant kind will be technically feasible. Jervis is far too kind to the level of strategic sophistication in the nuclear policy debate when he observes: "The problem, it should be noted, is not with the lack of a theory of victory, but with victory's impracticality." Ibid., p. 182, n. 30. Most people, Jervis honorably excepted, do not appreciate the need of current U.S. policy for a theory of victory in nuclear war. To understand the policy salience of victory, one has to think strategically; one has to think about converting military power into the achievement of political goals.

119.   Brown, *Department of Defense Annual Report, Fiscal Year 1979* (Washington, D.C.: USGPO, February 2, 1978), p. 6.

120.   These doubts are detailed and pursued in chapter 6.

CHAPTER 5

Strategic Stability

In an important article published in 1978, John Steinbruner claimed:

> As the United States force posture has evolved over the past 15 years, the idea of stability has emerged as the central strategic objective, and the asserted conceptual consensus seems to be organized around the objective.[1]

Five years later, the Scowcroft Commission report supported Steinbruner's claims:

> Whether the Soviets prove willing or not, stability should be the primary objective both of the modernization of our strategic forces and of our arms control proposals.[2]

The following concerns underlie this chapter: that the theories of stability most widely held in the West may be gravely deficient and that the integrity of the concept of strategic stability itself may be questionable.

A discussion of stability and its possible requirements is really a discussion of deterrence theory, which, in turn, is really a debate about the operational merits of different postures and doctrines. There can be no useful, doctrine-neutral exploration of the idea of stability. The discussion that follows makes no pretense of neutrality; instead, it endeavors, first, to explain the roots, meaning, and deficiencies of popular theories of stability and, second, to suggest a theory that has much greater internal and external integrity.

It is very important to recognize that for all its popularity, there is only limited consensus on the meaning and policy implications of the idea of stability. Most commentators—and certainly the U.S. government and NATO—acknowledge the value of the twin concepts of *arms race stability* and *crisis stability*. Arms race stability is understood to be a condition wherein neither party to an arms competition is strongly motivated to press military developments or deployments in quest of major advantage, because such advantage is judged to be unattainable, however desirable it may be. Crisis stability is understood to be a quality of strategic relations wherein, during periods of acute crisis, the instruments of war should not be the proximate cause of war.[3] These concepts, at this level of generality, have been widely understood and approved in the West since at least 1960.[4] However, consensus breaks down over particular policy implications. From an operational perspective, how is arms race stability to be achieved and maintained and how is crisis stability to be enforced—in both cases vis-à-vis a distinctively Soviet adversary?

My quest is for a theory of stability that should work "well enough" given the full dimensions of Western strategic security problems in the context of the military consequences of the unique "cultural thought-ways"[5] of a particular major adversary. As a working hypothesis, I contend that the ideas of arms race and crisis stability—and the theory of deterrence to which they most usually make reference (often implicitly)—have misled Western policy makers into neglecting the operational dimensions of strategy. Indeed, many politicians, officials, and analysts seem to believe that nuclear strategy cannot really have operational dimensions that have political meaning. An adequate theory of deterrence must encompass, as its first priority, a determination of military requirements in war itself. Extant, still-dominant deterrence theory—as the leitmotiv for Western strategic preparation—is fully consistent with a strategic force posture that is incredible as a threat because it would not be intelligently usable in practice. It is essential to recognize, as argued throughout this book, that the Western ideas on stability and the relevant contemporary Soviet approach to the determination of the principles that should guide defense preparation and war planning have deep cultural roots; they are not accidents of recent history.

For much of this chapter, as the context makes clear, *stable deterrence theory* refers to the proposition that stability, in arms competition and in time of crisis, is maximized when both sides are unambiguously vulnerable at home and when each side is confident that a large number of its strategic offensive weapons are invulnerable prior to launch and during mission execution.[6] This condition of mutual assured vulnerability has been identified for many years as a fact of military-technological life in the nuclear age that ensures that both superpowers, no matter what their yearnings to the contrary, cannot help but possess a mutual assured destruction (pejoratively, MAD) capability. Even today, orthodox Western stability theory rests very heavily on the assumption that mutual societal vulnerability is desirable and, allegedly, inescapable. Many critics of President Reagan's Strategic Defense Initiative (SDI) contend that it would be profoundly destabilizing were the Soviet Union to believe that the United States was in the process of rendering its homeland substantially invulnerable to nuclear damage. Such invulnerability, so the argument proceeds, would yield the United States a freedom of offensive action incompatible with minimum Soviet security needs and would tempt a U.S. president to behave recklessly. Needless to say, perhaps, the strategically interesting prospect is a context wherein both superpowers deploy "leaky" defenses.[7]

As an initial point of doctrinal reference for this chapter, it is my view that the strategic balance would be stable were it to permit Western governments to enjoy not-implausible prospects both of defeating their enemy (on its own terms) and of ensuring Western political-social survival and recovery. This admittedly somewhat muscular definition, which closely parallels the known Soviet approach to defense planning, is already well-established U.S. policy with respect to the requirement for the defeat of the enemy,[8] is not incompatible with the more familiar connotations of arms race and crisis stability, and is at least visible as a possibility in the SDI. The bedrock of this definition is the proposition that forces that do not lend themselves to politically intelligent employment in war are unlikely to be sufficient to deter—at least in those very rare moments when an adversary may be motivated to seek a military solution to its problems (that is, in those situations where deterrence might apply).[9] The costs of major war today are anticipated to be so high, and so many of the weapon systems on both sides lack realistic field tests,[10] that the definition's identification of the need for a war-survival capability would hardly be likely to encourage Western governments down the path of military adventure.

Reference to politically intelligent employment of nuclear weapons must accommodate consideration of probable Soviet style in the conduct of war. Deficiencies in this realm continue to plague U.S. and NATO defense planning. I do not dismiss the practical difficulties that must beset Western war-survival strategies. Escalation control may not be unilaterally achievable through defensive prowess. The U.S. SDI may well trigger a process of bilateral superpower defensive deployment, which, in extremis, could mean that offensive nuclear employment would be politically, but not technically, credible. Stability conditions pertain to the entirety of the East-West political-military relationship. However, the essential logic holds: offensive nuclear action, no matter how cunningly and carefully directed, is not credible as an extended deterrent unless the United States can deny the Soviet Union the ability to strike back in ways incompatible with U.S. survival and recovery. Efforts to evade this logic, by means of renewed emphasis on "conventional deterrence" (thereby reducing the needed writ of extended deterrence[11]) or by faith in "threats that leave something to chance,"[12] are precisely what they appear to be—evasions. The thesis of this chapter is that the West requires a concept of stability that will provide the theoretical guidance for the determination of military requirements sufficient for the defense of its vital interests. The stability theory dominant in the 1960s and 1970s was addressed to a relationship between two supposedly like-minded and ultimately (after détente processes had done their work) like-intending adversary-partners. In the mid-1980s, the burden of an obsolescent theory of strategic stability remains heavy.

STRATEGIC STABILITY AND STRATEGIC CULTURE

Recognition of the idea of strategic culture outlined in chapter 2 is important for several reasons. First, it should help explain how and why the concept of strategic stability took such firm root in the soil of the U.S. defense and arms control community. Second, it should facilitate more accurate comprehension of Soviet deeds and words. Third, it should help U.S. policymakers identify programs and doctrines that, while broadly compatible with U.S. values, are adequately responsive to Soviet developments.

The United States

The concept of strategic stability took firm root as a U.S. strategic desideratum long before it was tested substantially in the field in the military competition and before there was a directly relevant, formal arms control process. U.S. theoreticians reasoned that the multitiered arms competition between East and West could be stabilized through cooperative management effected through tacit or formal bargaining. Moreover, the literature of the early and mid-1960s conveys the very clear message that the U.S. defense community thought that it knew both what strategic stability was and how the fortune of the concept could best be forwarded. In 1964, a gifted Israeli commentator on the U.S. arms debate wrote:

> Stability has become a fundamental concept in nuclear strategy, and a magic formula. Strategic situations are measured by the degree of their stability. . . . Once a situation of stability has been achieved, the initiation of war by surprise no longer assures any gain or advantage. A situation is stable, therefore, when there is no temptation to force the issue; it is a situation of mutual neutralization in which both the householder and the burglar know that even if one slays the other, the latter will manage to retaliate posthumously.[13]

The U.S. defense community, with very few exceptions, decided that a stable military balance should mean a safer world, at less cost in resources expended on defense than would be the case with an unstable military balance; that it should be compatible with the support of U.S. foreign policy interests (though it is not at all clear that careful analysis was performed on this subject); and that it should eventually find favor with the USSR because of both its technological inevitability and its nearly self-evident desirability. In a book that probably merits description as the fullest and most mature statement of 1960s-style stability theory (through mutual vulnerability to second-strike retaliatory forces), Jerome Kahan wrote:

> A mutual stability approach, in the broadest sense, rests on the premise that the United States is benefited if the Soviet Union maintains a strategic deterrent capability comparable in overall strength to our own; it is an acceptance of both the mutual assured destruction relationship and numerical parity.[14]

A little earlier, Kahan had written:

> If then, the U.S.S.R.'s strategic doctrine is largely understandable and somewhat comparable to ours, it is possible to establish a relatively effective U.S. policy of mutual stability.[15]

Thus, the United States seemed to know what it wanted and seemed to believe that what was good for the United States would come to be seen by the USSR as if not good, at least unavoidable for the USSR also. A stable military balance, from the U.S. perspective, would be a balance wherein both sides' military forces looked roughly comparable and neither side would believe that it could achieve a significant military advantage by striking first, because neither side would be able to protect its domestic assets against retaliation. This set of stability elements initially derived, in good part, from discouraging analyses of the future promise of damage-limiting strategies. Military-technological prediction—that future societal vulnerability will be a fact, not a matter of choice—was transformed into normative terms. Far from being a problem for the freedom of action that U.S. policymakers might require to extend deterrence, mutual vulnerability was seen, instead, as an opportunity to establish more stable Soviet-U.S. strategic relations. The Soviet Union might prefer to compete for useful advantage so long as that was believed to be attainable, but technology was and is believed to have a logic that the Soviets must and will respect. In a 1970 publication, Roman Kolkowicz expressed the following then-popular, and perhaps even plausible, view:

Soviet strategic doctrine and capabilities appear to have lagged behind those of the United States by about five years . . . modern defense technology determines to a large extent the kind of strategic doctrines and policies that will be adopted by the superpowers. Thus, technology seems to have a leveling effect which subsumes political, ideological and social differences in various political systems.[16]

The convergence of strategic ideas that was hoped for in the late 1960s and early 1970s—actually meaning a Soviet convergence on the U.S. concept of a stable military balance—did not occur. By the mid-1980s, most U.S. commentators on Soviet-U.S. strategic policy issues accepted as a fact the existence of a conceptual gap between Soviet and U.S. thinking on strategic issues, which appeared to be enduring because each side's thought was rooted in what has come to be termed strategic culture.[17] Since the signing of PD-59 in July 1980, many critics of U.S. strategy have noticed, and lamented, an apparent conceptual convergence of U.S. on Soviet strategic thinking.[18] At first glance, the basis for this growing belief is not difficult to discern. The United States has embraced at least part of what is generally termed a war-fighting theory of deterrence.[19] However, appearances to the contrary notwithstanding, the official U.S. approach to nuclear strategy and nuclear war is very truncated. The public explanation for clarification that succeeded President Reagan's announcement in March 1983 of an intent to explore the feasibility of strategic defense made it unmistakably plain that the United States is not, or at least is not yet, approaching the issues pertaining to homeland protection in Soviet terms. The U.S. government, as of this writing, has not made a commitment to develop a damage-limitation capability.

An important difference between 1985 and 1975 (or 1965) is that what was plainly recognized as a possibility then—that the Soviet Union would not wish to engage in genuinely reciprocal measures for arms stabilization—has now taken on the character of a fact. Indeed, a major question that should be posed is whether, or perhaps how, the United States can conduct serious arms control business with a Soviet Union that shows no evidence of endorsing a recognizable or attractive concept of strategic stability. Through the 1960s and at least part of the 1970s, such a troublesome question could be, though should not have been, ignored or deferred. In the late 1950s and early 1960s, when U.S. arms control theory was being forged, uncooperative Soviet ideas and practices could plausibly be interpreted as reflections of a relatively backward technology or of a policy or intellectual lag. By the early 1970s, the SALT process appeared to carry promise for the partially cooperative management of strategic relations. It was appreciated both that the Soviet Union still had to catch up in some important military respects and that program momentum reflecting pre-SALT I thinking and practices would take some time to be amended so as to be compatible with the new relationship.

Today, the U.S. defense community has to grapple with the implications of the hypothesis that Soviet military ideas and activities are deeply rooted in local soil and, hence, are very likely to endure; that the Soviet General Staff is extremely well acquainted with Western ideas on stability—Soviet military thinking is not crude and uneducated;[20] and that there are no important apparent strains between the policy preferences of the Soviet military and the Soviet political leadership.[21]

It would be difficult to exaggerate the importance of the widespread, if somewhat belated, Western recognition of the strategic-cultural distinctiveness of the USSR. The distinctiveness diminishes markedly, of course, as Robert Jervis has observed, if Soviet military thinking is compared with U.S. professional military thinking.[22] The U.S. military establishment prepares to fight and, if possible, to win wars, and from preference probably would support a military doctrine as traditional in its concerns as that espoused by the Soviet Union.[23] However similar the doctrinal preferences of Soviet and U.S. soldiers, it is only in the Soviet Union that those preferences are fully expressed in postural terms. As in Germany between the Franco-Prussian War and World War I, Soviet strategic planning appears to be wholly a professional military product.

Soviet thought on the military dimensions of statecraft—what is loosely called strategic theory in the West—is distinguished by its rarity.[24] Soviet writings tend to focus on efficient force preparation and implementation—generically, *operational* matters—or on grand-strategic, highly politicized topics. There are no direct Soviet equivalents to the Western theories of deterrence, limited war, and arms control, just as the key Western concepts spawned by and in those theories—stability, escalation control, bargaining, sufficiency/adequacy, and the rest—appear to play no identifiable role in guiding Soviet military planning. In the half-light of the growing appreciation of the alien character of Soviet strategic culture, U.S. policymakers have to reassess the relevance and prudence of the strategic ideas that have held intellectual and declaratory sway (in policy, if not war-planning) for the past twenty years.

Despite the accumulating evidence on Russian/Soviet strategic culture and the implications of that culture for future momentum in military programs, Western commentators continue to deny, implicitly, that stability is a condition describing a military-political *relationship*. The vision of stability that pervades much of U.S. theorizing about deterrence questions is essentially static and absolute. It tends to be bereft both of the idea of competition and of the essential referents of foreign policy interests and geopolitical relationships. On this narrow logic, the United States has a deterrence problem of finite physical dimensions. The complex military balance is stable if the Soviet urban-industrial target set is adequately covered and if the United States looks, and preferably is, resolute in its willingness to retaliate.

The question of what kind of damage a Soviet leadership would most likely judge unacceptable has been posed and even answered in recent years[25]—with conclusions that cast grave doubts on the merits of the society-destruction bedrock of the theory that identifies stability with mutual vulnerability—but the covering of the urban-industrial target set is still accorded importance and even pride of place by many U.S. scholars of deterrence theory.[26]

It may be that this society-punishment-oriented theory can provide a robust basis for a stable military balance, even in the context of an adversary relationship with an alien Soviet strategic culture. It is possible that the Soviet political-military establishment is seeking the unattainable in its evident pursuit of a war-waging/war-winning capability and that the United States would be ill-advised to compete very vigorously with military programs designed to improve war-waging performance. However, it is generally recognized that the Soviet military effort marches to the beat of a distinctly non-American drummer. As the Soviet military competitive position continues to improve, there should be no serious resistance to consideration of the possibility that the consequences of mainstream Western stability theory may lead to underrecognized dangers.

The ideas that comprise the concept of a stable military balance reflect, fairly faithfully, the world view, values, and pertinent education of those commentators, policymakers, and theorists who have articulated U.S. strategic culture.[27] The United States is a satisfied power, with a fundamentally defensive strategic mission as its international responsibility. From the publication of Bernard Brodie's *The Absolute Weapon* in 1946[28] to the present, U.S. strategic theorists have tended to argue, explicitly or implicitly, that the development of nuclear weapons has imposed a technological peace. The existence of very large and diverse strategic nuclear arsenals may be held to have solved the problem of premeditated war between nuclear-armed states, because the initiator will know that it cannot deny the enemy the capability of destroying its society in retaliation. Moreover, as the theory maintains, the ability to destroy a society in a second strike can deter not only attacks on the U.S. homeland, but also—with only a modest and tolerable loss of credibility—attacks on at least some of the vital overseas interests of the United States. The balance of terror is thus massively indelicate. As Soviet strategic capabilities improved relative to those of the United States over the decade from 1965 to 1975, so the United States sought to retain or restore the credibility of strategic deterrence through the advertisement of more flexible targeting designs (the so-called Schlesinger doctrine).[29] However, it is important to note that 1970s-style strategic flexibility was, at root, an endeavor to retain the credibility of the ultimate sanction of the very large countersociety strike. What beliefs, attitudes, and perspectives are reflected in this theory? It reflects a belief that nuclear war either would mean or prudently should be presumed to mean the end of history. The assumed certainty or strong likelihood of unrestrained escalation and mutual destruction leads easily to the conclusion that there can be no intelligent way of preparing for or waging nuclear war.[30]

Even if some stable-balance theorists are prepared to admit that nuclear war might have a wide range of outcomes, they tend to reject the possible policy implication—that the United States should work hard to design a policy and posture that would minimize the prospective damage in war. U.S. political culture, unlike Soviet political culture, does not take an instrumental view of the value of the lives, and the quality of life of its citizens. In its potential need for military support, U.S. foreign policy rests heavily on nuclear threats. However, no operational nuclear strategy, contemplated in consequentialist perspective vis-à-vis wartime action, is compatible with U.S. societal values. An important reason why U.S. strategic commentators have focused so heavily on deterrence, as opposed to military operational questions, is that they have realized that U.S. society is profoundly unwilling to confront, let alone debate coolly, the prospect of losing millions of people.

For the better part of two decades, the United States has been highly dependent on latent nuclear threat, but U.S. society—and even the U.S. defense community—has shown little inclination to think beyond prewar deterrence, let alone to invest large resources in a capability to prevail in, survive, and recover from a nuclear war. Instead, many leading strategic theorists have taken refuge in two axioms that greatly simplify life: that deterrence is relatively easy to accomplish and that possible differences in the outcome of a nuclear war are really uninteresting. Michael Howard was close to the mark when he wrote:

> But such credibility [of nuclear response] depends not simply on a perceived balance, or imbalance, of weapons systems, but on perceptions of the nature of the society whose leaders are threatening such retaliation. Peoples who are not prepared to make the effort necessary for operational defense are even less likely to support a decision to initiate a nuclear exchange from which they will themselves suffer almost inconceivable destruction, even if that decision is taken at the lowest possible level of nuclear escalation.[31]

Also, stable-balance theory reflects a conviction that an enduring East-West political modus vivendi is possible, if only because nuclear arsenals mean that neither superpower dares intrude into regions understood to be of vital interest to the other. The relationship between intense arms competition—and its associated periodic first-strike alarms—and political tension remains poorly understood. However, a plateau of stable deterrence resting on total societal vulnerability and sufficient weapon invulnerability should, so the argument goes, calm many of the anxieties that the arms competition can foster.

The more reasonable supporters of SALT I tended to avoid asserting that the Soviet political leadership and General Staff had been educated into accepting U.S.-style stable-deterrence thinking. Instead, they assumed that U.S. strategic vigilance would deny the USSR any militarily meaningful future advantage and the Soviet leaders would rein in their programs in anticipation of the futility of a bid for superiority. In addition, it was widely assumed that the five-year Interim Agreement on strategic offensive arms would be superseded by a permanent treaty regime that would greatly assist stability through the survivability it would facilitate for offensive forces and the predictability it would provide for defense planning.[32] Although stability could be enforced through expensive competitive effort, the case for attempting to encourage stability through negotiated joint management of the strategic balance was assumed to be attractive.

In short, stable-balance theory was believed to reflect inescapable technological truths.[33] Those truths were to be codified, at least in part, via the SALT process, and the SALT process was to be both the centerpiece and the beneficiary of a multichannel and increasingly entangling détente venture.

Stable-deterrence theory indicated, quantitatively, "how much is enough."[34] U.S. strategic culture is oriented toward attempts to solve problems. The U.S. defense and arms control community has extreme difficulty accommodating the idea that it is condemned to an endless competition with the USSR. Stable deterrence plus the parity principle appeared to reduce the stress and strain of unwelcome and unfamiliar strategic thought to a fairly simple problem of efficient management.

Stable deterrence, with its logical implication of a finite need for weapons, appeals to the Western belief that peacetime defense preparation has an almost wholly negative social impact. An insular strategic culture such as that of the United States tends generally to view the allocation of scarce resources for defense functions as inherently wasteful. Such a culture supports substantial armed forces in peacetime with the attitude that they constitute, at best, a regrettable necessity. Major defense program initiatives are often taken belatedly and clearly reluctantly, and they have to be justified in very specific ways in terms of identifiable or very plausible threats.

Even on its own terms, it is legitimate to question the validity of mainstream stable-deterrence theory. For example, as Henry Kissinger has argued forcefully, in policy practice it constitutes "a revolution in the strategic balance as we have known it"[35] (which was not noticed, or was simply disregarded, by its proponents). It has nothing to say on the problem of self-deterrence—which is not a trivial deficiency, because, for geopolitical reasons, it would likely be the United States that would be under the most pressure to lead an escalation process in the hope of restoring deterrence; and it is not responsive to the fact that deterrent calculations are not always relevant in the sequence of events that lead to war. However, leaving such reservations aside, the most troublesome aspect of mainstream stable mutual deterrence theory is that it does not speak to what is known of Soviet reality.

The Soviet Union

Soviet thinking on the preferred character of the complex East-West military balance is easily identified as a product of the lessons perceived in Russian and Soviet history, the nature and rationale of the Soviet state, and what may best be termed strategic logic. The Soviet Union cannot endorse a Western-style concept of military stability. The legitimacy of CPSU rule in the Soviet imperium resides in its claim to be the sole authoritative interpreter of *the* scientifically correct theory of historical change—and the peoples and the physical resources of that imperium, allied to "progressive forces" everywhere, are the instruments for effecting that process of historical change. Except as a tactical ploy, the USSR cannot endorse a concept of stability in the relations between socialist and nonsocialist states. Richard Pipes almost certainly was correct when he argued that Marxism-Leninism became the state ideology in Russia because the grosser features of that ideology, and the practices they legitimized, fitted so well a Russian national political character marked by cunning, brutality, and submissiveness.[36] Soviet military thinking on this argument today is influenced by, and expresses, a strategic culture that is, at root, Russian rather than Marxist-Leninist.[37] The important point is that obligatory Soviet ideology and Russian historical impulse both drive Soviet military thinking in the same direction. It is worth recalling that pre-1917 Marxist-Leninist theory said nothing of note on the subject of how a socialist state should conduct its foreign relations or design and implement its national security policy, because it was not anticipated that socialist states would need a foreign policy or would need a national security policy with reference to other states.

The commitment to permanent struggle, the need for eternal vigilance, the militarized character of society, the fundamental distrust of independent power centers (domestic and foreign)—all are enduring features of Russian/Soviet strategic culture. "The revolution in military affairs," as evidenced in Soviet military programs and as discussed in detail in the Penkovskiy "Special Collection," was dramatically different from the revolution in strategic thinking caused by nuclear weapons in the West.

The Western nonoperational focus on deterrence *as opposed to* defense is totally alien to Soviet strategic culture and is, indeed, viewed as dangerous, irresponsible, and scientifically incorrect. Since 1956, the Soviet Union has rejected Lenin's "inevitability of war" thesis, but has continued to believe that war is possible, that the difference in the range of outcomes could encompass the distance between victory and defeat, and that more military power cannot fail to pay political dividends.[38] The notion of having enough military power is alien to Soviet thought and appears to be contrary to the Soviet reading of its own and other states' history.[39] Rough equivalence and approximate parity are recognized by the Soviet Union as the necessary rhetorical basis for East-West security relations, but that necessary basis is not, and cannot be, accepted as operationally sufficient.

Aside from any ideological imperative, Soviet geopolitics, like Russian geopolitics in times past, is the story of nearly continuous struggle against actual or potential enemies that posed, or might pose, a threat to the multinational existence.[40] Russian and Soviet history teaches the lesson that "those who fall behind, get beaten."[41] The Soviet Union is engaged in improving its security condition through attaining an increasing measure of control over its external environment. It does not matter whether one seeks to explain this outward pressure in terms of ideology, strategic calculation, or the absence of imagination. More power is sought for the purpose of being more powerful, which cannot fail to be useful in a world where the USSR is surrounded by enemies.

Even if one attempts to discard cultural and geopolitical explanations, the detail of Soviet military activity drives one to recognition of the deeper imperatives that have molded Soviet strategic culture. There is an enormous inertia behind the Soviet military establishment. Much of that inertia can be explained in Western military-rational ways, but much of it reflects what is difficult to explain except with reference to a seemingly mindless momentum. That momentum flows from habitual practices of "safesiding" through minimal decision making, of eschewing the taking of potentially dangerous initiatives, and generally of focusing on doing that which one knows one can do—all in the context of a society that is nearly obsessed with the fear of disruptive change and that seeks to avoid risks.[42]

Innovation is possible, of course, in the Soviet Union, although it generally has to be ordered and even organized from above. The Soviet military buildup and modernization programs of the past twenty years in particular speak to forces very deep within the character of the Soviet system. Some alarmed Western observers see clear evidence that the Soviet Union is building more military power than it needs for defense (a totally alien formulation in Soviet perspective) and is rejecting the Western concept of a stable military balance (as if that concept could possibly strike a genuinely responsive chord in Soviet breasts). However, it is probably more accurate to argue that what we see as the cumulative product of a bureaucratic-industrial system that finds it very difficult to change a course once set (not that there is any plausible evidence suggesting Soviet desire to change military direction) is steadily providing the military means to express the Soviet vision of a desirable military relationship with potential enemies (that is, preponderance).

Unless a thousand years of Russian history and the strategic-cultural attitudes that flow from that history can be expunged from Soviet consciousness, there is no way that the USSR is likely to join with the United States in genuinely cooperative ventures in the management of a more stable military balance. The Soviet commitment to competition for relative advantage, real or illusory, is so fundamental and so rational in Soviet terms that stability, by Western definition, can only be enforced.

The implications of this strategic-cultural theme could be very grim for Western security. The strategic concepts and attitudes of both sides are valid on their own terms. However, the quality of a strategic concept pertains not to its intellectual elegance but rather to its utility as a policy guide or reference in a context of dynamic competition with opponents that may, and in this case clearly do, hold to very different ideas.

By dint of fairly steady effort, and moved by an ethic of prudence that has expansive implications for military requirements, the Soviet Union could come to believe that in East-West crises it will be the United States that will or should back down. The ideas and military program details associated with the dominant Western concept of stability amount to a military and civilian posture that in many respects is not serious about the actual conduct of war. To itemize: The United States has a very limited prompt hard-target counterforce and countercontrol capability. It lacks command, control, communications, and intelligence (C^3I) assets that could survive and endure. It has no homeland defense. It has no real plans for timely industrial mobilization or for postwar recovery. It has no vision of how all parts of the military posture should cooperate in a global war. It has made only the most feeble preparations for strategic-force reconstitution. And it has no convincing story to tell vis-à-vis war aims and the political character of a postwar international order.[43]

All of the foregoing criticisms are leveled in the context of a Soviet adversary that attempts to provide adequately in those areas.[44] The idea that some weapons and operating practices promote stability, and that other weapons and practices promote instability, is alien to Soviet strategic culture.[45] For many years, the Soviet Union has attended in great detail to what might be called, from a Western perspective, the unilateral crisis stability of its military posture. Missile silos have been greatly hardened; some missiles are truly mobile (SS-20s and, in the future, SS-X-24s and SS-X-25s); political and military command-and-control facilities have been proliferated and in some cases superhardened, and so on. Whether because of political-cultural insensitivity or cold military calculation, the Soviet Union seems unwilling, or unable, to take a systemic approach to what Western analysts identify as stability problems. Judging by the evidence of Soviet deeds, and employing Western terminology, it is stabilizing, from the Soviet perspective, for Soviet strategic and combined arms forces to threaten successful surprise attacks against U.S. strategic systems and NATO's posture in Europe.[46] Similarly, Soviet military thinkers see nothing unstable about a strategic context wherein Soviet society is afforded some useful measure of protection via civil defense and air defense.

There is a distinct possibility that a U.S. government in the future could believe the Soviet Union to be deterred by the assumed short fuse from provocative Soviet military action to nuclear holocaust—a belief that projects Western stable-deterrence reasoning into Soviet decision-making processes—while a Soviet government could believe that it had a very good prospect of winning a war and that the U.S. government should appreciate its weak political position and back down. In short, each side might falsely project the perspective of its strategic culture onto the other, with very dangerous consequences. The virtue of uncertainty that looms so large in Western theories of deterrence could mislead us. Strategic uncertainty should provide powerful fuel for prudence, but it might also spark hope for success.

STABILITY DISSECTED

A focus on stability criteria that are oriented toward mutual vulnerability encourages a defense community to think astrategically. A strategic nuclear posture that is truly innocent on classically defined crisis or arms race instability grounds is likely to be a military posture that is poorly suited to coercive diplomacy (peace-time and crisis-time intimidation and muscular dissuasion for the restoration of deterrence in war itself). U.S. strategy should translate military posture into plans for the efficient and effective application of force in support of political goals. Strategic stability is fully compatible with policy paralysis in the context of what may be dangerous instabilities at lower levels of violence.[47]

If one postulates stability at every level of potential conflict,[48] the problem disappears. However, unless the United States can enforce multilevel stability, stability at the strategic nuclear level should mean that the United States could not responsibly exert strategic nuclear pressure in compensation for an unfolding theater defeat.[49] Indeed, the integrity of NATO's defense doctrine of flexible response requires that there be a measure of instability at the central war level—translated as a potential for U.S. advantage. However, this does not deny that even a very stable strategic-nuclear balance—one in which there is no discernible first-strike advantage—will exert some magnetic attraction for policymakers toward caution in statecraft. A heavily nuclear-armed world will never be judged truly "safe" for the conduct of conventional war, no matter what Western stability-instability theory may predict.

The concept of stability is used in a wide variety of senses. Among them, three in particular merit individual analytic attention: arms race stability, crisis stability, and stability in perception.

Arms Race Stability

The concept of arms race stability holds that the basic engine of competition is the first-strike fear encouraged by defense programs that are designed to threaten at least part of the opponent's ability to wreak massive societal damage in a second strike.[50] By this reasoning, a stable condition of the arms competition is one in which neither side invests in programs that the other would view as a challenge to its assured destruction capability and, hence, would be motivated to offset. This logic was elaborated in detail in the late 1960s. It was argued that the arms race was driven not so much by the reality of first-strike dangers as by the fears that flowed from anticipation of such dangers.[51]

The idea of sympathetic parallelism in armament programs was the logical corollary of the arms race spiral theory. It was argued that just as the superpowers could stimulate each other to build more and more capable weapons, so they should be able, through deliberate restraint and perhaps explicit cooperative management, to remove much of the anxiety that drives essentially anticipatory-reactive armament programs.

The concept of arms race stability, in terms of defense intellectual history, tends to carry with it the stable-deterrence ideas that incorporate the desideratum of mutual assured destruction capabilities. However, such a linkage is not inevitable. Arms race stability could be held to obtain in a context where one side maintains a permanent, variably substantial lead and is in a political, financial, and industrial position to deter most arms race challenges. With some qualifications, this kind of arms race stability characterized Great Britain's naval relations with its actual and potential rivals from the 1840s until 1914. However, this stability was not achieved easily, cheaply, or without recurring alarm in British defense circles; panics and anticipated gaps were familiar and repeated features of British naval debates.[52] Ronald Reagan, campaigning for the presidency in 1980, implied that because of the disparity between Soviet and U.S. industrial power, a United States competing very vigorously in armaments could achieve an enduring condition of superiority, or—in his phrase—a "margin of safety."[53] This view had been unfashionable for more than fifteen years. Whether the case for restoring a healthy margin of safety was to be an example of nostalgia—as former Secretary of Defense Harold Brown claimed by strong implication[54]—or a dictate of prudence was answered fairly plainly in the early 1980s. In his campaign for reelection in 1984, President Reagan claimed neither that a margin of safety, in the sense of a useful military advantage, had been achieved nor that such a goal would be sought in the course of a second term.

Also, stability can obtain in a period when there is a rapid change in technological generations and considerable unpredictability concerning the building programs of rivals, yet when a tolerable balance of military power is maintained, albeit nearly exclusively through competition. Indeed, as Bernard Brodie observed in assessing the complex naval competition of the later decades of the nineteenth century, there are periods in strategic history in which stability, by any reasonable definition, is best maintained through unconstrained competition.[55] Arms control processes are as likely to constrain the wrong (that is, ultimately "stabilizing") as the right (that is, ultimately "destabilizing") defense technologies, given human frailty in strategic prediction. Moreover, arms control constraint "entails the danger of losing the flexibility with which to adapt to change."[56]

In its loosest though most easily defensible sense, arms race stability could be held to pertain simply to the pace and degree of rival postural change, regardless of the character of that change. An unusually rapid succession of deployed weapons generations on both sides would appear to many people to constitute an unstable situation. However, such rapid change may reflect a particularly fecund period of parallel defense research activity, rather than unusual political hostility, and may be fully compatible with some important definitions of a stable condition. Nonetheless, it is reasonable to allow that rapid postural change would be likely to breed fears abroad that militarily significant, if transitory, breakthroughs were a distinct possibility.

Probably the major problem attending the concept of arms race stability was that it rested on an easily challengeable theory of arms race dynamics.[57] The 1960s-vintage stability theory posited an abstract and very simple model of arms competition. The banner carriers for arms race stability in the late 1960s leaped from abstract proposition to defense policy claims and arms control proposals (for example, not to deploy ABM or MIRV because they would be destabilizing). The arms race and crisis instability claims deployed to challenge ABM and MIRV (and, later, the Mk-12A RV and MX) were, by and large, both interesting and internally consistent—but were they true? And how might they be validated or invalidated? This argument applies, of course, to all sides in the ongoing U.S. defense debate.

President Reagan's SDI has revived the late-1960s claims that defensive deployments would trigger offensive force reactions. As a simple proposition, these claims have merit. No responsible proponent of the SDI denies that the Soviet Union would have a major incentive both to discourage the SDI politically and to offset any military product that might be deployed someday. However, Soviet defense planners can be provided with powerful reasons not to pursue the path of offensive-force counter-measures very far. These reasons could include U.S. target sets that are too elusive or agile to reward extensive counterforce attention and a level of anticipated defensive prowess for a weaponized SDI such that massive offensive-force assault would be profoundly cost-ineffective.

It is possible that Soviet offensive-force deployments in the 1970s would have been greater than they actually were if the United States had proceeded with Safeguard or Site Defense BMD deployment in the absence of the ABM Treaty. However, in the presence of United States BMD deployment, opponents of that deployment would very likely be attributing the pace and much of the character of the Soviet ICBM and SLBM programs to alleged Soviet BMD-offset motivations. The kinds of Soviet offensive-force deployments that should lack for a strong strategic rationale in the absence of U.S. BMD, assuming a mutual assured destruction framework to Soviet thinking, have occurred anyway.

Notwithstanding the often ambiguous and incomplete evidence available, the U.S. defense and arms control community should recognize that Soviet arms programs are driven not by a determination to overcompensate for U.S. programs that could threaten Soviet maintenance of an adequate capability to destroy U.S. society, but rather by some combination of a doctrinal imperative to improve Soviet war-waging/war-winning ability and a bureaucratic defense-industrial momentum. This suggests that for many years, U.S. arms control surgeons may have diagnosed falsely and, hence, may have sought to operate inappropriately on the causes of the arms race disease.

Many people who debate arms race stability-instability charges are really concerned lest continuous competitive military-technological innovation might open temporary windows of opportunity for possible exploitation. Gaps may occur with respect to comparison of some elements in superpower postures, but they should not be of such a kind as to call into serious question the overall quality of deterrent effect purchased by the United States through its military investment. Deterrence stability is compatible with a formidable rate of change in competing postures.

Crisis Stability

The concept of crisis stability refers to a strategic condition wherein the very character and mobilization procedures of armed forces in confrontation should not comprise the proximate cause of war. Very often, crisis stability-instability is deemed to inhere in particular kinds of weapons. However, as Thomas Schelling has argued persuasively, to focus on weapons technology is to miss a good part of the potential problem:

To impute this influence on the likelihood of the outbreak of war to "weaponry" is to focus too narrowly on technology. It is weapons, organizations, plans, geography, communications, warning systems, intelligence, and even beliefs and doctrines about the conduct of war that together have this influence. The point is that this complex of military factors is not neutral in the process by which war may come about.[58]

Particulary valuable is the distinction Schelling draws between the static and dynamic dimensions of crisis stability:

> The static dimension reflects the expected outcome, at any given moment, if either side launches war. The dynamic dimension reflects what happens to that calculation if either side or both sides should *move* in the direction of war, by alert, mobilization, demonstration, and other actions that unfold over time.[59]

It is not difficult to slip into self-congratulation concerning the stability that appears to have obtained with respect to both the military standoff in Europe and the central nuclear relationship. However, the stability of those balances is not tested day by day, nor even by the kinds of crises registered over Berlin, Hungary, Cuba, and Czechoslovakia (and perhaps Poland someday). In none of those cases is it very plausible to argue that either the Soviet Union or NATO was strongly motivated to launch a theater or general war. The real road test for crisis stability would be that one occasion in forty or fifty years when nearly everything appeared to be at stake and one or both leadership groups could not see any nonmilitary solutions to their political problems.[60] A force posture and strategic doctrine that are good enough for one crisis may not be good enough for another. Those who are inclined to believe that U.S. and NATO forces are broadly resilient to crisis stress should ask themselves what it might take to dissuade a very desperate Soviet leadership.

Robert Jervis has argued, quite rightly, that rival schools of thought about the requirements of deterrence differ over how much deterring it is prudent to assume the Soviet Union might need:

> Thus there is a disagreement over "how much credibility is enough": two policy analysts therefore might agree on how likely the Russians thought it was that a limited war would escalate and disagree over whether they could be deterred.[61]

If taken to its logical extreme, the more pessimistic argument might lead to the conclusion that, at some point in the future, the Soviet Union might be so desperate as to be "beyond deterrence"—meaning, again logically, that considerations of crisis stability, however rigorous, would be irrelevant. The only question remaining would be: "How well would the West fare in the war?" A Soviet leadership might be beyond deterrence because it firmly believed that war was inevitable; because it could discern no nonmilitary solutions to political problems; because it stumbled into an expanding conflict without considering carefully the broader possibilities of whither today's actions could lead; or because it believed that a war could be won by the side that struck hard enough and fast enough. Different analysts may agree on the general characteristics of a crisis-stable military balance, and even on the character of Soviet strategic culture, yet they may disagree on whether particular U.S. military postures are sufficiently crisis-stable. The reason for disagreement lurks in the different range of political crises that each is willing to consider relevant to the sizing and character of the U.S. defense effort. Some interpretations of the military implications of the concept of crisis stability bear the potentially dangerous hallmark of a managerial, as opposed to a strategic, perspective on security issues. Crisis stability is fully compatible with a U.S. strategic-force posture that could take the initiative, compete for escalation dominance, and—if need be—fight the war through to a favorable military decision. However, crisis stability is often considered narrowly either in the context of a rigid application of mutual assured destruction reasoning or, beyond that in sophistication, in the addendum of flexible targeting design. Typically, any capability that threatens Soviet strategic forces, prelaunch or during mission execution, is held to be an affront to crisis stability. Crisis stability, properly understood, does not lend its conceptual authority to such judgments. For reason of extended deterrence duties, the United States cannot afford a quality of crisis stability that precludes first U.S. use of strategic nuclear weapons. Needless to say, perhaps, any strategic-force posture, or fraction thereof, could be used first. The point is that first use cannot be a credible threat and certainly should not be exercised in action, unless the United States could limit damage from Soviet second use.[62] As Nicholas Spykman has written:

> There is no possibility of action if one's strength is fully checked; there is a chance for a positive foreign policy only if there is a margin of force which can be freely used.[63]

However, Jerome Kahan has written:

> In order to establish a mutual stability policy, it is necessary to classify strategic systems as either stabilizing or destabilizing and to avoid the latter.[64]

Following classical mutual vulnerability theory, Kahan has claimed that weapons threatening to the countervalue mission performance of strategic offensive forces are destabilizing, "since they can directly negate an opponent's deterrent capability."[65] Examples of "stabilizing" weapons include inaccurate SLBMs, MRVs (or inaccurate MIRVs), long-range cruise missiles, manned bombers, and missile site (or bomber base) BMD. "Destabilizing" weapons include accurate MIRVs, strategic ASW systems, area BMD, area air defense, and ASATs.

This simple classification is only as useful as its doctrinal premises. For example, if the Soviet Union does not equate the quality of its deterrent with its ability to devastate urban-industrial America, then defense of the urban-industrial U.S. homeland would not threaten the Soviet deterrent. Moreover, one could argue, as noted earlier, that overall stability in the East-West military-political relationship requires that the United States be able to initiate strategic nuclear use in defense of forward-located allies. Such central war initiation, no matter how selective, cannot be credible in the event unless a U.S. President is confident that physical damage to the U.S. homeland could be severely limited. If Soviet leaders were to think in terms of stability, it could be argued that strategic defense of U.S. society would be destabilizing because it would, or might, yield that freedom of offensive action that would restore a quality of strategic utility to U.S. offensive forces. There can be no doubt that the threat to U.S. society is very important to the Soviet Union as a counterdeterrent. However, that threat can have little, if any, relevance to operational planning. The "defeat" of U.S. society, no matter how significant a prospect for deterrent purposes, would contribute nothing to Soviet success in war. The United States should discern no interest in cooperating with the Soviet Union for the purpose, functionally, of supporting a condition of stability that denies strategic utility to U.S. strategic forces.

Given the Soviet traditional military approach to nuclear war planning, strategies and tactics that, in the West, tend to be judged as destabilizing almost certainly have no such implications in Soviet thinking.[66] Soviet political and military planners would be very unlikely to view programs intended to provide active and passive defense of the U.S. homeland as signaling anything other than common sense.[67] To the extent that those programs threatened the success of Soviet plans for the military conduct of the war, they would be candidates for some Soviet response, just as they would be potent sources of deterrent effect. However, the mechanistic *yin-yang* envisaged in some simple-minded defense-offense, action-reaction theories of the arms race is the stuff of the U.S. seminar room, not of the real world of Soviet defense decision making.

Until very recently, the small strategic theory community has paid little attention to the place, let alone the details, of C^3I in its strategic visions.[68] Like peace and security, everyone, from every school of thought, is for good C^3I. Understandably, it would be difficult to generate a debate over the issue: "Does the United States require high-quality C^3I?" Noncontroversial subjects tend to escape attention. John Steinbruner has argued:

The most severe problems with the concept of stability result from the fact that its technical definition has not included a critical dimension of strategic capability: namely, the physical and organizational arrangements for exercising deliberate command of strategic forces.[69]

As Steinbruner proceeds to argue, when the concept of stability is expanded to accommodate C^3I desiderata, the preferred force structure (given classic stability themes) might alter markedly. For example:

The submarine-based strategic force which is clearly the most stable under the conventional definition is just as clearly the worst in terms of command stability.[70]

The Reagan administration has yet to invest in the kind of C^3I architecture that could survive and endure for months through a protracted conflict; from the onset, however, it has insisted that C^3I modernization be accorded top priority—certainly priority equal to new weapon systems. This policy determination was expressed forcefully in NSDD-12 in 1981.

Those theorists who believe that deterrence is a function of mutual societal vulnerability should be concerned lest command instability result either in unintended armed conflict or in essentially uncontrolled escalation in the course of a war. Those theorists who believe that deterrence flows from the promise of proficient military conduct should be concerned lest command instability deny the armed forces the ability to wage war in a militarily intelligent fashion.

Almost certainly, a good fraction of the strategic debate of the 1970s and early 1980s rested on unrealistic assumptions concerning the survivability of U.S. and NATO C^3I assets. There was much weaving of interesting strategic-targeting tapestries in the 1970s, but most of the targeting schemes that envisaged the protracted and progressive unfolding of a deliberate design of destruction, for carefully calculated military and political effect, failed to take adequate note of likely or probable U.S. and Soviet command instability phenomena.

There is ample evidence that classic stability theory, which encourages the belief that nuclear war would be the end of history, promoted a relaxed climate concerning the many details of actually managing a central war campaign. A dominant belief that nuclear forces would fail if they were ever used is hardly likely to lead officials to think very realistically about command stability problems in a nuclear war. Steinbruner's persuasive advocacy of the need to place command stability at the center of nuclear planning concerns failed to recognize that the relative neglect of command stability issues flowed in good part from the widespread acceptance of a classic stability theory (based on the assumption of the desirability of mutual societal vulnerability), of which he seemed generally to approve.

Furthermore, when he suggested that "the conceptualization of national strategy should be organized not around deterrence but rather around the much broader issues of managing modern strategic operations,"[71] he was ignoring the fact that those who tend to worry about stability, as classically defined, are not merely fundamentally uninterested in the improvement of the U.S. ability to manage a central nuclear war; they are profoundly suspicious of any such improvement. It is far from certain that the arms control community could be persuaded to purchase a really robust quality of command stability—encouraging politicians with poor judgment, or very limited knowledge, in the mistaken belief that nuclear war can be waged, controlled, and survived—notwithstanding Steinbruner's argument:

> *The preservation of a strong deterrent effect and the actual prevention of war are not the same thing.* Indeed the most serious threat of war under current circumstances probably lies in the possibility that organizationally and technically complex military operations might override coherent policy decisions and produce a war that was not intended.[72]

It is worth noting that although PD-59 (July 25, 1980) attracted a substantial and typically unfriendly literature, most commentators failed to notice that it was, above all, a document about C^3I. Critics were so excited, positively or negatively, about the allegedly increased stress the document placed on counterforce targeting that they ignored the fact that PD-59 called for a U.S. ability to command and employ strategic forces in war over a period of perhaps months, with the benefit of real-time, or nearly real-time, strategic-target intelligence-gathering assets. The counterforce theme, in historical terms, was a call for more of the same; the survivable C^3I theme was genuinely novel.

Stability in Perception

For many years, it has been recognized that military forces can cast a political shadow even when the assessment of probable relative military prowess is not conducted in what defense professionals would regard as a sophisticated manner. The 1970s saw a debate in the United States over the political value of military power,[73] particularly strategic-nuclear military power, wherein the contending schools of thought, not for the first or last time, appeared to be talking past each other. Harold Brown's annual reports tended to perpetuate the confused structure of this debate. In 1979, Dr. Brown wrote:

> Perceptions of the military balance, correct or not, affect political behavior both of our own nation and of others as well. Instability can result from swings in perceptions, which can be much greater than the

changes in the factual situation. The best way to avoid that instability is to avoid, to the maximum extent possible (it is a difficult task), expressing the balance in tendentious terms or, even worse, shading it whether this be in order to excite alarm or to calm fears.[74]

A year later, Dr. Brown explained:

> The need for essential equivalence reflects the fact that nuclear forces have a political impact influenced by static measures (such as numbers of warheads, throwweight, equivalent megatonnage) as well as by dynamic evaluations of relative military capability. It requires that our overall forces be at least on a par with those of the Soviet Union, and also that they be recognized to be essentially equivalent. We need forces of such a size and character that every nation perceives that the United States cannot be coerced or intimidated by Soviet forces.[75]

Without denying that appearances (reflected in the cruder static indices of relative capability) can matter, the major thrust of those who argued in the 1970s that perceptions of strategic nuclear (and theater-force) imbalance, real or imaginary, should have a political impact was to the effect that the disadvantageous trends in some of the more visible or static indices had real military significance.[76] Harold Brown suggested that perceptions of imbalance in megatonnage, throwweight, warhead numbers, and the like, can influence observers. That may be true, although it remained—notwithstanding many years of repeated assertion in the 1970s— almost entirely a matter of conjecture. Perceptions of U.S. and Soviet will and capability more likely flow far more from cultural stereotyping (what kind of a country, performing what kind of roles, is the United States?) and from assessment resting on observation of U.S. and Soviet deeds. Most of the foreign opinion leaders that were depicted year after year in U.S. Department of Defense annual reports as being susceptible to influence on the basis of learning of crude throwweight or megatonnage imbalances would not know a cold launch from a cold lunch. The quality and quantity of U.S. and Soviet actions, reflecting to some indeterminate degree U.S. and Soviet perceptions of their relative military standing, is the raw material influencing foreign perception of who is ahead or of which way the Soviet-U.S. political-military competition is tending.

For understandable reasons, some U.S. commentators appeared to believe that the debate over the foreign policy implications of alleged military imbalance was a debate over military "appearances" only. In the 1970s, it was fairly popular to argue that, ultimately, a military imbalance would have political significance only if it plausibly had military significance.[77] Since classic stability theory—with its focus on sufficiency in the region of the elbow of the equivalent megatonnage to casualties/ economic damage curve—was antagonistic or antipathetic to the idea that the United States could score political points through competing in militarily (by MAD definition) meaningless ranges of values on static indices, adherents to that theory naturally focused on the "appearances" dimension of the debate. Those who argued that comparison of Soviet and U.S. competitive performance on the static indices was important had some severe problems of evidence.

Although it is sensible to insist that the United States should not sign arms control agreements that prohibit U.S. pursuit of Soviet advantages (as under the launcher and heavy missile ceilings of SALT I and the heavy missile carryover to SALT II) while allowing the Soviet Union to pursue U.S. advantages (as in missile accuracy, payload fractionation, and reliability), I would not endorse the argument that militarily meaningless numerical advantages must have, or even are very likely to have, a destabilizing effect in the realm of perception. Those static indicators so heavily maligned by classical stability theory adherents happen to have major capability implications. Equivalent megatonnage, for example, can be related directly and graphically to anticipated population loss;[78] and missile throwweight is relevant to the issues of fractionation, warhead yield, and decoy deployment (vis-à-vis BMD). In short, the static indicators that many commentators in the mid-1970s assessed purely in a political context have major potential military operational meaning.

Where it matters most (for example, in Moscow, Washington, Beijing, and some European capitals), stability in perception should be held to refer to a military capability that could actually defeat Soviet military plans. The debate over the political meaning of a perceived military imbalance should not focus on the arguable merits of forces developed solely for the purpose of ensuring a perceptual symmetry, in the minds of the strategically illiterate, with those of the Soviet Union. The U.S. defense community has never really understood the issue of the political meaning of perceived military imbalance. To repeat, the issue is not one of appearances, except in very minor key. The hypothetical Third World leader or editorial writer who is deemed to be impressed, in his presumed ignorance, by crude ICBM launcher or ICBM throwweight counts almost certainly is a mythical person. Moreover, even if he is real, his unsophisticated perception of who is ahead or who is behind should not influence the course of U.S. defense policy. The perception that matters most is the Soviet perception, and that is colored by a war-fighting/war-winning perspective. To impress Soviet observers, the United States needs to invest in the kind of military muscle and societal protection that could yield war-waging advantage or enforced denial of war-waging success. As noted in the Scowcroft Commission report:

> We cannot afford the delusion that Soviet leaders—human though they are and cautious though we hope they will be—are going to be

deterred by exactly the same concerns that would dissuade us. Effective deterrence of the Soviet leaders requires them to be convinced in their own minds that there could be no case in which they could benefit by initiating war.[79]

STABILITY AND U.S. STRATEGY

John Newhouse, the chronicler of the NSC perspective on the SALT I negotiations, asserted that stability was "a truly divine goal."[80] Today, it is apparent that the theories of arms race and crisis stability that permeated the U.S. approach to SALT I were either wrong or misleading. At a general conceptual level, arms race and crisis stability are unexceptionable, of course. No one favors frenetic arms race activity per se or military postures that could themselves precipitate war; this much is well-nigh axiomatic. Where the mainstream of U.S. strategic theorizing erred was in tying the multifold concept of stability to a particular theory of deterrence that did not match the burgeoning evidence. That theory of deterrence held that each superpower had an assured destruction (countervalue) requirement vis-à-vis the other and that an enduring stable deterrence relationship could be constructed only on such a basis.

This theory of arms race stability was wrong because it could not explain the course of the strategic arms competition in the 1970s (under the aegis of SALT I or in the shadow of SALT II). Whatever mix of motives and institutional forces drove Soviet weapons procurement in the 1970s, a leitmotiv of sufficiency resting on the idea of assured destruction, let alone mutual assured destruction, clearly was not prominent among them. It is a matter of unambiguous historical record that since 1972, the Soviet Union has worked hard to undermine whatever degree of strategic stability, based on mutual societal vulnerability, there may have been at that time. In its ICBM, air defense, BMD (by and large in research and development), ASW, and civil defense programs, the Soviet Union has been providing persuasive evidence that its view of the arms competition is dramatically different from the view adhered to by succeeding U.S. administrations. It has sought, and continues to seek, "useful advantage" through whatever degree of preponderance the United States permits.[81]

The classical theory of crisis stability may or may not be correct. Fortunately, the 1970s and 1980s have not provided a field test. However, the Soviet perspective on strategic matters suggests that the explanatory power of the theory may be poor. Richard Burt expressed this skepticism:

> Central strategic war, according to Soviet literature, is not likely to stem from mechanistic instabilities within the super-power military

relationship, but rather from real and enduring differences between competing political systems and national interests.[82]

In principle, certainly, it is sensible to argue that it would be undesirable for the superpowers to deploy forces that lend themselves to first-strike destruction. However, it is no less sensible to argue that "the reciprocal fear of surprise attack"[83] as the principal proximate cause of war merits probable identification as a U.S. "mechanistic" fantasy. This is not to endorse a total indifference to Burt's "mechanistic instabilities," but rather to suggest that the traditional theory of crisis stability, on the basis of which particular weapons and doctrines are praised or vilified, needs considerable amendment. It overemphasizes the probable role of such instabilities in an acute East-West crisis while taking a wholly apolitical approach to an inherently political phenomenon. Moreover, the popular view of crisis stability is inimical to the extended deterrence requirement that the United States be able and appear willing to take the strategic initiative.

Many of the elements of a new theory of strategic stability have already been expressed in official prose and action over the past decade. However, the theoretical revolution remains incomplete. What is missing, above all, is both a recognition of the pervasiveness and longevity of competition and a positive approach to the functions of strategic nuclear forces. An adequate concept of stability has to be anchored in a prospectively effective theory of deterrence at the highest levels of violence. Crisis stability should be approached in terms of the calculations of probable war-waging prowess made by the several parties involved. Concern about mechanistic or technical crisis instability would be policy-appropriate only in a condition of such intense antipathy that overall central war campaign analyses would likely dominate decision processes. As a prediction, the Soviet Union would not "go to war" because a large fraction of its ICBM force was theoretically vulnerable either to U.S. first use or to U.S. BMD deployments,[84] any more than the United States would under reverse circumstances. Crisis stability would flow from a Soviet belief that any escalation of the military conflict would produce negative military and, hence, political returns. The U.S. Department of Defense acknowledges this logic, but it does not adequately recognize that the United States is most unlikely to be able to enforce stability if damage to the U.S. homeland cannot be limited.

Strategic stability should not be equated with strategic stalemate. The United States cannot afford to endorse a strategic concept that implies thoroughgoing mutual U.S.-Soviet strategic deterrence. If strategic stability is to retain its preeminence as a policy goal of the United States, it must be redefined for compatibility with the extended-deterrent duties that the geopolitics of the Western alliance place on the U.S. strategic-force posture. From the U.S.-NATO perspective, a stable strategic balance is one that would permit the United States to do the following:

- Initiate central strategic nuclear employment in expectation of advantage or disadvantage prevented (a requirement of NATO stategy)—or "compellence" for recovery of positions lost.
- Seize and hold a position of "escalation dominance."
- Deter Soviet escalation, or counterescalation, both by reason of the potent threat posed to the most vital assets of the Soviet state and by reason of the ability of the United States to limit damage to itself.[85]

Escalation dominance is a prerequisite for escalation control. Moreover, given authoritative Soviet views on "the terrible logic of war," escalation dominance prudently has to be a matter of capability, not of a political mechanism of intrawar deterrence.[86] A Soviet Union confronting a United States with military and civilian programs appropriately supportive of the foregoing objectives would have little incentive either to effect a military "breakout" from a regional crisis or to engage very persistently in a competition in risk taking at high levels of violence. Crisis stability would be enforced through the Soviet perception of the United States as a very tough wartime adversary indeed. It might be objected that a U.S. president should not be trusted with the capabilities suggested.[87] However, even if such a concern is valid (which is extremely dubious), it must be weighed against the greater danger of a president not being able to have recourse to such capabilities. The concept of strategic stability envisaged here is the only one that speaks persuasively to Soviet strategic culture, and it is intended, of necessity, only to minimize that self-deterrent element that is the most crippling deficiency in existing official U.S. strategic policy. Self-deterrence cannot be removed altogether, because the United States would know that even under the aegis of a stable military balance, as defined here, millions of U.S. casualties would likely result from central war. Nonetheless, the United States would have a guiding concept from which military requirements could be derived in support of militarily and politically intelligent strategic targeting plans. This concept relates robustness in crisis regimes to anticipation of success or defeat in war and to a judiciously competitive program of peacetime armament.

In the event that the late 1980s and the 1990s should see a structural shift in U.S. and Soviet strategic postures in favor of defensive capabilities, a new approach to stability would be required. Indeed, it is far more likely than not that a United States seeking to provide a quality of stability as outlined here would eventually trigger or encourage Soviet programs for nationwide ballistic missile defense and more effective air defense. A situation could evolve wherein offensive nuclear arms would cease to play even close to a dominant role in deterrence. Unless compensation is provided, such a development could produce great instability in theater security structures. The solution would have to lie in providing robust nonnuclear deterrence—in terms of both ready forces and mobilizable potential—for problems of regional security.[88]

It may well be that no matter how formidable U.S. war-fighting capabilities might seem in Soviet estimation, the Soviet Union would never negotiate an agreement that would truly foreclose on the prospect of defending the Soviet state (except, perhaps, as a matter of temporary tactical necessity, as a price to be paid for arresting the momentum in U.S. programs).

The identifiable Soviet approach to arms competition is steady acquisition of a more and more formidable war-fighting/war-survival capability. It is highly improbable that the Soviet Union could be dissuaded from pursuing this approach. The evidence of the 1970s and early 1980s suggests that although, in principle, a particular U.S. theory of stability might be encouraged through negotiated SALT/START restraints—whereby both sides agree to forgo those capabilities that the mutual vulnerability theory of stability holds to be undesirable—it is far more likely that stability, by any definition, has to be enforced solely through competition. It is virtually self-evident that Soviet strategic culture precludes the negotiation route to enhanced stability, except in the context of vigorous U.S. strategic effort. There is growing agreement within the Western defense community to the effect that stability cannot rest intelligently on the threat of massive societal destruction (except, possibly, as an ultimate threat). Such damage certainly would be unacceptable to the United States, but it may be insufficiently unacceptable to Soviet politicians. If the U.S. concept of a stable military balance in extremis makes more or less formal reference to the assured destruction threat, the United States has a deterrence theory that is fundamentally unsound. The "ultimate threat" posed by the United States would be incredible because it would never be in the U.S. interest actually to implement it. Execution of such a threat would be the negation of strategy; in and of itself it would solve no military or political problems, whereas it would almost guarantee a Soviet retaliation that would preclude U.S. recovery from war.

The strategic nuclear targeting review of the late 1970s, as summarized in PD-59 and subsequently endorsed with few amendments by the Reagan administration in NSDD-13, has prepared the way for serious discussion of the concept of stability suggested in this chapter. The U.S. government recognizes that Soviet military and political assets should be the primary focus for strategic offensive attention;[89] that "limited nuclear options" have little promise unless the United States has a good theory of escalation dominance (and the forces to match); and that Soviet economic "recovery" targets are difficult to identify and probably of relatively little interest. However, notwithstanding President Reagan's SDI, Washington does not yet recognize that crisis and intrawar stability cannot rest on intelligent strategic offensive planning alone.[90] The U.S. SIOP can have integrity only in the context of the ability to limit damage. Fortunately, there is good reason to believe that the technologies of air and missile defense, with substantial civil defense assistance, could restore a much more even relationship between offense and defense and could restore stability in the relationship between U.S. foreign policy commitments and U.S. military power.

Notes

1. John Steinbruner, "National Security and the Concept of Strategic Stability," *Journal of Conflict Resolution* 22, no. 3(September 1978): 413.

2. President's Commission on Strategic Forces, *Report* (Washington, D.C.: The White House, April 1983), p. 3.

3. The classic case was the interlocking of the mobilization moves of the Great Powers in July–August 1914. There was instability in the military relations of the powers in that Austrian mobilization against Serbia triggered Russian mobilization against Austria (and Germany), which triggered German mobilization against Russia and France—and mobilization for Germany meant war. As Jack Snyder has emphasized, a very important reason why there was a crisis slide to a general European war in 1914 was the nearly universal belief in the superiority of offensive over defensive modes of war. See Jack Snyder, *The Ideology of the Offensive: Military Decision Making and the Disasters of 1914* (Ithaca, N.Y.: Cornell University Press, 1984). Also see Jack Snyder, "Civil-Military Relations and the Cult of the Offensive, 1914 and 1984," *International Security* 9, no. 1(Summer 1984): 108–46; and Stephen Van Evera, "The Cult of the Offensive and the Origins of the First World War," *International Security* 9, no. 1(Summer 1984): 58–107.

4. For example, see Thomas C. Schelling, *The Strategy of Conflict* (Cambridge, Mass.: Harvard University Press, 1960). "It is not the 'balance'—the sheer equality or symmetry in the situation—that constitutes mutual deterrence; it is the *stability* of the balance. The balance is stable only when neither, in striking first, can destroy the other's ability to strike back" (p. 232).

5. Ken Booth, *Strategy and Ethnocentrism,* (London: Croom, Helm, 1979), p. 14.

6. "Hostages must remain unambiguously vulnerable and retaliatory forces must remain unambiguously invulnerable." Ian Smart, *Advanced Strategic Missiles: A Short Guide,* Adelphi Papers No. 63 (London: ISS, December 1969), p. 28.

7. The problems even with strategic defenses that "work" are analyzed in Charles L. Glaser, "Why Even Good Defenses May Be Bad," *International Security* 9, no. 2(Fall 1984): 92–123. Glaser's argument is a useful contribution to debate, but it should be noted that proponents of the SDI do not deny that there would be problems even with good defenses.

8.   This thought, central to PD-59, was expressed clearly in Harold Brown, *Department of Defense Annual Report, Fiscal Year 1981* (Washington, D.C.: USGPO, January 29, 1980), pp. 65, 67.

9.   See Colin S. Gray and Keith Payne, "Victory Is Possible," *Foreign Policy*, no. 39(Summer 1980): 14–27.

10.   See Stanley Sienkiewicz, "Observations on the Impact of Uncertainty in Strategic Analysis," *World Politics* 30, no. 1(October 1979): pp. 90–110.

11.   See John J. Mearsheimer, *Conventional Deterrence* (Ithaca, N.Y.: Cornell University Press, 1983).

12.   This is the core of the argument in Lawrence Freedman, *The Evolution of Nuclear Strategy* (London: Macmillan, 1981); and Robert Jervis, *The Illogic of American Nuclear Strategy* (Ithaca, N.Y.: Cornell University Press, 1984).

13.   Y. Harkabi, *Nuclear War and Nuclear Peace* (Jerusalem: Israeli Program for Scientific Translations, 1966), p. 48.

14.   Jerome H. Kahan, *Security in the Nuclear Age: Developing U.S. Strategic Arms Policy*, (Washington, D.C.: Brookings, 1975), p. 272.

15.   Ibid.

16.   Roman Kolkowicz et al., *The Soviet Union and Arms Control—A Superpower Dilemma* (Baltimore: Johns Hopkins University Press, 1970), pp. 35–37.

17.   See Fritz Ermarth, "Contrasts in American and Soviet Thought," *International Security* 3, no. 2(Fall 1978): 138–55.

18.   For example, see Donald W. Hanson, "Is Soviet Strategic Doctrine Superior?" *International Security* 7, no. 3(Winter 1982/1983): 61-83; and Leon Wieseltier, *Nuclear War, Nuclear Peace* (New York: Holt, Rinehart and Winston, 1983), chap. 2.

19.   See Colin S. Gray, "War-Fighting for Deterrence," *Journal of Strategic Studies* 7, no. 1(March 1984): 5–28.

20.   See Jonathan S. Lockwood, *The Soviet View of U.S. Strategic Doctrine: Implications for Decision Making* (New Brunswick, N.J.: Transaction, 1983); and Benjamin S. Lambeth, "On Thresholds in Soviet Military Thought," *Washington Quarterly* 7, no. 2(Spring 1984): 69–76.

21.   See William E. Odom, "Who Controls Whom In Moscow?" *Foreign Policy*, no. 19(Summer 1975): 109–23; and Dan L. Strode and Rebecca V. Strode, "Diplomacy and Defense in Soviet National Security Policy," *International Security* 8, no. 2(Fall 1983): 91–116.

22.   Robert Jervis, "Why Nuclear Superiority Doesn't Matter," *Political Science Quarterly* 94, no. 4(Winter 1978/80): 630.

23.   See Benjamin S. Lambeth, "The Political Potential of Soviet Equivalence," *International Security* 4, no. 2(Fall 1979): 23–39.

24.   An excellent presentation of this important point is Robert Legvold, "Strategic 'Doctrine' and SALT: Soviet and American Views," *Survival* 21, no. 1(January/February 1979): 8–13.

25.   See Leon Sloss and Marc Dean Millot, "U.S. Nuclear Strategy in Evolu-

tion," *Strategic Review* 22, no. 1(Winter 1984): 19–28; and Desmond Ball and Jeffrey T. Richelson, eds., *Strategic Nuclear Targeting*, forthcoming.

26.   See Jervis, *The Illogic of American Nuclear Strategy*.

27.   See Booth, *Strategy and Ethnocentrism*; and Ken Booth, "American Strategy: The Myths Revisited," in Ken Booth and Moorhead Wright, eds., *American Thinking About Peace and War* (Hassocks, Sussex [U.K.]: Harvester, 1978), pp. 1–35. Also useful is Matthew P. Gallagher and Karl F. Spielmann, *Soviet Decision-Making for Defense: A Critique of U.S. Perspectives on the Arms Race* (New York: Praeger, 1972).

28.   Bernard Brodie, ed., *The Absolute Weapon: Atomic Power and World Order* (New York: Harcourt, Brace, 1946).

29.   See Henry Rowen, "Formulating Strategic Doctrine," in Commission on the Organization of the Government for the Conduct of Foreign Policy, Vol. 4, Appendix K, *Adequacy of Current Organization: Defense and Arms Control* (Washington, D.C.: USGPO, June 1975), pp. 219–34.

30.   See Leon V. Sigal, "Rethinking The Unthinkable," *Foreign Policy*, no. 34(Spring 1979): 39; and Jervis, *The Illogic of American Nuclear Strategy*.

31.   Michael Howard, "The Forgotten Dimensions of Strategy," *Foreign Affairs* 57, no. 5(Summer 1979): 983. Howard has made it very plain in his subsequent writings that he, too, does not view nuclear weapons as politically useful weapons of war (as opposed to war prevention). See his essays, "On Fighting a Nuclear War," and "Reassurance and Deterrence," in Howard, *The Causes of Wars and Other Essays* (London: Unwin, 1983), pp. 133–50 and 218–376, respectively.

32.   Notwithstanding the retrospective wisdom that claimed, with strict accuracy, that "they [SALT I and SALT II] did not create the problem of Minuteman survivability and cannot be expected to cure it" (Secretary Brown in U.S. Congress, Senate, Committee on Foreign Relations, *The SALT II Treaty, Hearings*, Part 1, 96th Cong., 2d sess. [Washington, D.C.: USGPO, 1979], p. 159), the historical record shows, unambiguously, that SALT I was officially advertised in 1972 as imposing important constraints on Soviet "light" missile programs. The SS-19 problem, as it is known, entailed an uncertain mix of U.S. official incompetence, dishonesty, and cowardice. See David S. Sullivan, *Soviet SALT Deception* (Boston, Va.: Coalition for Peace Through Strength, 1979), p. 1–3; and William R. Harris, "Breaches of Arms Control Obligations and Their Implications," in Richard F. Staar, ed., *Arms Control: Myth Versus Reality* (Stanford, Calif.: Hoover Institution Press, 1984), p. 142.

33.   See Wolfgang K. H. Panofsky, "The Mutual Hostage Relationship Between America and Russia," *Foreign Affairs* 52, no. 1(October 1973): 109–18. These claims have been repeated ad nauseam in the mid-1980s in the context of public debate over the SDI.

34.   See Alain Enthoven and K. Wayne Smith, *How Much Is Enough? Shaping the Defense Program, 1961–1969* (New York: Harper & Row, 1971), chaps. 5, 6.

35.   Henry Kissinger, "The Future of NATO," *Washington Quarterly* 2, no. 4(Autumn 1979): 6.

36.   Richard Pipes, "A Reply," to Wladislaw G. Krasnow, "Anti-Soviet or

Anti-Russian?" *Encounter* 54, no. 4(April 1980): 67–72; Pipes's reply is on pp. 72–75. Also relevant is Richard Pipes, "How to Cope with the Soviet Threat: A Long-Term Strategy for the West," *Commentary* 78, no. 2(August 1984): 13–30.

37. See Richard Pipes, "Why the Soviet Union Thinks It Could Fight and Win a Nuclear War," *Commentary* 64, no. 1(July 1977): 21–34.

38. See Lambeth, "The Political Potential of Soviet Equivalence"; and Joseph D. Douglass, Jr., and Amoretta M. Hoeber, *Soviet Strategy for Nuclear War* (Stanford, Calif.: Hoover Institution Press, 1979). For a usefully skeptical view, see Karl F. Spielmann, *The Political Utility of Strategic Superiority: A Preliminary Investigation into the Soviet View*, IDA Paper P-1349 (Arlington, Va.: Institute for Defense Analyses, May 1979). Still more skeptical is Robert L. Arnett, "Soviet Attitudes Towards Nuclear War: Do They Really Think They Can Win?" *Journal of Strategic Studies* 2, no. 2(September 1979): 172–91. Also useful are Derek Leebaert, ed., *Soviet Military Thinking* (London: Allen and Unwin, 1981); and Robert Legvold, "Military Power in International Politics: Soviet Doctrine on its Centrality and Instrumentality," in Uwe Nerlich, ed., *Soviet Power and Western Negotiating Policies, Vol. I: The Soviet Asset: Military Power in the Competition Over Europe* (Cambridge, Mass.: Ballinger, 1983), chap. 3.

39. I find great merit in the following judgment offered by Benjamin Lambeth: "It would probably not be overly facetious to suggest that for Soviet military planners, the favored measure of strategic sufficiency is the notion that 'too much is not enough.' " *How to Think About Soviet Military Doctrine*, P-5939 (Santa Monica, Calif.: RAND Corporation, February 1978), p. 7.

40. See Richard Pipes, *Russia Under the Old Regime* (New York: Scribner's, 1974), chap. 1; and Colin S. Gray, *The Geopolitics of the Nuclear Era: Heartland, Rimlands, and the Technological Revolution* (New York: Crane, Russak [for the National Strategy Information Center], 1977), chap. 3.

41. Stalin speech in 1931, quoted in Arthur J. Alexander, *Decision-Making in Soviet Weapons Procurement*, Adelphi Papers Nos. 147–48 (London: IISS, Winter 1978–79), p. 2.

42. On Soviet weapons acquisition, see ibid.; David Holloway, *The Soviet Union and the Arms Race* (New Haven: Yale University Press, 1983); and Matthew A. Evangelista, "Why the Soviets Buy the Weapons They Do," *World Politics* 36, no. 4(July 1984): 597–618.

43. These allegations were presented and defended in detail in Colin S. Gray, "Nuclear Strategy: The Case for a Theory of Victory," *International Security* 4, no. 1(Summer 1979): 54–87; and in Gray and Payne, "Victory Is Possible." Some improvements have been registered since 1980, but the United States continues to eschew pursuit of a war-survival posture.

44. See Douglass and Hoeber, *Soviet Strategy for Nuclear War*.

45. See Johan J. Holst, "Strategic Arms Control and Stability: A Retrospective Look," in Johan J. Holst and William Schneider, Jr., eds., *Why ABM? Policy Issues in the Missile Defense Controversy* (New York: Pergamon Press, 1969), pp. 245-84.

46. Such capabilities discourage adventure on the part of the imperialists.

47. On the stability-instability paradox, see Jervis, *The Illogic of American Nuclear Stategy*, pp. 31–33, 147–57.

48. On multistable deterrence, se Herman Kahn, *On Thermonuclear War* (Princeton, N.J.: Princeton University Press, 1960), pp. 141–44.

49. See Paul Nitze, "Deterring Our Deterrent," *Foreign Policy*, no. 25(Winter 1975/77): 195–210.

50. See Jerome Wiesner, "The Cold War Is Dead, but the Arms Race Rumbles On," *Bulletin of the Atomic Scientists* 23, no. 6(June 1967): 6–9; and George W. Rathjens, "The Dynamics of the Arms Race," *Scientific American* 220, no. 4(April 1969): 15–25.

51. See Lawrence Freedman, *U.S. Intelligence and the Soviet Strategic Threat* (London: Macmillan, 1977); and John Prados, *The Soviet Estimate: U.S. Intelligence Analysis and Russian Military Strength* (New York: Dial, 1982).

52. Anxiety is a part of the price paid for preeminence. For an authoritative discussion of Britain's problems with naval supremacy, see Paul M. Kennedy, *The Rise and Fall of British Naval Mastery* (New York: Scribner's, 1976), particularly chaps. 6–8.

53. See "Excerpts from Reagan Interview on Policies He Would Follow," *New York Times*, October 2, 1980, p. B 13. Also see Ronald Reagan, "Strength: Restoring the Margin of Safety," Address to the American Legion National Convention, Boston, Mass., August 20, 1980.

54. Brown, *Department of Defense Annual Report, Fiscal Year 1981*, p. 68.

55. Bernard Brodie, *Sea Power in the Machine Age* (Princeton, N.J.: Princeton University Press, 1941), pp. 246–52. This is a modest expansion of Brodie's point, but it is faithful to his plain meaning.

56. Laurence Martin, *The Two-Edged Sword: Armed Force in the Modern World* (London: Weidenfeld and Nicolson, 1982), p. 72. By way of analogy, even if hospitals cannot cure a disease, one should insist that they not be permitted to spread it.

57. I have challenged that theory at some length in *The Soviet-American Arms Race* (Farnborough, Hampshire [U.K.]: Saxon House, 1976).

58. Thomas C. Schelling, *Arms and Influence*, (New Haven: Yale University Press, 1966), p. 234.

59. Ibid., p. 236.

60. One school of thought among modern historians believes that the leaders of Imperial Germany saw themselves in just such a situation in 1912–14. See Van Evera, "The Cult of the Offensive and the Origins of the First World War," particularly pp. 79–85. But also see Richard Ned Lebow, "Windows of Opportunity: Do States Jump Through Them?" *International Security* 9, no. 1(Summer 1984): 147–88.

61. Jervis, "Why Nuclear Superiority Doesn't Matter," p. 622.

62. *First use* of nuclear weapons is conceptually distinctive from a *first strike*. The operational consequences may be identical, in that anticipation of U.S. central nuclear use, let alone actual implementation, would be likely to trigger a

very large Soviet countermilitary assault. Conceptually, *first use* implies a relatively modest level of attack intended more to signal political will than to have a particular military effect in and of itself. *First strike* in popular usage, has come to imply strongly a thoroughgoing attempt to disarm the enemy forcibly.

63. Nicholas J. Spykman, *America's Strategy in World Politics: The United States and the Balance of Power* (Hamden, Conn.: Archon, 1970; first pub. 1942), p. 21.

64. Kahan, *Security in the Nuclear Age*, p. 272.

65. Ibid., p. 273.

66. For example, early strikes against command-and-control facilities.

67. Note the judgment on this point in Howard, "The Forgotten Dimensions of Strategy," pp. 982–83, 985–86.

68. Works by Desmond Ball and Paul Bracken have helped greatly to bring questions of command and control "out of the closet" for technically minded theorists and commentators. See Ball, *Can Nuclear War Be Controlled?* Adelphi Papers No. 169 (London: IISS, Autumn 1981); and Bracken, *The Command and Control of Nuclear Forces* (New Haven: Yale University Press, 1983). Both of these works, notwithstanding their many virtues, tend to obscure the central truth that there is nothing *inherently* uncontrollable about *nuclear* war. Survivable command and control can be purchased, albeit at a high dollar price. A superior treatment is Bruce G. Blair, *Strategic Command and Control: Redefining the Nuclear Threat* (Washington, D.C.: Brookings, 1985).

69. Steinbruner, "National Security and the Concept of Strategic Stability," p. 417.

70. Ibid., p. 422.

71. Ibid., p. 424.

72. Ibid. For a fuller appreciation of Steinbruner's concerns, see his article "Beyond Rational Deterrence: The Struggle for New Conceptions," *World Politics* 28, no. 2(January 1976): 223–45; and his book, *The Cybernetic Theory of Decision: New Dimensions of Political Analysis* (Princeton, N.J.: Princeton University Press, 1974).

73. See R. J. Vincent, *Military Power and Political Influence: The Soviet Union and Western Europe*, Adelphi Papers No. 119 (London: IISS, Autumn 1975). Also see Edward N. Luttwak: *The Missing Dimension of U.S. Defense Policy: Force, Perceptions and Power* (Alexandria, Va.: Essex Corporation, February 1976); "Perceptions of Military Force and U.S. Defence Policy," *Survival* 19, no. 1(January/February 1977): 2–8; and *Strategic Power: Military Capabilities and Political Utility*, Washington Papers, Vol. IV, No. 38 (Beverly Hills, Calif.: Sage, 1976).

74. Harold Brown, *Department of Defense Annual Report, Fiscal Year 1980* (Washington, D.C.: USGPO, January 25, 1979), p. 64.

75. Harold Brown, *Department of Defense Annual Report, Fiscal Year 1981*, p. 69.

76. This argument over the instability potential of perceptions of disparity in strategic capability has largely vanished from the public debate in recent years.

In the section entitled "Preventing Soviet Exploitation of Their Military Programs," the authors of the Scowcroft Commission report focused on the political dangers of unmatched military capabilities, rather than on the dangers in perception of advantage. See President's Commission on Strategic Forces, *Report*, pp. 5–7. Careful readers of Caspar Weinberger's *Annual Report to the Congress, Fiscal Year 1985* (Washington, D.C.: USGPO, February 1, 1984) will look in vain for analysis of the problems with perception of military disadvantage.

77. This view is found in Walter Slocombe, *The Political Implications of Strategic Parity*, Adelphi Papers No. 77 (London: IISS, May 1971); and Paul C. Warnke, "Apes On A Treadmill," *Foreign Policy*, no. 18(Spring 1975): 12–29.

78. See the testimony of Donald G. Brennan in U.S. Congress, Senate Committee on Foreign Relations, *The SALT II Treaty, Hearings*, Part 4, p. 365.

79. President's Commission on Strategic Forces, *Report*, p. 6.

80. John Newhouse, *Cold Dawn: The Story of SALT* (New York: Holt, Rinehart and Winston, 1973), p. 9.

81. See John Erickson, "The Soviet Military System: Doctrine, Technology and 'Style,' " in John Erickson and E. J. Feuchtwanger, eds., *Soviet Military Power and Performance* (Hamden, Conn.: Archon, 1979), pp. 28–29.

82. Richard Burt, "Arms Control and Soviet Strategic Forces: The Risks of Asking SALT to Do Too Much," *Washington Review* 1, no. 1(January 1978): 22.

83. This is the title of chapter 9 in Schelling, *The Strategy of Conflict*.

84. Notwithstanding the enormous significance the Soviet Union attaches to the surprise disruptive-disarming blow, their operational practices vis-à-vis their strategic forces have never approached the day-in, day-out instant readiness ethos of SAC and the U.S. SSBN force. See Graham T. Allison, Albert Carnesale, and Joseph S. Nye, Jr., eds., *Hawks, Doves, and Owls: An Agenda for Avoiding Nuclear War* (New York: Norton, 1985).

85. I explored this thesis in some detail in my article, "Targeting Problems for Central War," *Naval War College Review* 33, no. 1(January-February 1980): 3–21.

86. In an interview with *Krasnaya Zvezda* on May 9, 1984, Marshal Ogarkov offered some pertinent observations on the question of the character of nuclear war.

> The calculation of the strategists across the ocean, based on the possibility of waging a so-called "limited" nuclear war, now has no foundation whatever. It is utopian: Any so-called limited use of nuclear facilities will inevitably lead to the immediate use of the whole of the sides' nuclear arsenal. That is the terrible logic of war. Their arguments about the possibility of a so-called "limited" nuclear strike without retaliation against the enemy's main centers and control points are even more groundless. Such arguments are pure fantasy.

"Ogarkov on Implications of Military Technology," reprinted in *Survival* 26, no. 4(July/August 1984): 188.

87. In discussion of President Reagan's SDI, several senior officials from NATO-European countries have told me that they would not trust the United

States to behave wisely with a major military advantage. A defended United States (to some important degree), so the argument proceeds, might well choose to take bold political decisions on the use of force that would be paid for, in the first instance, by far more vulnerable allies.

88. For contrasting analyses, see Keith B. Payne and Colin S. Gray, "Nuclear Policy and the Defensive Transition," Foreign Affairs 62, no. 4(Spring 1984): 820-42; and Glaser, "Why Even Good Defenses May Be Bad."

89. See Harold Brown, Department of Defense Annual Report, Fiscal Year 1981, pp. 66, 67, 86; and President's Commission on Strategic Forces, Report, pp . 2-3, 6.

90. I remain skeptical of the merit in crisis stability theory. As a matter of elementary prudence, it is sensible to minimize the basis for perceptions of first-strike advantage. However, the proposition that war could be triggered by technically unstable military postures is generally accorded too uncritical an endorsement. See Stephen Peter Rosen, "Foreign Policy and Nuclear Weapons: The Case for Strategic Defenses," in Samuel P. Huntington, ed., The Strategic Imperative: New Policies for American Security (Cambridge, Mass.: Ballinger, 1982), p. 141-61. Crisis stability theorists have a way of finding in the historical record that which suits their purposes. For example, I believe that both Van Evera and Snyder, though saying many sensible things, go much too far in the importance they assign to "the cult of the offensive" in 1914. Also, they are less empathetic to German dilemmas than they probably should be. See Van Evera, "The Cult of the Offensive and the Origins of the First World War"; and Snyder, The Ideology of the Offensive.

CHAPTER **6**

Escalation Control
and Crisis Management

STRATEGIC IDEAS AND "THE MCNAMARA STABLE"

This chapter develops the thesis that many defense policy problems continue to evade successful, or convincing, assault because the U.S. defense community does not address strategic questions in strategic terms. Military officers and civilian analysts who should have been trained by the writings of Sun Tzu, Clausewitz, and Thucydides[1] instead were trained on the ideas promoted in Charles Hitch and Roland McKean's *The Economics of Defense in the Nuclear Age*[2] and Thomas Schelling's *The Strategy of Conflict*.[3] The economic wizardry of "Hitchcraft," as the new defense economics have been called, brings to mind the awe-struck comment of General Pierre Bosquet, who observed the charge of the Light Brigade at Balaclava: "*C'est magnifique, mais ce n'est pas la guerre.*" The largely chimerical wonders of the bag of analytical techniques collectively termed *systems analysis*[4] might have had a net beneficial effect if the United States were already plentifully endowed with an institutionalized tradition of strategic thinking.[5] As it was, systems analytic techniques constituted the *schwerpunkt* for the domination of the official defense community by a new breed of essentially "glorified accountants."[6] For reasons of budgetary self-defense, the armed forces followed suit.

These are harsh words, but consider the strength of the grounds for the indictment. Coinciding in time with "the occupation of the Pentagon"[7] by the largely RAND-schooled economists, appearing to be strategists:

169

- The United States lost a major war in Southeast Asia. (Policy is judged by the quality of its outcome, not by the elegance of design of its inputs—that is, "Did it work?" not "Was it well made?")

- The United States enunciated a strategic doctrine (of stable mutual deterrence deriving from assured-destruction-based ideas of crisis and arms race stability) that was devoid of *strategic* merit.[8] That is, it neglected to relate military power to the accomplishment of political objectives. Although Robert McNamara apparently did not intend his preferred doctrinal leitmotiv of assured destruction to pertain in detail to actual strategic-operational plans, the fact remains that the stable deterrence ideas of the late 1960s did have a major impact on the course and kind of weapons acquisition[9] and contributed in a lasting way to the cumulative strategic debility that began to afflict the United States seriously by the mid-1970s.

There is an apparent paradox: How could a defense establishment whose sophistication in management was the envy of the Western world (and perhaps also the Eastern world)[10] contrive to lose a major war and so mismanage its end of the strategic arms competition with the Soviet Union that by March 1982, President Reagan could say: "The truth of the matter is that on balance the Soviet Union does have a definite margin of superiority."[11] Could it be that sound management and sound strategy need have no necessary close relationship with one another?[12] This is not to argue that sound management is not, ipso facto, desirable; rather, it is to suggest that the U.S. defense community has often approached strategic questions as if they were only problems in efficient management. If Robert McNamara had attended to Carl von Clausewitz as well as to Charles J. Hitch, he might have learned:

> War plans cover every aspect of a war, and weave them all into a single operation that must have a single, ultimate objective in which all particular aims are reconciled. No one starts a war—or rather, no one in his senses ought to do so—without first being clear in his mind what he intends to achieve by that war and how he intends to conduct it. The former is its political purpose; the latter its operational objective. This is the governing principle which will set its course, prescribe the scale of means and effort which is required, and make its influence felt throughout down to the smallest operational detail.[13]

Clearly, how a war is to be conducted has to be congruent with the aims to be achieved. In Vietnam, the United States violated Clausewitz's principle with predictable consequences. Explicit defense analysis can promote efficiency in the acquisition, maintenance, and employment of military means—always provided that somebody is minding the strategy store (that is, determining policy ends and the connections between ends and means).

In the wake of the Cuban missile crisis of October 1962, Robert McNamara is reported as having offered the revealing opinion that "there is no longer any such thing as strategy, only crisis management."[14] Moreover, Alastair Buchan, the principal founder and first director of the Institute for Strategic Studies in London and scarcely less representative a standard-bearer for Western strategic culture than Robert McNamara, felt moved in 1966 to characterize crisis management as "the new diplomacy."[15] The two very closely related concepts that are the subject of this chapter—escalation (and its control) and crisis management—speak very directly to their roots in U.S. (and, more generally, Western) strategic culture. As with virtually every major concept analyzed in this book, they constitute good ideas that became less good when they were taken too far. My problem here is to identify and develop what is of value and should be retained, while no less rigorously specifying the specious and the dangerous and misleading. Lest there be any misunderstanding, I favor the control (as opposed to the absence of control) of escalation, just as I favor the management (as opposed, presumably, to the mismanagement or absence of management) of crises.

THE DISCOVERY OF THE OBVIOUS

Escalation and crisis management briefly achieved what amounted to fashionable status in the mid-1960s among strategic and diplomatic commentators.[16] Crisis management was "discovered" in the course of the intermittent Berlin crisis of 1958–61 and—most particularly—during the Cuban missile crisis of October 1962; and escalation was the "in" idea during 1964–66 as the United States flexed its military muscles in a very selective and deliberate way over Southeast Asia.[17] These are very much cases of pouring old wine into new bottles. Foreign offices have always known about crisis management, and many governments have practiced controlled escalation,[18] even if they did not so label their activities. However, the theory-conscious social-scientific community in the United States wrote as if gold had been discovered.

As a historical aside, it is not self-evident that the appearance of an overarching theory pertaining to a long-practiced reality necessarily improves the quality of policy. For example, notwithstanding its genuine gratitude to Alfred Thayer Mahan for his services as a publicist, it is a fact that the British Royal Navy had *practiced* the doctrine of "seapower," as expounded by Mahan, for more than two centuries prior to his detailed exposition.[19] In fact, his seapower thesis assisted Admiral von Tirpitz in selling a battle fleet theory that was quite inappropriate for Imperial Germany.[20] For a further example, U.S. limited war theorists of the mid-1950s erected a fragile theory overwhelmingly on the basis of one historical case, Korea, although practice of limited war has been a hardy perennial throughout recorded history.[21]

The argument in this chapter is leading toward an indictment of poor instant theory by ahistorical strategists looking virtually backwards to a single or very small population of events and seeking therefrom the elements of a general theory—not to an indictment of theory creation writ large. I believe that from a close study of direct historical evidence, from the folklore of statecraft, and from the viewpoint of political-military logic, it might be possible to derive useful theories of escalation control and crisis management. To date, the United States does not enjoy the services of such theories. Escalation control remains, as it began, almost solely a deductive theory resting almost exclusively on inexplicit U.S. cultural values. Also, because it burst forth as a fashionable concept/theory in 1964–66, its further evolution was stifled when its real-world referent in Vietnam lost favor with most defense intellectuals.[22]

By 1968–69 at the latest, one could argue that the idea of controlled escalation, and limited conventional war more generally, was missing in action somewhere in Southeast Asia. However, although public scholarly development of the escalation concept virtually stopped in 1967–68, the concept—reflecting, after all, long-standing practice in statecraft—did take firm root in NATO and U.S. general war planning. Unfortunately, official endorsement of the concept, as in NATO's "flexible response" document MC-14/3 of 1967 (a very important example), virtually coincided with a period of defensiveness and even complacency[23] on the part of strategic theorists, meaning that NATO (and the United States, in its ideas pertaining to the conduct of central war) was bequeathed an undeveloped infant of a concept, not a mature theory. Moreover, the controlled escalation concept embraced by NATO-allied officials reflected all too accurately the ethnocentric weaknesses of the strategic theories outlined in the West as of the mid-1960s. The "Golden Age" of U.S. strategic theorizing, for all its deductive merits, was as culturally insular as apple pie.

Crisis management, like escalation control had immediate appeal to a management-skill-oriented U.S. defense community. Here was "how to do it" advice—which is always popular. More often than not, when scholars brief officials on their academic findings, those "findings" amount to the conclusion that "the subject is more complicated than you think." (The discovery and elaboration of complications is an academic specialty. In the words of science fiction writer Poul Anderson: "I have yet to see any problem, however complicated, which, when you looked at it the right way, did not become still more complicated."[24]) In short, crisis management was touted in the mid-1960s as a body of knowledge that constituted the distilled lessons believed to be largely derivable from the Cuban missile crisis. The first wave of commentaries on crisis management tended to focus almost exclusively on the events (and nonevents) of October 1962,[25] with some references to the recent crisis experience over Berlin.[26] Scholarly social science, ever eager to pursue quantifiable wisdom, was scarcely less eager to leap aboard the crisis study train. The product of many years of prodigious social-scientific inquiry into crisis has been, with a few noteworthy exceptions,[27] a literature of almost monumental inutility. For example, one unquestionably scholarly compendium offers its unfortunate readers an appendix with no fewer than 311 "propositions." Without evidence of irony, proposition 302 holds: "The credibility of threats increases when there is consistency between verbal statements and action."[28] The appropriate response has to be: "Amen."

Notwithstanding the pomposity and naiveté that permeate the crisis management literature, it should be remembered that this literature was catalyzed by a particular event and that it had a very serious—indeed, an unquestionably praiseworthy—motive. First, in the early and mid-1960s, difficult though many people find it to recall today, there was a sense of crisis management achievement; in October 1962, the U.S. decision-making system at the highest level had been tested almost *à outrance* and had not been found wanting.[29] Second, and scarcely less important, there was a belief that although we were successful, we were also fortunate. Third, it was believed by many commentators, analysts, and theorists that through proper codification of the rules of crisis management, the element of *fortuna* in future crises could be reduced in favor of deliberate (partially preplanned), prudent calculation.[30] Among the most penetrating descriptions of the intent behind the crisis management theorizing of the early to mid-1960s was that by Robert Osgood and Robert Tucker:

> There is, of course, nothing novel in the aspiration, as such, to manage diplomatic crises. What is novel in contemporary "crisis management" is the intensity of aspirations to exercise a far greater measure of control over those critical junctures in state relations than men have exercised in the past and the confidence that this may indeed be done through exhaustive analysis, imaginative speculations, and careful planning for future actions. Whereas in the past crises all too often "broke" on men who, being unprepared and having no time, were made the prisoners of events, crisis management would reverse this ancient and today dangerous form of servitude and make men the masters of events.[31]

Almost needless to say, the optimism to which Osgood and Tucker referred stemmed from reflections on the course and outcome of the recent experience with Cuba in October 1962.

The Theory of Escalation Control

The Western (really, U.S.) theory of escalation, to stretch terminology a little, holds that force can be applied purposefully in measured, graduated quantities of specified quality to a point or zone at which an enemy will decide that its expectation of future loss exceeds its expectation of gain; hence, the enemy will acquiesce in a process of war termination.[32] As a very bare framework of rational decision making, escalation theory can accommodate a wide range of deterrence theories. Also, if it is left sufficiently sparse of detail, the theory need not be vulnerable to charges of strategic ethnocentricity or wishful thinking. To have a vision of escalation need not be to endorse that particular vision as prospective reality.[33] Nonetheless, defensible though the theory of escalation is, in very general terms, against theoretical assault from all quarters, in practice the theory has had a powerful, specific impact on Western defense thinking. Aside from what a wise strategist might make of the theory of escalation, U.S. and NATO-European officials have tended to the following beliefs:

- That war, particularly nuclear war, is a bargaining process or a process of competition in risk-taking.[34]

- That a bargaining process or competition in risk-taking has thresholds likely to be recognizable as such by both parties.

- That escalation is a process of graduated punishment (and the threat thereof). Both sides will have opportunities (at the thresholds) to consider carefully whether or not the stakes of the war are worth the damage yet to be inflicted and suffered.

- That neither side will have grave difficulty understanding the strategic-political meaning of the military actions taken by the other.[35]

- That neither side will be beyond deterrence.

- That a "seamless web" of escalation possibilities and probabilities means that militarily convincing defense capability is not needed at any level of the process, though particularly at the lower levels, because deterrence works through the fear of the damage that can be inflicted at ever-higher levels of violence. Indeed, a truly convincing denial capability with respect to theater-conventional/or theater-nuclear forces, might well undermine the "great chain of deterrence" that reposes in the escalation connections between different kinds of military forces.[36]

The foregoing constitutes only a very modest caricature of orthodox NATO deterrence thinking.[37] In practice, the theory of escalation, as interpreted by very self-interested NATO members, has tended to function as an alibi for a fundamentally nonserious in-theater (European) defense posture. As Kenneth Hunt argued more than ten years ago, the principal duty of NATO's conventional forces in Europe is to guarantee the Soviet Union a "major war" if they should invade Western Europe.[38] That major war raises the very credible prospect of a theater-nuclear war, and a theater-nuclear war renders very credible the prospect of intervention by central nuclear systems. In short, the strength of NATO's defense posture for deterrence, appraised in a fairly narrow military way, lies in the existence of and the believed escalation chains interconnecting the NATO triad of conventional, theater-nuclear, and strategic-nuclear forces.

In principle, this theory, with its multiple synergisms, has much to recommend it—particularly if the prospective adversary shares Western values and would engage in rational decision making in familiar Western terms. Unfortunately, there is no good reason to make these assumptions. Some Western commentators have sought to argue that "in the event," Soviet decision makers would likely prove far less idiosyncratic and indifferent to limitation of military activity than might be believed on the basis of study of Russian/Soviet national style and the evidence of Soviet literature and military exercises.[39] The proposition is that Soviet operational strategy would demonstrate a sensitivity to thresholds relevant to a process of relatively early war termination, far beyond any signals received in the West in peacetime.[40] I am not scornful of this proposition, but neither am I particularly respectful of it.[41] Unwelcome though the judgment is, it is difficult to find an evidential base to controvert Jack Snyder's 1977 argument:

> Countercultural strategic analysis is not well-developed in the Soviet Union and has been in retreat since the Cuban Missile Crisis. As a result, there has been no discernible effort to explore the advantages of flexible-option strategies. Based on what is visible to the outside observer, Soviet crisis decision-makers would appear intellectually unprepared for real-time improvisation of a doctrine of intrawar restraint.[42]

In short, although the Soviet Union may identify some potential thresholds in an East-West military conflict, it is not at all obvious—on the basis of the admittedly imperfect evidence available—that the Soviets embrace any political theory of intrawar deterrence or escalation control that could function as a combat dampener in conjunction with Western policies.[43] This is not to suggest that the thin reed of intrawar thresholds is not worth grasping, however fragile, for reasons of the damage implications of an absence of escalation control; rather, it is to suggest that a U.S. theory of escalation control has to take explicit account of the strong possibility that the Soviet Union will seek to wage war according to its understanding of the logic of armed conflict.

Western theorists of escalation, no matter how well they hedged their theoretical frameworks with caveats, provided Western decision makers with a dangerous concept. Herman Kahn's hypothetical escalation ladder may be a metaphor—really, a heuristic device to stimulate creative thought— but in practice, it may have encouraged some particularly dangerous illusions concerning the potential for the control of conflict. By way of summary:

- Many politicians and officials who are unused to strategic theoretical thinking have difficulty distinguishing between "what can be conceived" and "what is likely to happen."

- The logical structure of a "44-rung" escalation ladder may be too explicit for official minds in search of answers rather than aids to constructive thought.[44]

- Theoreticians' caveats notwithstanding, some officials may have acute cultural difficulty understanding that the rungs and thresholds (if any) most obvious in Moscow almost certainly are substantially different from those most obvious in Washington.

- Finally, and perhaps of greatest significance, to many strategically ill-educated persons, escalation theory may seem to offer a "management offset" to a major decline in relative military muscle.

As with the concept of crisis management, the concept of escalation control contains an inherent tension that may prove fatal for its efficacy in policy practice. In the enduring absence of substantial domestic damage-limitation capabilities, U.S. enthusiasm for the control half of the escalation control concept promises to be fatally erosive of the desired deterrent effect. In the "Disney World" of some U.S. theorists, fearful Soviet leaders either are deterred by the "great chain of escalation" reasoning or—in the worst case—are brought to their senses abruptly by sharp escalatory initiatives by the United States.[45] That is, deterrence is restored. Yet no explanation is offered of why the United States would be willing to escalate an unfolding conflict while the Soviet Union would be unwilling to continue that escalation process; there simply is no basis presented for anticipating such U.S. boldness or Soviet caution. Indeed, there is some evidence to suggest that just the inverse might be the case. As already argued extensively in this book, no one can predict with high confidence which superpower would lead an escalation process; geopolitical logic suggests, however, that it should be the United States, because of local military weakness in Eurasian theaters, although Soviet preemptive strategy may recognize and then outrun and overwhelm that logic.

If the logic of geopolitics holds true and the United States is in the driver's seat of escalation, seeking to reverse the course of some local conflict, then the U.S. cultural attraction to escalation control in the context of a totally vulnerable U.S. homeland could well vitiate the efficacy of the escalation concept as a structure of credible, or not-incredible, threats. The more carefully the United States seeks to control a process of escalation, the less menacing its deterrent profile may seem in Soviet eyes.

Thus far, the argument in this section has sought to establish the danger that is immanent in much of the contemporary American thinking about controlled escalation for deterrence restoration and early war termination. By way of a counterpoint, it is worth noting the argument that there would be considerable deterrence advantage for the United States in a situation wherein U.S. policymakers would manage to persuade Soviet policymakers that the United States was convinced that escalation could (or even *would*) be controlled and Soviet leaders were not so convinced. In other words, Moscow would have to face a Washington apparently convinced that nuclear force, even central nuclear force, truly was usable in a graduated, controllable manner—all the while itself believing that a slide to nonrecoverable catastrophe could not be averted.

Whatever the abstract merit in this counterpoint argument, it founders on the U.S. inability to manipulate Soviet perceptions reliably. In practice, the United States has achieved probably the worst of all situations; senior officials of the Carter and Reagan administrations have articulated variants of the controlled escalation thesis but then have proceeded rather hastily to say that "we do not really believe this." In the United States, to date at least, it is not politically (really, culturally) acceptable to articulate a belief in wageable and survivable nuclear war.

THE THEORY OF CRISIS MANAGEMENT

For a rather crude, though not wholly misleading, caricature, crisis management attained the status of being a chic concept in the early to mid-1960s. Apparently, it had cultural appeal to some of those Americans whom David Halberstam described, ironically, as "the best and the brightest."[46] The concept of crisis management, and the theory (or theories) that was woven around it, spoke to some enduring U.S. cultural themes.

First, crisis management suggested toughness, or at least a tough-minded approach to problems. Adversaries of the United States would do well to remember that, as Ronald Reagan is demonstrating, the United States is fundamentally a very macho country. Gary Cooper in *High Noon* and George C. Scott in *Patton* may have been cultural stereotypes, but those stereotypes should not be dismissed lightly by America's friends and foes. Cooper and Scott (and, indeed, "The A-Team" and "Rambo") truly spoke to, and for, U.S. culture.

Second, crisis management appealed to the U.S. proclivity to solve problems and to define conditions as problems. By definition, a crisis is, or may be, a problem-solving mechanism (as war is).[47] Third, crisis management was attractive to Americans as a concept because it was both optimistic (crisis *management*) and skill-oriented. The concept, in its very structure, suggests that crises can be managed, and Americans have never lacked for confidence in their ability to manage effectively.

Fourth, crisis management seems to imply that the (inferred) pacific management of crises is the natural order of affairs. The prevalence of lawyers or—more realistically, perhaps—of people with some legal training in the U.S. government has the skill-bias effect on policy planning of encouraging the belief that "a deal" can always be struck between fundamentally reasonable advocates for their state-clients. The concept of crisis management has immediate appeal to a U.S. policymaking community heavily populated by lawyers, temporarily lapsed lawyers, or lawyers manqués, who have been socialized by the unhealthy net effect of a legal perspective imbued at an impressionable age with the belief that reasonable people will eventually come to terms to manage a crisis to the satisfaction of all interested parties. In other words, the very concept of crisis management encourages the view that every crisis can be managed successfully if only the right package of incentives (and disincentives) can be assembled and negotiated. There is what may be termed a fallacy of negotiability.[48]

For example, Roger Fisher, professor of law at Harvard, has long advised U.S. governments to "give them a yesable proposition"[49]—in other words, to seek a way of packaging U.S. desires such that the adversary will feel moved to say yes. This is yet another example of a good idea that all too easily becomes a poor idea. There are occasions—as, for example, over "Who rules South Vietnam?" or "Shall the American hostages be released?"—when "men of good will" on both sides cannot attain a mutually satisfactory crisis outcome. It is worth recalling the rather obvious historical points that not all crisis landscapes are well populated with men of good will (for example, Munich in September 1938). Sometimes the issue at stake does not lend itself to a compromise decision; and not all crises permit one party to make an offsetting side payment in return for acquisition of the major prize in the conflict. In practice, Roger Fisher's advice to "give them a yesable proposition" serves as a temptation to appeasement (although Fisher does not, of course, intend it as such). Fisher advocated his "yesable proposition" option in relation to the U.S. hostages in Tehran, but no one, including Professor Fisher, succeeded in designing a proposition that appealed to Shiite zealots. If there are no "yesable" propositions on the horizon, and if the issue truly is a matter of vital national interest, one has little recourse other than to send in the Marines. The final resolution of the hostage crisis in January 1981 had little or nothing to do with the quality of U.S. diplomacy.

As Osgood and Tucker have suggested (quoted earlier), the crisis management theorists of the early and mid-1960s were reacting to the perceived fact that, as they believed, the world was fortunate to have been spared nuclear war in October 1962.[50] It seemed sensible to argue that although every crisis has distinctive features (of time, place, strength of commitment of adversaries, alliance complications and assistance, correlation of forces, and so on), at a fairly high level of generality one should be able to specify some guidelines for crisis management, some "conventions of crisis,"[51] that would have value apart from the details of one or two particular passages of foreign policy or diplomatic arms.[52] Although I am very friendly to the idea that policymakers should be forearmed for crisis with appropriate general wisdom, I am also concerned lest policymakers enter acute international crises forearmed either with wisdom so general in character that it can offer no guidance to policy determination or with apparent wisdom that offers a false sense of security. One can conceive of situations in which it probably would be preferable for policymakers to enter a period of crisis with something approaching a tabula rasa of prior thought on the subject at issue, rather than with their minds full of half-relevant (or less) precanned contingency plans.

Notwithstanding the prodigious efforts of scholars to provide an explicit data base of historical crises, the (possibly unfortunate) fact remains that the historical and social-scientific education of the average senior U.S. policymaker remains lamentably elementary. His understanding of the dynamism of crises tends to be limited to any crisis decision making in which he participated personally; the Cuban missile crisis of October 1962; the crisis slide of 1936–39; and the crisis slide of 1914.[53] Unfortunately, each of these historical cases for easy reference constitutes a distinctive "dominant scenario." Moreover, with respect to October 1962 and, particularly, 1914, it is far from obvious that scholars agree at any useful level concerning the lessons of successful (1962) and unsuccessful (1914) crisis management. Indeed, 1914 is an extreme case of crisis pathology;[54] one might well learn more from the successful crisis management practiced by the Great Powers in 1908–1909 over the Bosnian crisis.

Notwithstanding the major scholarly endeavor undertaken to dissect crisis phenomena, the end result—at least to date—has been disappointingly obvious. For example, one distinguished scholar, Ole R. Holsti, having engaged in scrupulous, painstaking research, has informed us that the following are the most important items of crisis management advice:[55]

Perhaps the first prerequisite is a sensitivity to the adversary's frame of reference. [*Comment:* Sun Tzu said much the same in the China of the Third Century B.C. "Know the enemy" is good advice, but its propagation is hardly a triumph of scholarship.]

Avoid taking steps which seal off "escape routes."

Reducing the adversary's incentives to escalate will probably require a combination of incentives and threats. [*Comment:* This is so obvious as to be banal and without value.]

In crisis diplomacy, as in other forms of communications, actions tend to speak louder than words. [*Comment:* This is good advice, but again, it is stupefyingly obvious.]

Make every effort to slow the pace of crisis events. [*Comment:* This was good advice for October 1962; it was irrelevant for 1939; it was believed by the best military brains of the time to be bad advice in July 1914;[56] and it could be disastrous advice for NATO.[57]]

During a crisis, responsible policymakers should be in control not only of broad strategic decisions, but also of the details of implementation. [*Comment:* Clearly, and sensibly, Professor Holsti does not want a battalion commander in the U.S. Fifth Corps starting World War III on his own initiative. However, the long-standing U.S. tradition of trusting "the man on the spot" should not be discarded too lightly. Far from starting World War III, prompt and resourceful action taken by a battalion commander might just resolve a military problem that could otherwise have escalated had it been left to the judgment of the man with the global perspective in the White House.]

Although there should be policy value in wisdom derived from the careful historical study of statecraft and from a high-level theory of crisis management, the fact remains that the U.S. record of crisis management prior to enunciation of crisis management theory was not obviously inferior to the postenunciation record. This, of course, does not necessarily indict the theory. Any theory, of any degree of explanatory power, may be ignored or misapplied by fallible and fumbling policymakers—not to mention the distressing fact that adversary policymakers either may hold to a very different set of rules of crisis management or may read your theory and ambush its application in detail.[58]

To lend some much-needed reality to this discussion, readers are invited to consider Holsti's six items of crisis management advice in the light of the protracted Iranian hostage crisis of 1979–81 and the protracted and prospectively permanent Soviet military intervention in Afghanistan. I suggest that a U.S. president would have been no more likely to know how to direct U.S. grand strategy vis-à-vis those two protracted crises after having studied Holsti's advice than he would have been before. In the Iranian hostage crisis, the U.S. government crippled the effectiveness of its diplomacy first by attaching, or appearing to attach, far too much importance to the lives of the hostages and then by being overly concerned that it not antagonize Iran further (drive it into the arms of still less friendly elements, and so on). What happened is that the United States lost face over the hostages, and as Thomas Schelling has argued:

> "Face" relates not to a country's "worth" or "status" or even "honor" but to its reputation for action. If the question is raised whether this kind of "face" is worth fighting over, the answer is that this kind of face is one of the few things worth fighting over.[59]

Finally, as with the concept of escalation control, there is an inherent tension in the concept of crisis management that can subvert the effectiveness of U.S. policy. The term *crisis* implies a short period of time, an important issue at stake, a turning point, a decision, and danger.[60] *Management*, on the other hand, implies deliberate and purposeful control, careful planning, and the efficient and measured application of resources. If deterrent effect, to some important though indeterminate degree, is believed to flow from the fear that one is making threats "that leave something to chance," in Schelling's phraseology,[61] then making public play of careful management of the crisis may largely negate putative deterrent effect. In principle, at least, the term *management* is neutral in its implied policy content. One could manage, carefully, to place one's armed forces on a genuine war footing. However, *management* tends not to carry that implication in the Western perspective.

It is probably no exaggeration to argue that just as it may be held that deterrence has failed if force has to be used, so crisis management is often judged to have failed when war breaks out nonetheless. In terms of Western culture, wherein peace is normal and war is abnormal, crises tend to be viewed either as acts of God (or of a capricious nature) or as the acts of a malevolent adversary. It would be almost inconceivable to describe as successful a case of crisis management that resulted in war. U.S. strategic theory and strategic policy makes no provision for the coercive use of crises.[62] Indeed, the very idea of crisis fomentation as a deliberate act of policy is a challenge to U.S. strategic and political culture. This is probably unfortunate, though culturally inevitable, because a new rule of crisis diplomacy, generally neglected by stability-minded theorists in the United States, is to the effect that "you should be more likely than not to win a crisis that you yourself initiate" (because you choose the time, place, and issue of the crisis).

Although they carry some risk of a wider war erupting, local crises are occasionally the deliberate and intended outcomes of the policies of the Soviet Union. Even if Western policymakers are unable to foment local crises in the prospect of political gain, they should not forget that Soviet policymakers, although they do not want war, do see some local crises as advancing Soviet influence. Disorder, instability, crisis, and war are all—

by definition—undesirable in the Western perspective, but not necessarily in the Soviet view.

THE SOVIET PERSPECTIVE

The U.S. defense community, although it acknowledges, belatedly, the distinctiveness of Soviet strategic thought, has yet to recognize many of the logical implications of that alien way of thinking. For example, the United States has yet to begin to come to terms with the plausible implications of the following assertion in the Soviet *Officer's Handbook:*

> In wartime, military doctrine drops into the background somewhat, since, in armed combat, we are guided primarily by military-political and military-strategic considerations, conclusions, and generalizations which stem from the condition of the specific situation. Consequently, *war, armed combat, is governed by strategy, not doctrine.*[63] (emphasis added)

Although the Soviet Union holds to a supremely political view of war, there is good reason to believe that the Soviet General Staff, theorizing and planning in peacetime, anticipates that in a future war the *Stavka* (Headquarters of the Supreme High Command) would function much as it did in World War II.[64] The *Stavka* is a fully integrated policymaking body of senior civilians and soldiers, and the General Staff is its executive agency. There are no good grounds for believing that, in the event, civilians in that body would view problems of strategy very differently from their military colleagues. By and large, Western models of civil-military relations do not apply to the USSR.[65] Colonel P. A. Sidarov, the author of the foregoing quotation, was not voicing a highly personal opinion that was intended to stimulate debate, nor was he engaged in the propagation of misinformation. *The Officer's Handbook,* with an original printing of 83,000, should be taken at face value. It is intended to assist "officers in broadening their outlook and in resolving many practical problems related to the training and education of subordinates."[66] Moreover, the Soviet-Clausewitzian view that war is a political instrument is not in any way challenged by the proposition that "war . . . is governed by strategy, not doctrine." Although the Soviet Union would not engage in war lightly or for frivolous reasons, once bent upon combat Soviet military professionals appear to expect to be permitted to conduct military operations according to sound military criteria.

Sensibly enough, Soviet officials and military professionals are committed to the view that war should be waged only for the most serious of reasons, only in pursuit of clearly defined (*in advance*) political goals, and only with a level and kind of violence that is appropriate to the political goals sought.

Whereas Western theorists of limited war have been means-oriented in their search for ways of limiting war, Soviet military thinkers are obliged by Soviet military doctrine (grand strategy) and the state ideology behind that doctrine to be ends-oriented in their consideration of the kinds of force that may be permitted in particular kinds of war (defined politically, not technologically). The long-standing Soviet denial of the validity of U.S. limited war theory almost certainly has reflected a genuine professional repudiation of what has been believed to be an erroneous approach to conflict.[67] The Soviet Union does not have an undifferentiated view of war. Of particular relevance to this discussion, Soviet authorities appear to recognize the difference between a theater conflict in Europe and a superpower homeland-to-homeland war—always provided that the theater conflict in Europe does not encompass nuclear strikes against Soviet home territory.[68] Also, they recognize a variety of local "just wars" in the Third World. However, doctrinal recognition of possibilities need not be matched by war plans that are constrained in major ways. I have suggested in this chapter that although Soviet officials acknowledge, in practice, the somewhat basic concepts of escalation control and crisis management, much of the detail appended to those concepts by Western theoreticians is simply not relevant to the Soviet view of diplomacy and war.[69]

Although Soviet writers do not deny the potential for catastrophe inherent in nuclear weapon use (although, in Soviet perspective, it is hoped to be a *survivable* catastrophe),[70] they do not, by and large, endorse the idea that military operations should be conducted with a view to manipulating adversary expectations of further damage.[71] In short, once combat begins in pursuit of clear political goals, the Soviet armed forces would not, on the literary evidence available, be engaged in a "diplomacy of violence" or in "the manipulation of risk." Instead, political objectives, translated into military terms, would be sought. Consistent with political guidelines, Soviet military professionals would be unleashed to solve military problems in proper military fashion. The leading Western authority on Soviet military thought and military practice, John Erickson, has offered the following relevant judgments:

> It is worth noting in passing that the founders of the Soviet strategic missile force were not strategic theoreticians but experienced and distinguished artillery commanders, doubtless having little or no patience with American strategic constructions and high-falutin' nonsense about zero-sum games.[72]

In the sequence of strikes, *the maximum number should be allocated to the first launch,* in order to maximize survivability, though the phasing of launches can afford a certain degree of flexibility, which after survivability is certainly a Soviet objective.[73]

In the United States, escalation theory has been something of an academic plaything. With great ingenuity, richly differentiated logical sequences of escalatory actions were invented. Unfortunately, perhaps, it appears that the Soviet Union is not attracted to the idea of engaging in a very carefully graduated "diplomacy of violence." The Soviets seem to believe that the "grammar" of war is largely sui generis and that there is thus an internal logic or integrity to military operations that must be permitted to run its course, albeit within predetermined political parameters. In other words, military action has political meaning in the sense that war must be conducted only for appropriate political ends, but not in the sense that war comprises a series of violent political messages.

If there is an alternative direct-control option, it is not the Soviet way to place reliance on self-restraint being exercised by others. Deterrence, prewar and intrawar, is believed by Soviet theoreticians to be the consequence of anticipation of war-waging success or of net prowess in combat.[74] Although a Soviet government may surprise us in the event, it is virtually inconceivable that the Soviet Union would edge its way onto and up an escalation ladder, hoping that political decisions by very frightened Western politicians would yield victory at relatively modest cost. In the Soviet perspective, the political character of the war would (or should) determine the strategy and tactics of military operations. Historical experience does not encourage a Soviet leader to expect major gains to be secured at low cost,[75] whereas the price of victory against a first-class enemy (the Third Reich or the United States) is known, and expected, to be very high indeed. Wishful thinking is not a trait known to be highly developed among Soviet leadership cadres, civilian or military.

Soviet thinking on the set of problems and possibilities encompassed by the concept of escalation control has to be considered both in the light of Soviet attitudes and beliefs and, scarcely less important, in the context of a major war. Even if the Soviet Union is judged to be a status quo power seeking primarily to ensure the stability of its existing imperium, that essentially defensive aim is fully compatible with expansive and offensive strategy and tactics. Careful escalation control, for motives easily recognizable in the West, probably is not consistent with Soviet strategic culture. In a war embracing the whole European theater of operations, the Soviet Union would anticipate the employment of any, and perhaps all, theater weapons (conventional, chemical, battlefield-oriented theater-nuclear, and deep-strike theater-operational nuclear weapons). Although Soviet military literature and military exercises accommodate the idea of the possibility of a nonnuclear phase in a European conflict, I know of no persuasive Soviet evidence that would suggest Soviet anticipation of the likelihood of a theater-wide, totally nonnuclear conflict.[76] In Soviet terms, and in the Soviet estimation of NATO-European terms, the political stakes of the war would be so high that both sides would be expected to use their most effective weapons. This is not to deny the small possibility of Soviet planning for some very limited-purpose military operations west of the existing dividing line, which would not entail expectation of resort to nuclear combat.

If the Soviet Union should decide to attack NATO-Europe—a decision emerging, perhaps, as a consequence of Soviet frustration in attempting to deal with dissent in Eastern Europe—then it should be presumed that the Soviet leaders would have thought through the potential costs of an assault against a very heavily nuclear-armed adversary. By way of sharp and even embarrassing contrast to the thinking that underlies NATO's doctrine of flexible response, the Soviet Union gives every evidence of believing that "war is war"; and because wars are either won or lost (stalemate would probably translate into "lost" in the Soviet political context), it is mandatory to try very hard to win. In Soviet military and, one must presume, authoritative political terms, victory is not a nostalgic idea clung to by old soldiers, and it is not simply a morale-boosting concept.[77] Rather, it is the operational objective of the Soviet armed forces at whatever level of violence they are committed to action. For ideological and sensible analytically based military reasons, the Soviet Union remains convinced that victory is possible in wars of all kinds.[78]

Once a Soviet government makes the decision to fight, it should not be expected that the Soviet military establishment would be much constrained by political considerations of escalation control. The Soviet Union would not employ force needlessly (in its estimation), but neither should Western countries anticipate a Soviet willingness to risk paying a major military price in return for a considerable lowering of the risks of further escalation.

Although Western defense analysts have discerned some evidence of Soviet identification of a possible geographical threshold between theater war and superpower homeland-to-homeland war (a central war, as U.S. theorists are wont to express it, parochially), I am not wholly convinced that Soviet military planners place any credence on the serious possibility of a theater war remaining confined to Europe—which is not to deny their evident interest in such an option. In the Soviets' perspective, they confront a multistate adversary

- whose societal assets in Europe constitute "the principal prize" in world politics. Thinking geopolitically, as they do, Soviet planners must notice what was obvious to Nicholas Spykman—that control of the Eurasian rimlands should ultimately mean control of the world.[79] In terms of its long-range competitive prospects, the United States cannot afford to permit the assets of Europe to fall totally under Soviet control (or even *contrôle*[80]).

• that has roughly 350,000 Americans in uniform (plus their dependents) deployed forward, by and large, in the European theater. The Soviet Union cannot wage war against NATO-Europe alone.

• that is in the process of modernizing its nuclear strike systems to provide at least the beginnings of a convincing-looking theater-based threat to the Soviet homeland. Soviet leaders probably understand that in the eyes of NATO leaders, the Polish-Soviet frontier does not constitute an appropriate political-geographical threshold for the containment of a war in Europe.[81]

• whose fundamental strategic concept embraces the idea of a seamless web of deterrent effect—flowing from the "planned deficiencies" of the lower levels of the NATO triad (or "tripod"). Year after year, Soviet leaders observe NATO's intramural conflicts over the credibility of the connection between events pertinent to NATO's Central Front in West Germany and U.S. central strategic systems. Those Soviet leaders cannot afford to take very seriously Henry Kissinger's gloomy judgment "that our European allies should not keep asking us to multiply strategic assurances that we cannot possibly mean or if we do mean, we should not want to execute because if we execute, we risk the destruction of civilization."[82] (However, Western defense planners, for their part, cannot prudently assume that Henry Kissinger is wrong.)

For these reasons, it is improbable that the Soviet Union anticipates at all seriously the prospect of confining a war initiated in Europe to Europe. Probably the most appropriate way to express this inferred Soviet perspective is to suggest that although a Soviet government would prefer a war to be confined to Europe and would not be eager to accelerate the expansion of the geographical domain of military operations, it would— for reasons of elementary prudence—both expect and have to anticipate U.S. resort to the employment of central strategic systems. Moreover, by way of a truly vital qualification, the Soviet Union almost certainly would not be willing to initiate armed conflict in Europe unless it was reasonably confident that the central war, down the road, could be won. No Soviet government should be expected to place total reliance on the counterdeterrent efficacy of its strategic-forces posture.[83]

As best one can tell on the basis of several different kinds of evidence, the Soviet Union, though not willing to "waste" nuclear weapons on politically or militarily meaningless targets, would wage war in the European theater or beyond it with an overriding determination to win. In terms of targeting tactics, this determination—in a central war—should translate into very large-scale strikes directed against such elements of the U.S. strategic-forces posture as could be struck (perhaps even very cost-ineffectively); against the National Command Authorities (NCA); against C^3I nodes; against key transportation targets; against immediate war-supporting industry; and against the national power grid.[84] The Soviet targeting "withhold" suggested here vis-à-vis urban areas of no immediate relevance for war-waging is of no great military relevance. It could be interpreted as applied escalation control, but it probably is better viewed simply as military common sense. Readers of this book should be aware of the fact that Western strategic theorists who are advertising ideas for the control of escalation in central war are condemned to listen to the echoes of their own voices. Except for very negative commentary on U.S. theories of strategic flexibility, escalation, and limited war,[85] the Soviet military theory establishment simply has not produced a literature on the subject of escalation and its possible control.

Aside from political-propagandistic motives for not joining a transnational debate on the subject of escalation (or on "the rules of engagement or exchange" in nuclear warfare), the Soviet defense establishment probably has not felt moved to advance down the escalation theory road because the very concept of escalation, at least in terms familiar via the U.S. theoretical literature of the mid-1960s, is alien in the Soviet context. In the Soviet perspective, political leaders decide if, when, where, and for what objectives Soviet military power will be applied in action, following which the "how" of combat is a matter for professional military determination.

The concept of the political control of escalation is very much the product of an insular, as opposed to a continental, strategic culture. The insular situation of Great Britain and the United States and a good part of their actual (as opposed to romanticized) histories have lent credence to the view that a country could "take as much and as little of the war as he will."[86] Prior to the maturing of the means of long-range aerial and space bombardment, insularity, in the context of superior friendly seapower, meant that the United States or Great Britain (more precariously, because of the narrowness of the Straits of Dover) would, or should, retain the initiative in the direction of war.[87] Those countries enjoyed the luxury of being able to decide, unilaterally, just how much effort to apply to a particular political-military venture, because—essentially—the center of national power was not immediately at risk in war.[88]

Insular countries—particularly insular democracies like Great Britain and the United States—are unusually vulnerable to the siren appeal of a concept such as escalation control. This concept presumes the feasibility of deliberate manipulation of the military environment in favorable ways (which was long a *condition* for these two countries by virtue of their geographical location). It appeals to the pragmatic, engineering-manipulative impulse that is dear to the U.S. (and, to a much lesser degree, the British[89]) self-image;[90] and, virtually by definition, it affirms the insular-democratic axiomatic preference for order (meaning stability consolidated through explicitly or tacitly negotiated compromise).

Readers may recall the discussion in chapter 3, which made explicit the strategic-cultural implications of continental heartland political location. The Soviet Union shares none of the deep cultural drives that incline U.S. politicians and officials to look with favor on the concept of escalation control. One can imagine a Soviet leadership group so fearful of the "next" or the anticipated "next but one" step in U.S. strategic targeting execution that it develops an overwhelming interest in the control of escalation. However, proceeding inductively rather than deductively, one can see few, if any, grounds for the still widespread U.S. and NATO-European belief that "on the night," the Soviet Union actually would conduct its military operations paying very close attention to the escalatory potential of those operations.

SOME IMPLICATIONS

The analysis in this chapter, though admittedly hampered by lack of evidence from the Soviet side—not to mention the obvious point that there is no hands-on, real-world experience of the functioning of escalation processes in a nuclear war—reinforces the conclusions reached in the prior discussion of deterrence and stability. Looming over all of these subjects is the apparent fact of a Soviet "battlefield" view of the proper use of nuclear weapons in war.

As with U.S. theories of deterrence through the threat of punishment and of strategic stability, so the U.S. theories of escalation control and crisis management are pervaded with U.S. cultural desiderata. The issue is not whether those desiderata are or are not praiseworthy; rather, it is whether or not those cultural desiderata encourage, in practice, the evolution of military postures and policies that would be unlikely to be able to withstand the traffic of Soviet policies driven by Soviet culturally-derived impulses.[91] The basic idea of escalation control, on the surface at least, appears to be compatible with both U.S. and Soviet strategic cultures. The idea that more and more (or different) force may be applied in discriminating ways for the achievement of political objectives is hardly culture-specific. Similarly, the idea of intrawar deterrence—even if alien in the Soviet context—once understood, potentially has to be a major candidate for policy influence. It is not difficult to believe that Soviet leaders, in the course of a war, would prefer not to conduct military operations in such a way that the United States might feel strongly moved to begin to execute a series of strike options against Soviet political-control targets. The caveat is the thought that once the decision to fight has been taken, Soviet leaders would be unlikely to jeopardize the achievement of their war-waging goals for reason of real-time anticipation of damage likely to be inflicted by the United States. The prospect of such damage would have been assessed before the decision to fight was made.

Those relatively optimistic thoughts aside, U.S. defense planners have no prudent choice other than to assume a strategic-culturally distinctive Soviet adversary in time of acute crisis. I believe that the Soviet Union is slow to anger to the point where a decision is confronted on the proximate use or nonuse of military power. Soviet leaders, thanks to their Russian/ Soviet historical and Marxist-Leninist ideological inheritances, almost axiomatically think the worst of their adversaries. (There are no disillusioned liberals in the Politburo.) In short, there is typically little emotional input to Soviet decision making on foreign policy.[92] Soviet government is very much committee government, and Soviet political leaders know, or think they know, that they are beset by actual or potential enemies. A major problem in Soviet-U.S. understanding is the extent to which the U.S. government is highly personal—in the hands of one man who has few, if any, ideological preferences and probably little sense of historic mission and responsibility at all comparable to those familiar to the men in the Kremlin. The very structure of the Soviet mode of leadership, since 1964 at least, lends it a degree of predictability that is quite absent from the U.S. presidential scene.

In addition to the dampening effect imposed by committee government on policy initiative, the apparent Soviet belief that "war will run its course" should also serve to discourage boldness in prediction of putative chains of escalation logic. Furthermore, it should not be forgotten that although the Soviet Union has been elected by History (that is, Lenin with a revolver) to lead and guard the transformation of capitalism-imperialism into socialism (thence, eventually, to communism), the Soviet Union is both the vanguard and the principal asset of proletarian internationalism. Soviet leaders are not supposed to place the citadel of socialism (that is, the USSR) at serious risk through adventurous diplomacy.

Although the Soviet Union traditionally has been, and should be expected to continue to be, relatively slow to anger, once the decision to fight is taken Soviet leaders are unlikely to endorse any outcome short of military and, hence, political victory. Unlike the United States, the Soviet Union is very unlikely to stumble into a war, thinking about its political objectives in the course of fighting. If the Soviet Union should decide to fight NATO—for whatever mix of the most compelling reasons—it is fairly safe to predict that any tentative Soviet consideration of escalation control factors would be rapidly overwhelmed by the will to win (and the sense of duty to try to win).

As a consequence of many living historical memories, the Soviet Union knows that war is a very serious business. A theory of escalation control that poses a potentially major threat to military efficacy is unlikely to secure many converts in Moscow, even under the dire pressure of wartime events. Soviet leaders know, through historical and personal experience, that if a war can be won, virtually any kind of damage sustained can eventually be made good. Recognition of this perspective, alien though it is, did not permeate the writings of U.S. theorists on escalation in the 1960s, nor has it gained a solid footing in policy thinking since.

The final word in this chapter is provided by a leading Soviet defense scientist:

> Let's turn first to the conception of "limited" nuclear war, which is used to "legitimize" the use of nuclear weapons and nuclear war as such. This conception—and this conclusion follows from the analysis of official American documents and works by American military theorists which have appeared over the last decade—has been elaborated to such a degree that its very existence in the arsenal of American strategic thought increases the possibility of a rapid slide toward nuclear conflict. Today it comprises plans for "selected nuclear strikes" against Soviet territory, a "limited" nuclear war in Europe, and plans to use nuclear munitions during "Rapid Deployment Force" operations in the developing countries.
>
> With regard to the possibility of limited strikes, escalation control, protracted and graduated nuclear exchanges, Western specialists often talk about the first use of nuclear weapons as though it were some isolated, almost symbolic act, following which both sides would immediately rush to settle the conflict on the basis of a mutually acceptable compromise. Nothing could be more dangerous than these suppositions. The use of nuclear weapons is not some *"démarche* in a crisis."* It would signify the crossing of the Rubicon and would set in motion an irreversible chain of events. Use of nuclear weapons would threaten the vital interests of the other side, and would evoke a retaliatory strike designed to achieve the maximum possible destruction of the opponent. Nuclear war is not a "joint enterprise," not a game with established rules and constraints. Because of the physical characteristics of nuclear weapons and the consequences of their use, such a war would be the greatest catastrophe in history.[93]

NOTES

1.   Sun Tzu, *The Art of War* (trans. Samuel B. Griffith) (Oxford: Clarendon Press, 1963); Carl von Clausewitz, *On War* (Michael Howard and Peter Paret, eds.) (Princeton, N.J.: Princeton University Press, 1976; first pub. 1832); Thucydides, *The Peloponnesian War* (London: Penguin, 1954).

2.   Charles Hitch and Roland McKean, *The Economics of Defense in the Nuclear Age* (New York: Atheneum, 1966; first pub. 1960).

3.   Thomas Schelling, *The Strategy of Conflict* (Cambridge, Mass.: Harvard University Press, 1960).

4.   See E. S. Quade, ed., *Analysis for Military Decisions: The RAND Lectures on Systems Analysis* (Chicago: Rand McNally, 1964); and E. S. Quade and W. I. Boucher, eds., *Systems Analysis and Policy Planning: Applications in Defense* (New York: Elsevier, 1968).

5.   See Russell F. Weigley, *The American Way of War* (New York: Macmillan, 1973); and John Shy, "The American Military Experience: History and Learning," *Journal of Interdisciplinary History* 1(Winter 1971): 205–28.

6.   Edward N. Luttwak, *Strategy and Politics: Collected Essays* (New Brunswick, N.J.: Transaction, 1980), p. 263. A little earlier, Luttwak offered the thought that "our defense planners take pride in knowing nothing of military history" (p. 261).

7.   Arthur M. Schlesinger, Jr., *A Thousand Days: John F. Kennedy in the White House* (London: Deutch, 1965), p. 283. For a positive assessment of the new defense economics by a participant-commentator, see Ralph Sanders, *The Politics of Defense Analysis* (New York: Dunellen, 1973).

8.   See chapters 4 and 5.

9.   See Sanders, *The Politics of Defense Analysis*, p. 9.

10.   Quantified defense analysis was hardly novel in the 1960s; what was novel was the invention, at RAND in the early 1950s, of systems analytic techniques that basically comprised operations research without fixed and given goals. For example, whereas one might ask in operations research, "What is the most cost-effective mix of air defense weapons to deploy and maintain against particular levels of threat?" one could ask in systems analysis, "Should the United States maintain any mix of air defense weapons?" The Soviet General Staff is no less enthusiastic about explicit defense analysis than the U.S. Office of the Secretary of Defense. For example, see V. V. Druzhinin and D. S. Kantorov, *Decision Making and Automation: Concept, Algorithm, Decision (A Soviet View)*, Soviet Military Thought Series of the U.S. Air Force, No. 6 (Washington, D.C.: USGPO, 1975; Moscow, 1972), which explains the science of automated troop control. Soviet criteria identify military cybernetics as constituting the third phase of the ongoing "revolution in military affairs."

11.   Quoted in Strobe Talbott, *Deadly Gambits: The Reagan Administration and the Stalemate in Nuclear Arms Control* (New York: Knopf, 1984), p. 6.

12.   This concern permeates James R. Schlesinger, *Selected Papers on National Security, 1964–68*, (Santa Monica, Calif.: RAND Corporation, September 1974).

13.   Clausewitz, *On War*, p. 579.

14.   Quoted in Coral Bell, *The Conventions of Crisis: A Study in Diplomatic Management* (London: Oxford University Press, 1971), p. 2.

15.   Alastair Buchan, *Crisis Management: The New Diplomacy* (Boulogne-sur-Seine: Atlantic Institute, 1966).

16. For an explanation of the historical context favoring the emergence of these concepts, see Colin S. Gray, *Strategic Studies and Public Policy: The American Experience* (Lexington: University Press of Kentucky, 1982), pp. 107–30.

17. The "in" book of the period was Thomas C. Schelling, *Arms and Influence* (New Haven: Yale University Press, 1966).

18. See Richard Smoke, *War: Controlling Escalation* (Cambridge, Mass.: Harvard University Press, 1977).

19. This is hardly surprising, given the fact that Mahan's theories were devised inductively from meticulous study of the operational practice of the Royal Navy *in the age of sail*. At the very time he was writing, changes in the weapons of sea warfare rendered obsolete his theory of decisive action for command of the sea. See James Goldrick, *The King's Ships Were at Sea: The War in the North Sea, August 1914–February 1915* (Annapolis, Md.: Naval Institute Press, 1984). For an excellent recent treatment of the entire war at sea, see Richard Hough, *The Great War at Sea: 1914–1918* (Oxford: Oxford University Press, 1983).

20. See Holger H. Herwig, *"Luxury Fleet": The Imperial German Navy, 1888–1918* (London: Allen and Unwin, 1980), particularly pp. 15, 17, 40. Also useful is Paul Kennedy, "Strategic Aspects of the Anglo-German Naval Race," in Paul Kennedy, *Strategy and Diplomacy, 1870–1945: Eight Studies* (London: Allen and Unwin, 1983), pp. 127–60.

21. The best overviews of limited war theory and practice are Robert E. Osgood, *Limited War Revisited* (Boulder, Colo.: Westview Press, 1979); Robert E. Osgood, "The Post-War Strategy of Limited War: Before, During, and After Vietnam," in Laurence Martin, ed., *Strategic Thought in the Nuclear Age* (Baltimore: Johns Hopkins University Press, 1979), pp. 93–130; and Stephen Peter Rosen, "Vietnam and the American Theory of Limited War," *International Security* 7, no. 2(Fall 1982): 83–113.

22. "Period classics" include Herman Kahn, *On Escalation: Metaphors and Scenarios* (New York: Praeger, 1965); and Bernard Brodie, *Escalation and the Nuclear Option* (Princeton, N.J.: Princeton University Press, 1966).

23. This argument is developed in detail in Gray, *Strategic Studies and Public Policy.*

24. Quoted in Arthur Koestler, *The Ghost in the Machine* (London: Pan, 1970), p. 77.

25. For example, see Harland Cleveland, "Crisis Diplomacy," *Foreign Affairs* 41, no. 4(July 1963): 638–49.

26. See Buchan, *Crisis Management.*

27. Honorable exceptions include Ole Holsti, *Crisis, Escalation, War* (Montreal: McGill-Queen's University Press, 1972); Smoke, *War: Controlling Escalation;* Phil Williams, *Crisis Management: Confrontation and Diplomacy in the Nuclear Age* (New York: Wiley, 1972); and Richard Ned Lebow, *Between Peace and War: The Nature of International Crisis* (Baltimore: Johns Hopkins University Press, 1981). A worthy essay is Richard Ned Lebow, "Practical Ways to Avoid Superpower Crises," *Bulletin of the Atomic Scientists* 41, no. 1(January 1985): 22–28.

28. Charles F. Hermann, ed., *International Crises: Insights from Behavioral Research* (New York: Free Press, 1972), p. 320. For a more recent social-scientific assault on crisis phenomena, see Michael Brecher and Jonathan Wilkenfeld, "Crises in World Politics," *World Politics* 34, no. 3(April 1982): 380–417.

29. A popular and reliable book that provided a graphic firsthand record of the achievement was Robert F. Kennedy, *13 Days: The Cuban Missile Crisis* (London: Pan, 1969; first pub. 1968). Graham Allison's vigorous and theoretically rich study, *Essence of Decision: Explaining the Cuban Missile Crisis* (Boston: Little, Brown, 1971), provides an essential scholarly view of the crisis, set within the framework of a much more general concern to interrogate public policy decisions with different sets of questions.

30. Lebow is suitably skeptical of the potential benefits of crisis management techniques. See his conclusions in *Between Peace and War*, p. 335.

31. Robert Osgood and Robert Tucker, *Force, Order and Justice* (Baltimore: Johns Hopkins University Press, 1967), pp. 342–43.

32. See Alexander George, David K. Hall, and William E. Simons, *The Limits of Coercive Diplomacy: Laos, Cuba, Vietnam* (Boston: Little, Brown, 1971).

33. However, provision and discussion of a particular metaphorical ladder of escalation (as in Kahn, *On Escalation*) will mislead those who are easily misled. Kahn recognized this problem, although—with justice—he argued that theorists should not desist from developing interesting and occasionally sophisticated ideas just because some officials will fail to understand them properly.

34. This proposition permeates Robert Jervis, *The Illogic of American Nuclear Strategy* (Ithaca, N.Y.: Cornell University Press, 1984).

35. This is held to be true only because the incentive to understand will be so high. I find this assertion grossly optimistic. Aside from the blinkering effect of cultural stereotype thinking, the plain physical facts of the "fog of battle" must impede timely receipt, let alone analysis, of information concerning military activity. Moreover, in the event of nuclear conflict, information-gathering assets for attack and damage assessment might be early victims of the assault.

36. See John D. Steinbruner and Leon V. Sigal, eds., *Alliance Security: NATO and the No-First-Use Question* (Washington, D.C.: Brookings, 1983); David N. Schwartz, *NATO's Nuclear Dilemmas* (Washington, D.C.: Brookings, 1983); and Paul Buteux, *Strategy, Doctrine, and the Politics of the Alliance: Theatre Nuclear Force Modernization in NATO* (Boulder, Colo.: Westview Press, 1983).

37. It is worth noting that considerable ambiguity exists regarding the character of the deterrent function of NATO's battlefield and longer range theater-nuclear forces. On the one hand, there is the idea that nuclear use should restore deterrence primarily through its value as a signal of political determination and because of the fear it should induce that military events might be sliding out of control. On the other hand, there is the view that nuclear use should restore deterrence by inflicting such military damage that the battlefield situation would be rectified thereby—meaning that the burden of further escalation should be placed on Soviet shoulders.

38. Kenneth Hunt, *The Alliance and Europe: Part II. Defence with Fewer Men*, Adelphi Papers No. 98 (London: IISS, Summer 1973), p. 20, passim.

39. For a penetrating analysis, see Nathan Leites, *Soviet Style in War* (New York: Crane, Russak, 1982).

40. Readers friendly toward this possibility should consider carefully the arguments in Benjamin S. Lambeth, "On Thresholds in Soviet Military Thought," *Washington Quarterly* 7, no. 2(Spring 1984): 69–76. Maximum discouragement may be located in "Ogarkov on Implications of Military Technology," *Survival* 26, no. 4(July/August 1984): 187–88. For sharply contrasting analyses of Soviet willingness to withhold nuclear weapons in a theater war, see Phillip A. Petersen and John G. Hines, "The Conventional Offensive in Soviet Theater Strategy," *Orbis* 27, no. 3(Fall 1983): 695–739; and Ilana Kass and Michael J. Deane, "The Role of Nuclear Weapons in the Modern Theater Battlefield: The Current Soviet View," *Comparative Strategy* 4, no. 3(1984): 193–213.

41. The historical record of prediction on the character and duration of future war is sufficiently replete with error on a massive scale that the defense analyst today is well advised to be very careful in his prognostication. On the subject of why defense planners in peacetime often go astray, and on the implications for policy, see Colin S. Gray, *Protracted War: The Lessons of History* (Fairfax, Va.: National Institute for Public Policy, 1984). For a classic case of generally accurate prediction that was ignored, see Michael Howard's analysis of the writings of Ivan Bloch (1836–1902), "Men Against Fire: Expectations of War in 1914," *International Security* 9, no. 1(Summer 1984): 41–57.

42. Jack L. Snyder, *The Soviet Strategic Culture: Implications for Limited Nuclear Operations*, R-2154-AF (Santa Monica, Calif.: RAND Corporation, September 1977), pp. 39–40.

43. Studies by Joseph Douglass over the past decade have made this central point very persuasively. See Joseph D. Douglass, Jr.: "Strategic Planning and Nuclear Insecurity," *Orbis* 27, no. 3(Fall 1983): 667–94; *Soviet Military Strategy in Europe* (New York: Pergamon, 1980); and *The Soviet Theater Nuclear Offensive*, Studies in Communist Affairs, Vol. 1 (Washington, D.C.: USGPO, 1976). Also see Joseph D. Douglass, Jr., and Amoretta M. Hoeber, *Soviet Strategy for Nuclear War* (Stanford, Calif.: Hoover Institution Press, 1979). In addition, see John Erickson: "Soviet Theater-Warfare Capability: Doctrines, Deployments, and Capabilities," in Lawrence L. Whetten, ed., *The Future of Soviet Military Power* (New York: Crane, Russak, 1976), pp. 117–56; and "The Soviet Military System: Doctrine, Technology and 'Style'," in John Erickson and E. J. Feuchtwanger, eds., *Soviet Military Power and Performance* (Hamden, Conn.: Archon, 1979). A study that emphasizes the importance attached to achieving military objectives as rapidly as possible is Peter H. Vigor, *Soviet Blitzkrieg Theory* (New York: St. Martin's, 1983).

44. See Kahn, *On Escalation*, pp. 37–41.

45. Initial nuclear use in Europe and execution of one or more sub-SIOP-level limited nuclear options are widely viewed in this light—as shocks to "restore deterrence." European critics of President Reagan's SDI have expressed anxiety that even a modest scale of nationwide ballistic missile defense deployment by the Soviet Union would deny NATO the "coupling" benefits of LNOs.

46. David Halberstam, *The Best and the Brightest* (New York: Random House, 1972).

47. An interesting analysis of this aspect of crisis is Lebow, *Between War and Peace*, particularly chap. 9.

48. In U.S. culture, traditionally, a stigma attaches to obvious failure in negotiations. The idea that a U.S. government might have performed well (even succeeded, in terms of protecting the national interest) by not reaching agreement remains somewhat alien. This strain to agreement in the U.S. body politic can be a severe handicap in the arms control context, for example. As several commentators have observed, the long history of the SALT II negotiations showed a fairly steady U.S. retreat from negotiating goals judged to have been sensible in 1972–73. See Paul Nitze's prepared statement in U.S. Congress, Senate, Committee on Foreign Relations, *SALT II Treaty, Hearings*, Part 1, 96th Cong., 1st sess., (Washington, D.C.: USGPO, 1979), pp. 441–42. Appropriate commentary on Mr. Carter's almost indecently rapid retreat from his ambitious and praiseworthy "comprehensive" SALT II package of March 1977 may be found in Foy D. Kohler, *How Not to Negotiate with the Russians* (Washington, D.C.: Advanced International Studies Institute, in association with the University of Miami, 1979), pp. 17-18. Also see Strobe Talbott, *Endgame: The Inside Story of SALT II* (New York: Harper & Row, 1979), chaps. 3, 4. There may be much to criticize in the Reagan administration's conduct of arms control business from 1981–85 (in which regard see Talbott, *Deadly Gambits*), but it remains far from self-evident that any ambitious arms control agreements of genuine value to Western security were negotiable by the United States in the early 1980s. For excellent reasons, the Reagan administration would not sign on for pseudo arms control after SALT I and SALT II, and pseudo arms control was the only product offered by the Soviet Union. Critics of President Reagan too often neglect the point that arms control worthy of the name simply was not available.

49. See Roger Fisher, *International Conflict for Beginners* (New York: Harper Colophon, 1970; first pub. 1969), chap. 2; and his more recent work (with William L. Ury), *Getting to Yes* (Boston: Houghton Mifflin, 1981). Similar in good intention and approach is William L. Ury, *Beyond the Hotline: How Crisis Control Can Prevent Nuclear War* (Boston: Houghton Mifflin, 1985).

50. In retrospect, President Kennedy's crisis management success in October 1962 looks somewhat less impressive than it did at the time. The United States had the local and strategic military power to insist on withdrawal of the missiles. Nikita Khrushchev knew that he had no choice other than to back away. This is not to deny that there was some danger of the military dynamics of the crisis escaping political control, but it *is* to deny that there was any substantial risk of the Soviet Union *choosing* to fight.

51. See Bell, *The Conventions of Crisis*; "Crisis Diplomacy," particularly pp. 173-82.

52. The point is often lost that foreign policy and diplomacy are not synonymous. Diplomacy is but one among many instruments of foreign policy. The State Department is in charge of diplomacy, but it does not have under its direct control the full range of foreign policy instruments.

53. As is well known, Barbara Tuchman's book, *The Guns of August— August 1914* (London: Constable, 1962), had made a deep impression on President

Kennedy, who was determined that, by way of contrast to what occurred in the July crisis of 1914, he would not permit himself to become the prisoner of any preplanned logic of military events.

54.   See Ole R. Holsti, "The 1914 Case," *American Political Science Review* no. 2(June 1965): 365-78. Also see Paul Kennedy, ed., *The War Plans of the Great Powers, 1880-1914* (London: Allen and Unwin, 1979); L. C. F. Turner, *Origins of the First World War* (London: Arnold, 1970); and H. W. Koch, ed., *The Origins of the First World War: Great Power Rivalry and German War Aims*, 2d ed. (London: Macmillan, 1984).

55.   Holsti, *Crisis, Escalation, War*, pp. 222-25.

56.   It was believed by most competent military professionals at the time that any unilateral slowing in the pace of execution of mobilization would invite defeat. See L. C. F. Turner, "The Significance of the Schlieffen Plan," in Paul M. Kennedy, ed., *The War Plans of the Great Powers, 1880-1914*, pp. 252–68. Also see Jack Snyder, *The Ideology of the Offensive: Military Decision Making and the Disasters of 1914* (Ithaca, N.Y.: Cornell University Press, 1984).

57.   Because of its known preference for blitzkrieg-type campaigning, the Soviet Union might be accorded the 24 or 48 hours that it needs to out-mobilize NATO and thereby prepare the way for a short-war victory, if NATO capitals should seek to "cool the crisis" beyond the point when the Soviet Union has decided to fight. A useful analysis is in Richard K. Betts, "Surprise Attack: NATO's Political Vulnerability," *International Security* 5, no. 4(Spring 1981): 117-49.

58.   As Herman Kahn has written:
If one nation uses the threat of escalation to coerce an opponent, the escalation will be more effective in exerting pressure if it does not depend too explicitly and publicly on "escalation theory." (Indeed, it probably is a serious error to look as if one has read a book.)
"On Establishing a Context for Debate," in Frank E. Armbruster et al., *Can We Win in Vietnam? The American Dilemma* (London: Pall Mall, 1968), p. 51.

59.   Schelling, *Arms and Influence*, p. 124.

60.   For an excellent theoretical dissection of the phenomenon of crisis, see Charles A. McClelland, "The Acute International Crisis," in Klaus Knorr and Sydney Verba, eds., *The International System: Theoretical Essays* (Princeton, N.J.: Princeton University Press, 1961), pp. 182-204.

61.   See Thomas C. Schelling: *The Strategy of Conflict* (Cambridge, Mass.: Harvard University Press, 1960), chap. 8; and *Arms and Influence*, chap. 3.

62.   Even in the cases discussed in George, Hall, and Simons, *The Limits of Coercive Diplomacy*, the U.S. intent was fundamentally, or strategically, defensive. "Coercive diplomacy" was a muscular approach to compel an adversary to desist from inimical activity or to disgorge gains already made. In Soviet terms, of course, active U.S. resistance to regional imperialism (masquerading as a war of national liberation, as in Vietnam) is, by definition, an example of the waging of unjust, aggressive war. See General-Major A. S. Milovidov and Colonel V. G. Kozlov, *The Philosophical Heritage of V. I. Lenin and Problems of Contemporary War (A Soviet View)*, Soviet Military Thought Series of the U.S. Air Force, No. 5 (Washington,

D.C.: USGPO, 1975; Moscow, 1972), chap. 2; and General-Major S. N. Kozlov, ed., *The Officer's Handbook (A Soviet View),* Soviet Military Thought Series of the U.S. Air Force, No. 13 (Washington, D.C.: USGPO, 1977; Moscow, 1971).

63. Kozlov, *The Officer's Handbook,* p. 65.

64. See Harriet F. Scott and William F. Scott, *The Armed Forces of the U.S.S.R.* (Boulder, Colo.: Westview Press, 1979), particularly pp. 99-102. Also of interest is Richard Pipes's judgment that the organization and procedures of the Soviet High Command are such that "it taxes the imagination how, under these circumstances, there could develop in the Soviet Union two distinct military doctrines." "Militarism and the Soviet State," *Daedalus* 109, no. 4(Fall 1980): 12, n. 21.

65. Although the USSR has a tradition of civilian supremacy at least as strong as that in the United States, for reasons of history and political prudence (and KGB practice), the dividing line between soldier and civilian in the USSR is considerably blurred (not least because of Party supervision of all aspects of military activity).

66. Kozlov, *The Officer's Handbook,* p. vii.

67. See the informative and persuasive discussion in Benjamin S. Lambeth, *Selective Nuclear Options in American and Soviet Strategic Policy,* R-2034-DDRE (Santa Monica, Calif.: RAND Corporation, December 1976). Also see Thomas W. Wolfe, *The SALT Experience* (Cambridge, Mass.: Ballinger, 1979), pp. 162-66.

68. See the excellent and appropriately tentative discussion in Douglass, *Soviet Military Strategy in Europe,* pp. 187-93.

69. Phil Williams offers the sensible thought that "merely because there is no formal Soviet recognition of crisis management as a distinct type of behavior does not necessarily mean that the Soviet leaders have not developed procedures and techniques designed to contain within tolerable limits their confrontations with the opposing superpower." *Crisis Management,* p. 10. However, there is a problem of evidence, beyond the inferences that may be drawn concerning Soviet motives behind policy action and inaction.

70. There is no question that since the mid-1970s, Soviet political leaders have been describing nuclear war in apocalyptic terms, in the long tradition of Western official pronouncements. What this may mean is analyzed in Dan L. Strode and Rebecca V. Strode, "Diplomacy and Defense in Soviet National Security Policy," *International Security* 8, no. 2(Fall 1983): 91-116. We are acutely short of authoritative evidence concerning Soviet views on the prospects for survival through and recovery from nuclear catastrophe. I believe that the Soviet leaders hope and plan for the best but fear the worst. Of more significance is the apparent fact, on the evidence of activity observed, that the Soviet Union is ideologically and culturally incapable of following a policy that would amount to a resignation to a condition of near-total state and societal vulnerability.

71. The "by and large" qualification intrudes in the text because there has been a very modest level of discussion in the Soviet military literature of strategic targeting designed to attack the political will, or morale, of an enemy. See Douglass and Hoeber, *Soviet Strategy for Nuclear War,* pp. 17-18. However, it is not totally clear from the Soviet texts that terror strikes for assault on morale either are what the Soviet authors had in mind or have met with official Soviet approval.

72. John Erickson, "The Soviet View of Nuclear War," Transcript of broadcast on BBC Radio 3, June 19, 1980, p. 8.

73. Ibid., p. 10

74. An interesting Soviet commentary by a highly qualified author is Henry Trofimenko, *Changing Attitudes Towards Deterrence*, ACIS Working Paper No. 25 (Los Angeles: UCLA, Center for International and Strategic Affairs, July 1980). Notwithstanding the disinformation this publication provides in large measure, the author may have revealed more than he intended in places.

75. Nor does even his personal historical experience. See the career details of members of the Soviet High Command provided in Scott and Scott, *The Armed Forces of the U.S.S.R.*, pp. 120–26. Senior civilian and military leaders in the United States appear to be amateurs by comparison. This is not to suggest, of course, that long experience is the only virtue; nonetheless, the Soviet High Command is distinguished by both the quality and quantity of the experience of its members.

76. It is fashionable today to discern a growing Soviet interest in all-conventional attack options, but the evidence available to Western analysts on the subject is ambiguous, at best. Flat denial of Soviet anticipation even of a conventional phase in a war in Europe is argued strongly in Kass and Deane, "The Role of Nuclear Weapons in the Modern Theater Battlefield." Kass and Deane may be wrong, but the evidence they present is certainly no less impressive than that advanced for the contrary view.

77. For a view that is skeptical of the judgment in the text, see Robert L. Arnett, "Soviet Attitudes Towards Nuclear War: Do They Really Think They Can Win?" *Journal of Strategic Studies* 2, no. 2(September 1979): 172-91. A useful balanced discussion is David Holloway, "Military Power and Political Purpose in Soviet Policy," *Daedalus* 109, no. 4(Fall 1980), particularly pp. 18-21. Also helpful is Vigor, *Soviet Blitzkrieg Theory*, particularly chaps. 4, 5.

78. Western commentators should never forget that Soviet military professionals believe that war, in all its aspects, lends itself to "scientific" study. Soviet texts on "military science" should be taken at face value as reflecting the genuine Soviet approach to the subject. See Kozlov, *The Officer's Handbook*, pp. 47-61; Milovidov and Kozlov, *The Philosophical Heritage of V. I. Lenin and Problems of Contemporary War*, chap. 4; General-Lieutenant G. T. Zavizion and Lt. Col. Yu. Kirshin, "Soviet Military Science: Its Social Role and Functions," in *Selected Soviet Military Writings, 1970-1975 (A Soviet View)*, Soviet Military Thought Series of the U.S. Air Force, No. 11 (Washington, D.C.: USGPO, 1977), pp. 76-85. Zavizion and Kirshin claim that "military science is one of the important factors for attaining victory in war." As the U.S. editor of this collection of important articles, William F. Scott, observes: "In Soviet military writings, nothing less than 'victory' ever is considered" (p. 64).

79. "Who controls the rimland rules Eurasia; who rules Eurasia controls the destinies of the world." Nicholas J. Spykman, *The Geography of the Peace* (New York: Harcourt, Brace, 1944), p. 43.

80. The French *contrôle*, which translates as a somewhat distant general supervision, is close to the usual meaning ascribed to a "Finlandized" Western Europe. It is consistent with Soviet hegemony.

81. Until very recently, Soviet theater-operational strike assets have been deployed overwhelmingly on Soviet rather than Eastern European soil. Forward deployment of nuclear missile systems has been advertised as a timely and suitable response to NATO's deployment of GLCM and Pershing II missiles. However, it is just possible that Soviet forward deployment may be intended to encourage the United States to preserve the Soviet homeland as a sanctuary in the event of a war in Europe.

82. Henry Kissinger, "The Future of NATO," "Washington Quarterly 2, no. 4(Autumn 1979): 7.

83. The U.S. defense community has been outstandingly lax in addressing problems relevant to issues of military transition—from theater-conventional to theater-nuclear operations and from theater to central war. Notwithstanding the difficulty of the subject matter, the absence of well-conducted studies of transition matters is as notable as it may prove fatal one day.

84. Unclassified Western commentary on this subject is rare. For lonely examples of such commentary, see Douglass and Hoeber, Soviet Strategy for Nuclear War, chap. 6; and Benjamin S. Lambeth and Kevin N. Lewis, "Economic Targeting in Nuclear War: U.S. and Soviet Approaches," Orbis 27, no. 1(Spring 1983): 127-49.

85. For example, see Trofimenko, Changing Attitudes Towards Deterrence, particularly pp. 21-26. Also useful is Jonathan S. Lockwood, The Soviet View of U.S. Strategic Doctrine: Implications for Decision Making (New Brunswick, N.J.: Transaction, 1983), parts III, IV.

86. Sir Francis Bacon, quoted in Bernard Brodie, War and Politics (New York: Macmillan, 1974), p. 178.

87. See Michael Howard, "The British Way in Warfare: A Reappraisal," in Michael Howard, The Causes of Wars and Other Essays (London: Unwin, 1983), pp. 189-207. Also pertinent is Howard's masterly short study, The Continental Commitment: The Dilemma of British Defence Policy in the Era of the Two World Wars (London: Temple Smith, 1972).

88. For some negative considerations, however, see Brian Bond, Liddell Hart: A Study of His Military Thought (New Brunswick, N.J.: Rutgers University Press, 1977; first pub. 1976), particularly p. 75.

89. The British have elevated "muddling through" to the level of a distinctive national approach to strategic policymaking.

90. See Stanley Hoffmann, Gulliver's Troubles: Or the Setting of American Foreign Policy (New York: McGraw-Hill, 1968), chap. 5.

91. Very much to the point is Steve F. Kime, "The Soviet View of War," in Graham D. Vernon, ed., Soviet Perceptions of War and Peace (Washington, D.C.: National Defense University Press, 1981), pp. 51–65.

92. This judgment clearly does not apply to the Khrushchev period.

93. E. Velikhov and A. Kokoshin, "Iaderno oruzhie i dilenny mezhdunarodnoi bezopasnosti" ["Nuclear Weapons and the Dilemmas of International Security"], MEMO no. 4(April 1985):36.

CHAPTER 7

Arms Competition and Arms Control

THE CRISIS OF ARMS CONTROL

For the better part of twenty years, arms control considerations have been in or close to the forefront of U.S. policy deliberations over research and development on and acquisition of strategic nuclear weapons.[1] Indeed, younger civilian officials and military officers have not known, firsthand, a strategic policymaking process that did not have to accommodate "the SALT/START factor." For sixteen years, SALT/START has either been underway or temporarily "on hold." The purpose of this chapter is to examine the nature of the arms competition that supposedly was the object of attention of the arms control negotiating endeavor and the character of the arms control process.

Because of its ongoing character since November 1969, because of the political dynamics that have driven it forward, and because of its longevity even when preconditions for negotiating success are very plainly absent, it is not unjust to observe that there has been a "mad momentum" to the SALT process.[2] That pejorative characterization is not intended to imply, ipso facto, that national or international security necessarily has been harmed by the arms control process; rather, it is to imply that the process has been endorsed and continued even as expectations of substantively worthwhile outcomes have withered.[3] Indeed, it is no exaggeration to argue that, somewhat strangely, many people discern merit in the SALT/START process even though they deplore, or at least are not impressed by, the direct outcomes produced by that process to date. A major reason why the debate over SALT II seemed never, or only very rarely, to rise above the level of dispute over secondary, essentially technical details was that neither "side" (to simplify) in the debate had thought through the criteria that should be applied for the assessment of the SALT II Treaty. Hence, had the debate over SALT II ratification gone its full course in 1979—to a vote on the floor of the Senate—whichever "side" won would very possibly have won for the wrong reasons.[4]

Barry Blechman, former assistant director of the U.S. Arms Control and Disarmament Agency (ACDA), offered the following judgments on the course of the SALT II debate of the late summer and fall of 1979:

> Although passage was far from certain, betting in Washington was that approval by the full Senate would be in hand by Thanksgiving. The subsequent travails of the treaty are traceable not to the surfacing of any new arguments about the agreement itself, nor to new information about the balance of strategic weapons, but to other types of events (Soviet combat brigades in Cuba; the Tehran hostage crisis; and, finally, the Soviet occupation of Afghanistan).[5]

Blechman's words again raise a basic question: "What are the right reasons for approving or disapproving an arms control agreement?" It is quite evident from the historical record that, by the late 1970s, the SALT process and agreements were markedly different from the dominant U.S. expectations of the early 1970s.[6] In and of itself, that fact was of no great consequence. However, few public officials took the time and trouble to stand back from the quest for a new agreement to ask fundamental questions of their activity. Ultimately, as a consequence of this neglect of basic, or strategic, issues—as the debate in 1979 was to reveal—neither side developed a very persuasive story to tell. What was lacking was a robust theoretical center to the debate—a common framework for the conduct of debate. Although senators and the general public could assess rival point-scoring on individual issues—for example, "heavy" missiles or promised restraint in Backfire production, basing, and operations—they had no doctrinal guide to which arguments were more, rather than less, important. In the fall of 1980, Andrew Pierre, who is certainly not hostile to arms control, wrote as follows:

> Arms control is, indeed, in crisis. There is a need to rethink its aims and reconceptualize some of its basic premises before commencing the next stage, rather than automatically moving on into SALT III (if and when SALT II is ratified).[7]

The debate over SALT II has been raised here to introduce and illustrate the thesis that the U.S. defense community has never benefited from an arms control theory worthy of the name—essentially because, to quote

Johan Holst, "We just do not have an adequate explanatory model for the Soviet-American arms race."[8]

Holst offered that pessimistic judgment more than twelve years ago. The intervening years—years of fairly intensive, if intermittent, superpower arms control interaction and even more intensive arms competition— still have not seen the presentation of "an adequate explanatory model," although several false or partial models have been identified for what they are.[9] As a consequence, this chapter presents, in an appropriately tentative manner, at least the broad outlines of a model of the Soviet-U.S. competition. The following points cannot be stressed too vigorously: if a proponent of one or another approach to arms control policy problems lacks a theory of arms race dynamics, he literally cannot know what he is about; and, if he reposes confidence in a theory of arms race dynamics that is demonstrably false, his advice on arms control would similarly be flawed.[10]

To date, the Reagan administration—to its credit—has not negotiated arms control agreements that are, more or less arguably, actually harmful to U.S. security. In 1981, the new administration was determined to reverse the approach taken by President Carter in 1977. Specifically, it decided that the United States must have its new defense program visibly in place, and gaining momentum, before reinitiation of the nuclear arms control negotiating process would be appropriate. In 1977, the Carter administration had its arms control proposals in order—though prompt Soviet rejection was to place them precipitately in disorder—long before it had determined the shape of its defense program.[11]

Neither the early Carter approach nor the Reagan approach to SALT/ START worked, if by "worked" one means the achievement of an agreement that forwards the classical goals of arms control. The Reagan administration has failed, so far, to achieve any negotiated outcome, let alone an outcome that would meet the criteria of constituting "real" arms control, essentially for three reasons.

First, arms control negotiations are not, and cannot be, conducted in a foreign policy vacuum. All of the negotiating parties have to want to achieve an agreement, and, more generally, they have to want their political relations to improve and to be seen by the world as a whole, not to mention their domestic public, as improving. Over the 1981–84 period, the Soviet Union almost certainly did not want improved political relations with the United States. In those years, through late 1983 at least, the Soviet Union was employing the arms control process as an instrument of political struggle for the attempted manipulation of Western European public opinion with respect to cruise missile and Pershing II deployments. START was hostage to progress, or lack thereof, in the negotiations on intermediate-range nuclear forces (INF). It is a general truth that the arms control process can prosper, indeed function, as a positive rather than a negative element in interstate relations only when there is a prior and continuing tacit foreign policy agreement on at least some of the terms of political engagement and on the language that will be used to describe those terms. In the light of this point, it is quite evident that START and INF could not possibly succeed.

Second, as Richard Pipes has reminded anyone willing to be attentive to historical and cultural realities:

> What really matters in dealing with Soviet diplomats is not diplomatic technique and well-prepared positions, but rather the strength with which one enters the negotiations.[12]

In the early 1980s, the Soviet Union plainly was unwilling to be much moved by U.S. weapons programs that Congress might well abort (MX) or that were scheduled to mature many years in the future (Trident II, D-5). Whether or not the U.S. government was suitably creative and flexible in its START position (and I believe that the United States changed its position so frequently that it encouraged the Soviet Union to anticipate a series of better offers down the road), it is probable that the procession of Soviet leaders was fundamentally unwilling to look for an agreement. An agreement in START would have undercut the principal thrust of Soviet foreign policy toward the West. Pipes's argument for negotiation from strength is unexceptionable. However, when considered in the light of the Reagan administration's actual proposals in START and INF, it is very apparent that even with his strategic-forces modernization program, the president lacked the near-term leverage to ask legitimately (in Soviet eyes) for what would amount to the restructuring of the Soviet strategic posture. Ingenious formulas for "build-down" and "double build-down" were simply irrelevant,[13] both for the political reasons cited and because they did not change the reality that the United States was seeking "unequal reductions for equal results."

Third, even if the political climate had been permissive for agreement and even if the United States had in hand the leverage accorded by, say, an actually deployed, survivably based, MX force, it would have been extremely unlikely that the Soviet Union would have seen merit in President Reagan's ideas on what constituted real arms control.[14] Soviet leaders have always seen more merit in large forces than in small forces and have never evinced what appeared to be a genuine interest in a dramatic scale of nuclear force reductions. Soviet strategic style embraces the value of mass.[15]

It must be emphasized that the U.S. defense and arms control community should be interested in forwarding the objectives of arms control rather than particular processes of arms control negotiation, except insofar as those processes are believed to be likely to have instrumental value. Albeit on a modest scale, arms control as a set of widely accepted broad objectives of policy has spawned a constituency and even a vested interest in its support. As with all vested interests and constituencies, program maintenance can come to dominate considerations of probable policy outcomes.[16] The maximizing of arms control business has healthy short-term bureaucratic, political, and even financial implications for the arms control community.[17] From the vantage point of the mid-1980s, it is instructive to be told, on good authority:

> Even in its early days, the experience of the Carter Administration demonstrated conclusively that neither the American political system nor the contemporary condition of relations among nations is capable of sustaining arms negotiations on a broad front.[18]

In short, what are needed are "tangible accomplishments."[19] Unfortunately the arms control paradox has done its worst; in other words, those areas most in need of negotiated attention have proved, unsurprisingly, to be the most difficult.[20] It is important to lay out very explicitly the causes of the crisis of arms control.

Although there is very general agreement on the identity of the broad objectives of arms control—to reduce the risk of war, to reduce the damage that might be suffered should war occur, and to reduce the burdens of peacetime defense preparation—there are no authorities on the subject of rendering those objectives operationally effective in U.S. defense policy. To be specific, there is no generally accepted theory of the causes of war. So, which postures and doctrines reduce the risk of war, and which do not? Furthermore, in good part because of its heavy focus on the problems of prewar deterrence, the U.S. defense community has never developed a mature theory of intrawar deterrence that could withstand the probable traffic of Soviet General Staff-authored targeting plans.[21] Although it is relatively easy to save money on defense, there is much to recommend the argument that because of the geopolitics of the Western Alliance, it is particularly foolish to cut costs close to the margin of sufficiency in the strategic-forces region. The strategic-force posture places only a modest burden on the defense budget,[22] in comparison to manpower-intensive general-purpose forces, and it encompasses that high end of the technology competition spectrum wherein Soviet officials know that they are at a major and almost certainly an enduring disadvantage.

It would be difficult to argue with Leslie Gelb's assertion:

> Arms control has essentially failed. Three decades of U.S.-Soviet negotiations to limit arms competition have done little more than to codify the arms race.[23]

The fact remains, however, that since the United States has yet to decide just what it is about in arms control negotiations, it is perhaps too harsh to conclude that "arms control has essentially failed." Failed to accomplish what? There can be no doubt that the U.S. arms control community, in reviewing the 1970s and early 1980s, must judge that its performance was unsatisfactory.[24] However, given the realities of a Soviet strategic culture that has no known concept of "sufficiency" and a U.S. political system both profoundly suspicious of the Soviet Union and insecurely attached to the idea that "rough parity" is good enough, it is not obvious that arms control policy failed in the 1970s and early 1980s.

Following directly from the foregoing line of argument, a very important aspect of the current crisis of arms control is profound uncertainty over the proper operational objectives of arms control. How high should the criteria be set for policy success or failure? Burt has noted: "For the most part, SALT agreements have tended to ratify, rather than restrain, the expansion of Soviet forces"[25]—but could they do anything else? If the arms control process can only reflect political and military reality, is it fair or enlightening to criticize its U.S. part-authors for failing to accomplish the impossible?

It is an open question whether negotiated arms control agreements are politically feasible for a U.S. government, given both the kind of foreign policy pursued by the Soviet Union under the banner of "peaceful coexistence" and what is beginning to be understood about the internal dynamics of the Soviet weapon procurement process.

If the charge can be sustained that, in some important respects, an ongoing or imminent arms control process contributes to the astrategic skewing of Western defense programs away from the path of policy rationality and toward the psychological disarmament of noteworthy political constituencies in the West, then it may be that the West cannot afford arms control. Richard Burt has argued:

> SALT, during the last decade, did not become a forum for American and Soviet doctrinal convergence. In fact, it tended to mask the different directions in which the two sides were moving.[26]

As phrased, this judgment is misleading. SALT masked nothing, though one may argue that the existence of a SALT process encouraged U.S. officials and commentators to believe, falsely, that the Soviet Union had "signed up" for some rough facsimile of standard Western theories of strategic stability.[27] In retrospect, it is quite evident that such delusions of SALT as there may have been were U.S. self-delusions. A United States respectful of Soviet proclivities to behave in accordance with Soviet strategic culture should not have been deluded.

If it was true that after nearly seven years of very hard and diverting labor, the best that the SALT II negotiators could do was to achieve an agreement that comprised essentially a photograph of the contemporary strategic balance[28]—which permitted both sides to proceed with force modernization unhindered in important ways—then the SALT process, and prospectively even the START process, may be vulnerable to the charge of military triviality or irrelevance. It has been precisely President Reagan's insistence that the Soviet Union must effect "drastic cutbacks in the most modern, potent Soviet weapon already deployed . . . [while] no comparable reductions should be considered in existing American forces"[29] that has helped provoke the charge of a lack of realism, or even seriousness, in U.S. policy. If President Reagan is to be condemned for proposing arms reductions that are intended, at least, to meet U.S. criteria of stability, what alternatives does he have? Should he propose an arms control regime that is more equitable to the Soviet Union in required reductions of deployed forces but that affronts stability criteria in its consequences? There is a dilemma: to be "realistic" is to suggest the trivial, while to suggest constraints that should assist stability is to be "unrealistic."

Ultimately, the protracted crisis of arms control, if that is the correct description, has its roots in the insufficiency of the base of common interests as perceived by Soviet and U.S. governments. As observed earlier, the arms control process cannot possibly prosper in the absence of a framework of foreign policy agreement on rules of political engagement over a wide range of policy areas. It should be recalled that the SALT I agreements of 1972 were an integral part of a process of political détente; they were never intended to stand alone without a supportive foreign policy environment. What has happened since 1972 is that the supportive foreign policy environment has disappeared, leaving the arms control process essentially "twisting in the wind."

Candidate villains in the crisis of arms control are in plentiful supply. In addition to the points already made here, cases can be made for the harmful impacts of inadequate momentum in U.S. strategic weapon modernization— thereby diminishing Soviet incentives to reduce the capabilities of most concern to the United States; the evident steadiness of the Soviet commitment to change favorably the balance of military power; the pace and detailed character of technological change; the Soviet cultural attachment to a level of secrecy, secretiveness, and willingness to seek competitive advantage beyond the bounds permitted by treaties; and finally, the absence of even an approximately common understanding of what comprises stable deterrence. (It is all too likely that Soviet comprehension of the meaning of stability is not merely different from the U.S. comprehension but is actually incompatible with it.)

Although it has become commonplace to argue that there is a crisis of arms control, I am not convinced that, in general, the crisis is correctly characterized. There is a crisis—if by that one means that negotiated agreements with strategic merit would seem to be beyond achievement.

Also, there is a crisis if one refers to the fact that on the basis of careful analysis, many people have come to wonder whether, judged on the official record, arms control really is or ever can be as important as successive U.S. adminstrations, including the present one, have asserted. It is difficult to avoid the judgment that arms control debate tends to direct attention to matters of only secondary significance to national security. For example, the real defense debate of 1979 should not have been over the merits of SALT II; rather, it should have been over the adequacy of Western defense programs.[30] Also, an arms control process such as SALT or START encourages the paying of attention to "a *symbolic* balance based on static hardware counts," not to "an *operational* balance reflecting the real capabilities of the two sides to engage in sustained nuclear conflict."[31]

This book, though certainly sympathetic to the argument that the United States could and should improve the quality of its negotiating performance in the future, is rather more sympathetic to the proposition that the poverty of tangible accomplishments in arms control to date must largely be laid, first, at the doors of an inadequate momentum in Western defense programs and a principal adversary that is incapable, for strategic-cultural reasons, of cooperating in any arms control endeavor that exceeds in its mandate the registration of facts.

Unfortunately, many people appear to have difficulty understanding that the crisis of arms control is really only a crisis of *formally negotiated* arms control. A poor or only marginally useful START agreement would not be a triumph for arms control. Arms control should be about reducing the risks of war, reducing the damage that might be suffered should war occur, and possibly reducing the burden of peacetime defense preparation. Those goals should be forwarded through a well-designed defense policy. Moreover, if they can be forwarded through formal interstate negotiations, it will only be because of the well-designed defense policy that U.S. negotiators have as the "hand" with which they can play.

UNDERSTANDING THE ARMS RACE: TOWARD A NEW MODEL

In company with Albert Wohlstetter,[32] I believe that employment of the term *arms race* to characterize the Soviet-U.S. military relationship misleads as much as it informs. However, this book is not about scoring rather easy debating points on the subject of "when is an arms race an arms race." It is a fact that , with some justification, the world at large believes that there is a nuclear arms race. In macroscopic terms, at least, this belief is not unreasonable:

- The United States and the Soviet Union have identified each other as principal adversaries.

- Each country is almost desperately attentive to the course *and detail* of the arms programs of the other.

- Each country attends carefully to its relative position on the multilevel military balance.

However, these three facts do not qualify the Soviet-U.S. military relationship as an arms race. Unfortunately, many of the pejorative connotations of arms *race* are all too lightly attached to Soviet-U.S. military rivalry, notwithstanding the absence of supporting evidence.[33] Arms races tend to be associated, popularly, with the risk of war.[34] Somewhat paradoxically, they also tend to be viewed as an expensive exercise in futility. (A particularly mindless mechanistic model of arms race dynamics still attracts a great many commentators.)

Insofar as history offers any general wisdom on the subject, it is to the unhelpful effect that some wars have been preceded by arms races and some have not.[35] A fundamental theoretical problem that awaits scholarly attention pertains to the identification of cases. States that anticipate the possibility of fighting one another naturally and responsibly seek to achieve or maintain a favorable relationship of military power. Since political rivalry very often is expressed, in part, in military rivalry, and since wars tend not to occur between states that had not considered each other prospective enemies until the eleventh hour of peacetime, a historical sequence of arms race and war is only to be expected. Notwithstanding the empirical knowledge claimed and the theoretical ingenuity displayed, the possibility remains that arms races are more the invention of polemical writers and social scientists in search of cross-historical general theory than they are genuinely identifiable event sequences that do, or may, have dynamics different from peacetime defense preparation as usual.

Heretical though the thought appears to be, it is worth considering the proposition that arms race theory has made so little progress largely because the concept of an arms race is mainly metaphor. The confusion of metaphor and reality may have encouraged Western arms controllers to seek what Robin Ranger termed "technical" as opposed to "political" arms control.[36] Because arms controllers could *conceive* of an arms race system distinct, to an important degree, from the framework of political relations, they came to believe that that system could be controlled in useful ways with only the most minimal reference to the political environment. Support for this claim has been provided by Barry Blechman:

> The American theory of arms control would isolate such negotiations [SALT] from politics. In theoretical terms, arms limitation talks should

be viewed as technical exercises, directed at constraining the risks which weapons themselves add to existing political conflict. As those espousing arms control made no pretense of solving political conflicts through the negotiations they proposed, they saw no relationship (other than that artificially instilled by politicians) between progress or lack of progress in settling underlying sources of conflict and progress or lack of progress in arms negotiations.[37]

Blechman proceeded to note: "In practice, however, the United States has closely linked movement in arms control with broader political accommodations with the Soviet Union." Nonetheless, the practice of "linkage" admitted, the fact remains that the political roots of competitive arms behavior continue either to escape the attention of or simply to be ignored by U.S. policymakers. Where many theorists of arms races and many policy proponents masquerading as arms race theorists have erred has been in focusing far too heavily on the putative interactive traffic in the alleged arms race system.[38] Indeed, the very concept of a largely autonomous arms race system encourages a quest for the military dynamics of military interaction. Scholars of Soviet-U.S. relations tend to be ignorant of the precise historical detail of the process of genesis of a weapon system in the United States and profoundly (and by and large excusably) ignorant of Soviet program details. This is a subject in which broad-brush characterization, deduced from first principles, can lead one astray all too easily.[39]

Consider the likely impact of the following "first principles" on one's understanding of the dynamics of arms competition and the prospects for negotiated restraint:

- The defense programs of each side are, and can be, greatly influenced by perceptions of the other side's programs—actual, anticipated, and possible.

- Both sides would like to reduce the burden of resource allocation for defense.

- The larger and more dynamic the defense programs of the two sides, the greater the influence over policy of defense-minded, hard-line officials.

- Both sides would like to be able to negotiate a plateau in weaponry, or at least to be able to set some "cap on the arms race," so that strategic predictability is enhanced—permitting both governments to deny requests for programs that plainly would provide "excessive" capability.

The foregoing short list encapsulates much of the theoretical, first-principle baggage with which the U.S. government conducted SALT and its end of the arms competition through much of the 1970s.[40] Each of the four principles was true *for the United States.* None of the four principles was true, or contained enough truth to be useful as a guide for policy, vis-à-vis the Soviet Union. It is difficult to improve on the words of Sun Tzu:

> Know the enemy and know yourself; in a hundred battles you will never be in peril.

> When you are ignorant of the enemy but know yourself, your chances of winning or losing are equal.

> If ignorant both of your enemy and of yourself, you are certain in every battle to be in peril.[41]

This book suggests that, to date, U.S. policymakers have not made adequate efforts to know the enemy and that even the level of U.S. self-knowledge has left much to be desired. The arms race metaphor, aside from its unhelpful pejorative aspects, encourages scholars and officials to consider Soviet-U.S. military relations apart from their local strategic-cultural soil. Although this discussion is cast in terms critical of past U.S. nuclear weapons and arms control policies, it should not be supposed that all, or even most, of the criticism of those policies that has been voiced in recent years is any better grounded in strategic-cultural realities than the policies assailed. One should not leap, with fashion, from a simpleminded theory of detailed interstate action-reaction to a scarcely less simpleminded theory of autonomous activity (or *eigendynamik*). In addition, however, one should not leap too precipitously from the erstwhile belief that the Soviet Union was in the process of converging upon the U.S. theory of strategic stability (through the maintenance of *mutual* assured destruction capabilities)[42] to the conviction that the Soviet Union is on the high road heading, deliberately, for the goal of strategic superiority or major military advantage.[43] All sides of the U.S. nuclear weapons policy debate are prone to project very American perspectives and concepts on an alien, though not unfathomable, Soviet strategic culture.

Several questions underlie the following analysis of the Soviet-U.S. race: Is there a sufficient basis of common interest for an arms control process to be able to achieve outcomes deemed at least minimally useful by the two sides? Even if a sufficient basis of common interest can be identified, what, and how strong, are the domestic political forces in the two superpowers likely to interdict the arms control process in a negative way? Finally, is it plausible to suggest that the future of arms control is likely to be as unimpressive, or short of "tangible accomplishments," as its past because of the very character of the Soviet Union? (In other words, to control the arms race do we need, first, to see a major change in the nature of the Soviet polity?[44])

What drives Soviet-U.S. military rivalry? The answer, at the macro level, is an antagonism that is partly geopolitical, partly ideological; at the micro level, Soviet defense programs are driven very substantially by their own inertia and by a distinctively Soviet brand of bureaucratic politics.[45] Each country runs (or jogs) in the so-called arms race in a fashion to be expected given its very different political system.

Arms race model builders tend to err because, by and large, they have not recognized the critical importance of the "level of analysis" problem. As a result, apparently strong and certainly superficially plausible cases can be made both for the proposition that the superpowers may be likened to two swordsmen, thrusting and parrying, and for the proposition that there is so high a degree of autonomy in the arms programs of each side that the concept of an arms race is really very misleading. There is both value and error in the major rival schools of arms race analysis. Therefore, rather than indulging in a protracted, eventually negative, exercise in critical review, I offer, instead, the outline of a new model for the understanding of the arms competition. Perhaps the most difficult idea to communicate—though it is commonplace to pay lip service to it—is that the two superpowers are genuinely different in their characteristic arms race behavior. Jonathan Steinberg, for example, has suggested:

> An arms race is, after all, an immense social, political, legal, and economic process. Its influences penetrate every corner of the societies involved, and its attendant manifestations are simply too complex to fit the standard categories of historical analysis. Even if the subject of study is only one of the participants in such a race, as is the case here [Imperial Germany], the number of elements in that nation's social, cultural, economic, and religious traditions which significantly affect the course of the arms race is very large.[46]

Thus, arms race activity cannot be explained satisfactorily exclusively either in macro or in micro terms; both must be accommodated.

The Ghost of Mackinder

The greatest geopolitical thinker of the twentieth century, Sir Halford Mackinder, predicted a major clash between the Eurasian land power, "heartland power" (the USSR), and the leader of the maritime alliance (the United States).[47] Peninsular Europe clearly is the major stake in Soviet-U.S. rivalry, although that stake may be secured more efficiently through effective control of its energy supplies at source, in the Persian Gulf, than through an attempt at outright direct conquest. Although in 1904 (when he began to write on geopolitics), Mackinder held the familiar standard

British view that Imperial Russia posed a potentially deadly threat to British India, his last geopolitical article, written in 1943,[48] pointed very clearly to the major enduring problem of the postwar world. Historians are wont to observe that the diplomatic history of the near-century from the early 1870s to perhaps the late 1950s was dominated by the fact of an overly powerful Germany, in actuality or in anticipation. The new, post-1870 Prussian-dominated Germany could not be accommodated within the European balance-of-power system.[49] Since 1945, with "the German problem" remaining essentially unresolved,[50] the Soviet Union has assumed the role formerly played by Germany. As Mackinder wrote in 1943:

> All things considered, the conclusion is unavoidable that: if the Soviet Union emerges from this war as conqueror of Germany, she must rank as the greatest land power on the globe. Moreover, she will be the power in the strategically strongest defensive position. The Heartland [redefined by Mackinder to encompass "the territory of the U.S.S.R."] is the greatest natural fortress on earth. For the first time in history, it is manned by a garrison sufficient both in number and quality.[51]

The Soviet Union, like Imperial Russia, has never viewed its frontiers as settled lines of reference. In the same way that the British acquired an Empire in India by controlling the hinterland behind the extant holdings and then the hinterland to yesterday's hinterland, so the Soviet Union will not feel truly secure in Eurasia until all potential threats to the stability of the extant Soviet "holdings" are controlled from Moscow.[52] Over the past 150 years, Russian imperialism has contended, successively, with three principal adversaries: Great Britain, Germany, and now the United States.[53] Each of these adversaries has sought to prevent Russian/Soviet domination of Eurasia. Russian/Soviet history is a story of endless struggle for survival, in sharp contrast to the history of insular polities. In the Soviets' view, sources of power that they do not control pose a threat to their security.

Motives are difficult to isolate. There is some sense in the claim that Soviet leaders seek power for its own sake. But there is probably more sense in the argument that Soviet, and Russian, rulers feel perpetually insecure—lacking, as they do, any very secure "mandate from heaven" to rule—and that this insecurity drives them to seek more and more control over their external environment.[54] Soviet, and Russian, history is replete with examples of political and military activity, which—though undertaken for reasons plausibly characterizable as defensive—nonetheless was grossly insensitive to the legitimate security interests of other states and peoples. That history, however sympathetically interpreted (apart from "court" or Party-approved versions, of course), is a story dominated by fear and the achievement of territorial or hegemonic aggrandizement.

The Weakest Link of Capitalism

Revolution should not have happened in Russia. A mere handful of ruthless adventurers successfully challenged, through action, the theories of nineteenth-century socialist philosophers. Communism, a desirable condition of mankind wherein the state has withered away, should be the product of a phase of socialism that, in its turn, would be created by the contradictions of the capitalist-bourgeois society that preceded it. Imperial Russia was viewed by Karl Marx and Friedrich Engels, reasonably enough, as very barren territory for implanting the seeds of socialism. That country was the most backward of all the major industrializing powers; it therefore had the least developed bourgeoisie and class-conscious proletariat and thus offered a very unpromising prospect for socialist revolution. Lenin pragmatically revised Marxist theory, with its consistent disdain for "the idiocy of rural life,"[55] and imposed his variant of autocratic, patrimonial rule on a society long accustomed to arbitrary central government. An understanding of Russian and Soviet history, and of the many major continuities between them, is essential for U.S. comprehension of the behavior of its arms race adversary. Until very recently at least, Soviet officials have been acutely aware of their enduring technological inferiority, whereas authoritative Soviet political attitudes (which underlie the arms programs), as Richard Pipes has suggested persuasively, may be traced very directly to the attitudes that paid in village life in a peasant society.[56] The Russian peasant knows that life (the weather and local and central political and religious authority[57]) can be cruel and arbitrary. When placed in a position of authority, the village strongmen have behaved with exactly the kind of ruthless, amoral rapacity that was to be expected. The crudeness of Soviet diplomacy, the lack of concern for "the decent opinion of mankind," and the general ruthlessness should have warned the U.S. defense community that the arms programs of the Soviet Union were being directed by a political elite that could not be understood in Western terms.[58]

This unflattering portrait could be extended in great detail. On a lower scale, however, it is not totally dissimilar from the problems faced by British and French statesmen in the 1930s in their dealings with Nazi Germany. Mr. Chamberlain, who was a decent English gentleman to the tip of his umbrella, could not understand that a civilized country like Germany had been captured by a criminal riffraff, essentially by gangsters. Even the proposition was inconceivable to him. The Soviet Union is Russia captured by village bullies, with all of the essential features of the Czarist regime left functionally intact: a patrimonial state; a quasi-mystical leadership; and an assumption that the world in general is hostile. U.S. policymakers would do well to ponder the implications of these colorful thoughts of Frank Barnett:

Some American entrepreneurs, anxious to sell technology to Moscow, still profess to believe the Russians are simply Slavic-speaking graduates of the Harvard Business School. They are not. They are an ideological Mafia in control of an empire with limitless designs on the rest of us, and with the guts, guile, and finesse to carry out their ambition. Our political heritage derives from the Magna Carta, Locke and Jefferson. The Soviet legacy is from Genghis Kahn, Ivan the Terrible and Lenin. The culture gap is wider, and perhaps more dangerous, than the missile gap.[59]

Permanent Struggle

The Soviet-U.S. arms race, in its Soviet dimension at least, is founded on the very character of the Soviet state. Quite aside from the geopolitical factors that drive Soviet-U.S. rivalry, the Soviet Union exists because it is the physical embodiment of a cause. By Soviet definition, the United States is—and in terms of capabilities has to be—the principal enemy. So as not to deny their Marxist-Leninist birthright and the very legitimacy of the rule of the CPSU, Soviet leaders are obliged to engage, or plausibly appear to be engaged, in a permanent struggle against other social systems.[60] This fact is very important to recognize because, not infrequently, commentators in the West argue that the Cold War and the arms competition that has flowed from it have been the product of mutual misperception. Also, it is argued that the arms rivalry might be damped down considerably if only an appropriate measure of U.S.-NATO self-restraint, or negotiating flexibility, were exercised.

Such a view totally misreads the political reality of the Soviet-U.S. arms competition. The fact is that regardless of what the West does or does not do, the Soviet Union is committed irrevocably, by its basic character, to permanent struggle. The Soviet Union cannot become just another, though a rather unusually powerful, authoritarian state. The past and present sacrifices of the Soviet peoples have to be justified in terms of a historic mission. Not only does the Soviet Union need a foreign enemy,[61] but the ideology that legitimizes the Soviet state very conveniently identifies such an enemy. The only choice open to the United States is whether or not it will compete effectively with the Soviet Union. There can be no peaceful settlement of basic differences with the Soviet state as it is today. A process of accommodation could have no foreseeable end point of that kind. The arms race must continue either until the USSR suffers domestic revolutionary (or cumulatively dramatic evolutionary) change of a character ultimately benign to the security condition of others or until there is a military decision between East and West.[62] This is hardly pleasant news, and it is scarcely surprising that prominent U.S. politicians generally have not shared this insight with their voters. Nonetheless, this argument rests on fact, not assertion, and the relevance of this argument to this book is the long-term, inalienable nature of the problem to which it points. The roots and sustaining fuel of the Soviet-U.S. arms race do not lie so much in the separate, very complex "domestic processes" that can be explored in detail by scholars of bureaucratic politics or the military-industrial complex, as they lie in the particular political character of Soviet state power and its cultural roots and in the facts of geopolitics.

THE ACTION-REACTION HYPOTHESIS

Arms race analysis in the West continues to be afflicted by theorists seeking to identify patterns of arms program interaction. It is my contention that although each superpower has sought to be responsive in a broad and general and certainly effective way to trends in the evolution of the military capabilities of its principal rival, there has been very little detailed action and reaction. Because of the nearly total absence of direct evidence on the motives behind individual Soviet weapons programs, I and the scholars I am criticizing are driven, more often than not, to argue by technical inference.

Although it would be an error to assert that Soviet defense programs are insensitive to perceived and anticipated threats, the historical facts of the 1964–85 period suggest that a claim for the very substantial autonomy of the Soviet defense effort (vis-à-vis change in the level of the U.S. defense effort) is unlikely to be far off the mark. In that extensive period, the rate of increase in the level of the Soviet defense effort roughly coincided with the rate of increase in the growth of the Soviet economy.[63] It is possible to argue that the absolute decline in the level of the U.S. defense effort in the early and mid-1970s encouraged the Soviet Union to compete more vigorously, but that argument lacks evidence to support it—notwithstanding both its logical appeal and its apparent fit with the facts. In Harold Brown's words:

> As our defense budgets have risen, the Soviets have increased their defense budget. As our defense budgets have gone down, their defense budgets have increased again.[64]

In short, the past twenty years have provided a happy playground for statisticians eager to establish positive and negative correlations. In practice, as is known from U.S. weapons program histories, much of the detail of a particular program is negotiated for reasons and to conclusions that have little or nothing to do with the anticipation of external threat. Determination of the key parameters of the MX ICBM program, both in its multiple protective structure (MPS) basing system (with a baseline configuration of 200 missiles and 4600 shelters) and certainly as 50-100 missiles to be housed in silos (after the Scowcroft Commission report of April 1983), has been affected very little by estimates of the Soviet threat. The 1979 Carter figure of 200 MX ICBMs was a compromise number negotiated between the Air Force and Senator MacIntyre of the Senate Armed Services Committee. The senator was opposed to a force size too obviously capable of posing a credible first-strike threat to Soviet silo-based ICBMs.[65] The 100-strong MX deployment recommended by Scowcroft was even less comprehensible in term of targeting rationality; however, there are pressing reasons of a more general character why 100 MX ICBMs are sorely needed in the U.S. strategic posture.[66]

Because the lead time for a major strategic weapon system is on the order of ten years or longer—to full operational capability (FOC), neither superpower can act and react in the mechanistic, deft manner suggested by some arms control theorists. There are so many technical, budgetary, political, and (in the U.S. case) even basic doctrinal hazards facing a weapon program over its very long gestation period that it simply is not possible to orchestrate agile reactions to Soviet offensive or defensive developments.[67]

Aside from the uncertainties of strategic intelligence predictions for a decade hence—the lead time pertinent to major weapon program evolution—each party to the arms competition has unique foreign policy duties to perform, very individual strategic preferences to express (in weaponry and C^3I), and particular domestic-process considerations to accommodate. In short, U.S. officials and extra-official commentators cannot sensibly support or oppose a particular weapon program—be it MX, a multiweaponized SDI, or whatever—solely on the grounds that the Soviet Union will (may?) respond in particular, specified ways.

Close study of such Soviet evidence as is available suggests that the Soviet Union strives to achieve maximum prospective combat effectiveness (in the interest of being more powerful, of discouraging imperialist adventures, and of plain common sense), but that it also is devoted to the preservation of stability on the home military-industrial front. Major rapid changes in resource allocation for defense vis-à-vis nondefense programs, or even between defense programs, are very expensive in the Soviet system. An economy that is centrally planned on a series of 5-year cycles is not the most agile vehicle for the conduct of an arms competition characterized by an action-reaction process. The more that is learned of Soviet defense industry—and that remains all too little—the less convincing becomes the image of a Soviet defense establishment willing and able to conduct a process of deft thrust and parry in the strategic arms competition. The Soviet defense system, writ large, is capable of effecting step-level jumps in effort, given sufficient notice. In other words, if a U.S. administration should decide to raise the level of U.S. defense expenditure by, say, 50 or 100 percent, one should expect the Soviet defense preparation machine to react. However, one should not expect the Soviet defense machine to react directly, in detail, to a new U.S. defense program, and neither should one assume that the Soviet Union necessarily *could* react, even in a gross fashion, as some action-reaction theorists tend to imply. It is not obvious that the Soviet Union could much increase the output of its high-technology industry for defense functions.[68]

A Soviet Union devoted to the improvement of its military condition at all levels easily lends itself to misassessment by Western theorists. Where Western theorists are inclined by strategic culture to see malign purposeful design, one should perhaps see only prudence (defined in Soviet terms). The Soviet Union has not imposed a condition of strategic inferiority or disadvantage on the United States. Strategic superiority may be general and geographically nonspecific if it is sufficiently awesome in physical terms. But if the strategic-force postures of the superpowers are approximately equivalent, the meaning of the relevant military balances is more likely than not to be dominated by such key factors as the political stakes of the players and their skill in manipulating perceptions of will. It is entirely possible that a strategic posture more than adequate to back-stop U.S. crisis moves in Central America or Western Europe would be critically inadequate as "top cover" for forward diplomacy in Southwest Asia, let alone as a "compellent" with respect to Soviet policy activity within its empire. A condition of superiority, if it exists,[69] is the product of steady momentum in Soviet weapons programs and an enduring deficiency in U.S. care about its strategic-force survival problems. The current (much exaggerated) problem with the stand-alone survivability of the U.S. ICBM force is not the result of a dramatic Soviet arms race challenge, nor need it be read as clear evidence of Soviet determination to achieve strategic superiority. Indeed, even to frame the problem in that way probably is to impose a very un-Soviet mode of thinking on the Soviet defense establishment.[70]

Believing that war can occur and that the quantity and quality of defense preparation can make the difference between victory and defeat, but all the while hoping that a direct military clash with the United States can be avoided,[71] the Soviet Union has pursued an orderly, affordable program of military modernization across the board of capabilities.[72] Soviet effort with respect to strategic offensive forces has been extraordinary in relation to other military programs, a fact that may be explained by reference to the comparative disadvantage of the Soviet Union in high-technology defense research, development, and production, and to the extraordinary significance of strategic nuclear weapons systems in the structure of Western strategy.[73] Although Western analysts may well over-price some of the more manpower-intensive military capabilities of the Soviet Union, they almost certainly underprice Soviet strategic nuclear programs.

As an arms race participant, the Soviet Union appears not to be racing to achieve any particular relationship of power, unless an appreciation of the political and military benefits of a growing (though necessarily fragile) degree of preponderance may be so characterized. The Soviet Union, driven both by fear of the outside world and by the general belief that coercive power is always useful, can never be satisfied that it has "enough" or "sufficient" military power. In a very dogged, steady manner, the Soviet defense establishment makes largely marginal improvements in its capabilities, year after year. Insofar as can be discerned, it is not performing at all consciously in a pattern of action and reaction of any kind. The enemy is clearly identified, and Soviet military doctrine provides a stability of guidance for military science from which flow military requirements. Thus, undramatically, the Soviet Union improves its ability to wage war, and hence enforce a deterrence condition, year by year.[74] The fragility to which I made brief parenthetical reference earlier lies in the inherent, structural limitations of Soviet high-technology industry. Soviet officials know very well that they cannot win or even sustain a rough parity in a high-technology arms competition with the United States (or with Japan or West Germany). The evident Soviet alarm at President Reagan's SDI seems to reflect a very genuine anxiety lest the strategic gains secured over the past 20 years be substantially cancelled by U.S. technological breakthroughs in defense.

The model of the arms competition implicit in the foregoing discussion should have an impact on Western debate over arms control policy. To summarize, the Soviet arms-race/arms-control adversary-partner has the following essential characteristics:

- A total, though long-term, commitment to the demise of Western governments. Détente, let alone near-entente, has to be solely a matter of tactical convenience.

- Both a geopolitical (realpolitik) and an ideological antipathy to the maritime alliance that continues to deny it total hegemonic imperium over Eurasia.[75]

- A very Russian, and certainly non-Western (and even premodern), suspicion of foreign ideas and, indeed, of any alien elements that are not controlled by Moscow.[76]

- A commitment, born of historical understanding and ideology, to global instability (in Western terms)—which is not to deny that Soviet leaders are supremely conservative with respect to putative change in the USSR and its hegemonic empire. Relationships of power and influence are not stable—they are dynamic; and the Soviet Union/ Russia has learned firsthand what apparent weakness can cost.[77]

- A commitment to seek victory if war should occur. Soviet defense programs are not guided or inhibited by any consideration of strategic stability favored by Western theorists.

- A stable military doctrine and a commitment to orderly, stable defense programs. This does not preclude intensive professional debates over tactics and strategy, nor does it preclude the probability that intraservice rivalry has a biasing effect on the evolution of broad categories of Soviet defense capabilities, but it is to suggest that the Soviet defense effort, as a whole, is not an instrument capable of playing new tunes on little notice.

Interaction between Soviet and U.S. defense capabilities therefore tends to be intermittent and necessarily somewhat broad in its effects at the higher levels of policy direction; to be all but absent at the level of particular major program development (the region classically assumed to be driven by a tight pattern of action-reaction); and to be quite intensive at the sharp end of tactical operating detail. Consideration of the evolution of weapons programs by arms race rivals from the early 1900s to the present suggests a surprising degree of autonomy in rationales. Whether it be with respect to Dreadnoughts and Super-Dreadnoughts prior to 1914 or to ABM, MIRV, MX, and the SDI in the 1960s, 1970s, and 1980s, the evidence (pertaining to the real detail of program genesis and evolution, as opposed to inferred strategic logic) of patterns of program interaction is, to be polite, extremely thin.[78]

The argument just presented may have major implications for U.S. weapons programs and arms control policies, because—as was explained in chapter 5—arms race stability is prominent, and allegedly preeminent, among the defense and arms control objectives of the United States. Western theories of arms race stability tend to posit a presumed, particular relationship between what we do and how we anticipate the adversary will react. Most of the Western theoretical literature on arms race stability, because it does not rest on any very persuasive understanding of what drives the race, must simply be discarded.

ARMS CONTROL

The principle obective of arms control is to reduce the risk that war will occur. It is time to introduce the thought, however, that there is no very obvious connection between arms control processes, as generally understood, and the likelihood that war will occur. If anything, the most prominent of the formal arms control processes of the 1970s, SALT, probably contributed in a very modest way to the enhancement of the likelihood that war will occur.[79] This apparently perverse judgment refers to the known, indeed quite explicit, Soviet theory of the prospects for war. The Soviet Union holds to the self-serving proposition that the stronger the forces of socialism, the stronger the forces for peace. According to Soviet logic, the prospects for the occurrence of catastrophic East-West war are reduced if Soviet-led forces are sufficient (and then some) to deter the forces of imperialism from intervening in local conflicts of national liberation (or "social progress"). SALT (and MBFR) should ratify Soviet counterdeterrent power, at least, with reference to the major military capabilities of imperialism, leaving Soviet, Soviet-proxy, and friendly local-indigenous forces free to subvert and "liberate" in the regions of political turmoil (South Asia, Africa, and Central America).[80]

Notwithstanding the importance of the central nuclear relationship and the political-military standoff in Europe, it has to be noted that those areas of competition are not "where the action is" on a day-to-day basis. The Soviet Union can make no major gains in Europe unless it is prepared to wage a major and probably nuclear war. The potential benefits that should flow from political-military success in Europe are very high, but so also are the risks. The East-West demarcation line in Europe has been frozen since the spring of 1948 (with the pro-Soviet coup in Czechoslovakia). In the Middle East, South Asia, and Africa, there are very few demarcation lines. Prospective gains—typically though not invariably—are modest when assessed individually, but so also are the risks.

Although I endorse the hallowed trinity of arms control objectives—to reduce the risks that war will occur, to reduce damage if war should occur, and to reduce the burden of peacetime defense preparation—I do not believe that interstate formal arms control processes, as pursued thus far in the 1920s and 1930s or in the 1970s and 1980s, have contributed very usefully to the forwarding of those objectives. At the least, a strong case can be made for reassessing the sense in such an institutionalized process as SALT/START. Western knowledge of the arms control process, the character of the negotiating adversary, and the relationship between arms control and other streams of foreign policy activity have advanced so greatly since the early 1970s that the case for a creative hiatus in activity in arms control almost seems to make itself. Critics of the Reagan administration argue, of course, that the world has suffered through 5 years of an uncreative hiatus. Sensible policymaking on arms control is at least as difficult today as it was in 1980 or 1981. The general elections of 1980 and 1984 were both characterized by gross pusillanimity toward the structure of the problem. Great debates, such as they have been, have focused on details of particular negotiations, actual or impending, and even on inferred attitudes toward arms control per se. What has been lacking, notwithstanding the political differences between the debaters, has been a willingness to articulate doubts about the promise in the enterprise.[81]

Without prejudice to one's final conclusions, and certainly without malice toward the people historically involved in the process assessed here, the following considerations of relevance to future U.S. arms control policy seem to be suggested by the protracted arms control experience of the past 15 years.

First, the Soviet adversary, though respectful of U.S. defense-industrial power and technological prowess (witness the ABM Treaty of 1972[82]), is not at all respectful of U.S. theories of strategic stability. The United States may enforce arms race discipline on the Soviet Union, thanks to Soviet anticipation of a net diminution in its security condition if the competition remains formally unconstrained, but the United States cannot induce cooperative Soviet arms behavior with reference to Western ideas of what is and what is not destabilizing.[83]

Second, the Soviet Union cannot be persuaded to sign arms control agreements that would forfeit the right to wage war, should it occur, as efficiently as feasible in defense of the Soviet homeland. A condition of mutual vulnerability is not negotiable. Mutual vulnerability and mutual deterrence may be strategic facts of life, but the Soviet Union will never endorse those ideas as desiderata.

Third, notwithstanding the juvenile rhetoric of disarmament that is standard official Soviet fare, the Soviet Union is not at all interested in major measures of mutual strategic nuclear disarmament. As in MBFR, in SALT/START (and INF), the Soviet Union has sought to register the facts of the competition and, insofar as possible, to help dissuade the U.S. defense community from competing effectively in regions of major Western comparative advantage. Central nuclear war is a variant of war that the Soviet Union hopes it will never have to fight, but its reading of the possible calculations of imperialists-in-desperation leads it to conclude that such a war is distinctly possible. Hence, there is no way that the Soviet Union would knowingly agree to a START regime that would have a noticeably negative impact on its prospective war-waging prowess. War is a truly serious business, and START agreements and their political ramifications may be beneficial, but they are several orders of magnitude less serious than defense capabilities.

Fourth, the SALT process as launched by Nixon and Kissinger was seen by both sides as an integral part of a much more general architecture of East-West détente. The historical record of Soviet foreign policy in the 1970s demonstrated conclusively what could easily have been deduced from Soviet statements. Specifically, the détente process, with SALT as its somewhat unfortunate centerpiece, was viewed in Moscow both as a reward for the great improvement in the correlation of forces it had secured and as a license for a more forward foreign policy.[84]

Fifth, the SALT/START process, bearing as it did and does on the dominant weapons of the superpowers,[85] could not possibly support the political traffic it was required to accommodate.[86] In fact, the relationship between foreign policy in general and arms control as a particular element in foreign policy was heroically misunderstood for many years. The U.S. SALT-commentary literature of the early 1970s was generally ambivalent on the subject of which was the dependent variable—the SALT process or Soviet-U.S. political relations writ large. The whole period of more or less active SALT and START interstate engagement, from 1969 until the present, tells the story that arms control, far from being an independent or even quasi-independent factor, was in fact very much at the mercy of shifting tactics in the conduct of political relations.

Sixth, as the debate over SALT II in 1979 began to point to problems for a SALT III, the U.S. defense community began to appreciate that the very integrity of a negotiating process—limited, for reasons of negotiating convenience, to so-called central systems—posed prospectively major problems for the credibility of NATO strategy. If, as Paul Nitze argued, the Soviet Union succeeded with SALT assistance in "deterring our deterrent" through the mechanism of a genuinely balanced SALT accord, what could remain of NATO's strategy of flexible response? How could a U.S. strategic-force posture that has been offset be invoked to help reverse a developing theater disaster? The Reagan administration perpetuated old sins by agreeing to separate negotiations on INF and on central systems (in START). If one views arms control negotiations principally as provision of political cover for the development and deployment of new weapons systems, one could find that INF was a great success. I recognize merit in the (domestic) political cover argument, but I see more merit in negotiating frameworks that make sense both in terms of Western strategic interests and in terms of the potential for agreement. U.S. acceptance of the INF negotiating format implied acceptance of the debilitating concept that there is a "Eurostrategic balance" (which there is not and will not be). This concept is fundamentally erosive of the deterrent logic behind NATO's strategy of flexible response.

It is attractive to argue, as many people do today, and as they also did back in 1980, that with respect to arms control:

- The United States needs to find "a new approach," since clearly the old approach has not produced satisfactory results.

- The United States needs "a better hand" with which to bargain. A new approach will accomplish little, if anything, if the United States continues to lack visible, credible momentum in weapon programs.

- The United States needs to attend to the quality of its negotiating tactics and strategy.

There is something to recommend all three of these items of advice. It is sensible to have an open mind on new approaches. It is true, virtually beyond argument, that in SALT and START, to date, strategically the least useful measures of capability have been the focus of attention.[87] Similarly, there is a growing realization that it is probably a poor idea to isolate so-called central systems (understood to refer to strategic arms) for negotiating treatment. However, it seems likely that the fundamental reasons why East-West arms control processes have contributed to international security either not at all, or only at the margin, cannot be finessed by imaginative "new approaches." Diplomatic engineering cannot solve problems of foreign policy. Much, though not all, of the well-intentioned advice proffered in the 1970s for the edification of U.S. SALT negotiators was analogous to proposals for deck-chair rearrangement on the *Titanic;* the SALT voyage of the 1970s was doomed from the start. The important question is whether any future START voyages might have a safer and more profitable passage.

In 1985 the Reagan Administration unveiled a new approach to arms control which outlined a three-phase transformation in Soviet-U.S. strategic relations. In the first phase—of perhaps ten years duration—there would be a radical scale of reduction of strategic offensive arms; in the second phase a transition would be effected towards a strategic stability imposed by a growing scale of deployment of non-nuclear defenses; and in a third phase the superpowers could move to eliminate all nuclear arms.[88] The new element in, the key to, this very ambitious scheme is the leverage hoped to be provided by active defenses. It would be difficult to exaggerate the difficulties that confront the United States in seeking to implement this new strategic concept. However, much of the criticism that has been levelled at the new U.S. approach to arms control, and at the SDI in particular, has not been well reasoned. For example, former Secretary of Defense James Schlesinger writes:

> At Geneva we shall be reading a sermon to the Soviets to which they are unprepared to listen. That sermon propounds the supposed mutual advantages of strategic defense that the Soviets specifically rejected. It is based upon a "strategic concept" that in fact is less a *strategic* concept than it is a rationalization for the President's vision. The concept itself is fundamentally flawed. According to the concept, when strategic defenses are deployed a so-called second phase will ensue. But the prospect of deployment of strategic defense in that second phase precludes attainment of the first phase, the radical reduction of offensive arms. This is because the prospective deployment of strategic defenses increases the premium on missile throw-weight and on offensive forces generally—to overwhelm any prospective defense. The Americans are now prepared not only to read to the Soviets a sermon to which they will not listen, but one that is internally inconsistent.[89]

Schlesinger here confuses a general strategic proposition of high plausibility—the Soviet incentive to *attempt* to construct offensive forces that could defeat defenses—with an undemonstrated technical claim that the Soviet Union will in fact be able so to augment or modify their offensive forces as to thwart the U.S. SDI. The Soviet Union should not be expected to respond cooperatively to the new U.S. strategic *concept*, as a concept, but only to U.S. technical realization of a highly cost-effective strategic defense. Whether or not such a defense is possible remains to be seen and is indeed what the SDI is all about.

The advice to hold "a better hand" in the negotiations is obviously sensible. However, it is not at all self-evident either that a strategically much stronger United States would be permitted by the Soviet Union essentially to shape a future strategic arms agreement (the Soviet Union may prefer not to negotiate with a strategically much stronger United States) or that an agreement "with teeth"—even with teeth that bit genuinely to the mutual discomfort—would be negotiable if Moscow should elect to continue negotiations. The least contentious of the three items of advice is the third—that the United States should negotiate in a professional and tough-minded manner and should be prepared to affront the sensitivities of that segment of Western domestic opinion that insists that its political leaders demonstrate "faith" in the arms control process. (Redemption through arms control?)

The First Law of Arms Control holds that you will receive through negotiations only that which you have demonstrated a willingness to achieve unilaterally (that is, there are no "free lunches" in arms control). The Second Law of Arms Control holds that you will not receive what you deserve unless you attend meticulously to every detail in the negotiations. Unlike the United States, the Soviet Union adheres to the precept of caveat emptor ("let the buyer beware"). Like the Russian peasants from whom they stem, Soviet arms control negotiators seek to secure a bargain that is weighted in their favor.

It remains an open question whether or not the arms control process and the diplomatic institutions of East-West arms control activity are a net liability or a net benefit to international security. On balance, it appears that the strategic arms control process probably is a net liability, because even if it is competently conducted on the Western behalf, at best it can register only a rough parity in the realm of military competition wherein the United States has major comparative advantage. It is to the Western advantage to negotiate agreements on the basis of parity in realms of military competition that are manpower-intensive rather than technology-intensive.[90]

Western arms control theory has foundered on the elementary fact that it has neglected to take account of the character (culture and style) of the principal adversary. Behind the talk about controlling the arms race remains the unpromising reality of the Soviet imperium. No new approach to negotiated arms control, suggested either by the Left or the Right in the West, merits serious policy consideration unless it takes explicit account of Soviet reality. Soviet arms control policy, as an integral part of Soviet grand strategy, is dominated—sensibly, in the Soviet view—by a conflict-oriented view of world politics. Soviet leaders do not endorse an arms control process in the hope that arms control may promote a lasting peace. Instead, they are obliged to endorse an arms control process because such a process may contribute usefully to the physical and/or psychological disarmament of clearly identified enemies. The genuine mutuality of Soviet-U.S. interest in avoiding nuclear war or entry on any "powder trail" that plausibly might lead to such an event cannot suffice to deflect Soviet policymakers from their duty to provide, as efficiently as possible, for the conduct of possible hostilities.

In seeking to control the arms race, Western officials are really talking about seeking to control a state (the USSR) that is obliged, by its theory of legitimacy, to seek prospective war-waging success; that cannot easily shift resource allocation from defense to nondefense functions; and that sees stability in terms of development of an ever more impressive Soviet counterdeterrent ability to discourage Western intervention in local conflicts.

In short, one wonders whether—given the values of Soviet strategic culture—there is any approach, strategy, or tactic that is more likely to promote success in arms control than what has been tried thus far. The Soviet drive to compete vigorously in armaments does not stem from misperceptions of Western hostility, nor does it stem from a desire to achieve any identifiable, particular relationship of relative power. Instead, the Soviet commitment to compete is inherent in the very character of the Soviet state. Moreover, Soviet military science, in line with superordinate doctrine, identifies dynamic goals for Soviet military development that are incompatible with mainstream Western thinking on the nature of a stable military relationship between East and West.

On the basis of observation of their programs and from a close reading of their military literature, one is quite safe in arguing that arms control has not been a major planning factor in the calculations of the Soviet General Staff. Unlike the situation in the Soviet defense community, the United States has negotiated over the period of a decade and a half in SALT and START while it has been bereft of a stable strategic doctrine.[91] Soviet military science, though it may err, does offer authoritative guidance to any Soviet official seeking wisdom with reference to a particular capability that is the subject of arms control attention. A career-professional General Staff, as in the Soviet Union, is tasked, inter alia, with providing "correct" military solutions to military problems. The United States, with its lingering suspicion of "Prussian-style" general staffs, continues to debate even the most basic question of nuclear strategy, while civilian policy-makers concoct strategies that affront the principles of war.[92] The impact of this contrast on the quality of arms control negotiating performance is obvious. The Soviet Union has a settled strategy that tells Soviet officials what particular military capabilities are worth and, therefore, what kind of price should be demanded for their control or abolition. U.S. negotiators have enjoyed no such doctrinal guidance.

It is probably sensible to adopt an essentially agnostic stance vis-à-vis the future of formal East-West arms control negotiations. To simplify, the problem does not lie in "the dynamics of the arms race"; rather, it lies in the character of the Soviet political system (which is perhaps the same thing). Although the superpowers share a common interest in the avoidance of war, it is reasonably obvious that Soviet officials see no incompatibility between their vigorous prosecution of strategic arms programs and that common interest (indeed, quite the contrary appears to be the case). Plausibly, if unconventionally in the Western perspective, Soviet officials appear to see no noteworthy danger of war in the dynamics of the arms competition itself. I agree with them.

The moral of this somewhat depressing story is to the effect that the United States should not inhibit its defense-planning activities with largely spurious so-called arms control considerations. To the best of our knowledge, the Soviet Union does not and cannot react program-for-program to U.S. arms race behavior. The only sound approach to negotiations on defensive space weapons, strategic and intermediate range nuclear forces, or MBFR, is for the United States to pursue an arms policy that is robust in defense of U.S. foreign policy interests. The more robust that policy, the better the "hand" available to U.S. arms control negotiators, and the less important will be agreement on arms control. After all, strategic arms control only reflects the rules of international politics—it does not change them. As already observed in this chapter, by 1979 the most noteworthy feature of the great SALT II debate was the degree to which it was really marginal to matters fundamental to national and international security.

The U.S. body politic should appreciate that the so-called nuclear arms race is driven essentially by the political character of the Soviet state. Although developments in the arms race can be registered through arms control agreements, anything more fundamental has to rest on a theory for (or purporting to explain) a benign alteration in the character of the Soviet state. The United States cannot seek security through arms control, because arms control merely expresses the real world. The true basis for any START accord, for example, lies in the perceptions of power relationships in START-less futures. Foolish proponents of arms control seek to frighten the U.S. public with prognoses of arms-control-unconstrained Soviet strategic deployments—ignoring Soviet systemic fears of U.S. arms competitive activity.

There has been no close match between SALT/START diplomacy, as conducted thus far, and the three classic goals of arms control. Moreover, so different are the Soviet and U.S. concepts of strategic stability that there is no strong case to be made, on the historic evidence, for formal East-West arms control institutions. The only sensible approach to the problem of strategic arms control is a U.S. determination to develop a strategic-forces posture that should deny victory to Soviet arms and that would extend a not-implausible prospect of success for the United States. Such a posture would mean that the United States would no longer be in the position of the *demandeur* and that U.S. officials could be genuinely relaxed over the fate of arms control negotiations.

It is entirely possible that "success" in arms control is beyond the grasp of the United States—no matter what the character of U.S. defense policy. U.S. politicians should not promise that new approaches to arms control will produce better arms control agreements. A United States with a robust strategic-forces program may be no more able to negotiate a security-enhancing arms control agreement than was the United States of the 1970s. This should be no great cause for dismay, however—security flows from programs, not from agreements.

NOTES

1. This claim, though deliberately phrased strongly, does not extend to the assertion that arms control has dominated U.S. strategic-force planning. On the significance of the arms control process, see Richard Burt, "The Relevance of Arms Control in the 1980s," *Daedalus* 110, no. 1(Winter 1981): 159–77. Burt's article makes interesting reading in the context of his later performance in office in the State Department. See Strobe Talbott, *Deadly Gambits: The Reagan Administration and the Stalemate in Nuclear Arms Control* (New York: Knopf, 1984).

2. Richard Burt made this point nearly six years ago in "A Glass Half Empty," *Foreign Policy*, no. 36(Fall 1979): 40–42. His argument is no less relevant in the mid-1980s.

3. For an important example, in the summer of 1984, the U.S. government signaled a willingness to enter a process of discussions on space weaponry (albeit without preconditions—that is, without a moratorium on U.S. ASAT tests announced in advance), even though the technical and political prospects for anything of value for Western security to be negotiable are close to zero. The official study of this issue could hardly be more discouraging. See U.S. Government, *Report to the Congress on U.S. Policy on ASAT Arms Control*, March 31, 1984. Very similar views are expressed in Colin S. Gray, "Why an ASAT Treaty Is a Bad Idea," *Aerospace America* 22, no. 4(April 1984): 70–74.

4. This view was echoed (by a supporter of SALT II) in Gregory F. Treverton, "Issues and Non-Issues," *Survival* 21, no. 5(September/October 1979): 194–97.

5. Barry Blechman, "Do Negotiated Arms Limitations Have a Future?" *Foreign Affairs* 59, no. 1(Fall 1980): 105.

6. I recommend that skeptical readers compare the Senate hearings held on SALT I in 1972 with the Senate (and House) hearings held in 1979.

7. Andrew Pierre, "The Diplomacy of SALT," *International Security* 5, no. 1(Summer 1980): 179.

8. Johan Holst, "Comparative U.S. and Soviet Deployments, Doctrines, and Arms Limitations," in Morton A. Kaplan, ed., *SALT: Problems and Prospects* (Morristown, N.J.: General Learning Press, 1973), p. 68.

9. See Graham T. Allison and Frederic A. Morris, "Armaments and Arms Control: Exploring the Determinants of Military Weapons," *Daedalus* 104, no. 3(Summer 1975): 99–129; Albert Wohlstetter, *Legends of the Arms Race*, USSI Report 75-1 (Washington, D.C.: United States Strategic Insititute, 1975); and Colin S. Gray, *The Soviet-American Arms Race* (Farnborough, Hampshire [U.K.]: Saxon House, 1976).

10. The policy case developed in opposition to ABM deployment in the late 1960s and early 1970s—whatever other merit it may have had—was not embedded in a robust theory of the arms race. For example, see George W. Rathjens, *The Future of the Strategic Arms Race: Options for the 1970s* (New York: Carnegie Endowment for International Peace, 1969). Rathjens talked about trying to "break the ABM-MIRV chain by focusing on control of MIRV's or ABM defenses" (p. 38). That alleged chain was a logical postulate, rational only according to one particular U.S. theory of arms race dynamics. Also see Herbert York, *Race to Oblivion: A Participant's View of the Arms Race* (New York: Simon and Schuster, 1971).

11. See Thomas W. Wolfe, *The SALT Experience* (Cambridge, Mass.: Ballinger, 1979), chap. 11; Strobe Talbott, *Endgame: The Inside Story of SALT II* (New York: Harper & Row, 1979); and Talbott, *Deadly Gambits*, for the Reagan era.

12. Richard Pipes, "Diplomacy and Culture: Negotiation Styles," in Richard F. Staar, ed., *Arms Control: Myth Versus Reality* (Stanford, Calif.: Hoover Institution Press, 1984), p. 160.

13. The history of, and case for, the build-down is presented in William S. Cohen, "The Arms Build-Down Proposal: How We Got from There to Here," *Washington Post*, October 9, 1983, p. C8; and Alton Frye, "Strategic Build-Down: A Context for Restraint," *Foreign Affairs* 62, no. 2(Winter 1983/84): 293–317.

14. A useful summary of Reagan administration objectives in arms control is provided in William R. Van Cleave, "The Arms Control Record: Successes and Failures," in Staar, ed., *Arms Control*, pp. 14–17.

15. See Rebecca V. Strode, "Soviet Strategic Style," *Comparative Strategy* 3, no. 4(1982): 319–39.

16. See the argument in Burt, "A Glass Half Empty," pp. 40–42.

17. I believe that it is undesirable for the U.S. government to have an agency whose sole mission is the promotion of arms control activity. The Soviet practice of having the Ministry of Defense and the General Staff develop strategic arms limitation positions would seem to be much sounder than the counterpart U.S. policymaking procedure. With reference to the SALT era of 1969–79, Thomas Wolfe speculated that the Main Operations Directorate of the General Staff (which directs military operations, helps formulate general military policy, and develops

targeting and war plans) probably had charge of most of the substantive prepara-tion of SALT options. See Wolfe, *The SALT Experience* pp. 62–64.

18.   Blechman, "Do Negotiated Arms Limitations Have a Future?" p. 119.

19.   Ibid., p. 125. Readers may recall that in 1984 the absence of such tangi-ble accomplishments was a leading charge in the Mondale arsenal. The successful endeavors of the White House in the fall of 1984 to postpone general release of the report on Soviet noncompliance of the General Advisory Committee on Arms Control and Disarmament demonstrated beyond argument how vulnerable the administration felt itself to be to the charge that it was not sufficiently serious about the arms control process. See Colin S. Gray, "Moscow Is Cheating," *Foreign Policy,* no. 56(Fall 1984): 141–52. The issue of Soviet noncompliance was translated from an important matter of concern for national security policy to the status of a political embarrassment.

20.   On the arms control paradox and related matters of a structural nature, see Colin S. Gray, "Arms Control: Problems," in R. James Woolsey, ed., *Nuclear Arms: Ethics, Strategy, Politics* (San Francisco: Institute for Contemporary Studies, 1984), pp. 153-69.

21.   I believe that the United States should seek to persuade the Soviet Union to exercise escalation discipline, but I admit to being skeptical that anything short of physical enforcement would work. See chapter 6.

22.   This is a judgment that might have to be altered if the SDI should move into weaponization.

23.   Leslie H. Gelb, "A Glass Half Full," *Foreign Policy,* no. 36(Fall 1979): 21.

24.   However, there usually are scapegoats upon whom some or most of the blame can be placed. Blechman, for example, writing in 1980 with the domestic political failure of SALT II very much in mind, believed that politicians and the public had come to ask arms control to achieve too much; see "Do Negotiated Arms Limitations Have a Future?" particularly pp. 118–19. Gerard Smith, with no less reason, has indicted the simultaneous (and uncoordinated) pursuit of two separate streams of negotiations (front and back channels) in *Doubletalk: The Story of the First Strategic Arms Limitation Talks* (New York: Doubleday, 1980. Reprint, Lanham, Md.: University Press of America, 1985). The title tells all—at least concerning the frustrations of a "chief negotiator" who was kept less than perfectly informed by an unusually devious national security advisor. Since January 1981, the arms control community, generally out of office, has had no difficulty locating domestic villains. See Talbott: *Deadly Gambits;* and *The Russians and Reagan* (New York: Vintage, 1984), particularly, pp. 51-52.

25.   Richard Burt, "Reassessing the Strategic Balance," *International Security* 5, no. 1(Summer 1980): 49.

26.   Ibid., p. 37.

27.   This belief permeates John Newhouse, *Cold Dawn: The Story of SALT* (New York: Holt, Rinehart and Winston, 1973). Of some interest are Ambassador Smith's recollections of some doctrinal explorations in the very early days of SALT I; see *Doubletalk,* pp. 85–88.

28.   Henry Kissinger, in U.S. Congress, Senate, Committee on Foreign Rela-tions, *The SALT II Treaty, Hearings,* Part 3, 96th Cong., 1st sess. (Washington, D.C.: USGPO, 1979), p. 166.

29. Talbott, *The Russians and Reagan*, p. 52.

30. I developed this argument at the time in "SALT II: The Real Debate," *Policy Review*, no. 10(Fall 1979): 7–22.

31. Burt, "Reassessing the Strategic Balance," p. 39. The long policy debate in 1981–83 over the evolving U.S. INF arms control position was noteworthy for the nearly total absence of strategy considerations.

32. See Wohlstetter, *Legends of the Arms Race*.

33. See Jack Kugler and A. F. K. Organski, with Daniel Fox, "Deterrence and the Arms Race: The Impotence of Power," *International Security* 4, no. 4(Spring 1980): 105–31. Also relevant are Miroslav Nincic, *The Arms Race: The Political Economy of Military Growth* (New York: Praeger, 1982); and Andrew W. Marshall, "Arms Competitions: The Status of Analysis," in Uwe Nerlich, ed., *Soviet Power and Western Negotiating Policies, Vol. 2: The Western Panacea, Constraining Soviet Power Through Negotiations* (Cambridge, Mass.: Ballinger, 1983), pp. 3–19.

34. See Michael Howard, *The Causes of Wars and Other Essays* (London: Unwin, 1984; first pub. 1983), pp. 17–18.

35. See Theresa C. Smith, "Arms Race Instability and War," *Journal of Conflict Resolutions* 24, no. 2(June 1980): 253–84.

36. Robin Ranger, *Arms and Politics, 1958–1978: Arms Control in a Changing Political Context* (Toronto: Macmillan of Canada, 1979), particularly chap. 1.

37. Blechman, "Do Negotiated Arms Limitations Have a Future?" p. 108.

38. Arms race theory of the simple (and *incorrect*) action-reaction kind was deployed in 1968–70 to oppose ABM and MIRV, just as it was deployed in 1978–80 to oppose MX/MPS and as it is used again today to show the futility of strategic defense. For example, on the MX/MPS case; note the unexamined action-reaction premise that permeates Peter D. Zimmerman, "Will MX Solve the Problem?" *Arms Control Today* 10, no. 1(January 1980): 7–9. On the SDI, the Union of Concerned Scientists rushed to this judgment: "Following an inevitable action-reaction pattern, the Soviets are certain to respond to an American BMD with new offensive measures." *Space-Based Missile Defense* (Cambridge Mass.: Union of Concerned Scientists, March 1984), p. 75. Far more careful treatment of the SDI issue may be found in Sidney D. Drell, Philip J. Farley, and David Holloway, *The Reagan Strategic Defense Initiative: A Technical, Political, and Arms Control Assessment*, Special Report (Stanford, Calif.: Stanford University Center for International Security and Arms Control, July 1984), particularly pp. 27–29.

39. I am grateful to my former colleague, Norman Friedman, for pointing out to me the many misassessments of alleged technical-strategic motives that Western naval analysts have (falsely) discerned with reference to Soviet and U.S. naval shipbuilding programs.

40. See Newhouse, *Cold Dawn*; Wolfe, *The SALT Experience*; Talbott, *Endgame*; and Smith, *Doubletalk*.

41. Sun Tzu, *The Art of War* (trans. Samuel B. Griffith) (Oxford: Clarendon Press, 1963), p. 84.

42. See Thomas W. Wolfe, "The Convergence Issue and Soviet Strategic

Policy," in *RAND 25th Anniversary Volume* (Santa Monica, Calif.: RAND Corporation, 1973), particularly p. 149.

43.   See the detailed discussion of strategic superiority in chapter 8.

44.   If this is judged to be the case, one can only be pessimistic about the future of arms control.

45.   Useful works include Matthew P. Gallagher and Karl F. Spielmann, Jr., *Soviet Decision-Making for Defense: A Critique of U.S. Perspectives on the Arms Race* (New York: Praeger, 1972); David Holloway, "Technology and Political Decision in Soviet Armaments Policy," *Journal of Peace Research*, no. 4(1974): 257–79; Karl F. Spielmann, Jr., *Analyzing Soviet Strategic Arms Decisions* (Boulder, Colo.: Westview Press, 1978); Arthur J. Alexander, Jr., *Decision-Making in Soviet Weapons Procurement*, Adelphi Papers Nos. 147–48 (London: IISS, Winter 1978–79); David Holloway, *The Soviet Union and the Arms Race* (New Haven: Yale University Press 1983), chap. 6–8; and Matthew A. Evangelista, "Why The Soviets Buy the Weapons They Do," *World Politics* 36, no. 4(July 1984): 597–618.

46.   Johnathan Steinberg, *Yesterday's Deterrent: Tirpitz and the Birth of the German Battle Fleet* (London: MacDonald, 1965), p. 28.

47.   See Sir Halford Mackinder, *Democratic Ideals and Reality* (New York: Norton, 1962), which contains the title manuscript and three important additional articles. A thorough, if overly repetitive, study of Mackinder's theory is James Trapier Lowe, *Geopolitics and War: Mackinder's Philosophy of Power* (Washington, D.C.: University Press of America, 1981). An excellent biographical study is W. H. Parker, *Mackinder: Geography as an Aid to Statecraft* (Oxford: Clarendon Press, 1982).

48.   Sir Halford Mackinder, "The Round World and the Winning of the Peace," reproduced in *Democratic Ideals and Reality*.

49.   For a masterly study, see Gordon Craig, *Germany, 1866–1945* (New York: Oxford University Press, 1978).

50.   Although many West German politicians, of the Left and the Right, continue to adhere to the idea of a single German nation, prominent among the common views of East and West (except for the Federal Republic and the German Democratic Republic) is the determination that the division of Germany is both permanent and desirable.

51.   Mackinder, *Democratic Ideals and Reality*, p. 269.

52.   For a detailed justification of this argument, see Colin S. Gray, *The Geopolitics of the Nuclear Era: Heartland, Rimlands, and the Technological Revolution* (New York: Crane, Russak [for the National Strategy Information Center], 1977), particularly chap. 3. Also relevant is Edward N. Luttwak, *The Grand Strategy of the Soviet Union* (London: Weidenfeld and Nicolson, 1983).

53.   Plus Japan in minor key—though defeat by Japan in 1904–5 nearly brought down the Russian Empire.

54.   On the drives behind Soviet external policy, see Richard Pipes: "Soviet Global Strategy," *Commentary* 69, no. 4(April 1980): 31–39; "Militarism and the Soviet State," *Daedalus* 109, no. 4(Fall 1980): 1–12; and *Survival is Not Enough: Soviet Realities and America's Future* (New York: Simon and Schuster, 1984). Pipes

insists that the hardships imposed on the Soviet peoples need to be justified by a siege rationale. It would seem that Soviet leaders are confident of domestic control only in the context of a fortress condition, and they also believe that their empire is genuinely imperiled by the very existence of other powerful and politically independent states.

55.   Imperial Russia was nothing if not dominated, at least quantitatively, by "rural life."

56.   See Richard Pipes, "Why the Soviet Union Thinks It Could Fight and Win a Nuclear War," *Commentary* 64, no. 1(July 1977): 21–34.

57.   The Czar was not only the supreme secular authority; he was also God's representative in Russia. The CPSU claims a functionally analogous religious-based obedience in the name not of God, but of the correct "scientific" theory of history.

58.   On leadership issues in the Soviet Union, see Jerry F. Hough, *Soviet Leadership in Transition* (Washington, D.C.: Brookings, 1980); Seweryn Bialer, *Stalin's Successors: Leadership, Stability, and Change in the Soviet Union* (Cambridge: Cambridge University Press, 1980); and Archie Brown, "Gorbachev: New Man in the Kremlin," *Problems of Communism* 34, no. 3(May-June 1985): 1–23. On the contemporary domestic condition of the Soviet Union, see Richard Pipes, "Can the Soviet Union Reform?" *Foreign Affairs*, 63, no. 1(Fall 1984): 47–61.

59.   Frank Barnett, "Conflict Chess in a Global Mode," Speech at Pepperdine University, January 15, 1980, p. 3 of printed text. Some useful complementary points are made in Bryan I. Fugate, *Operation Barbarossa: Strategy and Tactics on the Eastern Front, 1941* (Novato, Calif.: Presidio Press, 1984), pp. 1–12.

60.   Whatever Soviet motivations may truly have been, the détente policy line of the 1970s did pose some serious public relations problems. As Dimitri Simes argued: "For decades, portrayal of the U.S.S.R. as fiercely fighting the imperialist enemy was a dominant theme in public Soviet diplomacy." "The Death of Detente?" *International Security* 5, no. 1(Summer 1980): 6. Even though the Soviet Union remains a largely closed society, the Soviet government has had problems, from time to time, keeping separate its messages to the outside capitalist world and to its population at home. Alliance leadership, even Soviet-style in the command mode, also becomes more complicated for a Soviet leadership that is pursuing a policy line of limited accommodation with the West. However, when leadership from Moscow is uncertain, as has been the case in recent years, the Eastern European client-states seek policy room to assert local priorities in aid of much-needed domestic support—even when Soviet policy is rigidly and unimaginatively hostile toward the West. For a sophisticated analysis of East-West relations at the end of Reagan's first term, see Dimitri K. Simes, "America's New Edge," *Foreign Policy*, no. 56(Fall 1984): 24–43.

61.   It is needed as the reason, or excuse, for requiring continuing domestic sacrifice and vigilance. In the interests of discipline at home, the USSR would have to invent foreign enemies if they were not already so conveniently identified by ideology and geopolitics. On the prospects for change in the Soviet system, see Pipes, "Can the Soviet Union Reform?" Pipes argues that Western resistance to the Stalinist forces in the Soviet Union carries some hope for benign reform.

62.   Logically, there is another alternative: that Soviet-U.S. antagonism will wither and die—much as Christian-Moslem and later Reformation-Counterreformation antagonism did as state and religious interests clearly diverged in the evolution of modern Europe. It is possible that someday the rise of new centers of first-class power—China, Japan (or China-Japan), Western Europe, or Germany–Western Europe—will subsume Soviet-U.S. rivalry into a broader and more complex pattern. Nonetheless, such a possibility is of less than pressing relevance to U.S. policymakers today.

63.   At least as averaged over the years. Typically, as well as one can judge, the Soviet defense effort in the Brezhnev period registered roughly a 4- to 5-percent rate of real growth each year. Such a rate was somewhat below the rate of growth in Soviet GNP in the better years of the 1960s, somewhat above the rate of growth of the late 1970s, and *well above* the current and expected future rate of growth of Soviet GNP. As the Soviet Union entered a period in the 1980s of a rate of economic growth averaging roughly 1.5 to 2 percent per annum, so the rate of growth in defense allocation began to decline (though spending on procurement increased sharply in 1983 over 1982, 5 to 10 percent). One should not forget that we are talking about the rate of growth in defense effort from a very high base, not about any absolute decline. See U.S. Congress, Joint Economic Committee, Subcommittee on International Trade, Finance, and Security Economics, *Soviet Defense Trends: A Staff Study*, 98th Cong., 1st sess. (Washington, D.C.: USGPO, September 1983); and "Soviet Military Spending Increased," *Air Force Magazine* 67, no. 9(September 1984): 33, 35, 37.

64.   Harold Brown, *Department of Defense Annual Report, Fiscal Year 1980* (Washington, D.C.: USGPO, January 25, 1979), p. 6

65.   For studies of President Carter's MX/MPS program, see Colin S. Gray, *The MX ICBM and National Security* (New York: Praeger, 1981); John Edwards, *Super Weapon: The Making of MX* (New York: Norton, 1982); and Lauren H. Holland and Robert A. Hoover, *The MX Decision: A New Direction in U.S. Weapons Procurement Policy?* (Boulder, Colo.: Westview Press, 1985).

66.   See R. James Woolsey, "The Politics of Vulnerability: 1980–83," *Foreign Affairs* 62, no. 4(Spring 1984): 805–19; and Barry R. Schneider, Colin S. Gray, and Keith B. Payne, eds., *Missiles for the Nineties: ICBM's and Strategic Policy* (Boulder, Colo.: Westview Press, 1984).

67.   Threat manipulation for purposes of scoring points in policy debate is a well-established habit. In 1980, Admiral Turner, then director of central intelligence, waged a campaign via the national intelligence estimates to dissuade President Carter from continuing with MX/MPS. The CIA allegedly predicted a Soviet response to MX/MPS at the high end of the possible threat range, comprising well in excess of 20,000 ICBM warheads. The basis for this estimate range was largely CIA strategic logic—it was not *Soviet* evidence. See Richard Burt, "Soviet Nuclear Edge in Mid-80s Is Envisioned by U.S. Intelligence," *New York Times*, May 13, 1980, p. A12. In 1983–85, it has been fairly commonplace for opponents of President Reagan's SDI to assert, rather casually, that the Soviet Union could and would deploy sufficient additional offensive forces to run U.S. strategic defenses out of ammunition.

68. It is only fair to point out that the U.S. defense community is divided in its assessment of Soviet mobilization potential vis-à-vis defense high technology.

69. Some interesting reflections on the perils and pitfalls of strategic analysis may be found in Richard Ned Lebow, "Misconceptions in American Strategic Assessment," *Political Science Quarterly* 97, no. 2(Summer 1982): 187-206; Thomas A. Fabyanic, "Triad Without Trilogy: Strategic Analysis, Strategy, and Strategic Programs in the Reagan Administration," in Stephen J. Cimbala, ed., *National Security Strategy: Choices and Limits* (New York: Praeger, 1984), pp. 237–65; and Stephen Peter Rosen, "Systems Analysis and the Quest for Rational Defense," *Public Interest*, no. 76(Summer 1984): 3–16.

70. It is far from obvious that the USSR recognizes a concept of strategic superiority outside the enveloping framework of the correlation of forces. See Bialer, *Stalin's Successors*, pp. 241–53.

71. In Paul Nitze's words: "The Kremlin leaders do not want war; they want the world." "Strategy in the Decade of the 1980s," *Foreign Affairs* 59, no. 1(Fall 1980): 90.

72. For an outstanding presentation of Soviet doctrinal tenets (for the guidance of military science), see John J. Dziak, *Soviet Perceptions of Military Power: The Interaction of Theory and Practice* (New York: Crane, Russak [for the National Strategy Information Center 1, 1981), pp. 27–28. Among those tenets is the following: "The basic political objective in *any* war is victory."

73. See Henry Kissinger, "The Future of NATO," *Washington Quarterly* 2, no. 4(Autumn 1979): 6.

74. See John Erickson, "The Soviet View of Deterrence: A General Survey," *Survival* 24, no. 6(November/December 1982): 242–51.

75. Sino-American détente-entente provides yet more fuel to the basic antipathy. On the geopolitical roles of the U.S.-led maritime alliance see Gray, *The Geopolitics of the Nuclear Era*, chap. 4. On Soviet strategic options vis-à-vis China, see Luttwak, *The Grand Strategy of the Soviet Union*, chap. 6.

76. Soviet/Russian political culture is not merely ill-fitted to accommodate Western ideas; it is fundamentally suspicious for reasons that have nothing to do with the performance of the current generation of Western leaders. Although it is very imperfectly balanced by a largely romantic myth of the virtues of the Russian peasant and his ties to the soil of Mother Russia and to the Orthodox Church, Russian/Soviet commentators continue to be afflicted by a deep sense of inferiority vis-à-vis the West. This assessment is necessarily difficult to document. I recommend that readers examine Russian cultural history; for example, see James H. Billington, *The Icon and the Axe: An Interpretive History of Russian Culture* (New York: Knopf, 1966).

77. This point refers to the fact that the Soviet Union, quite aside from the more local elements deriving from the Mongol memory and the rest, has a distinctive "continental," as opposed to "insular," strategic culture. Since there is, as yet, no literature of direct comment on the continental perspective, readers can approach this perspective via its Anglo-Saxon obverse. See Michael Howard, *The*

Continental Commitment: The Dilemma of British Defence Policy in the Era of the Two World Wars (London: Temple Smith, 1972). There tends to be a quality of geopolitical necessity about the national security policies of great continental states that typically is absent from the calculations of the statesmen of insular powers. In reviewing the protracted debate about the scale of German responsibility for the outbreak of World War I, H. W. Koch has provided a useful reminder of this realm of necessity:

> One factor often forgotten when discussing German war aims, or for that matter German military strategy at the outbreak of war, is the factor of geography. It would be well to remember at all times G. P. Gooch's dictum, that: "Geography is the mother of history." Germany's geographic position was to say the least highly vulnerable. And the historical memories of nations are not short. Most of the Germans who in 1914 marched to war were aware that in the centuries of Germany's weakness and fragmentation she had been the battleground of Europe.

The Origins of the First World War: Great Power Rivalry and German War Aims, 2d ed. (London: Macmillan, 1984), p. 10.

78.   There is no evidence worthy of note that would suggest either that the developers of MIRV in the 1960s rigorously considered the implications of this technology when married to the superior throwweight of Soviet ICBMs, or that the official proponents of MX/MPS in 1979–80 gave very much thought to possible Soviet reactions. However, for reasons developed in detail in Gray, *The MX ICBM and National Security*, MX/MPS almost certainly would have been very competition-viable.

79.   See the prepared testimony of Donald G. Brennan in U.S. Congress, Senate, Committee on Foreign Relations, *The SALT II Treaty, Hearings*, Part 4, pp. 369–76.

80.   Very much to the point is Keith B. Payne, "Are They Interested in Stability: The Soviet View of Intervention," *Comparative Strategy* 3, no. 1(1981): pp. 1–24.

81.   For some historical light on this dark subject, see Charles Burton Marshall, "Arms Control: History and Theory," in Staar, ed., *Arms Control*, pp. 180–88.

82.   Evaluation of Soviet motives vis-à-vis the ABM issue in 1972 continues to be controversial. However, a consensus appears to be emerging to the effect that, at the time, the Soviet Union judged itself unable to compete effectively with the United States in that area. Also, Soviet leaders may have believed that their ABM system could not cope with the offensive prowess of MIRVed Minuteman III and Poseidon C-3. For contrasting analyses, see the contributions by Sayre Stevens and Raymond L. Garthoff in Ashton B. Carter and David N. Schwartz, eds., *Ballistic Missile Defense* (Washington, D.C.: Brookings, 1984), chaps. 5 and 8, respectively.

83.   Notwithstanding 15 years of intermittent public and private SALT/START diplomacy, I have yet to hear a plausible item of evidence, or even candidate evidence, suggesting authoritative Soviet endorsement of the Western idea that it is strategically desirable for *both* superpower societies to be totally vulnerable.

84. This central theme of Soviet policy logic was not concealed, but it lacked a knowledgeable Western audience.

85. See Col. B. Byely et al., *Marxism-Leninism on War and the Army (A Soviet View)*, Soviet Military Thought Series of the U.S. Air Force, No. 2 (Washington, D.C.: USGPO, 1974; Moscow, 1972), p. 217.

86. This point is well argued in Lawrence Freedman: "Arms Control: No Hiding Place," *SAIS Review* 3, no. 1(Winter-Spring 1983): 3–11; and "Weapons, Doctrines, and Arms Control," *Washington Quarterly* 7, No. 2(Spring 1984): 8–16.

87. Note, however, the ingenuity with which "build-down" and "double build-down" proponents approached their task. See Frye, "Strategic Build-Down: A Context of Restraint."

88. For an authoritative statement of this concept see Paul H. Nitze, "The Objectives of Arms Control," *Survival* 27, no. 3(May/June 1985): 98–107.

89. James Schlesinger, "The Eagle and the Bear: Ruminations on Forty Years of Superpower Relations," *Foreign Affairs* 63, no. 5(Summer 1985): 960–61.

90. Studies of START and of arms control more generally have yet to address issues as basic as this.

91. The true seriousness of this charge tends to elude official comprehension. Unless one is trained to think strategically, one cannot easily understand that the United States has no business negotiating arms control if it lacks a stable strategic direction for weapon acquisition and if there are no authoritative doctrinal criteria for allocating funds for research and development.

92. The beneficial ethos of general staff work is almost totally alien to the U.S. defense environment. To be specific: unlike the Soviet case, there is an absence in the United States of official organizations charged with finding and disseminating authoritative answers to important military questions.

CHAPTER **8**

Strategic Superiority

THE CONCEPT

Superiority, like leprosy, is something that responsible people are afraid to touch. In the presidential campaign of 1980, Ronald Reagan chose to refer to the need for a "margin of safety," while his principal defense advisor, William Van Cleave, felt moved to endorse publicly only the idea of a "selective superiority."[1] "Selective superiority," of course, may be intellectually indistinguishable from the erstwhile authoritative concept of "essential equivalence."[2] For the better part of 20 years, U.S. officials and strategic commentators have professed to finding it difficult to comprehend the meaning of the concept of strategic superiority. Without prejudice to arguments suggesting that superiority is or is not technically attainable, strategic superiority should mean that the United States could, not implausibly:

- deter arms race challenges;

- deter crisis challenges;

- deter military crisis breakouts;

- take the military initiative;

- enforce escalation discipline on an adversary;

- impose defeat on an adversary (on its terms) and physically defend essential Western assets.[3]

Since the mid-1960s, the U.S. defense community has accepted as a fact the *proposition* that it cannot regain, let alone maintain, strategic superiority. It is necessary, first, to clear the air and demonstrate intellectually that the concept of strategic superiority does have meaning in the nuclear age. One can identify exactly what strategic superiority should mean in terms of freedom of foreign policy decision.[4]

The U.S. government never explicitly decided to move from a condition of strategic superiority to one of parity. Such a shift was permitted to occur through the mechanism of freezing the number of strategic missile launchers at the levels attained in 1967 and deliberately eschewing investment in weapons prospectively capable of enforcing damage limitation on a major scale;[5] the momentum in the Soviet strategic modernization program did the rest. It is only fair to observe that the demise of a condition of U.S. strategic superiority was so unduly unlamented largely because many commentators and officials believed that acceptance of parity or sufficiency really entailed merely making a virture of necessity. Today there are many people, including not a few defense professionals, who believe that strategic superiority is uninteresting as a concept because it is unattainable. Busy, pragmatic people do not waste their time on theoretical exploration of an impossible dream.

For reasons that have to do with a change, perhaps even a permanent one, in U.S. political culture in the late 1960s—or that may pertain only to a temporary, though major oscillation away from traditional U.S. insistence on being Number One—the concept of strategic superiority has ceased to be respectable even among generally conservative defense professionals. Few people appear to be comfortable with the concept. Although the United States has largely recovered from the collective identity and self-confidence crisis substantially triggered and fed by the Vietnam War, the idea that strategic superiority is both strategically necessary and technically feasible for Western security has yet to stage a truly convincing comeback.

The proposition central to this chapter is that strategic superiority refers to the ability to *win* or *prevail* in arms competition, crises, and wars. The concept is clear, even if the detail of effective, high-confidence implementation is uncertain. In his prepared testimony on the SALT II Treaty for the Senate Foreign Relations Committee, Henry Kissinger offered some much-quoted wisdom on the subject:

> After an exhausting negotiation in July 1974, I gave an answer to a question at a press conference which I have come to regret: "What in the name of God is strategic superiority?" I asked, "What is the significance of it . . . at these levels of numbers? What do you do with it?" My statement reflected fatigue and exasperation, not analysis. If both sides maintain the balance, then indeed the race becomes futile

and SALT has its place in strengthening stability. But if we get out of the race unilaterally, we will probably be faced eventually with a younger group of Soviet leaders who will figure out what can be done with strategic superiority.[6]

It was one thing to believe, as most U.S. defense officials did in the mid-1960s, that damage limitation—which, if sufficiently expansive in scale, is synonymous with superiority—would not be feasible for inescapable technical reasons. However, it was quite another to make a virtue of that believed necessity to the point where, retrospectively, it is legitimate to wonder whether the loss of U.S. strategic superiority was, to an identifiable degree, a self-fulfilling prophecy. This suspicion is strengthened when one reads the following historical assessment by one of the "high priests" of parity, Jerome Kahan:

> The stated policy of Presidents Kennedy and Johnson was to consider the effect of U.S. strategic weapon decisions on the Soviet Union's programs and the overall stability of the balance. This was explained by Assistant Defense Secretary John McNaughton as early as 1962 and later formalized by Secretary McNamara in his description of the action-reaction phenomenon. The decisions to eliminate vulnerable systems, limit the number of U.S. strategic vehicles to the levels of the mid-1960s, and emphasize assured destruction rather than damage limitation were influenced by a desire to avoid stimulating Soviet reactions or disrupting the stability of the balance, and the fight against the deployment of a large U.S. ABM system was increasingly motivated by arms race concerns.[7]

There can be no doubt that through most of the 1960s and 1970s, the U.S. defense community, at civilian policymaking levels at least, did not want to pose a major threat to the prelaunch or penetration survivability of Soviet strategic forces.[8] Whether or not such a threat could have been posed is another matter. As I explained in chapters 5 and 7, the theories of crisis and arms race stability to which Kahan refers have to be judged today—on the historical evidence and in the light of careful study of Soviet style—to be severely flawed. In short, the doctrinal basis for opposing the concept of strategic superiority is demonstrably false or, to be very generous, extremely fragile.

SUPERIORITY AND STRATEGY

Superiority carries with it a burden of largely substantively irrelevant negative baggage, which inhibits intelligent discussion. Some of this negative baggage may be sidestepped if one refers to military advantage rather than to superiority. It should be understood that, like credibility, superiority—at least below some threshold of truly splendid war-winning capability—is not a simple matter of either/or. Superiority, or advantage, tends to be specific to place and, hence, to political issue. Moreover, its substance as political reality can generally be assessed only very approximately before a field test in crisis.[9] The case for a militarily and, hence, politically meaningful measure of strategic superiority is functionally identical to the case for strategy, properly defined. As strategy should relate military power to political objectives in a purposeful way, so superiority or advantage is the means for providing the freedom of action that is essential if policymakers are not to be paralyzed into inaction or driven to take paths of unpromising action in case of acute need.

All too often, strategic commentary in the United States remains mired in the bog of static indices of relative strategic power. This prevalent inclination to count defense inputs (launchers, warheads, equivalent megatonnage, and so forth) is understandable, because it places little intellectual strain on the commentator. However, defense professionals should not encourage such shallow "analysis," even though the temptation can be strong in the heat of a highly politicized debate over a defense issue. Although it is sensible to argue that the United States should not endorse, for example, prominently visible unfavorable asymmetries in permitted force levels in arms control agreements, it is not sensible to argue that perceptual criteria should play a large role in the U.S. strategic posture design. The principal advocate of such a development, Edward Luttwak, may have rendered a good idea bad by taking it too far.[10] The concept of strategic superiority was cheapened and even degraded by a succession of annual Defense Department reports in the 1970s that failed to elevate strategic balance analysis beyond the level of political perception of the relationship in strategic inputs. Year after year in the middle to late 1970s, it was asserted in annual Defense Department reports that "essential equivalence"—the contemporary conceptual leitmotiv—pertained to the perceptions by unsophisticated Third World politicians and officials of which side was ahead or behind on crude input comparisons of strategic inventories.

Parity, inferiority, and superiority were all applied with the brush of operationally meaningless input comparison by virtue of association with the way in which essential equivalence was explained. Richard Burt was very close to the mark when he claimed:

> "Parity," a political definition of force sufficiency, is not an adequate measure of military effectiveness because it fails to provide any operational requirements for long-range forces.[11]

Similarly, superiority could be defined in crude input terms that bear not at all on operational issues. The problem here is that the U.S. defense community has come to accept as fact a largely implicit distinction between political-perceptual and operational analysis. Many, and probably most, commentators who deplore conservative arguments for strategic superiority are persuaded that conservatives are really arguing only for optically relevant, as opposed to operationally meaningful, superiority. For example, I am friendly to the following argument advanced by Abram Chayes:

> The efforts of strategic analysis to demonstrate that numerical superiority remains meaningful or that present force levels can be justified in terms of plausible missions—for example, damage limitation or war fighting capability—have become increasingly labored and unconvincing. Countries should have little difficulty in drawing the political conclusions. The political value of weapons is ultimately derived from their military significance. If numerical or technical advantage at present levels doesn't convey the one, it will soon lose the other.[12]

Inferiority, parity, and superiority seem, almost universally, to be concepts appropriated by commentators bent upon drawing far-reaching political conclusions from essentially static relative assessments. Strategic superiority has meaning, first, in prospective operational terms and then, by way of positive feedback, in terms of probable prewar and intrawar deterrent effect. A defense debate should not be conducted around such a question as "the desirability of strategic superiority." Superiority is a code word for the ability to prevail in arms competition, crisis, and war. Perceptual issues are important largely insofar as they affect judgments on operational issues. When a conservative or defense-minded strategic analyst claims that strategic-force relationships can have political meaning, he should be referring not merely to static indices but also to the political shadow cast by a militarily more, as opposed to less, capable strategic force posture.

The debate over the meaning of strategic inferiority-superiority has been "owned" by people who held, as an a priori assumption, the belief that nuclear war could only be lost. Hence, there could be no operationally significant debate over superiority. This chapter, in keeping with the thrust of this book as a whole, endorses no such assumption. Although one must be properly fearful of the damage that could be wrought by nuclear use and respectful even of "nuclear winter" possibilities, there is no sound basis for asserting that the use of nuclear weapons cannot serve political purposes. In other words, there is no good reason to believe that nuclear *strategy* is impossible. To endorse the possibility of bilateral defeat in nuclear war is not to say anything at all profound or helpful with respect to U.S. policy choices. Critics of nuclear strategy, as strategy, tend to remind us simply that it is difficult to design nuclear operations that would be of political value and that the potential for a catastrophic slide to general disaster is very likely to remain a condition of our, and future, times.[13]

Strategic superiority is a composite concept. It need not imply a crude numerical preponderance on any particular indices of relative military power. However, one should be suspicious of commentators who offer superiority, or freedom of action, at little or no additional cost. There is danger, as well as sense, in Sun Tzu's dictum:

> In war, numbers alone confer no advantage. Do not advance relying on sheer military power.[14]

Clever strategy is inherently desirable, but ceteris paribus (including clever tactics and strategy), the larger side tends to win. Strategic superiority not only implies the amassing of effective weapons, it also implies, or should imply, a search for excellence in strategic ideas. To summarize some of the work conducted on targeting doctrine over the past decade, the United States should seek to exploit the facts that the Soviet Union is grossly overcentralized as a state structure; is a colonial empire unloved by its subject peoples; and is a state fundamentally nervous of its legitimacy, even among Great Russians.[15] However, there probably are no "clever" ways of attacking the Soviet state, as opposed to Soviet society, that can sidestep, or finesse, the need to defeat or impose stalemate on the Soviet armed forces. Soviet political control at home will be restored, even in the context of heavy damage, provided that the Soviet armed forces are successful.

Strategic superiority continues to be undervalued, because few people are willing to consider strategic nuclear weapons as instruments of foreign policy. I empathize with that unwillingness (and indeed plain horror), but I am obliged to take account of the following considerations:

- Soviet military science—the foundation for Soviet military strategy—considers nuclear weapons to be not merely usable but also potentially decisive in their effect.

- If strategic nuclear weapons are truly not usable—if they are not "weapons" in any accepted instrumental sense—then a significant fraction of U.S. and NATO strategy is no more than a bluff.

- Nuclear war could happen. Policies of prewar deterrence cannot be guaranteed to succeed forever.

- Usability and credibility for deterrence are one and the same (which is not to deny that an incredible threat *may* still deter under some circumstances).[16]

Although strategic superiority is easily defensible conceptually in terms of the familiar Western logic of the arms race, of crisis, and of the management of sequences of wartime escalation, it is also defensible with reference to a hypothetical case of total deterrence breakdown (prewar and intrawar). Ignoring doctrinal labels—"countervailing strategy," "essential equivalence," a "margin of safety," the "prevailing strategy," and the rest—Caspar Weinberger was really calling for a strategically superior U.S. defense condition when he specified the following requirement:

> We must plan for flexibility in our forces and in our options for response, so that we might terminate the conflict on terms favorable to the forces of freedom, and reestablish deterrence at the lowest possible level of violence, thus avoiding further destruction.[17]

Always assuming that operational flexibility would be possible in nuclear war, it is difficult to see how a United States bereft of very serious damage-limiting capabilities could so dominate a conflict that it could enforce an outcome "favorable to the forces of freedom." As the argument in chapter 9 makes plain, strategic flexibility is a valuable quality, but it falls heroically short of constituting a robust theory of escalation control.

Henry Kissinger has stated:

> I define strategic superiority as the ability by the United States to pose a risk, or at least a perceived risk, to the Soviet Union that it might lose most of its strategic retaliatory force if it pushed a crisis beyond a certain point.[18]

Notwithstanding this "born-again" partial comprehension of the concept of strategic superiority, expressed in 1979, Kissinger still did not recognize the essential connection between counterforce threats and homeland defense. In a generally favorable 1984 commentary on President Reagan's SDI, Kissinger saw some value in defense for supporting a concept of strategic stability that does not extend beyond the ability to defeat Soviet strategy.[19] To have political value for a U.S. government, a concept of strategic superiority has to embrace the idea of damage limitation.

Typically, as noted earlier, assessment of the Soviet-U.S. strategic balance is conducted almost solely in terms of the gross static inputs to the "balance." Instead, commentators should be encouraged to consider the dynamic prospect for each side of achieving its war aims. In the case of the United States, this involves the novel requirement that war aims be identified. In the absence of war aims, there can be no strategy, because one cannot know what one is trying to accomplish. However, if one were totally pessimistic concerning the ability of the United States to limit damage to its homeland, one might argue that although war aims might have some meaning for a central war conducted with a major degree of reciprocated targeting restraint and willingness (and physical ability) to negotiate early termination, the "end game" could be of no operational significance, because the scale of certain catastrophe would assuredly overwhelm any consideration of political advantage.

Superiority has meaning for strategy only when it is translated into operational terms. If the Soviet Union is judged to be strategically superior to the United States, that judgment subsumes and transcends such strategic force inputs as quantities and quality of weapons and communication-assessment assets and makes reference to a believed ability on the Soviet part to conduct conflict processes (including wars) with a very good prospect of achieving success. I am not convinced that Harold Brown was correct when he asserted:

> The need for essential equivalence reflects the fact that nuclear forces have a political impact influenced by static measures (such as numbers of warheads, throw-weight, equivalent megatonnage) as well as by dynamic evaluations of relative military capability. It requires that our overall force be at least on a par with those of the Soviet Union, and also that they be recognized to be essentially equivalent. We need forces of such a size and character that every nation perceives that the United States cannot be coerced or intimidated by Soviet forces. Otherwise the Soviets could gain in the world, and we lose, not from war, but from changes in perception about the balance of nuclear power.[20]

Richard Betts has offered a very sensible judgment on the "perceptual impact" dimension of the argument over essential equivalence:

> Budgetary politics and rational strategy preclude astronomically expensive investments rationalized by public relations criteria that diverge from military logic. It is fine to have a force impressive to foreign leaders who lack serious understanding of nuclear strategy, but only if it is consistent with what impresses the important perceivers who are *not* untutored: the Soviet General Staff and Politburo.[21]

When one discusses the political meaning of relative strategic nuclear power, one is not leaving behind considerations of probable operational effectiveness. Confusion has been created by all sides in the debate over the foreign policy implications of parity, inferiority, superiority, and essential equivalence. In particular, proponents of the thesis that perceptions of an unfavorable strategic nuclear imbalance can be important may well not have been as explicit as they should have been concerning the military-operational assumptions underpinning their arguments.[22] Much of the audience for this debate may have believed, and perhaps may still believe, that the debate was about appearances only. "Dovish" spokesmen were correct in arguing that it is foolish to expend scarce resources for militarily meaningless weapons. "Hawkish" spokesmen should have made it very clear that their doctrinal opponents were assailing a position that was not defended.

The static measures of strategic capability—particularly missile throw-weight—were and remain of great consequence, because they are the raw material from which operational effectiveness is extracted. In and of themselves, disparities—even large disparities—in launcher numbers and missile throwweight, though undesirable on political perceptual grounds, should not promote expensive efforts at postural correction. Those disparities are important because when they are married to navigational improvements permitting CEPs that approach 0.1 nm, they translate into a unilateral Soviet ability to conduct effective hard-target counterforce strikes promptly.[23] Dr. Kissinger, on one of his less defense-minded days in the mid-1970s, asserted that "throwweight is a phony issue." The world, and Dr. Kissinger, was to learn that throwweight, far from being a "phony issue," was instead the key to the growing, and as yet unmatched, Soviet hard-target counterforce competence. Moreover, in the 1990s and beyond, missile throwweight may be critical to the ability to deploy countermeasures to burgeoning strategic defenses.

Parity and superiority cannot be debated intelligently unless they are understood to be code words for particular kinds of capability. Strategic forces have meaning only in terms of their contribution to the support of foreign policy. One cannot sensibly debate the political or strategic merits of such summary concepts as parity or superiority in an intellectual context innocent of foreign policy considerations.[24] Similarly, some strategic commentators seem determined to debate the feasibility or infeasibility of achieving victory in nuclear war, without acknowledging the character of historical circumstances. When commentators seek to spell out just what they mean by victory and endeavor to explain that U.S. and NATO freedom of choice may well be severely restricted,[25] they are often assailed with arguments that amount to the accusation that they have been guilty either of indecent doctrinal exposure (of things best left hidden) or of nostalgia or romanticism "for the golden age of U.S. superiority."[26] This book is founded, inter alia, on the twin beliefs that a country with a foreign policy heavily dependent on generally implicit nuclear threats cannot responsibly avoid campaign analysis of nuclear war, and that there is nothing romantic about such a war (even a nuclear war that the United States might win).

BEYOND ESSENTIAL EQUIVALENCE

The case for strategic nuclear superiority has to embrace both a persuasive rationale and a persuasive theory of feasibility. It is virtually a definitional truth that a doctrinal leitmotiv of essential equivalence cannot be appropriate for a country, and alliance, that structures its strategy such that strategic nuclear compensation is required to offset local deficiencies in Eurasian theaters of potential combat. This doctrinal, intellectual truth does not necessarily mean that essential equivalence will not be "good enough." It may be that the prospect of the catastrophe of nuclear war is so deterring a fear that gradations in anticipated general-war prowess may be irrelevant to foreign policy decision making. However, such a thought, if translated into policy terms, constitutes a grave and possibly unnecessary risk, is not sensitive to the possibility of history surprising us and perhaps the Soviet Union also, and is dangerously asymmetrical with known Soviet doctrinal tenets.[27] In short, the West might muddle through with theoretically inadequate forces, but how can one justify conscious acceptance of such a policy path? No matter what theoretical elegance is achieved in attempted explanation of "Why Nuclear Superiority Doesn't Matter,"[28]

> whether or not they agreed what it meant or whether it existed, leaders have never been indifferent to the prospect of enemy nuclear superiority.[29]

Stripped of the unhelpful rhetoric that tends to surround the subject, the case for strategic superiority amounts to the claim that arms competition, acute crises, and wars are event sequences that can have a range of unpleasant outcomes that can be influenced, and probably influenced decisively, by conscious policy design well ahead of time. Moreover, given the growing recognition in the United States that deterrence and defense are intimately related,[30] the perceived or anticipated ability to do well in arms competition, crisis, and war should logically have a benign impact on the probability that some of those event sequences will occur. That is only a partial, though important, truth, because arms competition, de profundis, flows from the very character of Soviet-U.S. political relations, and crisis and war might occur virtually regardless of the quality of Western defense doctrine and posture.

The U.S. need for strategic nuclear superiority is a function both of geopolitics and of the imperial character of the Soviet state. It is a fact, regrettable but inescapable, that the Soviet Union is placed geographically with relatively easy access to U.S. vital interests around the Eurasian littoral. The Western alliance, notwithstanding its economic-technological strength and defense-mobilization potential, tends to lack political cohesion for a firm and steady containment policy and adequate depth of territory for high-confidence local military resistance. Even though history might surprise us pleasantly, it is all too easy to design scenarios wherein the maritime alliance, led by the United States, suffers an unfolding military catastrophe in Eurasia and, hence, needs U.S. strategic nuclear intervention to "restore deterrence."[31] Unfortunately, the U.S. defense community has not, in recent years at least, recognized the merit in the argument that one cannot responsibly initiate what is intended to be only a small central nuclear war unless one has a very good story to tell concerning the course of a large central nuclear war.

Appreciation of the fundamental character of the Soviet empire should also help drive the direction of U.S. strategic policy. It is paradoxical that when such a distinguished British commentator as Michael Howard sought to take fairly direct issue with my defense policy recommendations, among similar views by others, his supposedly more reassuring characterization of Soviet national style was fully compatible with the analysis presented in this book. In addition, Professor Howard claimed:

> no amount of argument or evidence to the contrary will convince a large number of sincere, well-informed, highly intelligent and, now, very influential people that the Soviet Union is not an implacably aggressive power quite prepared to use nuclear weapons as an instrument of its policy.[32]

His thumbnail sketch did violence to both the tone and the content of arguments such as those presented in this book. It is argued here that the Soviet Union:

- is trapped in the dynamics of empire.[33] Retreat anywhere is impossible for fear of the political consequences for the integrity of the whole; whereas the security of the extant imperial holdings requires an expanding degree of control over the external environment.

- has a strategic culture, born of historical experience, that anticipates and presumes hostility abroad. Such anticipation tends to generate the external referents that then function malignly in a system of positive feedback.

- does not view its foreign policy démarches as aggressive. Soviet foreign policy is about the business both of fulfilling the prudent security goals of a state surrounded by actual or potential enemies (the United States, NATO-Europe, China, Japan) *and* of forwarding the essential missionary purpose of Soviet power.

- though it views nuclear weapons as a form of superefficient artillery, has no difficulty understanding their unique properties and would employ them only in a condition of dire military necessity (in the Soviet estimation).

Professor Howard proceeded to argue:

> My own firmly-held belief, however, is that it would take a great deal to shift me from my own view, that the leadership of the Soviet Union, and any successors they may have within the immediately foreseeable future, are cautious and rather fearful men, increasingly aware of their isolation in a world in which the growth of Marxian socialism does little to enhance their political power, deeply torn between gratification at the problems which beset the capitalist world economy and alarm at the difficulties which those problems are creating within their own empire; above all conscious of the inadequacy of the simplistic doctrines of Marx-Leninism on which they were nurtured to explain a world far more complex and diverse than Marx or Lenin ever conceived.[34]

Howard is almost certainly correct in his characterization of the Soviet leadership. However, advocates of a U.S. war-fighting (for *deterrence)* strategic posture have not sought to deny the obvious sources of weakness in the Soviet system.[35] Indeed, some of the weaknesses and frustrations identified by Howard, assessed cumulatively, are worrying rather than reassuring. Paradoxically, perhaps a major danger flows from the known and probable fragility of the Soviet system as it is probably identified in Moscow. It would be very easy indeed for a Soviet defense planner to design an exceedingly pessimistic briefing on long-term security trends. Such a briefing would note the demise of détente and the resurgence in U.S. self-confidence and defense investment; the long-term modernization program of the Chinese People's Republic (and the quasi-security ties between Beijing and Washington); the potential for defense mobilization in Japan and Western Europe; the enduring fragility of Soviet control over Eastern Europe; the continuing inefficiency of the Soviet economy; the demographic problems of the USSR; the political instability/policy paralysis consequences of protracted succession problems in Moscow; the complex "time bomb" of the nationalities problem within the USSR itself; and so on.

Unfortunately, the leading item on the plus side in the Soviet assessment, in addition to the politically fractured nature of the hostile external world, is the reality of a multilevel Soviet military advantage that may endure well into the 1990s. Whatever else may be developing unsatisfactorily, the Soviet Union, under Leonid Brezhnev and briefly under Andropov and Chernenko, has noted, rejoiced in, and exploited the "third stage" in the shift in the correlation of forces—the U.S. loss of strategic superiority.[36] Soviet leaders have a dynamic view of the relationships of influence among competing power centers. Although they may be sincere (but in my opinion are not) in asserting that strategic nuclear parity is all that the Soviet Union seeks,[37] they can never assert that they require only an essential equivalence in all of the factors, assessed comprehensively, that comprise the correlation of forces. Geopolitically, rough parity in strategic nuclear forces translates into political advantage for the Soviet Union. Although Soviet leaders undoubtedly would welcome any measure of strategic nuclear advantage granted by U.S. program deficiencies, their fundamental requirement is for a strategic nuclear counterdeterrent.[38]

This argument, though logically sound, could easily mislead if it were taken too far. One should not assert that the Soviet Union wants parity. Instead, one should argue that the Soviet Union prudently anticipates the possibility that war could occur, is attentive to the necessity of homeland damage limitation, but may be reconciled to the long-term prospect of being unable to secure an enduring strategic nuclear advantage. It should not be forgotten that although it is plausible to argue that the Soviet Union is probably pessimistic concerning its ability to establish a lasting measure of strategic nuclear superiority, the Soviet defense effort, overall, does not proceed on the basis of any known algorithm of sufficiency.

I anticipate that some readers, though perhaps willing in principle to grant the nearly self-evident desirability of the United States reestablishing a condition of strategic superiority or military advantage, may be intensely skeptical about the feasibility of such an enterprise. The argument in this book is to the effect that superiority (the ability to wage arms competition, crises, and wars to outcomes that would merit characterization as politically successful) would be neither cheap nor easy to accomplish, but that it is both possible and well worth attempting. Indeed, it is so desirable, even necessary, that the burden of persuasive analysis should really fall most heavily on the shoulders of those who seek to argue that such a capability should *not* be sought. Nonetheless, it is incumbent upon me to outline the practical basis for my argument that superiority may be feasible.

A U.S. strategy with a war-waging focus (for improved deterrent effect) would accommodate the fundamental principle that defense of the U.S. homeland is more important than damaging the enemy. Above all, the U.S. political system has to appreciate that one need not, and should not, curl up and play dead in the face of society-wide catastrophe. Courageous peoples have faced prospective nuclear-war-level casualty lists in the past and have survived and recovered. England in the mid-1340s, and again in the mid-1660s, took casualties from disease that were unambiguously catastrophic (one-third and above)—yet England survived. Similarly, Central Europe (particularly Saxony, Thuringia, and Bohemia) suffered a war/disease death rate in the Thirty Years' War (1618–48) that exceeded anything likely to be imposed by nuclear employment, barring a "nuclear winter"—yet survival and recovery occurred. U.S. skeptics are also invited to examine the casualty lists of Poland and Yugoslavia in World War II to see just how much loss a society can stand.

Contrary to appearances, perhaps, I am not seeking to trivialize or even to "conventionalize" the phenomenon of nuclear war. Of course, nuclear war would be different from all previous experience of conflict. Of course, it does matter that damage would or might be suffered over a period of hours and days, rather than months and years. Of course, the particular effects of *nuclear* weapons would pose quite new kinds of problems for survival and recovery. Everybody can agree that nuclear war would be terrible—that is not at issue. However, neither should it be at issue that nuclear war could occur over a very wide range of damage possibilities and that purposive preparation to defend, survive, and recover could make a night-or-day difference to the consequences of such a war and could enhance the prospects for successful deterrence.

There probably is some point of damage beyond which a society truly could not survive, at least in recognizable social-political form. However, it is worth recalling the fact that many societies have survived and eventually recovered from casualty lists well in excess of one-third their prewar population levels. Although it is fashionable, indeed even trivially self-evident, to observe that the nuclear threat is unprecedented, such an observation can mislead. The multigenerational threat of nuclear warfare (that is, the long-term genetic damage) is indeed unprecedented, as is the totality of menace lurking in the very uncertain possibility of the "nuclear winter" assault on the ecosphere, but the threat posed by nuclear arsenals does have several, admittedly imperfect, historical precedents. Consider the threat posed by the Huns to European civilization in the fifth century and the threat posed by the Mongols (or Tatars) to the Near East and to Europe in the Twelfth and Thirteenth Centuries. The "civilized world" survived the Huns and the Mongols. There is reason to believe that it could survive nuclear wars through suitable provision of active and passive defenses in the context of U.S. adoption of a true "classical strategy."

Needless to say, one cannot demonstrate the technical feasibility of survival and recovery. However, one can and should vigorously assert the facts: that the nuclear age has come to stay; that nuclear weapons are and will remain important in the threat arsenals of the superpowers (inter alia); that useful levels of protection against nuclear damage can be purchased; and finally, that the U.S. government has no responsible choice other than to provide such protection.

Nuclear war should not be thought of as an act of God, to be endured as well as possible. The amount of damage likely to be suffered by North America would depend significantly on the quantity and quality of the preparations effected. When a U.S. defense analyst argues for "strategic superiority," behind that recommendation should lie a structure of offensive and defensive force postural proposals such that a concern to damage the enemy is balanced fully by a determination to enforce a severe limitation on the amount and kind of damage the United States would suffer at home.

U.S. defense planners face an apparently intractable moral-philosophical-strategic problem: What is acceptable (or unacceptable) damage? Pessimism over the ability of the U.S. defense community to limit damage to a noteworthy degree is so ingrained that it is almost heretical to suggest that a nuclear war could be waged, for sound political purposes, in expectation of suffering only "acceptable" casualties. War, nuclear or otherwise, against a first-class adversary is going to involve a horrific casualty rate.

The advocate of U.S. superiority is blind neither to the potentially catastrophic scale of casualties that may be suffered in war nor to the whole range of casualty-attenuating policy measures that can and should be taken. In common with Soviet defense authorities, the U.S. damage-limiter places only qualified faith in any one instrument of protection. By way of summary, damage-limitation programs for the U.S. homeland could comprise the following: offensive counterforce attrition of the threat at source; multilayered active missile defense through a weaponized SDI; air defense; and civil defense.

It is well understood today that the key to damage limitation is multilayering; faith will not be placed in one magically proficient interception system. Furthermore, it is not assumed realistically that even a BMD system architecture with three or four intercept layers would be totally leak-proof. However, the leakage through such a complex BMD system, in the context of U.S. civil defense preparation, should easily be compatible with U.S. societal survival. For deterrence and actual defense purposes, the key to effectiveness lies in the multilayering. I can envisage U.S. defenses having four or more opportunities to defeat an incoming missile attack. This is a situation wherein some warheads certainly penetrate, but given U.S. urban-area evacuation and some blast and fallout protection, it is not a situation wherein urban-industrial America is destroyed.[39] The amount of urban-industrial damage suffered by the United States would depend on the degree of targeting restraint shown by the USSR, the quantity of warhead allocation the Soviet General Staff felt obliged to dedicate to U.S. non-urban-industrial target sets, and, of course, the effectiveness of U.S. offensive and defensive war-fighting capabilities. The details have to remain imprecise, given the major unknowns in the equation, but no great optimism is required for the claim that urban-industrial America could essentially survive a World War III.

The point is frequently made that if Soviet defense planners confronted the novel problem of truly severe penetration difficulties against U.S. BMD, they would respond by concentrating their attacks against cities. Aside from the technical consideration that it is far from certain that a concentration of brute force effort would succeed against multilayered defenses, the major difficulty with this point is that coercive strikes against cities affront known Soviet strategic cultural preferences as well as military common sense.[40] If a mature U.S. SDI denies the Soviet Union a militarily rational plan of attack, it should follow that such an attack is most unlikely ever to happen.

Everyone, so it seems, has a favorite damage-limitation study. Many defense commentators assert that they can find no good grounds for anticipating less than 100 million prompt fatalities for the United States. At the opposite extreme, readers can find some Boeing studies that envisage U.S. losses (prompt fatalities) at only a very low level.[41] Everybody is honest, but people employ different assumptions. When I claim that "victory" is possible in a nuclear war, I envisage the kind of damage-limitation system layering that I have specified here. Nothing has been mentioned that requires advances in fundamental scientific knowledge. Indeed, the prospects for damage limitation are so promising, and the potential costs of failing to attempt to make such provision could be so terminal, that—to repeat—the burden of proof really should fall on those who argue against superiority.

For the sake of clarity, it should be understood that I favor U.S. development and deployment of strategic defensive systems whether or not they are expressive, by intent, of a U.S. policy to regain superiority. A defensive standoff between the superpowers would promote acute strategic problems for a Western alliance that has leaned on the crutch of the very variably credible U.S. extended nuclear deterrent for half a century (by the late 1990s). Nonetheless, I would prefer a future with those problems to a future wherein North America was assuredly vulnerable to any and all long-range nuclear threats.

THE USE OF STRATEGIC SUPERIORITY

There is no discernible enthusiasm for war in Moscow. The Soviet Union is a heavily militarized, but not militaristic, society. The current Soviet leadership, though the beneficiary of the most successful peacetime military buildup in Russian or Soviet history, does not appear to be at all eager to precipitate a "day of reckoning" with the West.

Whether or not U.S. officials and commentators choose to emphasize the matter publicly, there can be no denying the possibility that in the course of a general nuclear war, the USSR might disintegrate as a centralized political structure. That possibility is enhanced by the fact that contemporary U.S. strategic-nuclear targeting design reportedly is directed to seek to exploit the unique weaknesses in the political-bureaucratic architecture of the Soviet empire.

Quite literally, strategic superiority means, if pressed, the ability to win a war. This means the ability to defeat the military power of the Soviet state and to hold down to a tolerable level the quantity and quality of damage that the Soviet state might inflict on North America. In short, the concept of superiority has fairly clear implications pertaining to both offensive and defensive capabilities.

The political benefits of strategic superiority have been much underplayed in the defense literature of the past 20 years. I have no wish to engage potential critics, yet again, in retrospective historical arguments over the value of strategic superiority in the 1950s and the early to mid-1960s. Whether or not many Western commentators agree, it is a fact that contemporary Soviet leaders were unwilling to press local crisis claims (over, say, Berlin and Cuba) to a point where U.S. central strategic nuclear power might plausibly have been invoked. To repeat a controversial point made much earlier in this book, it seems very probable, indeed, that the United States could have forcibly disarmed the USSR of strategic nuclear weapons in the late 1950s and early 1960s. That period should be judged not as a mythical Golden Age, but rather as a Golden Age in prospective operational terms. The fact that U.S. politicians did not so understand it at the time is neither here nor there.

Considering the explicit and implicit reliance of the United States on nuclear threats in the crises of the 1950s and early 1960s, there is much to recommend Richard Betts's judgment:

> if this was a bluff, the Soviets never chose to force the issue and allowed the crises to be settled on terms acceptable to Washington.[42]

Earlier, also with reference to the crises of the 1950s and early 1960s, Betts offered the following pertinent thought:

> Although no one can prove that such threats [of U.S. nuclear employment] were effective, there is enough circumstantial evidence that Communist leaders took them seriously to invalidate confident dismissal of the utility of superiority.[43]

If it moves in the 1990s to effect a weaponized SDI for a genuinely balanced offensive-defensive force posture in line with classical strategy, the U.S. government could aspire to restore a strategic relationship that should have the functional merits identified earlier with strategic nuclear superiority. Such a condition requires both an unusual willingness in the United States to think strategically about its defense requirements and a willingness to consider damage limitation the dominant defense concept. The leitmotiv for the determinant of U.S. strategic-force requirements prudently cannot be the need to ensure that the USSR would suffer a great deal of damage by way of U.S. retaliation—an objective almost trivially easy to achieve, given the character of nuclear weapons. Instead, the U.S. leitmotiv should be the need to pose a credible threat of intolerable damage, in Soviet terms, all the while rendering it very unlikely that the Soviet Union would be able to inflict intolerable damage on the United States.

Many, and probably most, commentators recoil from the idea of superiority because they hold to notions of acceptable-unacceptable damage that are wholly inappropriate for nuclear war. In common with some generic critics of nuclear strategy, I am not indifferent to the moral aspects of the subject.[44] What, after all, could be "worth" tens of millions of lives? It is morally repugnant even to pose the question. Nonetheless, there is no nuclear posture and strategy likely to be available to the United States that would not, by way of a net assessment of its prospective operational consequences, cost U.S. society millions of lives—and that refers to a hypothetical war in which the United States would fare very well indeed. The problem is really one wherein choice is severely restricted. The range of real choice embraces survivable and nonsurvivable catastrophe. Also, quite probably, many of the survivors of a World War III would judge that the political issues supposedly at stake were trivial, relative to the casualty list.

The fact remains that East and West are locked into a threat and counterthreat system from which the nuclear weapons element cannot be removed.[45] Indeed, for reasons of elementary geopolitics, the NATO alliance depends on nuclear threat for security more than the Soviet Union does. It is an enduring fact that for good Russian/Soviet historical reasons, Moscow takes an amoral instrumental view of the "value" of its citizens.[46] Western strategists have to contend with the unfamiliar fact that the Soviet adversary, in extremis, should be expected to take a nuclear cannon-fodder approach to its civilian dependents. This is not to say that Soviet leaders are indifferent to the prospect of a catastrophic level of civilian casualties, but rather that such a level is likely to be deemed "acceptable" given the political issues anticipated to be at stake. As outlined in chapter 1, the United States has no choice other than to play in the threat system, and today that means the nuclear threat system. International politics has not changed its nature from ancient China and ancient Greece to the present. Affluent societies that are unwilling to act responsibly in defense of their own interests inevitably go down before the barbarians.

The uses of strategic superiority may be summarized as the possession of freedom of diplomatic action in peacetime; the ability to wage crises in expectation of securing acceptable political outcomes; and the capability, if need be, to wage and survive war at any level. On the last point, it is not a very telling argument to claim—accurately enough, in all probability—that the societal survival envisaged encompasses acceptance of millions of casualties. I do not find the prospect of 20 million, 1 million, or indeed any number of casualties any more "acceptable" than the next person does. However, war may occur for reasons that are currently un-predictable or only dimly appreciated, and historically, the United States could and would recover from such a catastrophe.[47] The problem is that there is no wide range of choice. The United States could vastly reduce the geopolitical extent of its security perimeter, but that would not alter the character of the international threat system; it would alter only the role and influence of the United States within that system.[48] A United States that seeks to withdraw into a continental bastion, insulated against a hostile world, far from improving its security condition would merely guarantee that the Soviet Union would truly dominate Eurasia-Africa. Such a Soviet Union, still bound by the dynamics of perennially insecure empire, could never feel truly secure in Eurasia-Africa until it had achieved hegemony over the external threat posed by the very existence of a politically independent and still powerful United States.

The case of strategic superiority virtually makes itself once one succeeds in discarding the astrategic dicta that have been fashionable for more than 20 years. For example, the following propositions summarize the mind-set that continues to enervate the U.S. defense community. These propositions are all either false or irrelevant:

- "Parity is the only criterion on which political agreement—both internal and external—can be built."[49] *Comment:* Of course the Soviet Union will negotiate no less than parity, but that admitted fact does not mean that strategic nuclear parity should be, or has to be, negotiated. A U.S. administration should have no difficulty explaining both to its domestic public and to its NATO allies why superiority is geostrategically essential.[50]

- Strategic superiority is unattainable. *Comment:* Not only is this claim untrue as a theoretical proposition, it is also in the process of being falsified by current Soviet programs. The vital qualification is the recognition that there are no cheap (in absolute terms) victories in nuclear war. If it so chooses, the United States could construct a strategic posture that should both defeat Soviet military power and, no less important, very substantially attenuate, though not totally preclude, the ability of Soviet military power to damage the United States.

- Perception or anticipation of strategic nuclear advantage has no relevance to political life. *Comment:* This proposition appears to be false vis-à-vis the U.S. crisis experience of the 1950s and 1960s and it appears especially false in the context of Soviet foreign policy behavior since the age of strategic parity dawned in the late 1960s. Over Berlin from 1958–61 and over Cuba in October 1962, the Soviet Union seems to have learned that small local crises may become large general crises and that there is a political unity to prospective military performance. In short, one should not knowingly accept the risk of small-scale local conflict unless one has a very plausible theory of victory relevant to the war that might ensue.

In the early 1980s, the Soviet Union was in the enviable, though well-merited position of being able to eavesdrop on a Western strategic debate confined to the issue of whether the United States had retained rough parity or was slipping into a condition of strategic inferiority.[51] Looking realistically at what Western high-technology industry could produce if unleashed by alarmed governments, the Soviet Union must be delighted by the apparent policy fact that the uppermost ambition discernible today in Western debate is restricted to the concept of rough parity.[52]

Soviet leaders appear to view the central strategic nuclear relationship in two very distinctive, though fully compatible contexts. First, they see the strategic nuclear balance in terms of its peacetime function as a major scene-setter for diplomacy. Behind every exchange of diplomatic notes and representations by ambassadors is mutual knowledge that the Soviet Union would certainly deny victory to the United States if a major war should ensue and that Moscow might just secure victory on its own terms. Second, Soviet leaders consider the "balance" with respect to its meaning for the conduct and outcome of war.

Reduced to its essentials, the attainment of a condition of strategic nuclear superiority (which, admittedly, will always be a matter of degree and will be subject to more or less severe analytical uncertainties[53]) means that a country need not engage in bluff when it affirms or reaffirms, a crisis stand. Without meaning to detract from the strength in that claim, I would remind readers that no country, regardless of the tenor of the net assessments provided by its general staff, would lightly accept the risks of nuclear war. Therefore, to claim that the Soviet Union either has achieved or is about to achieve some margin of strategic superiority is not to claim that the Soviet Union would welcome the outbreak of war. The Soviet leadership knows, through firsthand experience in the fall and winter of 1941–42, that military operations can be a close-run thing.[54]

Reasserting the case for strategic superiority may be politically impossible for any U.S. administration. The reason, simply, is that under pressure of appropriately rigorous questioning, an administration would have to anticipate being compelled to specify at least its range of expectations regarding U.S. casualties, and those have to be unacceptably high.[55] Ultimately, the case for strategic superiority descends to the level of stating that a time, or times, may come when the United States will want to say to the Soviet Union either "thus far, and no further" or, in extremis, "go back." The details of the local geography may well be less significant than the timing of the intended arresting challenge. As in British society, though not so clearly in the British government, over the Polish Corridor in the late summer of 1939, the issue will not be "Germany must not be permitted to achieve the conquest of Poland (over the pretext of the Corridor)"; rather, it will take the form, "We have determined to resist the next (Soviet) act of aggression"[56]—whatever the local details may be.

If it is truly determined to deny the Soviet Union political success through military intimidation, the United States requires a theory of conflict management, or escalation control/dominance, that embraces all levels of conflict interaction from subcrisis maneuvering up to and including military resolution in a global war. Strategic superiority:

- is required strategically, given the enduring deficiencies in U.S.-NATO theater capabilities.

- is attainable and sustainable, given U.S.-NATO manpower and defense scientific-industrial potential.[57]

- should not be thought of as foreclosing on arms control possibilities. However, as Edward Luttwak has argued, we should not "seek partial solutions without considering their effect on the general equilibrium of power."[58] The West should negotiate arms control in a forum, or forums, where its total slate of assets is considered. Negotiations confined to so-called central strategic nuclear systems are bound to favor the Soviet Union, no matter how equitable the narrow agreement that is achieved.[59]

CONCLUSIONS

Strategic superiority means a guarantee neither of peace nor of war without pain. Theoretically, arms races, crises, and even wars can be won in the nuclear age. Moreover, painful though a nuclear victory would certainly be, there is no good reason to suppose that such a victory must be virtually indistinguishable from defeat or that such a victory would not be worth attaining, given the alternatives. In practice, at some time in the future, Western political-military options may narrow to a point where fine-drawn considerations of political merit are all but irrelevant. The issue may be whether Soviet forward diplomacy should be halted here (wherever "here" happens to be).

The Soviet Union certainly would resist a U.S. bid to regain strategic superiority as vigorously as the political instruments of its statecraft would permit. Soviet "scholars" from the various institutes of the Academy of Sciences would travel extensively to spread the word. Almost above all else, perhaps, Westerners should learn to disdain the argument that the Soviet Union somehow is *owed* strategic parity. The Soviet Union is owed nothing. On its record, the USSR is not to be trusted with parity, let alone with marginal superiority or better. Arguments to the effect that rough parity is a fact of technological life are simply wrong. Most Soviet missiles and manned bombers could be kept out of North America by a mature U.S. SDI. It is probable that over the long run, the Soviets would be able to achieve an approximately strategically equivalent level of defensive prowess. In other words, they could enforce parity. As the United States proceeds to explore the technological possibilities of the SDI, it should be neither fearful of a future condition of Western strategic advantage nor dismayed by the prospect of a possible defense–defense standoff. The ability to enforce damage limitation is essential for a condition of strategic superiority; but even if that ability is shared by the superpowers, the West retains more than adequate political and economic strengths to sustain an adequate deterrent (albeit a deterrent on terms radically different from those familiar today).

To repeat, arms races, crises, and wars can be won in the nuclear age. A United States that chooses to settle for essential equivalence is inviting policy paralysis in time of direst need. Unfortunately, strategic-logical truths tend to lack persuasiveness in the absence of real-world, recent evidence in their support. The case for a margin of usable power can probably be made convincing only by painful or humiliating experience with the consequences of its absence. From such bitter experience, U.S. policymakers would learn firsthand what they should have learned from history–that escalation dominance is not an "optional extra" or a fanciful notion forwarded by irresponsible theorists. Instead, it is a prerequisite for survival.

Inexact terminology can impede productive discussion. Virtually the entire U.S. defense community today agrees that it is essential for the Soviet Union to be denied victory (in prospect, for an adequate deterrence regime).[60] However, it is important to recognize that, logically, the denial of Soviet victory is not necessarily identical either with Soviet defeat or with the denial of U.S. defeat (in U.S. terms). The Soviet Union might be denied achievement of its political goals through effective Western military action, but Soviet military power may be checked rather than defeated, and the price exacted from U.S. and U.S.-allied societies might well be incompatible with Western strategic-cultural definitions of political success. U.S. multilevel military superiority, as defined functionally at the beginning of this chapter (in terms of different kinds of conflicts—arms races, crises, escalation sequences), should bear the plausible promise of denying Soviet leaders victory on their own terms; defeating Soviet arms; and in extremis, defeating the Soviet state and ensuring the survival and recovery of U.S. society.

NOTES

1. See William R. Van Cleave's discussion of the superiority issue in "A Debate: Are U.S. Defenses Ready, Rusty, or Adequate?" *New York Times*, October 12, 1980, p. E-5.

2. The one quality that virtually all of the officially popular defense slogans in recent years have had in common has been imprecision. During the 1980 election campaign, Mr. Reagan succeeded in avoiding indication of just how broad or narrow a "margin of safety" he favored. This confusion is clarified in Warner R. Schilling, "U.S. Strategic Nuclear Concepts in the 1970s: The Search for Sufficiently Equivalent Countervailing Parity," *International Security* 6, no. 2(Fall 1981): 68-79; and Richard K. Betts, "Elusive Equivalence: The Political and Military Meaning of the Nuclear Balance," in Samuel P. Huntington, ed., *The Strategic Imperative: New Policies for American Security* (Cambridge, Mass.: Ballinger, 1982), chap. 2.

3. This daunting list of functional attributes cannot, of course, be achieved as a consequence of physical capabilities alone. Deterrent effect is a product of capabilities and perceived determination, and the relationship between the two is not mechanistic and predictable. The quality of determination displayed will vary from issue to issue and from leader to leader.

4. This is not to claim, necessarily, that such freedom of action is either required or feasible. Lest there be any misunderstanding, the discussion at this juncture in the text is conceptual. I am not at all confused between solving strategic problems verbally and physically. For allegations to the contrary, see Donald W. Hanson, "Is Soviet Strategic Doctrine Superior?" *International Security* 7, no. 3(Winter 1982/1983), particularly p. 73.

5. This is not to neglect the fact of the major U.S. initiative in moving rapidly to deploy MIRVs, but it is to assert that the warhead yields selected for Minuteman III and Poseidon clearly were not chosen for their prospective efficacy in hard-target counterforce. See Aaron L. Friedberg, "A History of the U.S. Strategic 'Doctrine'—1945-1980," *Journal of Strategic Studies* 3, no. 3(December 1980): 54-55, particularly n. 83.

6. U.S. Congress, Senate, Committee on Foreign Relations, *The SALT II Treaty, Hearings*, Part 3, 96th Cong., 1st sess. (Washington, D.C.: USGPO, 1979), p. 169.

7. Jerome Kahan, *Security in the Nuclear Age: Developing U.S. Strategic Arms Policy* (Washington, D.C.: Brookings, 1975), pp. 133-34. For a highly pertinent partial retrospect on the 1960s by a key architect of U.S. nuclear policy, see Robert S. McNamara, "The Military Role of Nuclear Weapons: Perceptions and Misperceptions," *Foreign Affairs* 62, no. 1(Fall 1983): 58-80.

8. "In the interests of stability, we avoid the capability of eliminating the other side's deterrent, insofar as we might be able to do so." Harold Brown, *Department of Defense Annual Report, Fiscal Year 1980* (Washington, D.C.: USGPO, January 25, 1979), p. 61.

9. A historical monograph of more general applicability on the difficulty, yet necessity, of assessing the balance of power realistically is Williamson Murray,

The Change in the European Balance of Power, 1938–1939: The Path to Ruin (Princeton, N.J.: Princeton University Press, 1984).

10.   See Edward N. Luttwak, "Perceptions of Military Force and U.S. Defense Policy," *Survival* 19, no. 1(January/February 1977): 2-8. On the other side of the argument, the case for the limited relevance of military capabilities is taken much too far in Richard Ned Lebow, "Misconceptions in American Strategic Assessment," *Political Science Quarterly* 97, no. 2(Summer 1982): 187-206.

11.   Richard Burt, "The Relevance of Arms Control in the 1980s," *Daedalus* 110, no. 1(Winter 1981): 170.

12.   Abram Chayes, "Nuclear Arms Control After the Cold War," *Daedalus* 104, no. 3(Summer 1975): p. 27.

13.   This is the message in Lawrence Freedman, *The Evolution of Nuclear Strategy* (London: Macmillan, 1981).

14.   Sun Tzu, *The Art of War* (trans. Samuel B. Griffith) (Oxford: Clarendon Press, 1963), p. 122.

15.   Soviet problems are well covered in Richard Pipes, *Survival Is Not Enough: Soviet Realities and America's Future* (New York: Simon and Schuster, 1984).

16.   See Robert Jervis, *The Illogic of American Nuclear Strategy* (Ithaca, N.Y.: Cornell University Press, 1984), pp. 167-70.

17.   Caspar W. Weinberger, *Annual Report to the Congress, Fiscal Year 1985* (Washington, D.C.: USGPO, February 1, 1984), p. 29. For a useful critique from the Left, see Jervis, *The Illogic of American Nuclear Strategy*, chap. 3.

18.   "Kissinger's Critique," *Economist*, February 3, 1979, p. 18.

19.   Henry A. Kissinger, "Should We Try to Defend Against Russia's Missiles?" *Washington Post*, September 23, 1984, p. C8.

20.   Harold Brown, *Department of Defense Annual Report, Fiscal Year 1981* (Washington, D.C.: USGPO, January 29, 1980), p. 69.

21.   Betts, "Elusive Equivalence," p. 121.

22.   I offer a tentative guilty plea. See Colin S. Gray, "Foreign Policy and the Strategic Balance," *Orbis* 18, no. 3(Fall 1974): 706-27.

23.   The United States could conduct hard-target counterforce strikes today, but only with expectations of lethality on the very modest side.

24.   However, it would not be true to claim that all, or even most, strong proponents of strategic parity in the late 1960s and early 1970s ignored foreign policy considerations. As Richard Betts has observed, it seemed to many people that "the apparent growth of political stability: detente, SALT I, agreements on European security, and mutual and balanced force reductions (MBFR) . . . negotiations" reduced the West's need to be able to threaten nuclear escalation. "Declining political anxieties reduced concern about abstrusely defined weaknesses in technical military deterrence." "Elusive Equivalence," p. 110. A similar point was argued in Richard Rosecrance, *Strategic Deterrence Reconsidered*, Adelphi Papers No. 116 (London: IISS, Spring 1975), p. 36.

25. See Colin S. Gray, "Nuclear Strategy: The Case for a Theory of Victory," *International Security* 4, no. 1(Summer 1979): 54-87; Colin S. Gray and Keith Payne, "Victory Is Possible," *Foreign Policy*, no. 39(Summer 1980): 14-27; and Colin S. Gray, "War-Fighting for Deterrence," *Journal of Strategic Studies* 7, no. 1(March 1984): 5-28.

26. For a sensible review of the U.S. experience with superiority, see Betts, "Elusive Equivalence," pp. 111-17. Also see the remarks in Brown, *Department of Defense Annual Report, Fiscal Year 1981*, p. 68.

27. See John J. Dziak, *Soviet Perceptions of Military Power: The Interaction of Theory and Practice* (New York: Crane, Russak [for the National Strategy Information Center], 1981).

28. The title of an article by Robert Jervis in *Political Science Quarterly* 94, no. 4(Winter 1979-80): 617-33.

29. Betts, "Elusive Equivalence," p. 109.

30. Gray, "War-Fighting for Deterrence." For a sharply contrasting view, see Jervis, *The Illogic of American Nuclear Strategy*, chap. 5. Notwithstanding the scale of our differences, Jervis' arguments tend to penetrate to the heart of the matter and, as a consequence, are a joy to read.

31. Particularly thoughtful recent contributions to the debate over U.S. global and NATO alliance strategy include the following: John J. Mearsheimer, *Conventional Deterrence* (Ithaca, N.Y.: Cornell University Press, 1983); David N. Schwartz, *NATO's Nuclear Dilemmas* (Washington, D.C.: Brookings, 1983); Robert W. Komer, *Maritime Strategy or Coalition Defense?* (Cambridge, Mass.: Abt, 1984); Keith A. Dunn and William O. Staudenmaier, *Strategic Implications of the Continental-Maritime Debate*, Washington Papers No. 107 (New York: Praeger [with the Georgetown Center for Strategic and International Studies], 1984); and Jeffrey Record, *Revising U.S. Military Strategy: Tailoring Means to Ends* (Washington, D.C.: Pergamon-Brassey's, 1984).

32. Michael Howard, "On Fighting a Nuclear War," *International Security* 5, no. 4(Spring 1981): 7.

33. See Richard Pipes: "Militarism and the Soviet State," *Daedalus* 109, no. 4(Fall 1980): 1-12; and *Survival Is Not Enough*, pp. 37-44. Also valuable is Edward Luttwak, "On the Meaning of Strategy . . . for the United States in the 1980s," in W. Scott Thompson ed., *National Security for the 1980s: From Weakness to Strength* (San Francisco: Institute for Contemporary Studies, 1980), pp. 272-73. Those intrigued by Luttwak's claims that "the Russians have a strategy, and it is an imperial strategy of classic form" could profit from consulting his book, *The Grand Strategy of the Roman Empire: From the First Century A.D. to the Third* (Baltimore: Johns Hopkins University Press, 1976). Luttwak's more recent work, *The Grand Strategy of the Soviet Union* (London: Weidenfeld and Nicolson, 1983), is particularly rich in bold theory.

34. Howard, "On Fighting a Nuclear War," pp. 7-8.

35. Many of Howard's arguments have close parallels in Colin S. Gray, "The Most Dangerous Decade: Historic Mission, Legitimacy, and Dynamics of the Soviet Empire in the 1980s," *Orbis* 25, no. 1(Spring 1981): pp. 13-28. Also, the

analysis in Pipes, *Survival Is Not Enough*, is not exactly indifferent to Soviet problems.

36.   Pipes, *Survival Is Not Enough*, pp. 1-2, 86.

37.   For an analysis of Soviet views that concludes that Soviet leaders do not believe that nuclear war can be won in any meaningful sense, see Robert L. Arnett, "Soviet Attitudes Towards Nuclear War: Do They Really Think They Can Win?" *Journal of Strategic Studies* 2, no. 2(September 1979): 172-91. On recent trends in Soviet doctrine, see Dan L. Strode and Rebecca V. Strode, "Diplomacy and Defense in Soviet National Security Policy," *International Security* 8, no. 2(Fall 1983): 91-116.

38.   One of the major problems with superpower strategic defense deployments is that they *could* promote a situation wherein NATO lacked a technically credible nuclear offset for its long-standing conventional deficiencies. See Charles L. Glaser, "Why Even Good Defenses May Be Bad," *International Security* 9, no. 2(Fall 1984): 99-100, 121. This problem is addressed in Keith B. Payne and Colin S. Gray, "Nuclear Policy and the Defensive Transition," *Foreign Affairs* 62, no. 4(Spring 1984): pp. 829-32. An outstanding overall discussion of the SDI is Keith B. Payne, *Strategic Defense: "Star Wars" in Perspective* (Lanham, Md.: Hamilton Press, 1986).

39.   See Payne and Gray, "Nuclear Policy and the Defensive Transition," p. 823.

40.   See the discussion in Glaser, "Why Even Good Defenses May Be Bad," pp. 102-6.

41.   See *Industrial Survival and Recovery After Nuclear Attack: A Report to the Joint Committee on Defense Production, U.S. Congress* (Seattle: Boeing Aerospace Company, November 18, 1976).

42.   "Elusive Equivalence," p. 117.

43.   Ibid, p. 112.

44.   See Colin S. Gray, "Strategic Defense, Deterrence, and the Prospects for Peace," *Ethics* 95, no. 3 (April 1985): 659-72.

45.   This thesis usefully pervades Harvard Nuclear Study Group, *Living with Nuclear Weapons* (New York: Bantam, 1983); and Robert Gilpin, *War and Change in World Politics* (Cambridge: Cambridge University Press, 1981). The impracticality of abolition is demonstrated all too clearly by the glaring weaknesses in Jonathan Schell, *The Abolition* (New York: Knopf, 1984).

46.   This is a point of great significance for U.S. deterrence policy that is cited to telling effect in Albert Wohlstetter, "Bishops, Statesmen, and Other Strategists on the Bombing of Innocents," *Commentary* 75, no. 6(June 1983): 27.

47.   At the time of this writing, not enough is known about the global climatic effects of nuclear war for those effects to be accorded anything more than a "wild card" status in this analysis. Several years from now, as a result of a program of careful research—including some controlled experimentation with large fires—it is possible that the U.S. government will know a great deal more about the climatic impact of soot and smoke at different altitudes. However, it is scarcely less likely that years of careful research will feed scientific controversy

more than it will suggest implications for nuclear weapons policy. As a prospective participant in at least the early stage of a hypothetical nuclear winter, I have no interest whatsoever in denying the possible phenomenon of nuclear winter its due in terms of policy. Should the nuclear winter thesis be sustained by further research, given that the nuclear age and its politics cannot be repealed, the policy case for working very energetically to make a multilayered reality of the strategic defense of urban areas will be usefully strengthened. This point is made in Payne and Gray, "Nuclear Policy and the Defensive Transition," pp. 839-41. However, there is a school of thought that sees nuclear winter as valuable support for the stability allegedly provided by capabilities for mutual assured destruction (MAD). In the context of the nuclear winter prospect, MAD becomes MASD (for mutual assured self-destruction). This argument is advanced by Admiral James Eberle in Letter to the Editor, *The Times* (London), October 3, 1984, p. 15. The implications of the nuclear winter hypothesis for strategic policy are discussed in Albert Wohlstetter, "Between an Unfree World and None: Increasing Our Choices," *Foreign Affairs* 63, no. 5(Summer 1985):962-94; and Colin S. Gray, "The Nuclear Winter Thesis and U.S. Strategic Policy," *Washington Quarterly* 8, no. 4(Summer 1985), pp. 85–96.

48.   A sophisticated treatment of U.S. choices in national security policy, focusing on the problems with extended deterrence, is Robert W. Tucker, "The Nuclear Debate," *Foreign Affairs* 63, no. 1(Fall 1984): 1-32. In common with Robert Jervis, Tucker has the rare virtue of penetrating flabby thinking—whether or not one agrees with him.

49.   Betts, "Elusive Equivalence," p. 117.

50.   That is, it is essential in the context of conventional and theater-nuclear inadequacy.

51.   Early in 1984, Caspar Weinberger wrote, accurately enough: "The Soviet drive toward superiority has been particularly pronounced in the realm of strategic nuclear forces." *Annual Report to the Congress, Fiscal Year 1985*, p. 21. Also see Caspar W. Weinberger, *Soviet Military Power, 1985* (Washington, D.C.: USGPO, April 1985).

52.   In September 1984, the Reagan White House would not even endorse a rhetorical call for superiority or advantage, as had been proposed for the Republican campaign platform.

53.   From time to time in the past, technical deficiencies in particular kinds of equipment would have produced catastrophic failure rates. For example, EMP and gamma radiation effects would have had devastating consequences for unhardened equipment. Of course, once a problem is discovered, the required technical fix is often quite simple to effect. War planners and JSTPS targeting teams have to worry that there may be weapon effect problems that are not merely underappreciated but may be totally unknown today. On one important dimension of what could go wrong, see Paul Bracken, *The Command and Control of Nuclear Forces* (New Haven: Yale University Press, 1983).

54.   Particularly inappropriate was Michael Howard's historical analogy in which he compared some U.S. (and perhaps Soviet) nuclear war-fighting theorists with those "European strategists who in 1914 promised their political masters decisive victory before Christmas." "On Fighting a Nuclear War," p. 14. No recog-

nized strategic theorist in the United States today is *promising* victory, let alone a victory that could be considered cheaply purchased. Professor Howard's misrepresentation undoubtedly was unintentional, but it demonstrates how difficult it can be for strategic thinkers to conduct a dialogue on this subject.

55. James Schlesinger walked into this particular minefield in 1974–75 when he chose to initiate a public debate over the dangers, opportunities, and possibility of limited-purpose counterforce attacks. See U.S. Congress, Senate, Committee on Foreign Relations, Subcommittee on Arms Control, International Organization and Security Agreements, *Analyses of Effects of Limited Nuclear Warfare*, 94th Cong., 1st sess. (Washington, D.C.: USGPO, September 1975).

56. The government led by Neville Chamberlain convinced itself that Hitler's Germany could be deterred from moving against Poland by a firm-sounding diplomacy. War was not expected by official London, and even after war was reluctantly declared on September 3, 1939, hopes were nurtured for a prompt political settlement. See Murray, *The Change in the European Balance of Power, 1938–1939*, chap. 9.

57. This need not be a matter of a narrowly technological hubris on the part of the United States. Strategic superiority embraces the idea of strategic-intellectual as well as material preponderance.

58. Luttwak, "On the Meaning of Strategy . . . for the United States in the 1980s," p. 270.

59. This logical point was advanced forcefully, with subsequent diplomatic embarrassment (and "clarification," as the saying goes), by Helmut Schmidt in his 1977 Alastair Buchan Memorial Lecture at the International Institute for Strategic Studies in London. See *Survival* 20, no. 1(January/February 1978): 3-4.

60. "If the Soviets recognize that our forces can and will deny them their objectives at whatever level of conflict they contemplate, then deterrence remains effective and the risk of war is diminished." Weinberger, *Annual Report to the Congress, Fiscal Year 1985*, p. 27.

CHAPTER **9**

Nuclear Strategy:
The Range of Choice

There are cylical trends, or oscillations, in the character and the dominant strain of U.S. strategic thought. Following Harold and Margaret Sprout,[1] I endorse the idea that the historically and culturally rich setting for U.S. defense policy provides a wide range of possibilities. U.S. strategic culture is viewed here not as a constraint, but as a quite tolerant license. The "American way of war" endorses strategies of both annihilation (*Vernichtungskrieg*) and attrition (*Ermattungskrieg*), to use the enlightening distinction drawn by the German military historian Hans Delbruck.[2] In the U.S. Civil War, Sherman's march through Georgia and the Carolinas exemplified the former, and Grant's painful campaign in the wilderness and then before Petersburg and Richmond illustrated the latter. The two were complementary; Grant's campaign of attrition permitted Sherman to wage a war of maneuver. In World War II, General Eisenhower pursued a strategy of attrition in a broad-front advance to and beyond the Rhine, for reasons of both Anglo-American accord, or tolerable discord, and logistic convenience,[3] while MacArthur and Nimitz pursued the theme of maneuver-annihilation in their island-hopping campaigns. MacArthur's Inchon landing during the Korean War was a further illustration of the U.S. capacity for pursuit of the maneuver-annihilation choice.

More often than not, the United States has been denied freedom of choice between attrition and maneuver by circumstances of geography and the combat skills of the enemy. Obvious examples include the campaigns in Sicily, Italy,[4] and Normandy,[5] where the superior fighting power of the German Army,[6] greatly aided by highly defensible terrain, precluded agile maneuver for rapid decision. The maneuver by George Patton's Third Army that very nearly trapped the German forces in the Falaise "pocket" was possible only because of the prior 6 weeks' campaign of attrition, particularly around Caen, that had worn down German strength.

Although one may speak of cultural proclivities with respect to strategy,[7] it is reassuring to appreciate that U.S. military experience points to a wide range of policy options. Nonetheless, a close observer of the U.S. defense debate of the past 15 years could not help but notice the doctrinal rigidity that has characterized different schools of thought. This is a somewhat bizarre phenomenon for a nation and culture that prides itself on its pragmatism. Americans should be the least likely people to coalesce into doctrinally dogmatic, apparently exclusive groups.[8] Bernard Brodie wrote, accurately, that "strategic thinking, or 'theory,' if one prefers, is nothing if not pragmatic. Strategy is a 'how to do it' study, a guide to accomplishing something and doing it efficiently."[9]

It is fashionable to argue that a thousand flowers should be encouraged to bloom and that one person's theory is as good as the next. However, this book prefers to hew closely to the ideal of U.S. pragmatism and to argue that many of the candidate concepts for nuclear policy for the United States in the 1980s and 1990s have already been tested (short of battle, of course), have been found wanting, and should be identified clearly as inferior ideas.

In descending order of concern, the strategic nuclear forces of the United States are charged mainly with the deterrence of massive counter-urban/industrial strikes; the deterrence of massive counterforce/counterpolitical strikes; and the ability to exercise coercive influence on behalf of forward-placed allies or exposed U.S. forces by way of extended deterrence. These tasks were outlined by Herman Kahn in the early 1960s in his books *On Thermonuclear War*[10] and *On Escalation*.[11] Nonetheless, the fact remains that the functions of strategic nuclear forces are ill-appreciated today.

The required character of a strategic-force posture and the doctrine that it expresses is, or should be, determined by the character of U.S. foreign policy that it is required to support and by the political-military capabilities and nature of likely adversaries. For a leading contemporary example, the official in-house and public debate over the MX ICBM and its basing mode has been conducted in a near vacuum with respect to foreign policy supportive duties, strategy, and Soviet strategic culture—all of which are of central importance to the debate.[12]

The simplest task for the U.S. defense community is to design a strategic-force posture that is capable of deterring a tolerably rational enemy from launching a massive attack against U.S. cities. Unfortunately, U.S. planning problems cannot sensibly be restricted to such a task. Because the United States has global interests, its strategic forces have to be relevant, in the first instance, to the restoration of deterrence vis-à-vis some unfolding political-military catastrophe in a theater far from home. It is likely that it will be the United States that first feels moved to threaten and execute a central nuclear strike. This means that the question "Are we deterred?" may well be asked first in Washington, rather than in Moscow. This would be a reversal of the situation in the Cuban missile crisis of October 1962, when the Soviet Union had to decide whether or not to attempt to run the U.S. naval blockade.

One should respect the logical integrity of a policy-doctrinal opponent who marries a recommendation for a minimum U.S. strategic-force posture (designed to assure the destruction of perhaps the 100 largest Soviet urban areas) to a recommendation for the drastic retrenchment of U.S. foreign policy duties and interests. If the United States were to decide that it had no vital foreign policy interests beyond the Western Hemisphere, a far less expansive definition of force-postural adequacy might be appropriate.[13] Also, if a policy-doctrinal opponent were to recommend a general-purpose force posture (including tactical aviation, maritime assets, and theater-nuclear strength) that should, with the assistance of regional allies, be capable of defeating most local challenges, the deterrent and war-fighting burdens placed on the U.S. strategic nuclear force posture should be noticeably diminished.[14]

A defense analyst is not totally at liberty to select a personally favored strategic posture and doctrine. The United States does have global commitments. The policy arguments with reference to the balance of power in Eurasia-Africa vis-à-vis U.S. security that were persuasive in 1917 and in 1940–41 are no less valid today. The United States could function minimally in isolation, with the Soviet empire dominating the rest of the world outside the Americas, but that is not a world in which Americans would choose to live, and such an autarkic security condition of embattlement could have profound negative implications for the quality of U.S. domestic life.[15] On the defense-postural side, although the United States could choose to stress general-purpose force capabilities, there are some enduring problems of geopolitics. The Soviet Union enjoys interior lines of communications vis-à-vis theater conflict around much of Eurasia, if not Africa;[16] and scarcely less significant, the Eurasian allies of the United States have proved to be nervous about defense-postural/doctrinal "improvements" that appear to make the international political system safer for local or theater wars.[17] In extreme circumstances, a favorable transformation of the capability of U.S. (and U.S.-allied) nonnuclear forces may augment the incentives to nuclear employment on the Soviet side. As Richard Burt has argued:

> Although emphasizing conventional forces will tend to raise the "threshold" in local conflicts for the Western use of nuclear weapons, a con-

ventional-emphasis strategy could actually provide the Soviet Union with incentives to escalate in time of war.[18]

Among the worst sins committed by policy-contending defense analysts is an inability to listen to the arguments of "the other side." This chapter offers a preferred policy option, but that option is offered on the basis of characterizations of alternatives that doctrinal opponents should acknowledge to be fair. Opponents of the preferred option may cavil over the logic of that argument, but they should not be able to allege that their arguments have not been presented fairly.

Five nuclear strategy options for the United States are discussed here in detail:

1. mutual assured vulnerability;

2. mutual assured vulnerability with (targeting) flexibility;

3. counterforce and countercontrol preeminence;

4. damage limitation for deterrence and coercion ("classical strategy");

5. damage limitation with defense dominant.

The United States today, following President Carter's PD-59 and its associated NUWEP and President Reagan's NSDD-13, is at option 3 in terms of declaratory policy.[19] This chapter recommends a move to option 4—damage limitation for deterrence and coercion. Such a shift should affront relatively few current official shibboleths and should be technically feasible in the 1990s. A preference for damage limitation for deterrence and coercion, or classical strategy, lies squarely in the center of U.S. strategic culture. It can be advanced as essential today as the only concept that fully matches the foreign policy supportive duties that continue to be placed on the strategic nuclear forces. It is often easier to debate preferred, largely fictitious doctrinal adversaries than real ones. In the analysis of different postural and doctrinal ideas that follows, there is no conscious tailoring of opposing arguments for the purpose of easy demonstration of believed error. The proponents of different beliefs concerning the U.S. strategic-nuclear force posture may be judged, very substantially, to be in error, but their motives, patriotism, and so forth, are not in question. No one has any hands-on knowledge of bilateral nuclear war—all are rank amateurs; whereas virtually everything that is believed about what has or has not deterred is based largely on inferential, deductive reasoning.

Nuclear strategy, and deterrence more generally, tends to be taught in universities and war colleges in a doctrinally permissive mode. Students are exposed to rival theorists and are educated to believe that there is no source of authority on the subject. For example, at the Kennedy School of

Government at Harvard, students have been asked to compare and contrast my opinions with those of Robert Jervis.[20] The idea that there may be a "correct" theory is inimical to contemporary liberal scholarship.

OPTION 1: MUTUAL ASSURED VULNERABILITY

The United States could decide that nuclear war-fighting and intrawar deterrent ideas were an illusion and that security could best be forwarded by advertising and acting programmatically on the basis of that decision. The matching U.S. strategic posture would be designed to hold at risk, under all circumstances of attack, a very large number of Soviet urban areas and other economic targets believed to be essential to recovery from war. That number might be 100 or even more. U.S. strategic forces could be designed and sized for extravagant redundancy, in that one might require that each leg of the strategic triad be independently capable of effecting the identified level of damage.

This posture and doctrine is often termed one of finite or minimum deterrence. Not infrequently, when it is advocated, it is accompanied by the opinion that even a handful of nuclear weapons on a handful of cities would likely suffice to deter and, if executed would certainly be viewed as a societal catastrophe.[21] The implementing posture identified is typically quite substantial, however. Since the late 1960s, the United States has never had war plans that even approximated this idea.[22] Defense Department spokesmen in 1967 and 1968 often spoke and wrote in terms of the merits of mutual assured vulnerability, but critics (and admirers) of the idea of mutual assured vulnerability should not confuse rhetoric with operational policy.[23]

Nonetheless, the central core of reasoning at the heart of mutual assured vulnerability arguments remains as significant in terms of the public discussion of nuclear policy issues as it is insignificant, and of declining importance, in terms of recent defense planning. Although the defense intellectual and policy trend in the United States has been moving away from finite deterrence ideas, those ideas constitute an important and enduring landmark on the landscape of defense and continue to have a place, albeit frequently underrecognized, in the schemes of advocates of other, more complex postures and doctrines.[24] Although there is no logically necessary connection between them, the idea of mutual assured vulnerability underpins much of the reasoning in favor of the nuclear freeze. Many proponents of the freeze do not really care about the details of balance and imbalance or about the issue of exactly what is a candidate to be frozen and what is not. In the view of those freeze proponents, states are deterred by the general expectation that their principal urban centers would be devastated by nuclear weapons. Very plainly, both superpowers assuredly would retain considerable if not extravagant "overkill" against that elementary target set.[25]

Rival debaters from contrasting schools of thought should be discouraged from debating caricatures of their opponents' arguments, public relations acronyms, and pejorative slogans that are inaccurate. Nuclear strategy is a difficult enough subject when it is discussed fairly, without the added complication of deliberate or careless misrepresentation. Quite often, the first victim of the telling, oversimplified caricature is the author himself. For example, advocates of a finite deterrence approach to the quality and size of the strategic-force posture are interested in mutual vulnerability, not in executing mutual destruction. The politically effective acronym MAD, for *mutual assured destruction*, is not helpful for constructive debate. Similarly, proponents of a counterforce strategy, with or without homeland defense, design nuclear *war-fighting* or nuclear use theory *for deterrence*.[26] Theorists of different doctrinal persuasions are arguing over theories of deterrence and over what could and should be done in the event that deterrence fails.[27]

The discussion here and in subsequent sections of this chapter is organized by way of statements of key elements in each strategy option, with commentary, generally of a critical kind, immediately following every statement.

1. Nuclear war would be a catastrophe unparalleled in world history.

> *Commentary:* Nuclear war may or may not prove to be a catastrophe unparalleled in world history, but it is highly unlikely to be the functional equivalent of the cataclysmic biblical flood.[28] In the thirteenth and fourteenth Centuries, the Mongols and bubonic plague were viewed in much the same eschatological terms in which many people today view nuclear war. Those "visitations from God" were terrible, but mankind and even "civilization" survived. As Herman Kahn sought to establish more than 20 years ago, catastrophe can come in different sizes and with very different consequences.[29]

2. Nuclear war could not be controlled or limited.

> *Commentary:* Pessimists, or realists, may be correct in claiming, on the basis of no more evidence than that held by the people they criticize, that nuclear war cannot be controlled or limited.[30] Any nuclear strategist should be distrusted who claims limited and controlled nuclear wars as the wars that would happen if his version of the requirements of deterrence were to break down. Theorists of mutual assured vulnerability often do not appear to understand that their caricatured opponents are not offering nuclear wars of a pseudoguaranteed nature. Theorists who believe in intranuclear-war deterrence are gambling,

perhaps not unreasonably, that the Soviet High Command, in time of central nuclear war, would make decisions on the basis of an ethic of consequences that is functionally analogous to the U.S. ethic. They could be wrong. Counterforce/damage-limitation theorists do not exclude the possibility of catastrophe should the Soviet leadership either be unable or choose not to cooperate. Their argument is to the effect that mutual assured vulnerability guarantees unlimited catastrophe, whereas their preference at least holds open the hope of containing the scale of potential damage.

3. Probably the greatest risk of nuclear war will stem not from Soviet leaders who are insufficiently deterred, but rather from Western nuclear war-fighting theorists who may mislead policymakers into believing that nuclear weapons can be employed, like other weapons, as a political instrument.[31]

> *Commentary:* Western theorists do not promise political advantage from controlled nuclear employment. Those theorists note that nuclear threats are integral to NATO strategy, that war could occur regardless of the quality of NATO's posture and doctrine, and believe that a theory of limited nuclear war is preferable to no such theory. Even the severely constrained nuclear campaigns envisaged by defense-minded Western analysts are acknowledged to be very likely to entail a casualty rate so high as to give pause to, if not deter, any reasonable U.S. president.[32] No one is offering cheap nuclear wars or guarantees of very limited societal liability. Prudent commentators, regardless of doctrinal affiliation, are properly skeptical of the likelihood, though not the possibility, of controlled nuclear war.

4. Most of the Western strategic literature that focuses on the need for credibility in deterrent threats and that worries about the alleged delicacy of the balance of terror fails to understand how and why nuclear deterrence works.[33] Nuclear deterrence works because all (or nearly all) sensible people—policymakers and people in the street alike—are terrified by the prospect of nuclear war per se. No matter how large the escalatory leaps from a theater-conventional conflict to large-scale theater-nuclear war and then, most probably, to a large-scale central war,[34] any logical fragility in the credibility of the threat of such leaps is more than offset by the generalized fear of nuclear war. Statesmen, unlike theorists of nuclear strategy, do not confuse the logic of the real world of political responsibility with the abstract, consequence-free logic of the strategic theorists' seminar room.[35]

> *Commentary:* Western politicians are indeed frightened by the prospect of nuclear war *per se.* U.S. strategists have not questioned or ignored this general truth; rather, some of them have argued that Soviet gov-

ernments, historically, have approached domestic human loss from a perspective rather different from that of their Western counterparts. In the 1920s and 1930s, the Soviet governments killed close to 20 million of their own people, and some members of the current leadership group was a junior party to, and survivors of, that process.[36] Although it is possible that Soviet leaders are deterred by a generalized prospect of nuclear war writ large, the available evidence on the USSR may lead one to a different conclusion. Although the Soviet Union does not want nuclear war, and would not likely court the risk of its occurrence for reason of positive gain, there is reason to believe that Soviet leaders would view nuclear war not as the end of history, but rather as an experience to be survived and from which a resilient and objectively "progressive" society recovers. Moreover, it is very likely that Soviet leaders fear nuclear war not so much for the amount of human and property damage it would cause as for the risk it would pose to Soviet political control at home and abroad. Sensitivity to individual or even large-scale human loss has not been a prominent feature of Soviet (or Russian) political culture. Anyone who believes that nuclear war should mean the same to Americans and to Great Russians should reflect more deeply on the contrasting histories of the two societies.[37]

5. Nuclear weapons not only deter the employment of nuclear weapons by an enemy, they also deter the kinds of actions that would, or could, create a political-military situation wherein the use of such weapons would be judged to be much more likely. All people fear nuclear war; moreover, they fear it roughly to the same degree.

> *Commentary:* Although it is undoubtedly true that all people fear nuclear war, it is not necessarily true that all people fear nuclear war equally. Soviet military science teaches that nuclear missile weapons should be decisive in modern war and that although a bilateral nuclear war will place unprecedented burdens on military organizations, it will also offer unprecedented opportunities for swift success.[38] However much one may deplore the fact, authoritative Soviet military opinion sees nuclear firepower in the context of long-range artillery.[39] Where Western analysts tend to err is in their appreciation of the dynamics of an acute crisis. Soviet leaders are obliged by party doctrine to believe that their system will survive a nuclear war, and they also may well believe it because of the prudent provisions that have been made over the past 20 years. Mutual assured vulnerability, insofar as it refers to the USSR, is not a part of Soviet strategic culture. The evidence is not persuasive that the Soviet leadership is confident that it can wage and win a central nuclear war. However, Soviet leaders do believe that victory is possible (and important).[40]

6. Cultural nuance is not important in the nuclear deterrence system. A very large nuclear war means the same thing to all cultures.[41] In principle,

there is some political-analytical merit in pointing to possible cultural distinctions between countries that may affect deterrence reasoning. In practice, however, the sheer scale of damage that widespread nuclear war would impose renders discussion of operational nuclear strategy largely moot.

> *Commentary:* The level and kind of damage likely to be suffered in a central nuclear war cannot be assumed to constitute a given. Targeting "withholds" and other technical details such as yields selected, heights of burst, and so forth, could be critically important to the scale of the catastrophe effected. Although it is true that nuclear weapons come in inconveniently large packages of prompt energy release, it is also true that careful weapon design, extreme accuracy, and concern for unwanted collateral damage should reduce potential societal damage by many orders of magnitude.[42] Soviet targeting style almost certainly does not lend itself easily to the idea of waging nuclear war in a severely constrained manner,[43] but the possibility cannot and should not be discounted. Finally, almost no matter how an enemy chooses to wage war, a country can limit the damage it could suffer.[44]

7. Nuclear war, should it occur, would hold the participants and many bystanding states open to a limitless liability. Mutual assured vulnerability is not a posture and doctrine of choice. There *is* no choice. This posture and doctrine makes a virtue of necessity. Strategists who insist on seeking out operationally interesting nuclear employment options in pursuit of an improved quality of prewar deterrence, intrawar deterrence, or damage limitation have simply not come to grips with the nature of nuclear war. There are no plausible theories offering a reasonable promise of bearable, survivable, recoverable (let alone winnable) nuclear conflict.[45]

> *Commentary:* Nuclear war could prove to be a nonsurvivable, nonrecoverable catastrophe, but one can design war plans that should not lead to that dire result if the enemy follows the dictates of self-interest. No one is offering quarantees of nuclear war with strictly limited liability, but controlled and limited nuclear war is more likely to be a reality if it has been considered well ahead of time. The mutual assured vulnerability school of thought both discounts the Soviet evidence to the effect that Soviet society is unlikely to be in a condition even close to total vulnerability and forecloses, a priori, on the prospect of Western damage limitation in war. There would be an enormous difference between, say, 20 million and 120 million U.S. fatalities. Both are catastrophes, but the United States could recover from the former, whereas it could not recover from the latter. This is far from a claim that 20 million fatalities would be, let alone should be, "acceptable."[46]

8. Nuclear weapons cannot be tamed. There cannot be a nuclear strategy with a human face. However, by choosing a nuclear arsenal that manifestly lacks the capability to threaten even a generous Soviet definition of its second-strike retaliatory-force-level requirements, the United States can diminish both crisis and arms race instabilities.[47]

> *Commentary:* U.S. self-restraint in the region of strategic nuclear force deployment has had either no effect or an encouraging effect on Soviet defense planners. Soviet strategic force developments over the past decade have shown no evident sensitivity to U.S. crisis or arms race instability concerns. Whereas some Western theories of stability show very clearly, for example, that hard-target counterforce capability is destabilizing, Soviet weapons deployments do not betray any appreciation of this concern. In the Soviet view, the prevention of war is a political function; it is the task of the armed forces to prepare efficiently for the actual conduct of war.[48] The idea that the detail of military posture could be important for political decisions on the dynamics of crisis and perhaps even for military mobilization decisions relevant to the determination of war or peace, remains alien to the Soviet mind-set—at least insofar as it may affect Soviet program decisions.[49]

The foregoing characterization and commentary is offered as an intellectual anchor to one end of the policy-thought spectrum. It is not offered as an accurate representation of the contemporary beliefs of any particular individual or group of individuals.

Mutual assured vulnerability, though a vital part of U.S. thinking on defense, even today, has never truly dominated official thinking, let alone planning. An important issue not yet discussed here is whether or not the U.S. defense community can enforce a mutuality of societal vulnerability. As is well known, the Soviet Union has provided superhard protection for its top political leadership cadre, blast shelters for its essential work force, and evacuation plans plus fall-out shelters for its general urban population. These plans may not work very well in practice, but can a prudent Western defense analyst assume that they would fail catastrophically? More to the point, perhaps, can a prudent Western defense analyst afford to assume that Soviet leaders would lack confidence in their preparations for war survival? It is not good enough to argue by assertion, as Glenn Buchan does, that "no decision-maker can have confidence that any preparations for war, in case deterrence fails, would be successful or that any recovery plans are realistic."[50]

OPTION 2: MUTUAL ASSURED VULNERABILITY WITH FLEXIBILITY

The second option corresponds roughly and generically to the point whither most of the policy refugees from mutual assured vulnerability have evacuated intellectually.[51] It is probably no exaggeration to claim that this second option is the "thinking person's" version of mutual assured vulnerability. There is no need to reproduce here, yet again, the general arguments typically advanced in favor of mutual assured vulnerability. This policy option is particularly important because it represents an apparent way station on the nuclear war-fighting course. Many people associated with mutual assured vulnerability thinking will argue, perhaps with good reason, that they have never been opposed to flexibility in strategic employment planning; that they have known since 1961–62 that SIOP planning provided several preplanned options, albeit very large ones;[52] and that, in general terms, the conviction that mutual societal vulnerability is both a technological fact and desirable as a dampener of arms-competitive urges carries no particular implications vis-à-vis the size and sequencing of targeting options.[53] However, there are potential tensions between mutual assured vulnerability and flexibility in targeting. What follows are the essential characteristics of option 2, with commentary appended.

1. Because mutual vulnerability is considered the ultimate basis for deterrence stability, neither country should seek to acquire the physical means to limit damage to its homeland through active and passive defenses or through the development of offensive forces that threaten the survivability of the strategic retaliatory forces of the other side.

> *Commentary:* Option 2 suffers from the same fundamental weakness as option 1. If war should occur, and if the deterrent shock effect of initial, flexible strategic nuclear use should not function as hoped, the United States could well suffer a limitless catastrophe.[54] Moreover, as is very generally appreciated today, the Soviet Union, though not at all eager to engage in nuclear combat, unambiguously does not endorse the concept of *mutual* assured vulnerability.[55]

2. Because of the suicidal consequences of actually executing a major attack option against Soviet urban-industrial assets, the credibility of such a threat is not high under most circumstances. Therefore, both to augment perception of a link between theater forces and strategic forces and to provide a president with employment options that might serve to restore deterrence in the course of a war without necessarily producing mutual holocaust, targeting flexibility is desirable.[56]

Commentary: Flexibility per se does not solve the U.S. president's self-deterrence problem.[57] In principle, perhaps, it should be more credible for him to threaten small-scale rather than large-scale nuclear strikes, but he would have to be profoundly fearful of the consequences of such action. Option 2 does not contain a persuasive theory of escalation control, let alone dominance. If a political-military situation is sufficiently grave for a president to order the very limited employment of central nuclear forces, it is reasonable to assume that both parties to the conflict have a truly major stake in the political outcome to the conflict. It is just possible that the shock of homeland-to-homeland nuclear use would restore deterrence, but it is not very likely. It is far more likely that the Soviet Union would respond by beginning to execute its central nuclear war plan. Should the Soviet Union respond more or less in kind, contrary to what the U.S. defense community thinks it understands about Soviet strategic culture, what could the president try next? Among the more telling criticisms of limited nuclear options is the charge that they are very unlikely to succeed in restoring deterrence.[58]

3. Flexibility should enhance deterrence. The potential of flexibility for wreaking damage in the realm of crisis and arms race stability can be minimized through the endorsement of a posture that manifestly would be incompetent in fulfilling preclusive counterforce missions. Moreover, the absence of BMD and of serious air defense and civil defense should reinforce declarations to the effect that strategic flexibility is not, in any real sense, a move toward what is termed a war-fighting strategy.[59]

Commentary: Far from enhancing deterrence, option 2 could set in motion a process of escalation that the United States could neither discipline nor win. A posture that was obviously counterforce-incompetent—because of a determination not to enhance possible crisis and arms-race instabilities—would virtually invite a counterforce-dedicated Soviet Union to escalate rapidly in search of victory or, at the least, "useful advantage."[60]

4. Small nuclear-strike options would be intended both to provide a deterrent shock and to carry the clear threat of "more to come, unless . . ." By executing a limited nuclear option, one would have signaled determination through taking action to cross two major thresholds (use of central nuclear forces and employment most probably against the homeland of a superpower).[61] However, the small scale and the nature of the attack would also signal unambiguously a willingness to exercise restraint and would constitute an invitation for the restraint to be reciprocated. In short, such limited employment would be part of a political bargaining process, rather than constituting military action.[62]

Commentary: LNOs would more likely signal weakness than strength of will and capability. The Soviet Union, given its well-appreciated conflict style, probably would be more impressed by what the United States did not do or was unable to do than by what actually was effected. Very limited nuclear options, instead of signaling determination, would more likely be read in Moscow as signaling an extreme fear of nuclear war. Such fear is reasonable and sensible, but it is not the message that a U.S. president would want to transmit when he engages in what Thomas Schelling has termed a competition in risk-taking.[63]

The addition of flexibility of strategic employment to a mutual assured vulnerability posture and doctrine seems more likely to produce defeat on the installment plan than effective intrawar deterrence. It would be profoundly imprudent to begin a small nuclear war unless one had on hand a capability for waging, surviving, and recovering from a large nuclear war.

Proponents of mutual assured vulnerability with flexibility have not been unmindful of the perils of the option, in terms of their core beliefs about stability and about what deters.[64] The technical requirements for the execution of limited nuclear options plausibly could drive one toward endorsing deployment of very accurate ICBMs, which, so the argument goes, would be destabilizing because of their counterforce potential. Manned bombers and cruise missiles are inherently inappropriate for most (though not all) LNO/SNO (sub-SIOP nuclear options) missions, because Soviet air defenses would not have been suppressed in advance. Also, SLBMs would be inappropriate because there may not be submarines on-station to execute such missions; communication may not be adequate or even possible; and an SSBN comes with a distressingly large number of SLBM warheads (240 on the Ohio class), and betrays its position by launching even a single missile.[65]

With respect to the flexible and small-scale employment of nuclear weapons, extreme accuracy is desirable (as may be the use of single-warhead missiles), because the use of small warheads, creating the least possible collateral damage, is therefore feasible. In the future (in an era of zero-CEP or perfect accuracy), it is possible that strategic nonnuclear weapons could accomplish many of the counterforce tasks that currently either have to be allocated to nuclear-armed ICBMs or are not scheduled to be performed at all because of the problem of collateral damage.

In the immediate context of this discussion, flexibility implies very small-scale employment. However, there is no inherent reason why flexibility need refer only to the very limited end of the employment spectrum. Flexibility is a strategy-neutral concept, long appreciated as a political and military desideratum. Soviet military science, too, endorses flexibility, though with specific referents that are far removed indeed from the context of the U.S. debate of the mid-1970s.[66] Strategic flexibility at the level of principle is a difficult concept to oppose. It is no easy matter to argue for inflexibility.[67] Critics of so-called nuclear war-fighting strategies appreciate very well that endorsement of flexibility and the idea that central nuclear use might be controlled and limited places them on the unstable upper reaches of a doctrinal-postural slippery slope. Agreement to some kinds of flexibility may well open the floodgates to theories of controlled nuclear war—theories that generic adherents to option 2 emphatically do not endorse.

Option 2 is dangerous in the eyes of adherents to classical mutual assured vulnerability doctrine because it might encourage the view, which is strongly believed to be mistaken, that nuclear weapons are usable as political instruments and that nuclear war, in some very dire circumstances, would be a sensible course to pursue and would remain limited.[68]

OPTION 3: COUNTERFORCE AND COUNTERCONTROL PREEMINENCE

Option 3 is U.S. defense policy today. The U.S. defense community, coerced by the continuing adverse trend in the balance of forces, has addressed the vital strategic question of what Soviet leaders find most deterring and has decided, almost certainly correctly, that the most fearsome threat in Soviet anticipation is the attenuation or loss of political control over the Soviet empire at home and abroad. In addition, it is well appreciated in the United States that a fully effective strike against the Soviet political control system is highly improbable, which means that there are no easier options to the initial need to blunt Soviet military power directly.[69]

The most impressive defense-intellectual pyrotechnics of the nuclear era may have occurred in the Golden Age of 1955–65,[70] but the most valuable thought probably was registered in the late 1970s. The prospect of strategic inferiority, in the immediate context of the manifest failure of an erstwhile popular theory of strategic stability, stimulated the U.S. defense community to think through its evolving Soviet deterrence/war-fighting problem.[71] Unfortunately the intellectual task, in part for terms-of-reference reasons, was flawed with respect to its overall policy integrity. The principal flaw lay in the absence of a theory of damage limitation that was more substantial than aspirations for a reciprocity in targeting restraint.[72] However, for the first time in the nuclear age, the United States achieved a SIOP design that reflected a sophisticated view of the distinctively Soviet adversary. The major characteristics of option 3 are as follows:

1. Option 3 seeks to threaten the kind of damage that the Soviet Union should find most painful to suffer. The Soviet Union is deemed to fear not so much damage *per se*, but rather damage of particular kinds. Today, U.S. targeteers recognize that the relationship between state and society in the two superpowers is almost diametrically opposed. In the United States the state is, and ideologically is held to be, the servant of society, whereas the reverse is true in the Soviet Union. U.S. strategic targeting policy reportedly has now come to reflect this fact.

> *Commentary:* To the extent either that Soviet leaders can persuade Soviet citizens that the state interest is really their interest or that U.S. targeting policy cannot distinguish adequately between Soviet state and society, the fear and actual experience of war may serve to mobilize, rather than to fracture, patriotic sentiment in the USSR. The proposition that the Soviet leadership fears most for the continuity and effectiveness of its political tenure is almost certainly correct. However, many unanswered, and perhaps even unanswerable, questions remain with respect to the real vulnerability of the Soviet state to externally imposed shock. Even when they come with high accuracy and low yields, nuclear weapons inherently are weapons of mass destruction.[73] Much of the U.S. speculation about the possibility of forcing the political disintegration of the Soviet Union is really fanciful.

2. The essential assets of the Soviet state must be held at nuclear risk. These assets are preeminently, though by no means exclusively, military in character. In short, the United States requires a strategic-force posture that can inflict major damage on Soviet military power of all kinds. Above all, else, there is a need to be able to threaten second-strike counterforce missions that would offset, or more than offset, any benefit the Soviet Union might gain from a counterforce first strike. (Survivable U.S. strategic forces, in the second round of the war, would neutralize, or more than neutralize, whatever gains Moscow had achieved in round one.) Military power is the backbone and fundamental form of expression of the Soviet state, but it does not encompass the totality of "essential assets." Because a war may be relatively long—say, up to 6 months—and because one should worry about the postwar balance, directly war-supporting industry also has to be considered a prime target set.

> *Commentary:* The idea of the second-strike counterforce "equalizer" is attractive and has some theoretical merit,[74] but it appears to promise stalemate, which may or may not constitute a denial of Soviet victory. If the Soviet Union is faring well in a theater conflict, it is difficult to see why it should launch the first counterforce strike, to which the United States would need to provide an offsetting reply. The most

plausible reason for a massive Soviet counterforce blow against the United States would be a determination to achieve what John Erickson has termed a " 'disruptive strike,' not unlike Soviet artillery practice in World War II."[75] This would be a case of the Soviet Union striking first in the last resort in a central war, in preemptive anticipation of U.S. escalation. Plainly, the counterforce and countercontrol leitmotiv in U.S. nuclear strategy today is by no means confined in its relevance to the role of second-strike threats. In the words of the Scowcroft Commission: "The Soviets must continue to believe what has been NATO's doctrine for three decades: that if we or our allies should be attacked—by massive conventional means or otherwise—the United States has the will and the means to defend with the full range of American power."[76]

3. The single most essential asset of the Soviet state, dependent though it is on the power of the Soviet armed forces, is the political control structure.[77] The United States should hold at prompt risk Soviet political leaders, the Central Committee *nomenklatura* at large,[78] the means of communication and command from Moscow to the provinces, and critically important elements of the KGB. If Soviet leaders know that their political system, as opposed to their society, is targeted reliably, they know that the United States has the capability to deny them victory.

> *Commentary:* It is healthy for deterrence for the Soviet leadership to be told that it and its means for enforcing domestic and imperial political control are targeted reliably. However, countercontrol targeting has some severe problems. The United States does not have a fully comprehensive understanding of the workings of the control structure in peacetime, let alone in wartime; it does not know what are and what are not truly essential targets; it does not wish to foreclose totally, early in a central war, on the possibility of negotiated war termination; and it does not have the ability to neutralize or blunt the Soviet retaliatory strike that should be expected to follow as a consequence of U.S. execution of a major countercontrol strike option. The U.S. defense community has to consider whether a large countercontrol strike should be delivered "up front" as a bid for damage limitation, intended to destroy or paralyze the Soviet chain of political-military command, or whether the countercontrol strike option should be retained as "the threat of last resort" to protect U.S. cities.[79]

4. This strategy option has as its centerpiece a determination to deny victory to the Soviet Union, in Soviet terms.[80] The countervailing strategy of the second half of the Carter administration was dedicated to the mission of assuring effective deterrence through the promise of denying victory to the Soviet Union. The Soviet Union, so it was (and to a large extent still is) reasoned, would not initiate a war that it was convinced, with high

assurance, it could not win. Caspar Weinberger has been explicit in explaining that his idea of denying the Soviet Union achievement of its war aims cannot rest on a threat of action against Soviet cities: "We disagree with those who hold that deterrence should be based on nuclear weapons designed to destroy cities rather than military targets. Deliberately designing weapons aimed at populations is neither necessary nor sufficient for deterrence. If we are forced to retaliate and can only respond by destroying population centers, we invite the destruction of our own population. Such a deterrent strategy is hardly likely to carry conviction as a deterrent, particularly as a deterrent to nuclear—let alone conventional—attack on an ally."[81]

> *Commentary:* Denying victory to the Soviet Union prospectively is very important, indeed essential. Unfortunately, a focus on victory denial is compatible with acquiescence in the prospect of Western defeat. In practice, a U.S. president venturing up the escalation ladder in or toward central nuclear war is very likely to be much more interested in precluding U.S. defeat than in denying victory to the Soviet Union. U.S. officials and strategic theorists have tended to commit the somewhat elementary logical error of assuming that *the* problem is to determine what it is that Soviet leaders find most deterring. That question is exceedingly important, but it is no more important than its logical strategic corollary—what would deter a U.S. president? One should not design a U.S. strategic-force posture, and matching doctrine, that cannot at least alleviate the self-deterrence problem. If, as seems plausible, it were the United States that felt moved to consider initiating a central nuclear war, for reason of impending theater defeat, the major deterrence problem would be U.S. rather than Soviet.[82]

5. Option 3 rests on appreciation of the fact that relative to the USSR, U.S. strategic-force capability, on many important measures of merit, either has already slipped into the inferior category or is in peril of doing so.[83] As with the U.S. Army's characterization of its operational problem in the mid-1970s, the issue here is how to fight outnumbered and win. The idea central to former Secretary of Defense Harold Brown's concept of the countervailing strategy was that of superior strategy. Even if the Soviet Union purchased a more impressive quantity of qualitatively not-too-dissimilar strategic capabilities, the U.S. defense community would design targeting plans for deterrence that in the quality of fear they should produce, would offset or more than offset gross U.S. strategic muscular deficiencies. For example, if U.S. strategic nuclear forces could hold at risk (at least in the fearful Soviet perspective) the most essential of Soviet state assets, as opposed to societal assets, that should suffice to offset, through its prospective denial of Soviet victory in war, any advantage Soviet leaders might

anticipate as a well-merited consequence of their newly acquired advantages in the gross figures of merit of strategic capability.[84] If all else fails, the United States would retain, to the last moment, the ability to strike with devastating effectiveness against the Soviet economy. Survival and a superior recovery potential understandably are deemed vital by Soviet military science. The United States would be able, in extremis as its ultima ratio, to promise credibly to the Soviets that their ability to recover from World War III on a timetable likely to be politically acceptable could be fatally impaired.[85]

> *Commentary:* Superior strategy is always desirable. One must acknowledge that strategic competition between the superpowers embraces a dimension of doctrinal rivalry.[86] The countervailing strategy is very important, historically, in that it both recognizes the value of strategy and it seeks, explicitly, to exploit distinctive Soviet vulnerabilities. However, the countervailing strategy, for all its genuine sensitivity to Soviet culture, has neglected to consider a dominant reality of U.S. culture—namely, that a U.S. president could not intelligently hurt others if the certain consequence of such infliction of pain would be delivery by the Soviet Union of a nuclear strike likely to inflict 100 million or more U.S. casualties. The United States could never effect a major attack option against the Soviet economy, because such action would result in a Soviet retaliatory strike that the United States could not survive. What was and remains wrong with former Secretary of Defense Harold Brown's idea of a countervailing strategy was not that it promised to effect an inappropriate quality of damage on the Soviet Union, but that it neglected the problem of U.S. self-deterrence.

Contrary to the sense of many very strongly worded hostile Soviet commentaries, PD-59 did not provide guidance for a nuclear war-fighter's manual. PD-59, reflecting fairly accurately the two to three years of detailed research that preceded it, addressed adequately the question of what prospective damage Soviet leaders fear most. Nonetheless, PD-59 had two very major deficiencies—one internal, the other external.

First it reportedly outlined a vision of U.S. counterforce and counterpolitical control activity in the SIOP that is the better part of 10 years away from physical possibility (that is, U.S. strategic forces cannot do the job in the 1980s).[87] Second, as in its preceding strategic targeting review process, PD-59 ignored plausible connections between putative freedom of strategic offensive action and the ability to limit damage to the U.S. homeland.[88] Current nuclear policy is not so much wrong on strategic-logical grounds as it is incomplete (at least until the SDI evolves into a weapons program for homeland defense). PD-59 and NSDD-13 were not missteps, unless strategists choose to view them alone as the high-level doctrinal basis for strategic-force development over the years ahead.[89] Subsequent developments in policy guidance under the Reagan administration at least have recognized the importance of strategic defense.

By the end of the Carter administration, the small community of strategic targeting (for *deterrence*) afficionados was agreed, by and large, that sub-SIOP-level LNOs were relatively uninteresting;[90] that massive countereconomic recovery strike options were not obviously useful either for "up front" declaratory policy purposes or for operational reasons; and that World War III, should it occur, could be either very short or relatively long (perhaps 6 months).

Some defense analysts have worried about the issue of the endurance of strategic forces and the National Command Authority, and the idea that relatively long wars are possible moved from the status of idea to that of a planning assumption (among others) without benefit of very close strategic analytical scrutiny. On close inspection, one discovers that although 6-month wars are possible, 6-day or 6-week wars are no less possible and are probably no less plausible.[91] The problem here, as so often, is that the U.S. defense community tends to be dominated by technicians, not by strategic thinkers. Strategic technicians typically have scant appreciation of likely operational issues, let alone of genuinely strategic considerations. Other than in very exceptional cases, it is difficult to intrude strategic arguments into supposedly strategic policy decision processes. Typically, the major elements contending for preponderance are "technical fix" suggestions, considerations of managerial expediency, and the weight of vested bureaucratic interests in one weapon system, as opposed to an alternative. The official U.S. defense community is poorly organized either to generate or to respect truly strategic arguments.[92]

It is frustrating to recognize that option 3, where the United States officially aspires to be today, has already fractured the most important strategic cultural barrier; that is, option 3 recognizes the Soviet Union as a culturally distinctive adversary. Frustration lies in the appreciation that the United States, having broken free at the official level from strategic-cultural mirror-imaging, seems unable or unwilling to proceed logically the required additional mile to identification of a robust posture and doctrine. Having elected to take proper account of the uniquely Soviet aspects of the Soviet Union, U.S. officials are still resistant to the required further step of recognizing distinctively U.S. problems.

A U.S. official or extra-official defense analyst should know that his country is and has always been acutely sensitive to U.S. casualties. Except in the Civil War, high casualties have not been the U.S. military experience, and they have not been socially acceptable—hence, the traditional U.S. preference for profligate firepower to reduce U.S. casualty rates. Behind option 3 is full recognition of Soviet rejection of the concept of a strategic stability reposing on the basis of mutual assured societal vulnerability. However, option 3, or PD-59 (plus later refinements), accepts—

prospectively in perpetuity—the assured vulnerability of U.S. society. The Reagan administration has committed itself to exploration of the technical feasibility of strategic defense—and the president himself certainly has put the full weight of his office behind the vision of a United States no longer threatened by nuclear-armed ballistic missiles[93]—but that exploration and vision have yet to be translated into a damage-limitation policy for the enhancement of deterrence.

OPTION 4: DAMAGE LIMITATION FOR DETERRENCE AND COERCION ("CLASSICAL STRATEGY")

Option 4, the strategy preferred in this book, constitutes an evolution rather than a sharp break from the current posture and doctrine. It provides plausible answers to the more telling charges that can be leveled at option 3. In essence, option 4 would add a multifaceted homeland defense capability to the U.S. strategic posture. The title of this option was selected with care. The fundamental purpose of the strategic forces is to deter, or help deter, hostile acts against vital U.S. interests. The posture and doctrine outlined here should offer maximum discouragement to adventure and risk-taking on the part of the Soviets. However, deterrence is not a sufficient statement of the mission of U.S. strategic forces. Those forces, in addition to the negative task of dissuasion, also have laid upon them by foreign policy a range of possible "compellence" duties.[94] In other words, there may be occasions when the United States will have urgent political need to compel or coerce the Soviet Union to do things that it is most unwilling to do (for example, to recall armies that are fighting successfully in the Persian Gulf area or in Western Europe). Such a coercive mission is compatible with a broad definition of deterrence duties. A limited exercise of strategic nuclear power could be effected for the purpose of compelling a Soviet withdrawal; in short, it would be intended to "restore deterrence."

Characterization of option 4 as a war-fighting concept could be politically damaging, because the obvious elements of truth in the overall characterization tend to obscure the argument.[95] It is true that a commitment to damage limitation entails making preparations for the conduct of nuclear war, which is hardly a novel activity; the Soviet and U.S. defense communities have been making such preparations for 40 years. Proponents of a damage-limiting strategy believe that the United States has no sensible choice other than to attempt to implement this idea in planning. In fact, this is a task that is even worth doing badly.

Damage limitation is far from a new idea. Prior to the nuclear age, armed forces provided damage limitation by serving as a hard shell around a society. To damage an enemy's society, one had first to defeat his army and navy; long-range aircraft, ballistic missiles, and nuclear weapons appeared to change the situation drastically. Henceforth, it was believed, intolerable damage could be inflicted, whether or not an enemy's armed forces were defeated in the field (the bomber and missile would always get through).[96]

In their doctrinal "revolution in military affairs" in the late 1950s, Soviet military theorists accommodated the new technology by deciding that far from overturning the existing wisdom of Soviet military thought, nuclear-missile weapons would enable traditional tasks to be accomplished more swiftly and decisively. Neither then, nor since, did Soviet theorists accept fatalistically the proposition that nuclear weapons and their long-range means of delivery meant that Soviet state and society must, let alone should, be totally vulnerable. The massive air defense program developed in the United States in the mid to late 1950s, though largely abandoned subsequently, along with serious official interest in passive civil defense and the evolution of an impressive counterforce capability, reflected endorsement of the commonsense logic of damage limitation.[97]

Damage limitation was doctrinally preeminent in the United States in the very early years of Robert McNamara's tenure as secretary of defense. However, it was increasingly relegated to a backstage role, year by year, as Soviet strategic forces proliferated and were hardened and dispersed, and the U.S. government embraced theories of crisis and arms race stability (resting on the presumption of the inevitability and even desirability of the mutual vulnerability of societies).

Nonetheless, the idea of damage limitation persisted from the early 1960s to the present in the form of an aspiration for the functioning of restraint in targeting, reflecting the operation of an intrawar deterrence mechanism. For the past 30 years, the United States has been massively in the damage-limitation business with respect to the scale of allocation of SIOP-assigned assets to counterforce missions. Since the mid-1960s, however, there has been no expectation that truly effective damage limitation could be enforced through offensive counterforce action alone. With active and passive defenses eschewed for a mix of financial, technical, political, and strategic-theoretical reasons, the enduring hope for the limitation of damage has reposed in the belief in the possibility of reciprocated targeting restraint. One must deduce that even PD-59 and NSDD-13 endorsed the theory of damage limitation through the functioning of an intrawar deterrence mechanism. The logical flaws in this theory, and the lack of operational prudence in its derived policy advice, leads me, in this book, to identify option 4 as a superior strategy. The characteristics of option 4 are as follows:

1. In the absence of the ability to hold down U.S. casualties and economic damage to a level that is "acceptable" in the context of the most important political interests at stake, U.S. strategy either is a bluff or is heroically irresponsible.

> *Commentary:* Casualties and economic damage in nuclear war cannot plausibly be held down to "acceptable" levels. In the words of Bernard Brodie: "Whether the survivors be many or few, in the midst of a land scarred and ruined beyond all present comprehension, they should not be expected to show much concern for the further pursuit of political-military objectives."[98] Even if the United States were to endorse the multilayered damage-limitation instruments favored by option 4, it is probable that casualties would exceed the estimates of damage-limitation (for improved deterrence) proponents. Moreover, even if such proponents should be proved correct, how could a casualty list in the millions be politically or morally "acceptable"?[99]

2. It is essential that the United States have a SIOP designed and selectively advertised publicly, in general terms, to be able in prospective execution to promise denial of victory to Soviet leaders on their own terms.

> *Commentary:* Denying victory is all very well, but some considerable doubt remains over the real authority of the alleged Soviet official belief that victory is possible in nuclear war.[100] Also, denying victory encourages the atavistic urge on the part of some U.S. strategists to press a "theory of U.S. victory" on the U.S. government.[101]

3. No matter how intelligent or clever U.S. strategic targeting design may be, the credibility of execution of such design is very low so long as the United States makes no noteworthy provision for the protection of its homeland against inevitable Soviet retaliation.

> *Commentary:* The strategic logic of damage limitation is sound enough as strategic logic, but political decisions are not made totally in the light of abstract strategic logic. In practice, "our" leaders (and "theirs") would, quite properly and understandably, be terrified of the possibility of nuclear war. Strategic analysis promising "only" several million casualties, even if believed (which it would not be), would not strengthen presidential resolve. A president would not need to be told by the Congressional Office of Technology Assessment that "the effects of a nuclear war that cannot be calculated are at least as important as those for which calculations are attempted."[102] Proponents of damage limitation through intra-war deterrence do not claim that such a deterrent mechanism *will* work, only that it *might*. They do not choose the possibility of limiting central war through targeting restraints, as opposed to limiting such a war through measures of damage limitation,

because they do not believe that the choice is real. Opponents of option 4 deny that a worthwhile measure of damage limitation is feasible, and they worry that the implementation of programs for (ineffective) damage limitation may mislead U.S. policymakers into believing that nuclear war can be waged and survived at "acceptable" cost.

4. If the sole problem were the deterrence of a massive Soviet assault on North America, then the deterrence, though not prudential, case for homeland damage limitation would be far less persuasive. Unfortunately, each of the more plausible, or less implausible, scenarios that involve possible employment of central nuclear systems must be structured (because of the probable geography of conflict) such that it is the United States that most needs to restore deterrence through the issuing of credible threats and, if need be, the implementation of nuclear-strike plans.[103] The absence of protection for the U.S. homeland, in these most likely circumstances, should prove to have a paralyzing impact on the freedom of action of a desperate U.S. president.

> *Commentary:* There is abstract merit in the argument that a United States that could limit damage to itself to a major degree should be able to extend deterrence on behalf of distant allies more credibly and reliably. In practice, however, U.S. allies would fear that the United States would develop a "Maginot Line mentality." Moreover, even if extended deterrence does require a U.S. damage-limiting capability, the time is long overdue for NATO as a whole to diminish its security reliance on nuclear deterrence of all kinds—battlefield, theater, and strategic.[104] Extended deterrence was virtually a free gift, courtesy of the strategic-nuclear imbalance in favor of the United States that endured until the late 1960s. The challenge today should be defined not as ways in which that policy duty can be sustained in the face of a militarily far more capable Soviet opponent, but rather as ways in which NATO-Europe can diminish its politically debilitating client status vis-à-vis U.S. strategic forces.[105]

5. No one can predict the course of a central nuclear war. Intrawar deterrence may function as hoped. However, there is a significant chance that the superpowers would prove to be incapable of controlling a central war; and there is also a strong prospect that the Soviet Union would not be interested in any idea of control likely to prove tolerably congruent with U.S. wishes or interests. In short, for the extant official U.S. theory of strategic deterrence to prove robust in its hours of real test (acute crisis and war itself), a quite extraordinary degree of good fortune would have to bless its endeavors. Above all, perhaps, the Soviet war plan, in practice, would have to violate virtually every known precept of Soviet strategic culture.[106] Moreover, for tacit and explicit negotiations, the superpowers

would have to be willing and able to communicate in the most physically, administratively, and psychologically stressful environment the world has ever known.[107] They might succeed, given extraordinary resilience and redundancy of equipment, historically unusual qualities of statecraft, and a great deal of luck. However, a prudent defense posture and doctrine can hardly be constructed on the basis of such an expectation.

> *Commentary:* Citing the flaws in and problems with the prospective control and termination of a nuclear war, no matter how plausible the citation, does not answer such questions as "Is damage limitation really feasible?" and "Would a damage-limiting strategy increase the risk of war?" Many of the opponents of damage limitation as a policy goal are driven not by the kind of strategic ideology of a particular definition of stability that John Newhouse celebrated in his account of the SALT I negotiations,[108] but rather by a deep skepticism that the United States can achieve a genuine defense against large-scale nuclear assault.

Ideologically, the Reagan national security bureaucracy is not at all opposed to option 4. In practice, however, the shift from offense dominance to an offense-defense balance would strain any national security system. Defense decision makers wish to do the right things, but they often do not know what those things are. A secretary of defense may or may not be persuaded that a particular defense system would work adequately at the level of a "technical fix," but he may not be open to argument on the subject of basic U.S. deterrence philosophy. The Reagan administration entered office with a mandate to correct the adverse trend in relative military preparation, but not with a mandate to adopt any particular national security strategy.

The case for strategy is as strong in relation to the Reagan defense budgets of the 1980s as it was in relation to the declining defense budgets of the mid-1970s. The Reagan administration is committed to rebuilding U.S. military power, but it also needs to rethink the conceptual basis and the strategic purposes that should direct development of that power.[109] The administration is willing to pour funds into new programs, but it also has to be willing to engage long-standing domestic adversary constituencies in direct defense debate. The problem is very much one of political culture, for strategic culture and national style must reflect political culture.[110]

The kind of boldness shown by President Reagan in his endorsement of the promise of ballistic missile defense on March 23, 1983, stands in some contrast to the rhetorical caution displayed by the administration as a whole, after its first year in office, in expositions of its thinking on nuclear strategy. For reason of domestic and NATO-allied sensitivities, not to mention Soviet propaganda advantage, the administration has been anything but eager to expand public understanding of the essential elements of a true war-fighting, or "classical strategy," approach to nuclear deterrence. More troublesome even than the suspicion that policy declarations of a highly ambivalent kind may reflect or promote shifts in actual plans and programs, is the emerging fact that the administration has permitted important aspects of its strategic nuclear policy to slide into a hostage status. To secure the congressional votes needed to sustain the MX ICBM program, the administration entered into what may prove to be a somewhat imprecise Faustian pact with a powerful congressional arms control lobby. Congress is too diverse in the views it contains to provide true leadership on strategic issues,[111] but it is more than capable of discouraging an administration from pressing policy ideas that are controversial— whether or not those controversial ideas have strategic merit.

This is not to impugn anybody's motives. Rather, it is to suggest that a Congress that is determined to hold an administration's feet to the fire on the subject of arms control and an administration that recognizes that it can accomplish nothing of lasting value unless it can sustain a working consensus on its behalf in Congress can, between them, produce an unsatisfactory strategic policy.

Persuasive-sounding pro and con arguments can be designed for a wide range of strategic postures and doctrines. No one's theory of intranuclear-war deterrence or damage limitation has yet been road-tested, and the possible reasons why war is prevented are so various, and so impossible to assay, that one cannot sensibly point to the evidence of nuclear peace since 1945 as clear and unambiguous proof of the merit of any particular theory of deterrence. Option 4 is designed to cope with an unusually stressful set of circumstances wherein deterrence is particularly difficult to effect or simply does not apply. U.S. diplomacy, day by day, certainly does not need the support of option 4, but in the event of the true "war is in sight" crisis, nothing less than option 4 would likely be adequate—and even this option may not suffice to deter or to hold wartime damage down to an "acceptable" level.

OPTION 5: DAMAGE LIMITATION WITH DEFENSE DOMINANT

The reasoning behind option 5 to date has tended to be more prudential and technical than strategic.[112] As Donald Brennan wrote in 1969:

> I do not believe that any of the critics of BMD have even the beginnings of a plausible program for achieving major disarmament of the offensive forces by, say, 1980. Many of them seem committed to support a strategic posture that appears to favor dead Russians over live

Americans. I believe that this choice is just as bizarre as it appears; we should rather prefer live Americans to dead Russians, and we should not choose deliberately to live forever under a nuclear sword of Damocles.[113]

From the mid-1960s until the early 1980s, the United States endorsed a theory of strategic stability that held that the active and passive defense of a superpower homeland is not merely infeasible, it is undesirable. Nuclear peace was judged to rest, most reliably, on the accurate perception by all policymakers and policy-relevant publics that in the event of war, catastrophe could and probably would be unlimited. In keeping with this U.S. belief, SALT I and the abortive SALT II licensed an offense-dominant and unchallenged strategic nuclear environment.

It is not implied here that the dominance of the offense was chosen solely for reason of a particular strategic ideology (deterrence through mutual assured vulnerability), but it is claimed that ideology played a major role.[114] Proponents of offense dominance have political, technical, and strategic-theoretical cases to advance. From 1979 until the present, a stable deterrent—at least in its U.S. aspects—is a deterrent that Soviet leaders believe could deny them achievement of their objectives.[115] This essence of the countervailing strategy has yet to be translated very explicitly by officials into a careful reformulation of what is meant by strategic stability. The discussion that follows summarizes major elements in the case for option 5, with appropriate commentary:

1. Defense is possible. A defense-dominant world might be enforced through unilateral U.S. changes in posture, but it would be accomplished far more readily if strategic offensive arsenals were to be reduced drastically by formal arms control agreements.[116] The world envisaged here would be defense-dominant, not defense-exclusive. Perfect defenses are not possible, but even imperfect defenses would save many lives. In addition, strategic defenses, especially if they comprise a combination of different kinds of systems, would have to add greatly to the uncertainties that must promote deterrence-enhancing doubts in the minds of attack planners. Defense dominance should be thought of as a strategic condition wherein the current relationship of relative advantage between offense and defense is reversed.[117]

Commentary: It is not at all obvious that a defense-dominant world, as opposed to a useful level of defense for damage limitation, is technically feasible. Even if it is feasible, the pertinent time horizon for full operational capability is probably on the order of 20 to 30 years.[118] Furthermore, although the Soviet Union is known to favor assured survival, it is not known to favor mutual assured survival. There is no good reason to suppose that the Soviet Union would choose to cooperate in effecting an orderly transition from an offense-dominant to a defense-dominant world. An imperfect defense in the nuclear age is no defense at all, or, even worse, it is the illusion of a defense that could be dangerous if political leaders place undue confidence in it. So many and so troublesome are the uncertainties that beset planners and policymakers with regard to the prospective operational effectiveness of offensive forces alone, that it is far from self-evident that the additional uncertainties posed by the presence of active defenses are needed.[119]

2. There is nothing inevitable about the occurrence of major war, but July–August 1914 did happen. An international order enforced in part by latent (and irregularly explicit) nuclear threats is a world that is likely, one day, to see a nuclear war. Good management and good luck (in uncertain proportions), have seen us to the mid-1980s without a nuclear war, but the problem is the prevention of nuclear war *forever*. In an offense-dominant strategic world, it would take only one major, or possibly even minor, failure of the deterrence system for the United States to be out of business permanently. It is worth noting the judgment that the policymakers of the summer of 1914 were not noticeably less competent individuals than the policymakers of today. It is intolerable that Western civilization should forever be totally vulnerable to a single sequence of major crisis mismanagement.

> *Commentary:* Of course, a breakdown could occur in the existing system of nuclear threat; that is not at issue. However, none of the major players in the 1914 case tried as hard as they might to avoid war—a negligence that is hardly likely to be repeated in an era of nuclear risk.[120] What is at issue is whether such a breakdown would or would not be more likely to occur if the major powers should effect the postulated transition to defense-dominant strategic arsenals. It may be accurate to paint a glowing picture of a world freed from dread of the nuclear sword of Damocles—as President Reagan did on March 23, 1983—but such a world, by definition, would offer vastly reduced painful consequences for folly, adventure, and mismanagement. Such a reduction could well have a very marked negative impact on the incidence of major crises and wars.

3. Nuclear deterrence would not cease to function in a defense-dominant world. Active defenses, though very impressive, would not be totally leak-proof, and residual doubts would remain in the minds of politicians about just how efficient their untested defenses would prove to be in combat. However, those same doubts would have to be harbored on a magnified scale in the minds of policymakers in a government considering the risks of attack.

Commentary: It is all very well to argue that nuclear deterrence would still function in a defense-dominant world, but such a major reorientation in posture and doctrine could only be accomplished by means of very strongly phrased arguments to the effect that society would no longer be fatally at risk to the consequences of deterrence breakdown. If Soviet military theorists today, in an offense-dominant world, can argue that "victory"—embracing survival and recovery—is possible, how would the prospects of "victory" appear in a world where the balance of strategic armaments had deliberately been tipped massively in favor of defense? It seems as if proponents of defense dominance want to have it both ways: they argue that strategic defenses would strengthen deterrence, while—virtually in the same breath—they suggest that a defended world is a world that has transcended the perils of the nuclear deterrence system. Ben Adams, for example, has claimed: "Strategic defenses not only contribute to deterrence, they can repulse an attack, shield the homeland, protect the offense, and provide an opportunity to regain the initiative, rather than conceding it to an enemy *as a deterrent strategy does*"[121] (emphasis added). In theory, at least, there need be no opposition between defense and deterrence. As Glenn Snyder made clear nearly 25 years ago, one can deter by denial or by punishment.[122] Proponents of defense often seem to be needlessly ambivalent in their attitude toward deterrence.

4. The quantity and quality of societal damage that could be imposed on the Soviet Union would be reduced (assuming a bilateral superpower move to a defense-dominant posture) to the point where the United States and its friends and allies would worry about the feasibility of the extended deterrent duties that traditionally had been charged to the strategic offensive forces.[123] The argument probably would proceed as follows: The credibility of U.S. offensive action would be very high, because of the limited liability to which U.S. society could be held in a defense-dominant world, but the quality of nuclear deterrence would certainly be reduced by virtue of the same condition. (In effect, this world would be "safer" than the present one for war, nuclear and otherwise.) Aside from the residual uncertainty about the real operational effectiveness of heavily deployed active defenses, the Soviet Union should be compelled by U.S. and NATO-European (and Chinese) conventional and battlefield nuclear deployment to doubt its ability to prevail in the theater. Although extended deterrence prospectively would be both politically more credible and strategically less effective, its necessity would and should be diminished by a NATO prepared to conduct so staunch a local nonnuclear defense that the burden of decision to escalate or not to escalate would rest on Soviet shoulders.[124]

Commentary: Proponents of damage limitation through dominant defenses cannot cope plausibly with skeptical questions concerning the feasibility of extended deterrence. A residual fear of nuclear war certainly would exist in a supposedly defense-dominant world, but the risk calculus of a potential aggressor logically would have to be affected very negatively (for stability) as it considered the range of possible painful consequences of its actions. It is an exaggeration to claim that strategic defense dominance would make the world "safe for theater conflict" from the perspective of the superpowers, but that exaggeration does point to a certainty of crisis in U.S.-allied relations. The transition to a defense-dominated U.S. strategic nuclear posture would require a near-revolution in NATO capability, if not in agreed NATO strategic doctrine. MC-14/3 of 1967, with its endorsement of the concept of flexible response, could be retained as a general framework that it would be alliance-straining to seek to renegotiate, but the reality of where the balance of deterrent effect lay would have to shift down the scale of potential violence in favor of conventional forces.[125] It is worth mentioning that the necessity for more capable local denial forces that would seem to be a logical implication of Soviet strategic missile defense deployment, happens to be the direction that all NATO members *say* they favor anyway, for reasons that bear not at all on the U.S. SDI.

5. Proponents of option 5 may grant that they have a serious problem in the area of extended deterrence, or with respect to the feasibility of effecting a conventional-force partial substitute for extended deterrence, but they argue that that problem needs to be set against the prospect of removing the danger of unlimited nuclear catastrophe from the human race.

Commentary: It is highly improbable that the friends and allies of the United States would be willing to consider altruistically the possible merits of option 5 for the human race or, as Jonathan Schell has put it, "the fate of the earth,"[126] given that this option could have potentially adverse implications for their own national security. It is being argued today by NATO-European officials and commentators, in response to the U.S. SDI, that the United States may be choosing to place at risk the structure of mutual nuclear deterrence that helps to preserve peace.[127] For fear of the possible ultimate consequences for U.S. society, the United States would be designing an international military order wherein its allies would be expendable. European reactions to President Reagan's speech of March 23, 1983, were overwhelmingly negative.[128] European officials generally were less impressed with the idea that a defended United States might be a more reliable ally than with the fact that superpower strategic defenses would challenge the viability both of third-party nuclear missile deterrents and of U.S. LNOs threatened on behalf of NATO-Europe. Also, Europeans were, and remain, anxious lest a strong U.S. bid for strategic defenses lead to the demise of the ABM Treaty. Little comfort was drawn in Europe from the technical fact that space-based BMD systems could defend Western Europe as well as the United States. At an almost visceral level, some Europeans have seen in the president's proposal evidence, yet again, of a U.S. proclivity to seek security in technology rather than in political engagement.[129]

I am sympathetic to the motives of those who favor option 5, a defense-dominant strategy, and I have an open mind regarding the technical feasibility and strategic desirability of the idea. For example, it is possible that the current research on directed energy weapons will produce effective, though not leak-proof, defense against ballistic missiles, and defense against cruise missiles and penetrating manned bombers could also be successful (with sensing from and perhaps weapon platforms in space). However, such a prospect will serve to direct military research heavily into the region of offensive countermeasures, including the design of threats to the survivability of the defense system itself. To cite the certainty that each superpower would seek to neutralize the effectiveness of the defenses of the other is not, of course, to cast a vote against such defenses. The United States still builds tanks and aircraft, even though effective antitank and antiaircraft weapons exist.

Option 5 was advocated very strongly by Donald Brennan in the late 1960s,[130] but it has not attracted a politically significant following until very recently. Whether or not the Reagan administration is able to transform the President's vision of effective BMD into a real, sustained drive for homeland defense remains to be seen. Option 5 is compelling, notwithstanding the moderately skeptical commentary provided here. It really is intolerable, and foolish, to *choose* to live under a nuclear sword of Damocles indefinitely; someday that sword is likely to fall. However, if advocates of a defense-dominant strategy are to command the respectful hearing that their idea merits, they must show that they are aware of, and sensitive to, the major strategic, technical, and political objections to their preference.

There may seem to be a theoretical artificiality about the discussion of five discrete strategy options. After all, the U.S. government makes its strategic program decisions incrementally. There never seems to be a right time for shifting gears to a different strategy. Each administration is the legatee of the program decisions of its predecessors, and each inherits weapons programs and strategy and targeting plans, that cannot feasibly be terminated or substantially reoriented in the near term because of large sunk costs in hardware that would not be well suited to a new vision of strategy. Notwithstanding these considerations, the case for strategy assessment is overwhelming.

Individual weapons programs should make strategic sense within the framework of a coherent theory of war, both for improved deterrent effect and as insurance if war should occur nonetheless. The lead time for weapons development poses very serious problems for senior officials attempting to compose a coherent military posture, but at the least, those officials should have a clear vision of whither they are intending and why.

NOTES

1. Harold and Margaret Sprout, *The Ecological Perspective on Human Affairs with Special Reference to International Politics* (Princeton, N.J.: Princeton University Press, 1965).

2. Cited in Walter E. Kaegi, "The Crisis in Military Historiography," *Armed Forces and Society* 7, no. 2 (Winter 1980): 311. On the contemporary relevance of this distinction, see William S. Lind, "The Case for Maneuver Doctrine," in Asa A. Clark IV et al., eds., *The Defense Reform Debate: Issues and Analysis* (Baltimore: Johns Hopkins University Press, 1984), pp. 88-100. Of course very severe attrition can produce annihilation.

3. Russell F. Weigley, *Eisenhower's Lieutenants: The Campaigns of France and Germany, 1944-45* (Bloomington: Indiana University Press, 1981); and Martin van Creveld, *Supplying War: Logistics from Wallenstein to Patton,* (Cambridge: Cambridge University Press, 1977), chap. 7.

4. See John Ellis, *Cassino, the Hollow Victory: The Battle for Rome, January-June 1944* (New York: McGraw-Hill, 1984).

5. Useful recent studies include John Keegan, *Six Armies in Normandy: From D-Day to the Liberation of Paris* (New York: Viking, 1982); Carlo D'Este, *Decision in Normandy* (New York: Dutton, 1983); and Max Hastings, *Overlord: D-Day and the Battle for Normandy* (New York: Simon and Schuster, 1984).

6. On German military power, see Martin van Creveld, *Fighting Power: German and U.S. Army Performance, 1939-1945* (Westport, Conn.: Greenwood, 1982); and Trevor N. Dupuy, *A Genius for War: The German Army and General Staff, 1807-1945* (London: MacDonald and Jane's, 1977). It should not be forgotten that German military performance in North Africa, Sicily, Italy, and Normandy was flattered by the much less than stellar performance of the Anglo-American enemy. In addition, some scholars (including those cited in this note), in their praise of German combat skills, have a tendency to gloss over the glaring German weaknesses in communications security (and in intelligence more generally), in logistics, and *in strategy.* These points, inter alia, are made economically in Williamson Murray, "Ultra: Some Thoughts on its Impact on the Second World War," *Air University Review* 35, No. 5 (July-August 1984): 52-64. For a further corrective, see David Schoenbaum, "The Wehrmacht and G.I. Joe: Learning *What* from History?" *International Security* 8, no. 1(Summer 1983): 201-7.

7. See Russell F. Weigley, *The American Way of War* (New York: Macmillan, 1973); and Colin S. Gray, "American Strategic Culture and Military Performance," in Asa A. Clark IV et al, eds., *Military Technology* (Baltimore: Johns Hopkins University Press, forthcoming).

8.   This phenomenon was noted in John E. Mack, "Psychosocial Effects of the Nuclear Arms Race," *Bulletin of the Atomic Scientists* 37, no. 4(April 1981), particularly pp. 20–22; and in Theodore Ropp, "Strategic Thinking Since 1945," in Robert O'Neill and D.M. Horner, eds., *New Directions in Strategic Thinking* (London: Allen & Unwin, 1981), p. 5. A useful recent study of the history of the strategic advisory scene is Gregg Herken, *Counsels of War* (New York: Knopf, 1985).

9.   Bernard Brodie, *War and Politics* (New York: Macmillan, 1973), p. 452.

10.   Herman Kahn, *On Thermonuclear War* (Princeton, N.J.: Princeton University Press, 1960).

11.   Herman Kahn, *On Escalation: Metaphors and Scenarios* (New York: Praeger, 1965).

12.   This example is important because the MX ICBM epitomizes the kind of strategic capability that the United States needs because of its extended deterrent duties (largely in Europe).

13.   This would be true except for the consideration that a Soviet Union unconstrained by U.S. power in Eurasia-Africa should come to pose a far more substantial threat to the United States than is the case even today, by virtue of its ability to mobilize the economic assets of Eurasia. For detailed analyses providing background for these judgments, see James T. Lowe, *Geopolitics and War: Mackinder's Philosophy of Power* (Washington D.C.: University Press of America, 1981); and Colin S. Gray, *Basic U.S. Choices, 1982–2000* (Fairfax, Va.: National Institute for Public Policy, March 1983).

14.   An unusually clear-headed presentation of the structure of the problem is Robert W. Tucker, "The Nuclear Debate," *Foreign Affairs* 63, no. 1(Fall 1984): 1–32.

15.   See Donald G. Brennan, *National Security in Fortress America*, HI-1974-P (Croton-on-Hudson, N.Y.: Hudson Institute, May 2, 1974).

16.   However, see Albert J. Wohlstetter, "Illusions of Distance," *Foreign Affairs* 46, 2(January 1968): 242–55.

17.   The Reagan administration has rediscovered what Robert McNamara learned in the early 1960s—that forward-placed, potential battlefield countries are strongly resistant to that prospective status. An important, though indeterminate fraction of the hostile NATO-European official reaction to President Reagan's endorsement of the concept of homeland defense on March 23, 1983, flowed from anxiety lest a defended United States in the future would be far more relaxed over the dangers of a theater war than is the case at present.

18.   Richard Burt, "Reassessing the Strategic Balance," *International Security* 5, no. 1(Summer 1980): 49–50.

19.   This ignores the uncertain ultimate implications for policy of President Reagan's endorsement of the concept of homeland defense. See "President's Speech on Military Spending and a New Defense," *New York Times*, March 24, 1983, p. 20. See also Jeffrey Richelson, "PD-59, NSDD-13 and the Reagan Strategic Modernization Program," *Journal of Strategic Studies* 6, no. 2(June 1983): 125–46; and Desmond Ball, *Targeting for Strategic Deterrence*, Adelphi Papers No. 185 (London: IISS, Summer 1983), pp. 20–23.

20. To be specific, students were asked to compare and contrast Colin Gray, "Nuclear Strategy: The Case for a Theory of Victory," *International Security* 4, no. 1(Summery 1979): 54–87, with Robert Jervis, "Why Nuclear Superiority Doesn't Matter," *Political Science Quarterly* 94, no. 4(Winter 1978–80): 617–33.

21. See McGeorge Bundy, "To Cap the Volcano," *Foreign Affairs* 48, no. 1(October 1969): 10.

22. The character and scale of damage deemed feasible in 1946–48 were driven, of course, by severe contemporary stockpile limitations. See David Alan Rosenberg: "U.S. Nuclear Stockpile, 1945 to 1950," *Bulletin of the Atomic Scientists* 38, no. 5(May 1982): 25–30; and "The Origins of Overkill: Nuclear Weapons and American Strategy, 1945–1960," *International Security* 7, no. 4(Spring 1983): 3–71.

23. See Henry S. Rowen, "The Evolution of Strategic Nuclear Doctrine," in Laurence Martin, ed., *Strategic Thought in the Nuclear Age* (Baltimore: Johns Hopkins University Press, 1979), pp. 131–56.

24. Glenn Buchan was correct in asserting a distinction between finite deterrence and MAD, in that the former implies a relatively modest scale of nuclear weapon deployment, whereas the latter need not. However, like it or not, MAD is a theory or finite deterrence. See Buchan, "The Anti-MAD Mythology," *Bulletin of the Atomic Scientists* 37, no. 4(April 1980), especially p. 15.

25. For critiques of the nuclear freeze and its associated ideas, see Colin S. Gray and Keith B. Payne, eds., *The Nuclear Freeze Controversy* (Cambridge, Mass.: Abt, 1984). On the freeze movement, see Adam M. Garfinkle, *The Politics of the Nuclear Freeze*, Philadelphia Policy Papers (Philadelphia: Foreign Policy Research Institute, 1984).

26. Some liberal theorists, enraged by the MAD acronym, coined the rival acronym NUT (for *nuclear utilization theory*). See Buchan, "The Anti-MAD Mythology," p. 13n.

27. Even Robert Scheer concedes: "They [neo-hawks] are not eager for nuclear war anymore than I am." *With Enough Shovels: Reagan, Bush and Nuclear War* (New York: Random House, 1983; first pub. 1982), p. 121. However, he proceeds to assert: "They are as eager for confrontation as they are opposed to accommodation with the Soviet Union." Ibid. As one of the people identified by Scheer as a neo-hawk, I have some difficulty recognizing my views in his assertion—"eager for confrontation"?

28. See Paul R. Ehrlich et al., *The Cold and the Dark: The World After Nuclear War* (New York: Norton, 1984). For the argument that the possibility of the fatal destruction of the ecosphere should drive our approach to problems of security, see Jonathan Schell, *The Fate of the Earth* (New York: Knopf, 1982).

29. Kahn, *On Thermonuclear War*, particularly chap. 2.

30. See Desmond Ball, *Can Nuclear War Be Controlled?* Adelphi Papers No. 169 (London: IISS, Autumn 1981); and John D. Steinbruner, "National Security and the Concept of Strategic Stability," *Journal of Conflict Resolution*, 22, no. 3(September 1978): 411-28.

31. See Leon Wieseltier, *Nuclear War, Nuclear Peace* (New York: Holt, Rinehart and Winston, 1983), chap. 2. Wieseltier casts me as a major villain in what he terms "the Sovietization of American strategy" (see pp. 47–53).

32.   See Colin S. Gray and Keith B. Payne, "Victory Is Possible," *Foreign Policy*, no. 39(Summer 1980), particularly pp. 25–26.

33.   The classic statement remains Albert J. Wohlstetter, "The Delicate Balance of Terror," *Foreign Affairs* 37, no. 2(January 1959): 211–34.

34.   For an exceptionally clear statement of the structure of NATO's deterrence reasoning, see General Bernard W. Rogers, "Greater Flexibility for NATO's Flexible Response," *Strategic Review* 11, no. 2(Spring 1983): 11–19.

35.   See Bundy, "To Cap the Volcano," pp. 10–11, 13.

36.   Some critics of U.S. so-called war-fighting theorists have come to believe that war-fighters are arguing that because the USSR suffered some 20 million casualties in the Great Patriotic War, it would be willing to take casualties on a comparable scale again. Judiciously framed, the war-fighter's argument has the following elements: The Soviet state has a patrimonial view of its human and (other) economic "property"; it is indifferent to individual human suffering or loss; and it knows that the loss of 20 plus million people, in addition to vast economic devastation and dislocation, is "survivable" in "state entity" terms. One should not extrapolate Soviet human losses from 1917 to 1945 into a putative nuclear war case in a simpleminded fashion (for obvious reasons of the time scale for nuclear damage and the uniqueness of some nuclear weapons effects). However, it is a difficult exercise to seek to deny the qualitative difference between U.S. and Soviet views of human loss.

37.   Great Britain's mercenary Hessian soldiery of the 1770s may not have behaved like boy scouts, but the character and extent of their bestiality was light-years removed from the Russian experience of Mongol conquest and the subsequent "Tatar yoke."

38.   See Joseph D. Douglass, Jr., and Amoretta M. Hoeber, *Soviet Strategy for Nuclear War* (Stanford, Calif.: Hoover Institution Press, 1979), chap. 2.

39.   This is scarcely surprising, given the fact that the Soviet ballistic missile programs in the 1940s and 1950s delivered operational weapons to the artillery reserves of the Supreme High Command. The first commander in chief of the Strategic Rocket Troops was Marshal of Artillery M. I. Nedelin. See Harriet F. Scott and William F. Scott, *The Armed Forces of the U.S.S.R.* (Boulder, Colo.: Westview Press, 1979), pp. 133–41. Also see John Erickson, "The Soviet Military System: Doctrine, Technology and 'Style,' " in John Erickson and E. J. Feuchtwanger, eds., *Soviet Military Power and Performance* (Hamden, Conn.: Archon, 1979), pp. 23–31.

40.   See Robert Bathurst, "Two Languages of War," in Derek Leebaert, ed., *Soviet Military Thinking* (London: Allen and Unwin, 1981), p. 32; and Henry Trofimenko, *Changing Attitudes Toward Deterrence*, ACIS Working Paper No. 25 (Los Angeles: UCLA, Center for International and Strategic Affairs, July 1980), pp. 23–25. The quality of recent Western scholarship on Soviet military thinking is indicated by John Erickson, "The Soviet View of Deterrence: A General Survey," *Survival* 24, no. 6(November/December 1982): 242–51; William G. Hyland, "The U.S.S.R. and Nuclear War," in Barry M. Blechman, ed., *Rethinking the U.S. Strategic Posture* (Cambridge, Mass.: Ballinger, 1982), chap. 3; Mark E. Miller, *Soviet Strategic Power and Doctrine: The Quest for Superiority* (Washington, D.C.: Advanced International Studies Institute in association with the University of Miami, 1982); Na-

than Leites, *Soviet Style in War* (New York: Crane, Russak, 1982); David Holloway, *The Soviet Union and the Arms Race* (New Haven: Yale University Press, 1983); P. H. Vigor, *Soviet Blitzkrieg Theory* (New York: St. Martin's, 1983); and Douglas M. Hart, "The Hermeneutics of Soviet Military Doctrine," *Washington Quarterly* 7, 2(Spring 1984): pp. 77–88. The most recent authoritative statement of Soviet military thinking is Marshal of the Soviet Union Nikolay Vasilyevich Ogarkov, *Always in Readiness to Defend the Homeland*, trans. JPRS L/10412, March 25, 1982 (Moscow: *Voyenizdat*, January 1982). A replacement for Sokolovskiy's *Military Strategy* has reportedly been in preparation for a long while.

41. See Buchan, "The Anti-MAD Mythology," p. 17.

42. This is not to claim that nuclear war *will* be survivable, only that it is more likely than not that it will be, but only if the United States invests in multi-layered protection of U.S. society. This argument should have been settled definitively by Kahn's *On Thermonuclear War* in 1960. It is not helpful or sensible to argue, as Glenn Buchan does, that "the burden of proof must be on any decision-maker who would consider a general nuclear war to convince himself . . . that the risks of a nuclear war are manageable, and that the outcome could be predicted with sufficient certainty to make war a viable policy option." "The Anti-MAD Mythology," p. 14. Nuclear war is very important as a set of options in U.S. defense planning and has to be a viable policy option. Notwithstanding appearances to the contrary, this is not confusing logical necessity of policy with attainable reality. Whatever Mr. Hanson may believe, I can distinguish between verbal formulas and technical-strategic feasibility. See Donald W. Hanson, "Is Soviet Strategic Doctrine Superior?" *International Security* 7, no. 3 (Winter 1982), particularly pp. 72-73. Critics of counterforce, damage-limiting strategies often give the appearance of believing that they are saying something tolerably original and significant when they cite the horrors of nuclear war. Nuclear strategists do not need to be reminded of the penalty society would, or could, pay if deterrence should fail. See Colin S. Gray, "Nuclear Strategy: A Regrettable Necessity," *SAIS Review* 3, no. 1(Winter/ Spring 1983): 13–28.

43. See Trofimenko, *Changing Attitudes Toward Deterrence*, p. 25; and Leon Gouré and Michael J. Deane, "The Soviet Strategic View," *Strategic Review* 8, no. 4(Fall 1980): 79–84.

44. This is certainly the Soviet view. See Jacqueline K. Davis et al., *The Soviet Union and Ballistic Missile Defense*, Special Report (Cambridge, Mass.: Institute for Foreign Policy Analysis, 1979); and Michael J. Deane, *Strategic Defense in Soviet Strategy* (Washington, D.C.: Advanced International Studies Institute in association with the University of Miami, 1980).

45. This is a major conclusion in Lawrence Freedman, *The Evolution of Nuclear Strategy* (London: Macmillan, 1981), particularly chap. 26.

46. Robert Scheer has claimed, falsely, that in "Victory Is Possible" I have "specified that 20 million U.S. fatalities would represent an acceptable cost in a nuclear war." See Scheer, "Pentagon Plan Aims at Victory in Nuclear War," *Los Angeles Times*, August 15, 1982, p. 1. See the discussion in Gray, "Nuclear Strategy: A Regrettable Necessity," pp. 15, 21. Secretary of Defense Weinberger flatly denied the accuracy of Scheer's reporting in U.S. Congress, Senate, Committee on Foreign

Relations, *U.S. Strategic Doctrine, Hearing*, 97th Cong., 2d sess. (Washington, D.C.: USGPO, December 14, 1982), pp. 24–25.

47.   In its endorsement of military effectiveness as a requirement for effective deterrence, the Scowcroft Commission was sensitive to the instability arguments mentioned here in the text. In its report the Commission states that the deployment of 100 MX missiles "would provide a means of controlled limited attack on hardened targets but not a sufficient number of warheads to be able to attack all hardened Soviet ICBMs, much less all of the many command posts and other hardened military targets in the Soviet Union." The President's Commission on Strategic Forces, *Report* (Washington, D.C.: The White House, April 1983), p. 18. For a strong statement of the view that 100 MX missiles provides nowhere near an adequate quantity of prompt counterforce firepower to offset Soviet ICBMs, see A.G.B. Metcalf, "The Minuteman Vulnerability Myth and the MX," *Strategic Review*, Vol. 11, No. 2 (Spring 1983), pp. 7–8.

48.   Henry Trofimenko makes this point very clearly indeed in *Changing Attitudes Toward Deterrence:* "But if the mission of the military is to fight successfully and to win wars, then the mission of contemporary politicians is to prevent a nuclear war that can result in disaster for mankind" (p. 23). The Soviet view is portrayed sympathetically in Erickson, "The Soviet View of Deterrence." Erickson argues that the Soviet Union noted the U.S. theory of stability through MAD capabilities but was impressed by the reality of U.S. strategic force programs that exceeded the requirements of MAD (p. 246). An important, penetrating analysis of the Soviet perspective is Jonathan S. Lockwood, *The Soviet View of U.S. Strategic Doctrine: Implications for Decision Making* (New Brunswick, N.J.: Transaction, 1983).

49.   In the contexts of NATO policy over deployment of Pershing II and U.S. debate over the wisdom of deploying MX missiles in silos, Soviet spokesmen have been eloquent on the consequences of these developments for their missile-firing doctrine. Playing to Western anxieties, Soviet officials have suggested that they will be compelled to adopt some variant of a launch-on-warning or launch-under-attack firing rule.

50.   Buchan, "The Anti-MAD Mythology," p. 14.

51.   The state-of-the-art argument for this position, and against the offensive counterforce and damage limitation theses of options 3 and 4, is represented very well in Robert Jervis, *The Illogic of American Nuclear Strategy* (Ithaca, N.Y.: Cornell University Press, 1984).

52.   See Henry S. Rowen: "The Evolution of Strategic Nuclear Doctrine," p. 145; and "Formulating Strategic Doctrine," in Commission on the Organization of the Government for the Conduct of Foreign Policy, Vol. 4, Appendix K, *Adequacy of Current Organization: Defense and Arms Control* (Washington, D.C.: USGPO, June 1975), particularly pp. 226–33.

53.   As Jervis writes: "The missiles need not be fired all at once." *The Illogic of American Nuclear Strategy*, p. 167.

54.   See Gray and Payne, "Victory Is Possible," pp. 17–18.

55.   Soviet leaders do not believe that Soviet society should be a hostage, as envisaged in "the metaphysics of deterrence" as elaborated by Western schol-

ars. See Erickson, "The Soviet View of Deterrence"; and Lockwood, *The Soviet View of U.S. Strategic Doctrine*, chap. 10. The official U.S. view of the Soviet view is as follows: "Unfortunately, we face an adversary whose leaders have, through their writings, force deployments and exercises, given clear indications they believe that, under certain circumstances, war with the United States—even nuclear war—may be fought and won." Caspar W. Weinberger, *Annual Report to the Congress, Fiscal Year 1985* (Washington, D.C.: USGPO, February 1, 1984), p. 27.

56. This was the basic thrust of James Schlesinger's argument in 1973–75. A useful period piece, sympathetic to Schlesinger, was Richard Rosecrance, *Strategic Deterrence Reconsidered*, Adelphi Papers No. 116 (London: IISS, Spring 1975).

57. This point is well made in Jervis, *The Illogic of American Nuclear Strategy*, pp. 79–86.

58. James Schlesinger was criticized in 1974–75 on virtually every ground except the correct strategic one—that LNOs would be very unlikely to work. Critics waxed indignant over his alleged underestimation of likely U.S. casualties in a severely constrained counterforce exchange. However, those critics overwhelmingly tended to neglect the point that U.S. LNOs would be very unlikely to succeed in their policy purpose unless they were supported by forces expressing a brute-force, "backstop" theory of escalation dominance.

59. John Erickson has noted that U.S. lack of interest in active and passive defense, far from reassuring the Soviet Union, has evoked suspicions that the United States is so confident of offensive counterforce success that it need not allocate resources for homeland defense. "The Soviet View of Deterrence," p. 246.

60. Erickson, "The Soviet Military System: Doctrine, Technology, and 'Style,' " p. 28.

61. LNOs—or in more recent terminology, SNOs (sub-SIOP nuclear options)—could, of course, be executed against very discrete target sets in Eastern Europe. The strategic logic of GLCM and Pershing II deployment in Western Europe, as that of the national deterrents of Britain and France, is that the Soviet Union should not anticipate that its homeland would be accorded sanctuary status in the context of a theater conflict. On the probable consequences of the United States/NATO striking Soviet territory in the course of what the U.S. government defines as a theater war, see the sobering analysis in Benjamin S. Lambeth, "On Thresholds in Soviet Military Thought," *Washington Quarterly* 7, no. 2(Spring 1984): 69–76.

62. On the "selectivity" debate over strategic targeting in the 1970s, see Lynn Etheridge Davis, *Limited Nuclear Options: Deterrence and the New American Doctrine*, Adelphi Papers No. 121 (London: IISS, Winter 1975/1976); Warner R. Schilling, "U.S. Strategic Nuclear Concepts in the 1970s: The Search for Sufficiently Equivalent Countervailing Parity," *International Security* 6, no. 2(Fall 1981): 48–79; and Freedman, *The Evolution of Nuclear Strategy*, chap. 25.

63. See Thomas Schelling, *Arms and Influence* (New Haven: Yale University Press, 1966), chap. 3; and Jervis, *The Illogic of American Nuclear Strategy*, chap. 5. For an outstanding critical analysis of how wars can be lost if the United States thinks of military action not as war but rather as a process of diplomatic signaling and as a competition in risk-taking, see Stephen Peter Rosen, "Vietnam and the American Theory of Limited War," *International Security* 7, no. 2(Fall 1982): 83–113.

64. See Jerome H. Kahan, *Security in the Nuclear Age: Developing U.S. Strategic Arms Policy* (Washington, D.C.: Brookings, 1975), particularly pp. 223–37.

65. On the strategic potential of submarine-launched ballistic missiles, see Joel S. Wit, "American SLBM: Counterforce Options and Strategic Implications," *Survival* 24, no. 4(July/August 1982): 163–74; and Harold A. Feiverson and John Duffield, "Stopping the Sea-Based Counterforce Threat," *International Security* 9, no. 1(Summer 1984): 187–202.

66. See John Erickson, "The Soviet View of Nuclear War," Transcript of broadcast on BBC Radio 3, June 19, 1980, p. 10. For a useful and persuasive discussion of the importance that the Soviet General Staff accords flexibility in command (in weapon employment) and flexibility in planning, see Joseph D. Douglass, Jr., and Amoretta Hoeber, *Conventional War and Escalation: The Soviet View* (New York: Crane, Russak [for the National Strategy Information Center], 1981), pp. 58–63. Also valuable is Lockwood, *The Soviet View of U.S. Strategic Doctrine*, chap. 8.

67. However, see Francois de Rose, "Inflexible Response," *Foreign Affairs* 61, no. 1(Fall 1982): 136–50.

68. There is no debate over the proposition that both Soviet and Western leaders view nuclear weapons as instruments of political intimidation and that it is a rational act of policy so to employ (or brandish) these weapons. However, there is considerable disagreement over the extent to which it is accurate to describe Soviet military thought as Clausewitzian. Do Soviet leaders regard war, even nuclear war, as "simply a continuation of political intercourse, with the addition of other means"? Carl von Clausewitz, *On War* (Michael Howard and Peter Paret, eds.) (Princeton, N.J.: Princeton University Press, 1976; first pub. 1832), p. 605. On the meaning of Clausewitz for today, see Peter R. Moody, Jr., "Clausewitz and the Fading Dialectic of War," *World Politics* 31, no. 3(April 1979): 417–33; and Raymond Aron, *Clausewitz: Philosopher of War* (London: Routledge and Kegan Paul, 1983; first pub. 1976), part V. See also Erickson, "The Soviet View of Deterrence," p. 243; P. H. Vigor, *The Soviet View of War, Peace and Neutrality* (London: Routledge and Kegan Paul, 1975), pp. 80–96.

69. See Jeffrey T. Richelson, "The Dilemmas of Counterpower Targeting," *Comparative Strategy* 2, no. 3(1980): 223–37; Colin S. Gray, "Targeting Problems for Central War," *Naval War College Review* 33, no. 1(January–February 1980): 3–21; and Ball, *Targeting for Strategic Deterrence*, pp. 31–32.

70. See Colin S. Gray, *Strategic Studies and Public Policy: The American Experience* (Lexington: University Press of Kentucky, 1982), chap. 4.

71. See Desmond Ball, "Counterforce Targeting: How New? How Viable?" *Arms Control Today* 11, no. 2(February 1981): 1–2, 6–9; and Leon Sloss and Marc Dean Millot, "U.S. Nuclear Strategy in Evolution," *Strategic Review* 12, no. 1(Winter 1984): 19–28.

72. See Colin S. Gray, "Presidential Directive 59: Flawed but Useful," *Parameters* 9, no. 1(March 1981): 29–37.

73. Shocked, fearful, and possibly sick Soviet citizens are more likely to be desperate for the reassuring presence of a familiar Soviet authority (*faute de mieux*) than they are to be angry to the point of revolt.

74.   This theme was developed in Paul H. Nitze, "Deterring Our Deterrent," *Foreign Policy*, no. 25(Winter 1976–77): 195–210.

75.   Erickson, "The Soviet View of Deterrence," p. 247.

76.   President's Commission on Strategic Forces, *Report*, p. 6.

77.   See Harriet Fast Scott and William F. Scott, *The Soviet Control Structure: Capabilities for Wartime Survival* (New York: Crane, Russak [for the National Strategy Information Center], 1983). Paul Bracken was wide of the mark when he wrote:

> What is especially worth noting about PD-59 and NSDD-13 is the idea advanced as the key to victory over the Soviet Union in a nuclear war, which is to target the political and military control system of the Soviet Union, not just its military forces. Soviet military and leadership targets had always been included in earlier plans. PD-59 for the first time declared open threats against them. As a consequence, a spate of academic articles appeared about the benefits of "knocking out the Soviet control system." Most of these were superficial, almost nonsensical, for they never even defined "control system"; nor did they address what would happen if the Soviets shot back.

The Command and Control of Nuclear Forces, pp. 88, 89. Speaking from personal experience, I can say that those of us who speculated in public about threatening the Soviet control system did have some very specific Soviet target sets in mind. Whether or not we should have defined those target sets in detail in the open literature is another matter. Furthermore, the official U.S. defense community has assumed for many years that Soviet targeteers assign a very high priority to attacking U.S. control targets. Among many others, I have argued repeatedly that the vulnerability of U.S. C^3I systems constitutes a potentially fatal Achilles heel.

78.   The Central Committee *nomenklatura* are the holders of positions at the direct discretion of the Central Committee of the Soviet Communist Party—a system of highly centralized patronage.

79.   There is considerable merit in the following argument advanced by Samuel P. Huntington:

> The argument was sometimes made that "killing the top Soviet leadership would leave the U.S. no one to fight the war with." The destruction of the central political leadership of the Soviet Union and of the command and communications channels by which Moscow exercises control over its military forces and its satellites could well help precipitate the breakdown of Soviet authority that should be the wartime goal of American strategy.

"The Renewal of Strategy," in Huntington, ed., *The Strategic Imperative: New Policies for American Security* (Cambridge, Mass.: Ballinger, 1982), p. 33. Paul Bracken provided a contrasting perspective in *The Command and Control of Nuclear Forces*, pp. 91–97. For example, Bracken alleged that "since actually destroying the Soviet leadership group would serve no military useful purpose, targeting is a bargaining tool that is intended to *influence* the group" (p. 91). It is by no means obvious that actually killing Soviet leaders would *not* serve a useful military purpose.

80. See Harold Brown, *Department of Defense Annual Report, Fiscal Year 1982* (Washington D.C.: USGPO, January 19, 1981), pp. 38–40; and Caspar W. Weinberger, *Annual Report to the Congress, Fiscal Year 1984* (Washington, D.C.: USGPO, February 1, 1983), pp. 51, 57.

81. Weinberger, *Annual Report to the Congress, Fiscal Year 1984*, p. 55.

82. See Jervis, *The Illogic of American Nuclear Strategy*, particularly chap. 5.

83. Except for very occasional lapses of self-discipline, administration spokesmen have sought to avoid conceding in public their belief that the strategic nuclear balance of the early 1980s is in a condition of subparity to the U.S. disfavor. For example, Secretary Weinberger's *Annual Report to the Congress, Fiscal Year 1984* told the truth, but not the whole truth, when it said that "we are now faced with a Soviet Union that has deprived us of our advantage in nuclear arms" (p. 20). A more accurate gauge of official belief is the argument that has been deployed in opposition to the proposal that the superpowers should first freeze, then reduce, their nuclear arms. Officials have asserted, again and again, that "freezing now" would preclude necessary force modernization. I recognize the many difficulties pertaining to assessment of the state of the strategic balance.

84. As one would expect, these thoughts pervade the report of the Scowcroft Commission, which Harold Brown served as a consultant. See President's Commission on Strategic Forces, *Report*, pp. 2, 6, 7.

85. In his last annual report, Harold Brown emphatically registered the point that Soviet economic targets have not been removed from the U.S. SIOP (*Department of Defense Annual Report, Fiscal Year 1982*, pp. 42, 43). See also Benjamin S. Lambeth and Kevin N. Lewis, "Economic Targeting in Nuclear War: U.S. and Soviet Approaches," *Orbis* 27, no. 1(Spring 1983): 127–49; and Ball, *Targeting for Strategic Deterrence*, pp. 29–31.

86. See Holloway, *The Soviet Union and the Arms Race*, pp. 70–72. No less an authority than Sun Tzu advised that "what is of supreme importance in war is to attack the enemy's strategy." *The Art of War* (trans. by Samuel B. Griffith) (Oxford: Clarendon Press, 1963), p. 77.

87. Although one can imagine technical solutions to the targeting problems posed by the policy guidance of PD-59 and NSDD-13, in practice one wonders whether the pursuit of offensive counterforce prowess against ever more mobile Soviet strategic assets is the correct path to pursue. The proper solution to the damage-limitation problem posed by Soviet missile mobility almost certainly lies substantially in the realm of active defense. This is not to say the United States can deter with a shield only, but rather that the missions of offensive nuclear forces should be kept under constant review as targeting problems evolve.

88. For negative commentaries on this point that at least have the merit of understanding the argument (even though they mischaracterize the world that I envisage), see Robert C. Gray, "The Reagan Nuclear Strategy," *Arms Control Today* 13, no. 2(March 1983): 1–39; and Stanley R. Sloan and Robert C. Gray, *Nuclear Strategy and Arms Control: Challenges for U.S. Policy*, Headline Series No. 261 (New York: Foreign Policy Association, 1982), pp. 40–42.

89. A useful brief survey of the strategic doctrinal distance covered by the

Carter administration (prior to PD-59) is Desmond Ball, *Developments in U.S. Strategic Nuclear Policy Under the Carter Administration*, ACIS Working Paper No. 21 (Los Angeles: UCLA, Center for International and Strategic Affairs, February 1980).

90.   See Burt, "Reassessing the Strategic Balance," p. 50.

91.   However, there is an important case to be made for defense mobilization planning as an integral part of U.S. and NATO-allied defense policy. See Paul Bracken, "Mobilization in the Nuclear Age," *International Security* 3, no. 3(Winter 1978/1979): 74–93; Richard B. Foster and Francis P. Hoeber, "Limited Mobilization: A Strategy For Preparedness and Deterrence," *Orbis* 24, no. 3(Fall 1980): 439–57; and Colin S. Gray, "Mobilization for High-Level Conflict: Policy Issues," in Robert L. Pfaltzgraff, Jr., and Uri Ra'anan, eds., *The U.S. Defense Mobilization Infrastructure: Problems and Priorities*. (Hamden, Conn.: Archon, 1983), pp. 33–49. I have explored, generally sympathetically, the case for planning for long as well as short wars in my study *Protracted War: The Lessons of History* (Fairfax, Va.: National Institute for Public Policy, 1984).

92.   This claim underlies and pervades many of the essays in Clark et al. *The Defense Reform Debate.*

93.   See "President's Speech on Military Spending and a New Defense," *New York Times*, March 24, 1983, p. 20.

94.   Schelling, *Arms and Influence,* pp. 69–91.

95.   See Colin S. Gray, "War-Fighting for Deterrence," *Journal of Strategic Studies* 7, no. 1(March 1984): 5–25.

96.   This belief pervaded Bernard Brodie's contribution to *The Absolute Weapon: Atomic Power and World Order* (New York: Harcourt, Brace, 1946), pp. 21–110.

97.   On the fall of damage limitation from official favor, see Kahan, *Security in the Nuclear Age*, chap. 2; Fred Kaplan, *The Wizards of Armageddon* (New York: Simon and Schuster, 1983), chap. 23; and Ball, *Targeting for Strategic Deterrence*, pp. 10–15.

98.   Quoted in Michael Howard, "On Fighting A Nuclear War," *International Security* 5, no. 4(Spring 1981): 14.

99.   See Schilling, "U.S. Strategic Nuclear Concepts in the 1970s," pp. 64–65. As a general rule, moral philosophers and nuclear-age strategic theorists have argued past each other. I find three books in particular to have unusually high merit—which is not to say that I agree with them—in a rather arid field of enquiry: Geoffrey Best, *Humanity in Warfare* (New York: Columbia University Press, 1980); Philip J. Murnion, ed., *Catholics and Nuclear War: A Commentary on "The Challenge of Peace," The U.S. Catholic Bishops' Pastoral Letter on War and Peace* (New York: Crossroad, 1983); and Freeman Dyson, *Weapons and Hope* (New York: Harper & Row, 1984).

100.   See Robert L. Arnett, "Soviet Attitudes Towards Nuclear War: Do They Really Think They Can Win?" *Journal of Strategic Studies* 2, no. 2(September 1979): 172–91. But see Robert B. Berman and John C. Baker, *Soviet Strategic Forces: Requirements and Responses* (Washington, D.C.: Brookings, 1982), pp. 32–37; and Vigor, *Soviet Blitzkrieg Theory*, chap. 5. It is worth observing that even the Ground

Zero organization handled this issue very cautiously. See Ground Zero, *What About the Russians—And Nuclear War?* (New York: Pocket Books, 1983), pp. 169–70.

101.   I have been criticized by Michael Howard for proceeding from a focus on "denial of victory" to a focus on a "theory of U.S. victory." Howard, "On Fighting a Nuclear War," p. 10.

102.   U.S. Congress, Office of Technology Assessment, *The Effects of Nuclear War* (Washington, D.C.: USGPO, 1980), p. 3. Moreover, the nuclear winter thesis has been advanced since publication of the OTA study.

103.   U.S. strategic forces have a major duty in extending deterrence. See Edward N. Luttwak, "The Problems of Extending Deterrence," in *The Future of Strategic Deterrence, Part I,* Adelphi Papers No. 160 (London: IISS, Autumn 1980), pp. 31–37; Earl C. Ravenal, "Counterforce and Alliance: The Ultimate Connection," *International Security* 6, no. 4(Spring 1982): 26–43; Anthony H. Cordesman, *Deterrence in the 1980s: Part I: American Strategic Forces and Extended Deterrence,* Adelphi Papers No. 175 (London: IISS, Summer 1982); Tucker, "The Nuclear Debate"; and Walter B. Slocombe, "Extended Deterrence," *Washington Quarterly* 7, no. 4(Fall 1984): 93–103.

104.   A very strong statement of this thesis is Robert S. McNamara, "The Military Role of Nuclear Weapons: Perceptions and Misconceptions," *Foreign Affairs* 62, no. 1(Fall 1983): 59–80.

105.   Relevant analyses on these and closely related subjects are Michael Howard, "Reassurance and Deterrence: Western Defense in the 1980s," *Foreign Affairs* 61, no. 2(Winter 1982/83): 309–24; Eliot A. Cohen, "The Long-Term Crisis of the Alliance," *Foreign Affairs* 61, no. 2(Winter 1982–83): 325–43; and Hedley Bull, "European Self-Reliance and the Reform of NATO," *Foreign Affairs* 61, no. 4(Spring 1983): 874–92.

106.   See Jack L. Snyder, *The Soviet Strategic Culture: Implications for Limited Nuclear Operations,* R-2154-AF (Santa Monica, Calif.: RAND Corporation, September 1977), pp. 39–40.

107.   See Donald G. Brennan, "Soviet-American Communication in Crises," *Arms Control and National Security* 1:(1969): 81–8; and Ball, *Can Nuclear War Be Controlled?*

108.   John Newhouse, *Cold Dawn: The Story of SALT* (New York: Holt, Rinehart and Winston, 1973), chap. 1.

109.   Whether or not one agrees with his answers, Jeffrey Record asked many of the right questions in *Revising U.S. Military Strategy: Tailoring Means to Ends* (Washington, D.C.: Pergamon-Brassey's, 1984).

110.   See chapter 2.

111.   An exception to this rule was registered over the "build-down" proposal for START. See William S. Cohen, "The Arms Build-Down Proposal: How We Got from There to Here," *Washington Post,* October 9, 1983, p. C8.

112.   This will change as the policy debate over President Reagan's SDI gathers momentum. See Leon Sloss, "The Strategist's Perspective," in Ashton B. Carter and David N. Schwartz, eds. *Ballistic Missile Defense* (Washington D.C.: Brookings, 1984), pp. 24–48; Keith B. Payne and Colin S. Gray, "Nuclear Policy and

the Defensive Transition," *Foreign Affairs* 62, no. 4(Spring 1984): 820–42; Charles L. Glaser, "Why Even Good Defenses May Be Bad," *International Security* 9, no. 2(Fall 1984): 92–123; and Keith B. Payne, *Strategic Defense: "Star Wars" in Perspective* (Lanham, Md.: Hamilton Press, 1986).

113. Donald G. Brennan, "The Case for Population Defense," in Johan J. Holst and William Schneider, Jr., eds., *Why ABM: Policy Issues in the Missile Defense Controversy* (New York: Pergamon Press, 1969), p. 116.

114. For an exceptionally strong affirmation of this case, see Benson D. Adams, "In Defense of the Homeland," *U.S. Naval Institute Proceedings* 109, no. 6(June 1983): 44–49. Adams believes that "strategic defenses were rejected not on strategic grounds but because they did not conform to the theories of mutual deterrence and arms control which themselves have proved invalid" (p. 49).

115. On the ambiguities associated with "denying an enemy his objectives," see Jervis, *The Illogic of American Nuclear Strategy*, pp. 76–79.

116. Little by way of substantial argument was advanced in favor of a defense-dominant strategic environment during the 1970s. Following Donald Brennan's advocacy in the late 1960s (see Brennan, "The Case for Population Defense," particularly pp. 107–16), the public record was thin for many years. See Malcolm Wallop, "Opportunities and Imperatives of Ballistic Missile Defense," *Strategic Review* 6, no. 4(Fall 1979): 13–21; and Ellory B. Block, "BMD's Role in National Survival and Recovery: A First Assessment," in Jake Garn et al., *The Future of U.S. Land-Based Strategic Forces*, Special Report (Cambridge, Mass.: Institute for Foreign Policy Analysis, December 1980), pp. 64–80. However, true evidence of changing times was the appearance of Daniel O. Graham, *High Frontier: A New National Strategy* (Washington, D.C.: High Frontier, 1982).

117. For an examination of the meaning of defense dominance and problems and opportunities pertaining to it, see Colin S. Gray, *Towards Defense Dominance* (Fairfax, Va.: National Institute for Public Policy, September 24, 1984).

118. There is near-unanimity among technical experts that this is the earliest time frame in which a strategic defense system that relies heavily on directed energy weapons could be deployed. I have discussed this issue at length in *American Military Space Policy: Information Systems, Weapon Systems, and Arms Control* (Cambridge, MA/Lanham, MD: Abt/University Press of America, 1983). Also see Jeff Hecht, *Beam Weapons: the Next Arms Race* (New York: Plenum, 1984); and the excellent collection of essays in Uri Ra'anan and Robert L. Pfaltzgraff, Jr., eds., *International Security Dimensions of Space* (Hamden, Conn.: Archon, 1984).

119. See Stanley Sienkiewicz, "Observations on the Impact of Uncertainty in Strategic Analysis," *World Politics* 32, no. 1(October 1979): 90–110; and Benjamin S. Lambeth, "Uncertainties for the Soviet War Planner," *International Security* 7, no. 3(Winter 1982–83): 139–66.

120. However, see Jack Snyder, *The Ideology of the Offensive: Military Decision Making and the Disasters of 1914* (Ithaca, N.Y.: Cornell University Press, 1984); and George F. Kennan, *The Fateful Alliance: France, Russia, and the Coming of the First World War* (New York: Pantheon, 1984).

121.   Adams, "In Defense of the Homeland," p. 48. Plainly, Adams was contrasting defense and deterrence. Caspar Weinberger has also drawn a distinction between defense and deterrence. See Weinberger, *Annual Report to the Congress, Fiscal Year 1985*, p. 30.

122.   See Glenn Snyder: *Deterrence and Defense: Toward a Theory of National Security* (Princeton, N.J.: Princeton University Press, 1961), pp. 3–15; and "Deterrence by Denial and Punishment," in Davis Bobrow, ed., *Components of Defense Policy* (Chicago: Rand McNally, 1965), pp. 209–37.

123.   Critics of U.S. BMD are correct in assuming that BMD is a two-power-or-none phenomenon. See Albert Carnesale, "Reviving the ABM Debate," *Arms Control Today* 11, no. 4(April 1981): 8.

124.   The prospects for a nonnuclear defense of NATO-Europe have been debated for more than 20 years. A useful review of some fashionable ideas is Richard K. Betts, "Conventional Strategy: New Critics, Old Choices," *International Security* 7, no. 4(Spring 1983): 140–62. See the correspondence between Edward N. Luttwak and Richard K. Betts, triggered by this article, in *International Security* 8, no. 2(Fall 1983): 176–82.

125.   A useful study of NATO's nuclear strategy is J. Michael Legge, *Theater Nuclear Weapons and the NATO Strategy of Flexible Response*, R-2964-FF (Santa Monica, Calif.: RAND Corporation, April 1983).

126.   Schell, *The Fate of the Earth*.

127.   See David S. Yost, "European Anxieties about Ballistic Missile Defense," *Washington Quarterly* 7, no. 4(Fall 1984): 112–29.

128.   For example, see Elizabeth Pond, "European Reflections on Reagan's 'Star Wars' Defense," *Christian Science Monitor*, April 11, 1983, p. 5.

129.   I gleaned these critical observations, firsthand, from conversations held in Europe in 1983, 1984 and 1985.

130.   See Donald G. Brennan, "The Case for Missile Defense," *Foreign Affairs* 43, no. 3(April 1969): 633–48.

CHAPTER 10

Nuclear Strategy and National Style

This book has argued (1) that nuclear weapons have made an important but not fundamental difference to statecraft;[1] (2) that the national styles of the two superpowers are quite clearly distinctive, even with reference to theories, strategies, and tactics pertinent to nuclear-weapons policy; and (3) that there is a preferred nuclear strategy, compatible with U.S. values, that meets the unique needs for military support of U.S. foreign policy.[2]

Understanding across cultural lines is always useful, but international security problems cannot be defined solely in terms of misunderstanding. It is desirable that Western policymakers and publics understand that the Soviet threat is of an enduring character and has very deep roots in the Russian reaction to its unique historical experience. However, the predominant U.S. problem is to contain Soviet power. To the extent that Western policymakers can appreciate that they are dealing with a fundamentally unfriendly culture, rather than with an ephemeral unfriendly policy, cultural analysis may help remove illusions and wishful thinking from official deliberations.

It would be difficult to design two countries more likely to misunderstand each other than the United States and the Soviet Union, notwithstanding some superficial, macro-level similarities between them. Both countries have an unusual degree of insularity in their worldviews. In the U.S. case, there were the facts of oceanic distance isolating the new nation and the deliberate rejection of older models of political organization and practice. In the Russian case, there was, and remains, both geographical distance and the security apparatus of the state strictly controlling traffic

311

between Russia and the West. Also, both countries have messianic ideolo-gies—although in the U.S. case, the light that was lit on Plymouth Rock was to be a beacon that would inspire by example rather than command obedience at the tip of the bayonet.[3] The geopolitical basis for Soviet-U.S. rivalry lies in the simple process of Great Power elimination. World Wars I and II destroyed the multipolar balance-of-power system of Europe. By 1945, the United States was the only country capable of organizing a security system that could restrict the freedom of Soviet policy action, just as the Soviet Union was the only country capable of threatening to impose an imbalance of power in Europe.[4]

Soviet-U.S. rivalry is often difficult to explain to a general public that is not in the habit of thinking geopolitically.[5] After all, the Soviet Union does not appear to covet U.S. territory, and the threats it poses to U.S. *survival* interests flow most immediately from the U.S. assumption of security commitments around the periphery of Europe and Asia.[6] The U.S. quarrel with the Soviet Union is of the same kind as the British quarrel with Imperial Germany between 1900 and 1914. The insular power—Great Britain then, the United States today—cannot tolerate the domination of Europe, or of Eurasia, by a single continental power or coalition.[7]

The Soviet quarrel with the United States, in terms of geopolitics, is very fundamental indeed. In the Soviet perception, the political control the Soviet state exercises over the non-Great Russian regions of the USSR is supported by the firmness of Soviet political control over Eastern Europe. However, the political stability of Eastern Europe as an essential part of the Soviet empire is menaced by the attractive power of the independent states of Western Europe, and the security and political independence of Western Europe is underwritten by the United States.[8]

Whether Soviet patterns of thought and behavior, culture and style, are more Soviet than Great Russian is a matter of little interest—although a strong case could be advanced to the effect that the Soviet Union today is the Great Russian Empire of yesterday, with the overlay of a transna-tional ideology with global pretensions. What can be determined concern-ing Soviet/Russian strategic culture? Key characteristics include the following:

- An insatiable quest for national security that has no boundaries com-patible with the security of others. The USSR is seeking total security.

- An assumption that international politics is a permanent struggle for power. War and peace and "war in peace" (cold war or peaceful coexistence) are but different phases of a continuous process in which countries rise or fall.

- A belief that one cannot be too strong militarily, that one cannot achieve a sufficiency of national military power. The Soviet Union does not acknowledge even the idea that their weapons could be a threat to peace or could promote instability. The Soviet Union has a political and strategic, rather than a technical, view of what is and what is not stabilizing.

- A confidence in unilateral military prowess and a great unwillingness to repose important security functions in the anticipation of restraint on the part of others.[9]

- A recognition that war is always possible and that the duty of soldiers is to fight and try to win if the politicians make the decision to fight. Soviet strategic culture does not accommodate the idea that the USSR should design its forces according to important criteria that bear more upon Western-style theories of arms race or crisis management than upon war-waging effectiveness. In fact, by way of contrast, in the most important realm of stability analysis of a technical kind—that is, with reference to "command stability"[10]—the Soviet Union has practiced stability while the United States has confined itself largely to talking about it.[11]

- A military strategy that is the product of the Soviet military establishment. A decision to fight, and the definition of the political objectives, will of course be within the province of the civilians. However, once a decision to fight is taken, the Soviet military is unlikely to wage war in the tentative "bargaining" manner outlined by some U.S. theorists as being appropriate to the nuclear age.[12]

- A stable political backcloth provided both by the ideological underpinnings of the regime (which provide logical consistency at the least) and by the realpolitik wisdom inherited from centuries of semi-European Great Power experience.

- In Western eyes, a curious bifocal quality. Soviet strategic thinking can be traced at the grand strategy level of correlation-of-forces analysis and at the level of tactical detail of implementation, but Western-style strategic theory is notable by its absence.[13]

- A heavy reference to historical (including prenuclear) experience.[14]

By way of contrast, important characteristics of U.S. strategic culture include the following:

- A disinclination to prepare very seriously for the actual conduct of war. For 40 years, Americans have told themselves that their policy will have failed if ever a nuclear weapon is used. This is a limited truth that has served to discourage professional preparation for nuclear armed conflict. U.S. policy thinking, by and large, terminates abruptly with a putative breakdown in prewar deterrence.[15]

- An enduring conviction that somehow, and despite the evidence to the contrary, arms control agreements can help alleviate U.S. security problems (the "Valium theory" of arms control). Arms control activity is held to be activity for peace, and the United States must naturally abide by the spirit as well as the often ambiguous letter of agreements.[16]

- A faith in high technology and, indeed, generically in panaceas of a managerial and technical kind. Witness the contemporary confidence concerning the promise of smart-weapon technology for deep strike in Europe.[17]

- A continuing faith in progress—a faith that somehow, international politics can evolve toward a condition of greater security. No U.S. president has explained to the American people the enduring geopolitical basis of Soviet-U.S. rivalry. The American people believe, or want to believe, that things can change for the better.

- An arrogance of belief that the U.S. strategic enlightenment is *The Truth*. For years, in and around the SALT forum, Americans lectured Soviet officials on strategic stability, on what fueled arms races, and on what was dangerous in a crisis. In fact, Soviet officials seem not to have had any great difficulty understanding the dominant U.S. theory of stability—the conviction that societies should remain vulnerable to nuclear retaliation; they understood and rejected it.

- Intellectual domination by civilian theorists who have been intrigued by conceptual problems but who have little if any feel for likely operational realities and little appreciation of the significance of those realities.

- A heavy focus on the area that is substantially missing from the Soviet literature—strategic theory. U.S. strategic thinking is virtually silent at the level of grand strategy and is scarcely less active with respect to military operational details.

- A general disdain for historical experience.

Soviet intentions are written in Russian and Soviet history, are inherent in the geostrategic logic of the Soviet security condition as interpreted by Soviet officials, and cannot easily be deduced from Soviet military preparations. In common with the United States, the Soviet Union wishes to prevent war. However, Soviet leaders also seek to intimidate in "war in peace" through the shadow cast by their military power, and they believe that the better able the Soviet Union is to fare well in war, the less likely it is that war will occur.[18]

Just as the prospect of being hanged in the morning is supposed to concentrate the mind wonderfully, so the shift in the strategic balance in the 1970s served wonderfully to persuade U.S. governments that they needed a strategic-forces establishment that made military sense. A liberal democracy, contemplating armed conflict as a distant prospect, will be wont to indulge its hopes rather than its distant fears. There is some danger that if war should occur, the United States and NATO-Europe, in accordance with their "peacetime" strategic culture, will be striving to limit the war, control escalation, identify "firebreaks," and the like. Meanwhile, the Soviet Union, with its military machine firmly in military hands for military purposes "for the duration," will be waging the war to win, governed in its operational decisions only by considerations of military efficiency.

Superficially, it may be tempting to assert that many of the more important differences between the dominant stable of strategic ideas of the two superpowers have to do not so much with the deep-seated cultural differences that divide the two societies as with the identities of the pertinent strategic thinkers—although one might argue that these two are not unrelated. Strategic-missile doctrine in the Soviet Union was initially formulated by artillerymen, whereas in the United States, it was formulated by civilian university professors or "think-tank" analysts. However, as Soviet commentators are fond of observing, it is no accident that in the USSR nuclear-weapons doctrine is firmly in the hands of the professional General Staff, whereas in the United States, a Harvard professor of economics and a physicist on the RAND staff can exercise a great deal of intellectual and, ultimately, policy influence.[19]

Soviet nuclear strategy is designed and debated only by those who are properly licensed. That license is restricted to members of the appropriate organs of the General Staff and, possibly very occasionally, to full members of the Council of Defense (that is, some Politburo members).[20] The Soviet defense commentators who are most familiar personally to Western strategists—such people as Henry Trofimenko, Mikhail Milstein, and Alexei Arbatov—almost certainly play no role in Soviet defense policy formulation. Those people are variably expert on the details of U.S. strategy, not Soviet strategy. By way of analogy, CIA analysts are permitted only to study other countries; they are not permitted to engage in net assessment.

Although opinions will vary, of course, among individuals, it is nonetheless valid, on the evidence, both to talk of the Soviet approach to nuclear strategy and to relate that approach to a distinctive strategic culture and, back one step, to a distinctive political culture. The professional military domination of Soviet strategic thinking is a product of political expediency (on the part of the CPSU), historical experience, and what may be termed common sense.

To explain: in most possible, and certainly most plausible, circumstances, there is no question that the Soviet armed forces are loyal to the regime. However, the armed forces, albeit vastly penetrated by Party organs and personnel, constitute the one and only organization that could challenge CPSU authority with a fair prospect of success. Too much should not be made of this argument, but a historic, tacit bargain—of the "rendering unto Caesar" variety—has been struck between the Party and the armed forces. In other words, the armed forces are a loyal and reliable executive organ of the state, provided that they are permitted preponderant influence in determining the military requirements of national defense. As a general rule, there is little Party–armed forces tension, because both agree on the primacy of making very muscular provision for national defense. Soviet soldiers would not take kindly to being criticized on military matters by civilian amateurs, be they university professors or senior functionaries of the Party or government. Thus, although the Party has generally found it expedient to acquiesce in the predominance of the uniformed military in military matters, that expediency also reflects the belief that soldiers are indeed the experts on defense issues (but not on policy issues bearing on war or peace).

In the Soviet perspective, historical experience writ large also argues for military domination of military questions. Russian and Soviet military experience, successful and otherwise, has been the most vital single thread in the (multinational) experience. Up to the present, Russian/Soviet survival and expansion over the centuries has not been a function of diplomatic skill, economic strength, or attractiveness of culture; rather, it has depended on generation after generation of peasant conscripts willing to die for Mother Russia. In an increasingly complex and dangerous world, Soviet leaders know that the one element that is unlikely to fail them is the Russian/Soviet soldier.[21]

Finally, in the Soviet perspective it is no more than common sense to allow soldiers to determine military questions. The conduct of war is not a game, nor—for a centrally located, substantially land-locked power—can war be approached with a view to achieving some desirable measure of limited national liability. Soviet leaders have learned from their history, some of it at first hand, that war can be a matter of national survival or extinction. Although soldiers, in peacetime, may make terrible mistakes in planning, on balance they are more likely than civilians to design militarily sensible plans.

Quite unintentionally, this book may help to promote a pervasive fallacy—that although theories and theorists can be important, the world is frequently driven not so much by ideas as by the multitude of details pertaining to the implementation of ideas, and the connection those details have with the master ideas may be so tenuous as to be virtually nonexistent. Western strategists are prone to quote Clausewitz's *On War* to the effect that "its [war's] grammar, indeed, may be its own, but not its logic"[22] and to stress the nonmilitarily autonomous political logic of war.

This is sensible, but it could be fatal if it betrays an inadequate understanding of the grammar of war. It is virtually certain that a U.S. president, in peacetime, has no realistic understanding of just how the United States, let alone NATO, "goes to war." The operational details of going to war (what happens at DefCon2 or DefCon1?) are a mystery to civilians. Let it be added that this is not entirely their fault. For sound reasons of security (as well as clannishness), the U.S. military does not like to share the details of readiness and mobilization with civilians. The point of this discussion is to indicate that there is a military logic to the conduct of war that is considerably different from the logic of intrawar deterrence as typically advanced by civilian U.S. strategic theorists. Much of U.S. declaratory nuclear strategy—as explained in successive annual posture statements, for example—simply makes no military sense and would, one should expect, be disregarded "in the event." The political logic of deterrence in the West argues for a central nuclear war to be conducted, initially, with very great targeting restraint. Military logic, by way of sharp contrast, argues very strongly for large initial strikes, while forces and C^3I are still intact.

Soviet officials tell us that the Soviet Union does not believe in limited central nuclear war, although nuclear war limited to a particular geographical theater of operations may be something else. This claim should be taken at face value. The United States (in the British *insular* tradition) has in its strategic theory a strain of belief in voluntarism—a belief that "he that commands the sea is at great liberty and may take as much or as little of the war as he will."[23] The Soviet Union, in the continental tradition of strategic thinking, does not agree: war is war. In practice, a Soviet Politburo might seek to impose targeting restraint on its military machine, but such should not be expected with high confidence. Soviet military science says that the military character of a war is dictated by its political meaning, a consideration hardly conducive to restraint. In this context, Soviet war plans, and even the ideas behind those war plans, are the product of Soviet soldiers, not of Soviet civilian professors. This does not imply a lack of restraint in Soviet nuclear targeting; it implies only that such restraint as is exercised will likely accord more with military than with Western political algorithms.[24]

On the evidence available, it is prudent for the U.S. government to assume that in the event of central nuclear war, the Soviet Union would not only seek to deny victory to the United States; to terminate the war (on any terms?) as rapidly as possible; or generally, to engage in coercive nuclear diplomacy. The evidence suggests that in addition, or perhaps instead, the Soviet Union would seek political victory through military victory. It would attack U.S. forces, command and control, and essential war-supporting industry. Even if the Politburo would like to conduct the war with a view to the deterrent-restoring effect of particular, constrained targeting options, most probably it would find that the military would successfully resist such attempted political subversion of the orderly execution of the war plan.

I admit to being uncertain about whether my advocacy of a balanced offense-defense strategic posture in chapter 9 can fairly be termed an appeal to traditional U.S. pragmatism or whether I am asking more of the United States, an insular democracy, than should be expected in peacetime. This book has two distinct, though closely related, aspects. First, it has sought to analyze the cultural roots of the principal strategic ideas that have served to frame both debate and policy design in the United States in the nuclear era. Second, proceeding beyond analysis—and in the light of discussion of Soviet strategic culture as manifested in programs, plans, and attitudes toward nuclear weapons policy—this book has identified, in chapter 9, a preferred U.S. postural-doctrinal response.

The postural-doctrinal response specified here requires that the United States takes seriously the proposition that deterrence and defense are one and the same. It is strange to observe that although center-conservative opinion firmly endorses the idea that U.S. strategic-offensive capabilities should carry the promise of denying victory to the USSR, that opinion continues to have a mental block with regard to the limitation of damage to the U.S. (and allied) homeland. Relatively few people have grasped the almost sophomoric point that the quality of the deterrent threat posed in the SIOP is close to irrelevant if the United States cannot cope with the kind and quantity of Soviet strategic reply that is anticipated. The problem, in short, is one of self-deterrence.[25]

This problem appears to be as much intellectual as technical. By and large, U.S. strategists seem to be resistant to the idea that it will most likely be the United States, not the Soviet Union, that "goes first" (or very seriously considers "going first") with central nuclear systems, because of the enduring insufficiency of forward-deployed theater forces. In other words, the principal U.S. strategic problem is not the deterring of a Soviet first strike but rather the design of a total nuclear war campaign capability such that nuclear first use could be executed with a backstop of a robust theory of sequential escalation dominance.

Today it is popular, and politically prudent, to preface even very defense-minded analysis with the observation that the U.S. problem—first, foremost, and possibly exclusively—is deterrence. In other words, many people who are arguing, objectively, for "war-fighting" capabilities find it politically expedient to remind their audience that the name of the game is deterrence. Such preemptive surrender on the part of nuclear strategists may be politically intelligent, but it is not wholly sound strategically. Quite aside from the major qualification noted earlier—that the deterrent problem may be one of self-deterrence rather than other-deterrence—it is at least possible, and it may even be as likely as not, that if a nuclear war should occur, it would occur with a sequence of outbreak events to which deterrence is close to irrelevant. The most likely political scenarios for World War III entail, first, a truly desperate Soviet Union—convinced that its empire is collapsing and seeing no alternative to military action (regardless of nuclear vistas). Second, World War III could erupt out of an unplanned crisis that evolved according to the "grammar" of war and was not orchestrated by the strategic scenarists of either side. In short, by implication, the United States needs a defense posture that assures national survival both in cases where very high quality deterrence can make the difference in decision making for war or peace and in cases where deterrence simply does not apply.[26]

It is important that the arguments in this book not provide further support to the "scholarly fallacy" that understanding is analogous to the solution of a problem. It is not enough that U.S. policymakers acknowledge the strategic-cultural distinctiveness of themselves and their Soviet counterparts. What is required is that they carefully consider both the impact of strategic culture on defense programs and ideas and—above all—the probable fate of the two societies if they should ever find themselves locked in combat. How well would we do?

NOTES

1.   This was discussed in considerable detail in chapter 1. Many people are convinced that the advent of nuclear weapons has made a fundamental difference to world politics. They would echo the words reportedly uttered by Bernard Brodie on hearing of the dropping of the atomic bomb on Hiroshima: "Everything that I have written is obsolete." Quoted in Fred Kaplan, *The Wizards of Armageddon* (New York: Simon and Schuster, 1983), p. 10.

2.   Such a strategy is advanced for consideration in chapter 9.

3.   This is not to deny that the United States, particularly during the Progressive Era, has been known to adopt an expansive, even aggressive mandate in the realm of bettering mankind forcefully. An interesting though overstated study of the domestic roots of U.S. foreign policy is Robert Dallek, *The American Style of Foreign Policy: Cultural Politics and Foreign Affairs* (New York: Knopf, 1983).

4.   Capability has a way of defining rivalry, if not enmity. At the close of World War I, the U.S. government identified British and Japanese naval power as the principal threats to U.S. security, while in the same period, no less naturally, Great Britain was worried about the building program for the U.S. fleet and about the airpower imbalance that it predicted with France. As the dominant power on the continent of Europe in 1919, France inevitably excited British anxiety. Similarly, in 1944–45, the Soviet Union, through victory in war, assumed the erstwhile German role as principal threat to the balance of power in Europe.

5.   For an interesting example of an attempt to do so, see Thomas Powers, "What Is It About?" *Atlantic* 253, no. 1(January 1984): 35–55. "It" is the Soviet-U.S. global competition.

6. On the subject of U.S. national interests, see Donald E. Nuechterlein, *America Overcommitted: United States' National Interests in the 1980s* (Lexington: University Press of Kentucky, 1985); and Colin S. Gray, "Long-Range Planning and American Security Interests," *U.S. Naval Institute Proceedings* 110, no. 12(December 1984): 37–43. An outstanding discussion of the problems for U.S. nuclear strategy posed by overseas security commitments is Robert W. Tucker, "The Nuclear Debate," *Foreign Affairs* 63, no. 1(Fall 1984), particularly pp. 28–31.

7. Classic explanations of this reasoning are Sir Eyre Crowe, "England's Foreign Policy," in Robert L. Pfaltzgraff, Jr., ed., *Politics and the International System* (Philadelphia: Lippincott, 1969), pp. 384–86; and Nicholas J. Spykman, *The Geography of the Peace* (New York: Harcourt, Brace, 1944).

8. On the character and dynamics of Soviet territorial and hegemonic imperialism, see Edward N. Luttwak, *The Grand Strategy of the Soviet Union* (London: Weidenfeld and Nicolson, 1983).

9. See John Erickson, "The Soviet View of Deterrence: A General Survey," *Survival* 24, no. 6(November/December 1982): 242–51.

10. See John D. Steinbruner, "National Security and the Concept of Strategic Stability," *Journal of Conflict Resolution* 22, no. 3(September 1978): 411–28.

11. See John D. Steinbruner, "Nuclear Decapitation," *Foreign Policy*, no. 45(Winter 1981-82): 16-28; Desmond Ball, *Can Nuclear War Be Controlled?* Adelphi Papers No. 169 (London: IISS, Autumn 1981); Paul Bracken, *The Command and Control of Nuclear Forces* (New Haven: Yale University Press, 1983); Ashton B. Carter, "The Command and Control of Nuclear War," *Scientific American* 252, no. 1(January 1985): 32–39; and Bruce A. Blair, *Strategic Command and Control: Redefining the Nuclear Threat* (Washington, D.C.: Brookings, 1985). All five of these authors are pessimistic about the ability of *both* superpowers to control their nuclear forces in war. I find their pessimism understandable, but excessive.

12. This appears preeminently in the brilliant writings of Thomas C. Schelling. See his *Arms and Influence* (New Haven: Yale University Press, 1966).

13. See Robert Legvold, "Strategic 'Doctrine' and SALT: Soviet and American Views," *Survival* 21, no. 1(January 1979): 8–13.

14. This includes, particularly, the experience of the Great Patriotic War of 1941–45 and, to a lesser extent, the experience of the period of "war communism," November 1918–Spring 1921.

15. As numerous people have observed, U.S. strategic thinking leaves the field precisely when it would most be needed. This is not to say, of course, that the uniformed services have neglected their war-planning duties. In that regard, see David Alan Rosenberg, "The Origins of Overkill: Nuclear Weapons and American Strategy, 1945–1960," *International Security* 7, no. 4(Spring 1983): 3–71; Desmond Ball, *Targeting for Strategic Deterrence*, Adelphi Papers No. 185 (London: IISS, Summer 1983); and Colin S. Gray, *Nuclear Strategy and Strategic Planning*, Philadelphia Policy Papers (Philadelphia: Foreign Policy Research Institute, 1984). As often as not, what purports to be applied strategy is really little more than capabilities planning.

16. For analysis of a "back to basics" nature, see Colin S. Gray, "Arms

Control: Problems," in R. James Woolsey, ed., *Nuclear Arms: Ethics, Strategy, Politics* (San Francisco: Institute for Contemporary Studies, 1984), pp. 153–69.

17. See Daniel Gouré and Jeffrey R. Cooper, "Conventional Deep Strike: A Critical Look," *Comparative Strategy* 4, no. 3(1984): 215–48.

18. An important article discussing possible changes in the official Soviet attitude toward war and the utility of nuclear force is Dan L. Strode and Rebecca V. Strode, "Diplomacy and Defense in Soviet National Security Policy," *International Security* 8, no. 2(Fall 1983): 91–116. Notwithstanding the strength of competing convictions with which Western commentators debate the issue of whether or not the Soviet Union believes it could win a nuclear war, few people would dissent from the following characterization of the Soviet perspective, offered by David Holloway:

> The Soviet leaders have been forced to recognize that their relationship with the United States is in reality one of mutual vulnerability to devastating nuclear strikes, and that there is no immediate prospect of escaping from this relationship. Within the constraints of this mutual vulnerability they have tried to prepare for nuclear war, and they would try to win such a war if it came to that. But there is little evidence to suggest that they think victory in a global nuclear war would be anything other than catastrophic.

The Soviet Union and the Arms Race (New Haven: Yale University Press, 1983), p. 179.

19. I refer, specifically, to Thomas Schelling and Herman Kahn. The influence of these two theorists may easily be exaggerated, but it would be difficult to deny that each of them contributed very noticeably to the parameters of nuclear policy debate. At the very least, they both made large, obvious, and enduring contributions to the conceptual fuel of the debate. This claim is supported by Lawrence Freedman, *The Evolution of Nuclear Strategy* (London: Macmillan, 1981); and Robert Jervis, *The Illogic of American Nuclear Strategy* (Ithaca, N.Y.: Cornell University Press, 1984). On the question of policy influence, see Colin S. Gray, *Strategic Studies and Public Policy: The American Experience* (Lexington: University Press of Kentucky, 1982), chap. 11.

20. See Harriet Fast Scott and William F. Scott, *The Armed Forces of the Soviet Union* (Boulder, Colo.: Westview Press, 1979), pp. 97–99.

21. However, the declining percentage of Slavs among the Soviet citizenry has to be a source of Soviet anxiety for the future. The stake of non-Great Russians in the Great Russian imperial enterprise that is the Soviet Union today is judged by many Western experts to be a very important source of Soviet anxiety, if not actually a major vulnerability. See Vernon V. Aspaturian, "The Anatomy of the Soviet Empire: Vulnerabilities and Strengths," in Keith A. Dunn and William O. Staudenmaier, eds., *Military Strategy in Transition: Defense and Deterrence in the 1980s* (Carlisle Barracks, Pa.: U.S. Army War College, 1984), pp. 97–148; and Richard Pipes, *Survival Is Not Enough: Soviet Realities and America's Future* (New York: Simon and Schuster, 1984), pp. 178–86.

22. Carl von Clausewitz, *On War* (Michael Howard and Peter Paret, eds.) (Princeton, N.J.: Princeton University Press, 1976; first pub. 1832), p. 605.

23.   See Michael Howard, *The British Way in Warfare: A Reappraisal* (London: Jonathan Cape, 1975), p. 5.

24.   I have debated targeting restraint with Soviet officials and commentators on several occasions and have come to believe somewhat reluctantly, (1) that they genuinely mean what they say and (2) that they are probably correct. A useful recent discussion is Dennis M. Gormley and Douglas M. Hart, "Soviet Views on Escalation," *Washington Quarterly* 7, no. 4(Fall 1984): 71–84.

25.   A first-rate analysis that has the unusual merit of asking most of the right questions, although it provides the wrong answers, is Jervis, *The Illogic of American Nuclear Strategy*.

26.   The "irrelevance of deterrence" argument, advanced here, is a rank heresy—even among defense conservatives.

Bibliography

BOOKS

Abt, Clark C. *A Strategy for Terminating a Nuclear War.* Boulder, Colo.: Westview Press, 1985.

Allison, Graham T. *Essence of Decision: Explaining the Cuban Missile Crisis.* Boston: Little, Brown, 1971.

———. Albert Carnesale, and Joseph S. Nye, Jr., eds. *Hawks, Doves, and Owls: An Agenda for Avoiding Nuclear War.* New York: Norton, 1985.

Armbruster, Frank E., et al. *Can We Win in Vietnam? The American Dilemma.* London: Pall Mall, 1968.

Aron, Raymond. *Clausewitz: Philosopher of War.* London: Routledge and Kegan Paul, 1983; first pub. 1976.

Ball, Desmond, and Jeffrey T. Richelson, eds. *Strategic Nuclear Targeting,* forthcoming.

Basov, Colonel N. I., et al. *The Philosophical Heritage of V. I. Lenin and Problems of Contemporary War (A Soviet View).* Soviet Military Thought Series of the U.S. Air Force, No. 5. Washington, D.C.: USGPO, 1975; Moscow, 1972.

Beaufre, Andre. *Deterrence and Strategy.* London: Faber and Faber, 1965.

Beeching, Jack. *The Galleys at Lepanto.* New York: Scribner's, 1983.

Bell, Coral. *The Conventions of Crisis: A Study in Diplomatic Management.* London: Oxford University Press, 1971.

Berman, Robert B., and John C. Baker. *Soviet Strategic Forces: Requirements and Responses.* Washington, D.C.: Brookings, 1982.

Best, Geoffrey. *Humanity in War.* New York: Columbia University Press, 1983.

Betts, Richard. *Soldiers, Statesmen, and Cold War Crises.* Cambridge, Mass.: Harvard University Press, 1977.

Bialer, Seweryn. *Stalin's Successors: Leadership, Stability, and Change in the Soviet Union.* Cambridge: Cambridge University Press, 1980.

Billington, James H. *The Icon and the Axe: An Interpretive History of Russian Culture.* New York: Knopf, 1966.

Blair, Bruce G. *Strategic Command and Control: Redefining the Nuclear Threat.* Washington, D.C.: Brookings, 1985.

Blechman, Barry M., ed. *Rethinking the U.S. Strategic Posture.* Cambridge, Mass.: Ballinger, 1982.

Bond, Brian. *Liddell Hart: A Study of His Military Thought.* New Brunswick, N.J.: Rutgers University Press, 1977; first pub. 1976.

Boorstin, Daniel. *The Americans: The Colonial Experience.* New York: Vintage, 1958.

Booth, Ken. *Strategy and Ethnocentrism.* London: Croom, Helm, 1979.

Borklund, Carl. *Men of the Pentagon, from Forrestal to McNamara.* New York: Praeger, 1966.

Bracken, Paul. *The Command and Control of Nuclear Forces.* New Haven: Yale University Press, 1983.

Braestrup, Peter, ed. *Vietnam as History: Ten Years After the Paris Peace Accords.* Washington, D.C.: University Press of America, January 1984.

Bridge, F. R., and Roger Bullen. *The Great Powers and the European States System, 1815–1914.* London: Longman, 1980.

Brodie, Bernard. *Sea Power in the Machine Age.* Princeton, N.J.: Princeton University Press, 1941.

———, ed. *The Absolute Weapon: Atomic Power and World Order.* New York: Harcourt, Brace, 1946.

———. *Escalation and the Nuclear Option.* Princeton, N.J.: Princeton University Press, 1966.

———. *War and Politics.* New York: Macmillan, 1973.

Brogan, Sir Dennis. *American Aspects.* New York: Harper & Row, 1966.

Brown, A.H. *Soviet Politics and Political Science.* London: Macmillan, 1974.

Brown, Harold. *Thinking About National Security: Defense and Foreign Policy in a Dangerous World.* Boulder, Colo.: Westview Press, 1983.

Buchan, Alastair. *Crisis Management: The New Diplomacy.* Boulogne-sur-Seine: Atlantic Institute, 1966.

Bull, Hedley. *The Anarchical Society—A Study of Order in World Politics.* New York: Columbia University Press, 1977.

Buteux, Paul. *Strategy, Doctrine, and the Politics of the Alliance: Theatre Nuclear Force Modernization in NATO.* Boulder, Colo.: Westview Press, 1983.

Buzzard, Anthony, et al. *On Limiting Atomic War.* London: Royal Institute of International Affairs, 1956.

Byely, Col. B., et al. *Marxism-Leninism on War and the Army (A Soviet View).* Soviet Military Thought Series of the U.S. Air Force, No. 2. Washington, D.C.: USGPO, 1974; Moscow, 1972.

Carter, Ashton B., and David N. Schwartz, eds. *Ballistic Missile Defense.* Washington, D.C.: Brookings, 1984.

Chambers, James. *The Devil's Horsemen: The Mongol Invasion of Europe.* New York: Atheneum, 1979.

Clark, Asa A., IV, et al., eds. *The Defense Reform Debate: Issues and Analysis.* Baltimore: Johns Hopkins University Press, 1984.

Clark, Ian. *Limited Nuclear War: Political Theory and War Conventions.* Princeton, N.J.: Princeton University Press, 1982.

Clausewitz, Carl von. *On War* (Michael Howard and Peter Paret, eds.). Princeton, N.J.: Princeton University Press, 1976; first pub. 1832.

Collins, John M. *U.S.-Soviet Military Balance: Concepts and Capabilities, 1960–1980.* New York: McGraw-Hill, 1980.

Conquest, Robert. *The Great Terror: Stalin's Purge of the Thirties.* New York: Collier, 1973; first pub. 1968.

Craig, Gordon A. *Germany: 1866–1945.* New York: Oxford University Press, 1978.

Crankshaw, Edward. *The Shadow of the Winter Palace: The Drift to Revolution, 1825–1917.* London: Macmillan, 1976.

Creveld, Martin van. *Supplying War: Logistics from Wallenstein to Patton.* Cambridge: Cambridge University Press, 1977.

———. *Fighting Power: German and U.S. Army Performance, 1939–1945.* Westport, Conn.: Greenwood Press, 1982.

Dallek, Robert. *The American Style of Foreign Policy: Cultural Politics and Foreign Affairs.* New York: Knopf, 1983.

Deane, Michael J. *Strategic Defense in Soviet Strategy.* Washington, D.C.: Advanced International Studies Institute in association with the University of Miami, 1980.

d'Encausse, Helene C. *Decline of an Empire: The Soviet Socialist Republics in Revolt.* New York: Newsweek Books, 1979.

Dehio, Ludwig. *The Precarious Balance: Four Centuries of the European Power Struggle.* New York: Vintage, 1962; first pub. 1948.

D'Este, Carlo. *Decision in Normandy.* New York: Dutton, 1983.

Dinerstein, Herbert. *War and the Soviet Union.* New York: Praeger, 1962.

Douglass, Joseph D., Jr. *The Soviet Theater Nuclear Offensive.* Studies in Communist Affairs, Vol. 1. Washington, D.C.: USGPO, 1976.

———. *Soviet Military Strategy in Europe.* New York: Pergamon Press, 1980.

Douglass, Joseph D., Jr., and Amoretta M. Hoeber. *Soviet Strategy for Nuclear War.* Stanford, Calif.: Hoover Institution Press, 1979.

———. *Conventional War and Escalation: The Soviet View.* New York: Crane, Russak (for the National Strategy Information Center), 1981.

Drell, Sidney D., Philip J. Farley, and David Holloway. *The Reagan Strategic Defense Initiative: A Technical, Political, and Arms Control Assessment,*

Special Report. Stanford, Calif.: Stanford University, Center for International Security and Arms Control, July 1984.

Druzhinin, V. V., and D. S. Kontorov. *Decision Making and Automation: Concept, Algorithm, Decision (A Soviet View)*. Soviet Military Thought Series of the U.S. Air Force, No. 6. Washington, D.C.: USGPO, 1975; Moscow, 1972.

Duffy, Christopher. *Russia's Military Way to the West: Origins and Nature of Russian Military Power, 1700–1800*. London: Routledge and Kegan Paul, 1981.

Dyson, Freeman. *Weapons and Hope*. New York: Harper & Row, 1984.

Dziak, John J. *Soviet Perceptions of Military Power: The Interaction of Theory and Practice*. New York: Crane, Russak (for the National Strategy Information Center), 1981.

Edwards, John. *Super Weapon: The Making of MX*. New York: Norton, 1982.

Ehrlich, Paul R., et al. *The Cold and the Dark: The World After Nuclear War*. New York: Norton, 1984.

Ellis, John. *Cassino, the Hollow Victory: The Battle for Rome, January–June 1944*. New York: McGraw-Hill, 1984.

Enthoven, Alain, and K. Wayne Smith. *How Much Is Enough? Shaping the Defense Program, 1961–1969*. New York: Harper & Row, 1971.

Erickson, John. *The Soviet High Command, 1918–1941*. London: St. Martin's, 1962.

──────. *The Road to Stalingrad*. Boulder, Colo.: Westview Press, 1983; first pub. 1975.

Fisher, Roger. *International Conflict for Beginners*. New York: Harper Colophon, 1970; first pub. 1969.

──────, and William L. Ury. *Getting to Yes*. Boston: Houghton Mifflin, 1981.

Fox, William T. R. *The Super Powers*. New York: Harcourt, Brace, 1944.

Freedman, Lawrence. *U.S. Intelligence and the Soviet Strategic Threat*. London: Macmillan, 1977.

──────. *The Evolution of Nuclear Strategy*. London: Macmillan, 1981.

Frei, Daniel. *Risks of Unintentional Nuclear War*. Totowa, N.J.: Allanheld, Osmun, 1983.

Fugate, Bryan I. *Operation Barbarossa: Strategy and Tactics on the Eastern Front, 1941*. Novato, Calif.: Presidio Press, 1984.

Gaddis, John Lewis. *Strategies of Containment: A Critical Appraisal of Postwar American National Security Policy*. New York: Oxford University Press, 1982.

Gallagher, Matthew P., and Karl F. Spielmann. *Soviet Decision-Making for Defense: A Critique of U.S. Perspectives on the Arms Race*. New York: Praeger, 1972.

Garfinkle, Adam M. *The Politics of the Nuclear Freeze*. Philadelphia Policy Papers. Philadelphia: Foreign Policy Research Institute, 1984.

George, Alexander, et al. *The Limits of Coercive Diplomacy: Laos, Cuba, Vietnam*. Boston: Little, Brown, 1971.

George, Alexander, and Richard Smoke. *Deterrence in American Foreign Policy: Theory and Practice.* New York: Columbia University Press, 1974.

Gilpin, Robert. *War and Change in World Politics.* Cambridge: Cambridge University Press, 1981.

Goldhamer, Herbert. *The Soviet Soldier: Soviet Military Management at the Troop Level.* New York: Crane, Russak, 1975.

Goldrick, James. *The King's Ships Were at Sea: The War in the North Sea, August 1914–February 1915.* Annapolis, Md.: Naval Institute Press, 1984.

Gooch, John, and Amos Perlmutter, eds. *Military Deception and Strategic Surprise.* London: Frank Cass, 1982.

Gouré, Leon. *War Survival in Soviet Strategy.* Coral Gables, Fla.: University of Miami, Center for Advanced International Studies, 1976.

Graham, Daniel O. *High Frontier: A New National Strategy.* Washington, D.C.: High Frontier, 1982.

Gray, Colin S. *The Soviet-American Arms Race.* Farnborough, Hampshire (U.K.): Saxon House, 1976.

——. *The Geopolitics of the Nuclear Era: Heartland, Rimlands, and the Technological Revolution.* New York: Crane, Russak (for the National Strategy Information Center), 1977.

——. *The MX ICBM and National Security.* New York: Praeger, 1981.

——. *Strategic Studies: A Critical Assessment.* Westport, Conn.: Greenwood Press, 1982.

——. *Strategic Studies and Public Policy: The American Experience.* Lexington: University Press of Kentucky, 1982.

——. *American Military Space Policy: Information Systems, Weapon Systems, and Arms Control.* Cambridge, MA/Lanham, MD: Abt/University Press of America, 1983.

——. *Nuclear Strategy and Strategic Planning.* Philadelphia Policy Papers. Philadelphia: Foreign Policy Research Institute, 1984.

Gray, Colin S. and Keith B. Payne, eds. *The Nuclear Freeze Controversy.* Cambridge, MA/Lanham, MD: Abt/University Press of America, 1984.

Griffith, Paddy. *Forward into Battle: Fighting Tactics from Waterloo to Vietnam.* Chichester (U.K.): Antony Bird, 1981.

Ground Zero. *What About the Russians—And Nuclear War?* New York: Pocket Books, 1983.

Halperin, Morton H. *Limited War in the Nuclear Age.* New York: Wiley, 1963.

Harkabi, Y. *Nuclear War and Nuclear Peace.* Jerusalem: Israeli Program for Scientific Translations, 1966.

Harvard Nuclear Study Group. *Living with Nuclear Weapons.* New York: Bantam, 1983.

Heathcote, T. *The Afghan Wars: 1839–1919.* London: Osprey, 1980.

Herken, Gregg. *Counsels of War.* New York: Knopf, 1985.

Hermann, Charles F., ed. *International Crises: Insights From Behavioral Research.* New York: Free Press, 1972.

Herwin, Holger H. *"Luxury Fleet": The Imperial German Navy, 1888–1918.* London: Allen and Unwin, 1980.

Heyns, Terry L., ed. *Understanding U.S. Strategy: A Reader.* Washington, D.C.: National Defense University Press, 1983.

Hingley, Ronald. *The Russian Mind.* New York: Scribner's, 1977.

Hitch, Charles, and Roland McKean. *The Economics of Defense in the Nuclear Age.* New York: Atheneum, 1966; first pub. 1960.

Hoffmann, Stanley. *Gulliver's Troubles: Or the Setting of American Foreign Policy.* New York: McGraw-Hill, 1968.

Holland, Lauren H., and Robert A. Hoover, *The MX Decision: A New Direction in Weapons Procurement?* Boulder, Colo.: Westview Press, 1985.

Holloway, David. *The Soviet Union and the Arms Race.* New Haven: Yale University Press, 1983.

Holsti, Ole R. *Crisis, Escalation, War.* Montreal: McGill-Queen's University Press, 1972.

Horelick, Arnold, and Myron Rush. *Strategic Power and Soviet Foreign Policy.* Chicago: University of Chicago Press, 1965.

Hough, Jerry F. *Soviet Leadership in Transition.* Washington, D.C.: Brookings, 1980.

Hough, Richard. *The Great War at Sea: 1914–1918.* Oxford: Oxford University Press, 1983.

Howard, Michael. *The Continental Commitment: The Dilemma of British Defence Policy in the Era of the Two World Wars.* London: Temple Smith, 1972.

———. *The British Way in Warfare: A Reappraisal.* London: Jonathan Cape, 1975.

———. *War and the Liberal Conscience.* New Brunswick, N.J.: Rutgers University Press, 1978.

———. ed., *Restraints on War: Studies in the Limitation of Armed Conflict.* Oxford: Oxford University Press, 1979.

———. *The Causes of Wars and Other Essays.* London: Unwin, 1983.

Huntington, Samuel P., ed. *The Strategic Imperative: New Policies for American Security.* Cambridge, Mass.: Ballinger, 1982.

Jervis, Robert. *The Illogic of American Nuclear Strategy.* Ithaca, N.Y.: Cornell University Press, 1984.

Kahan, Jerome H. *Security in the Nuclear Age: Developing U.S. Strategic Arms Policy.* Washington, D.C.: Brookings, 1975.

Kahn, Herman. *On Thermonuclear War.* Princeton, N.J.: Princeton University Press, 1960.

———. *On Escalation: Metaphors and Scenarios.* New York: Praeger, 1965.

Kaplan, Fred. *The Wizards of Armageddon.* New York: Simon and Schuster, 1983.

Kaufmann, William W., ed. *Military Policy and National Security.* Oxford: Oxford University Press, 1956.

Kavanaugh, Dennis. *Political Culture.* London: Macmillan, 1971.

Keegan, John. *Six Armies in Normandy: From D-Day to the Liberation of Paris.* New York: Viking, 1982.

Kennan, George F. *The Fateful Alliance: France, Russia, and the Coming of the First World War.* New York: Pantheon, 1984.

Kennedy, Paul M. *The Rise and Fall of British Naval Mastery.* New York: Scribner's 1976.

———, ed. *The War Plans of the Great Powers: 1880–1914.* London: Allen and Unwin, 1979.

———. *The Rise of the Anglo-German Antagonism, 1860–1914.* London: Allen and Unwin, 1982; first pub. 1980.

———. *Strategy and Diplomacy, 1870–1945: Eight Studies.* London: Allen and Unwin, 1983.

Kennedy, Robert F. *13 Days: The Cuban Missile Crisis.* London: Pan, 1969; first pub. 1968.

Kintner, William R., and Harriet F. Scott, eds. *The Nuclear Revolution in Soviet Military Affairs.* Norman: University of Oklahoma Press, 1968.

Kissinger, Henry. *Nuclear Weapons and Foreign Policy.* New York: Harper Brothers, 1957.

———. *White House Years.* Boston: Little, Brown, 1979.

Knorr, Klaus, and Thornton Read, eds. *Limited Strategic War: Essays on Nuclear Strategy.* New Haven: Yale University Press, 1960.

Koch, H. W., ed. *The Origins of the First World War: Great Power Rivalry and German War Aims,* 2d ed. London: Macmillan, 1984.

Koestler, Arthur. *The Ghost in the Machine.* London: Pan, 1970.

Kohler, Foy D. *How Not to Negotiate with the Russians.* Washington, D.C.: Advanced International Studies Institute in association with the University of Miami, 1979.

Kolkowicz, Roman, et al. *The Soviet Union and Arms Control—A Superpower Dilemma.* Baltimore: Johns Hopkins University Press, 1970.

Komer, Robert W. *Maritime Strategy or Coalition Defense?* Cambridge, MA./Lanham, MD: Abt/University Press of America, 1984.

Kozlov, S. N., ed. *The Officer's Handbook (A Soviet View).* Soviet Military Thought Series of the U.S. Air Force, No. 13. Washington, D.C.: USGPO, 1977; Moscow, 1971.

Lebow, Richard Ned. *Between Peace and War: The Nature of International Crisis.* Baltimore: Johns Hopkins University Press, 1981.

Leebaert, Derek, ed. *Soviet Military Thinking.* London: Allen and Unwin, 1981.

Leites, Nathan. *Soviet Style in War.* New York: Crane, Russak, 1982.

Levine, D. C. B. *Russia and the Origins of the First World War.* London: Macmillan, 1983.

Lockwood, Jonathan S. *The Soviet View of U.S. Strategic Doctrine: Implications for Decision Making.* New Brunswick, N.J.: Transaction, 1983.

Lomov, Colonel-General N. A., ed. *Scientific-Technical Progress and the Revolution in Military Affairs (A Soviet View).* Soviet Military Thought Series of the U.S. Air Force, No. 3. Washington, D.C.: USGPO, 1975; Moscow, 1973.

Lowe, James T. *Geopolitics and War: Mackinder's Philosophy of Power.* Washington, D.C.: University Press of America, 1981.

Luttwak, Edward N. *The Grand Strategy of the Roman Empire: From the First Century A.D. to the Third.* Baltimore: Johns Hopkins University Press, 1976.

————. *Strategy and Politics: Collected Essays.* New Brunswick, N.J.: Transaction, 1980.

————. *The Grand Strategy of the Soviet Union.* London: Weidenfeld and Nicolson, 1983.

————. *The Pentagon and the Art of War.* New York: Simon and Schuster, 1985.

McElwee, William. *The Art of War: Waterloo to Mons.* London: Weidenfeld and Nicolson, 1974.

Mackinder, Halford. *Democratic Ideals and Reality.* New York: Norton, 1962.

Mahan, Alfred Thayer. *The Influence of Sea Power upon History, 1660–1783.* London: Methuen, 1975; first pub. 1890.

Mandelbaum, Michael. *The Nuclear Question: The United States and Nuclear Weapons, 1946–1976.* Cambridge: Cambridge University Press, 1979.

————. *The Nuclear Revolution: International Politics Before and After Hiroshima.* Cambridge: Cambridge University Press, 1981.

Martin, Laurence. *The Two-Edged Sword: Armed Force in the Modern World.* London: Weidenfeld and Nicolson, 1982.

Mearsheimer, John J. *Conventional Deterrence.* Ithaca, N.Y.: Cornell University Press, 1983.

Mellor, Roy E. H. *The Soviet Union and Its Geographical Problems.* London: Macmillan, 1982.

Miller, Mark E. *Soviet Strategic Power and Doctrine: The Quest for Superiority.* Washington, D.C.: Advanced International Studies Institute in association with the University of Miami, 1982.

Milovidov, General-Major A. S., and Colonel V. G. Kozlov. *The Philosophical Heritage of V. I. Lenin and Problems of Contemporary War (A Soviet View).* Soviet Military Thought Series of the U.S. Air Force, No. 5. Washington, D.C.: USGPO, 1975; Moscow, 1972.

Modelski, George. *Principles of World Politics.* New York: Free Press, 1972.

Morgan, Patrick M. *Deterrence: A Conceptual Analysis.* Beverly Hills, Calif.: Sage, 1977.

Morgenthau, Hans J. *Politics Among Nations: The Struggle for Power and Peace.* New York: Knopf, 1948.

Murnion, Philip J., ed. *Catholics and Nuclear War: A Commentary on "The Challenge of Peace," the U.S. Catholic Bishops' Pastoral Letter on War and Peace.* New York: Crossroad, 1983.

Murray, Williamson. *The Change in the European Balance of Power, 1938–1939: The Path to Ruin.* Princeton, N.J.: Princeton University Press, 1984.

Nacht, Michael. *The Age of Vulnerability: Threats to the Nuclear Stalemate.* Washington, D.C.: Brookings, 1985.

Nuechterlein, Donald E. *America Overcommitted: United States' National Interests in the 1980s.* Lexington: University Press of Kentucky, 1985.

Newhouse, John. *Cold Dawn: The Story of SALT.* New York: Holt, Rinehart and Winston, 1973.

Nincic, Miroslav. *The Arms Race: The Political Economy of Military Growth.* New York: Praeger, 1982.

Ogarkov, Nikolay V. *Always in Readiness to Defend the Homeland,* trans. JPRS L/10412, March 25, 1982. Moscow: *Voyenizdat,* January 1982.

Osgood, Robert E. *Limited War Revisited.* Boulder, Colo.: Westview Press, 1979.

Osgood, Robert E., and Robert Tucker. *Force, Order and Justice.* Baltimore: Johns Hopkins University Press, 1967.

Palmer, Bruce, Jr. *The 25-Year War: America's Military Role in Vietnam.* Lexington: University Press of Kentucky, 1984.

Palmer, Gregory. *The McNamara Strategy and the Vietnam War: Program Budgeting in the Pentagon, 1960–1968.* Westport, Conn.: Greenwood Press, 1978.

Parker, W.H. *Mackinder: Geography as an Aid to Statecraft.* Oxford: Clarendon Press, 1982.

Parkinson, F. *The Philosophy of International Relations: A Study in the History of Thought.* Beverly Hills, Calif.: Sage, 1977.

Payne, Keith B. *Nuclear Deterrence in U.S.-Soviet Relations.* Boulder, Colo.: Westview Press, 1982.

_____. *Strategic Defense: "Star Wars" in Perspective.* Lanham, Md.: Hamilton Press, 1986.

Peeters, Paul. *Massive Retaliation: The Policy and Its Critics.* Chicago: Regnery, 1959.

Pipes, Richard. *Russia Under the Old Regime.* New York: Scribner's, 1974.

_____. *Survival Is Not Enough: Soviet Realities and America's Future.* New York: Simon and Schuster, 1984.

Prados, John. *The Soviet Estimate: U.S. Intelligence Analysis and Russian Military Strength.* New York: Dial, 1982.

Pringle, Peter, and William Arkin. *SIOP.* London: Sphere, 1983.

Quade, E. S., ed. *Analysis for Military Decisions: The RAND Lectures on Systems Analysis.* Chicago: Rand McNally, 1964.

_____, and W.I. Boucher, eds. *Systems Analysis and Policy Planning: Applications in Defense.* New York: Elsevier, 1968.

Raeff, Marc. *Understanding Imperial Russia: State and Society in the Old Regime*. New York: Columbia University Press, 1984.

Ranger, Robin. *Arms and Politics, 1958–1978: Arms Control in a Changing Political Context*. Toronto: Macmillan of Canada, 1979.

Rathjens, George W. *The Future of the Strategic Arms Race: Options for the 1970s*. New York: Carnegie Endowment for International Peace, 1969.

Record, Jeffrey. *Revising U.S. Military Strategy: Tailoring Means to Ends*. Washington, D.C.: Pergamon-Brassey's, 1984.

Reynolds, Charles. *Modes of Imperialism*. Oxford: Martin Robertson, 1981.

Rogow, Arnold A. *James Forrestal: A Study of Personality, Politics, and Policy*. New York: Macmillan, 1963.

Roherty, James M. *Decisions of Robert S. McNamara: A Study of the Role of the Secretary of Defense*, Coral Gables, Fla.: University of Miami Press, 1970.

Rosecrance, Richard, ed. *America as an Ordinary Country: U.S. Foreign Policy and the Future*. Ithaca, N.Y.: Cornell University Press, 1976.

Sanders, Ralph. *The Politics of Defense Analysis*. New York: Dunellen, 1973.

Scheer, Robert. *With Enough Shovels: Reagan, Bush and Nuclear War*, 2d ed. New York: Vintage, 1983.

Schell, Jonathan. *The Fate of the Earth*. New York: Knopf, 1982.

———. *The Abolition*. New York: Knopf, 1984.

Schelling, Thomas C. *The Strategy of Conflict*. Cambridge, Mass.: Harvard University Press, 1960.

———. *Arms and Influence*. New Haven: Yale University Press, 1966.

Schelling, Thomas C., and Morton H. Halperin. *Strategy and Arms Control*. New York: Twentieth Century Fund, 1961.

Schlesinger, Arthur M., Jr. *A Thousand Days: John F. Kennedy in the White House*. London: Deutsch, 1965.

Schneider, Barry R., Colin S. Gray, and Keith B. Payne, eds. *Missiles for the Nineties: ICBMs and Strategic Policy*. Boulder, Colo.: Westview Press, 1984.

Schwartz, David N. *NATO's Nuclear Dilemma*. Washington, D.C.: Brookings, 1983.

Scott, Harriet Fast, and William F. Scott. *The Armed Forces of the U.S.S.R.* Boulder, Colo.: Westview Press, 1979.

Scott, William F., and Harriet Fast Scott. *The Soviet Control Structure: Capabilities for Wartime Survival*. New York: Crane, Russak (for the National Strategy Information Center), 1983.

Skirdo, Colonel M. P. *The People, the Army, the Commander (A Soviet View)*. Soviet Military Thought Series of the U.S. Air Force, No. 14. Washington, D.C.: USGPO, n.d.: Moscow, 1970.

Smith, Bruce. *The RAND Corporation: Case Study of a Non-Profit Advisory Corporation*. Cambridge, Mass.: Harvard University Press, 1966.

Smith, Gerard. *Doubletalk: The Story of the First Strategic Arms Limitation Talks.* New York: Doubleday, 1980. Reprint, Lanham, Md.: University Press of America, 1985.

Smoke, Richard. *War: Controlling Escalation.* Cambridge, Mass.: Harvard University Press, 1977.

Snyder, Glenn. *Deterrence and Defense: Toward a Theory of National Security.* Princeton, N.J.: Princeton University Press, 1961.

Snyder, Jack. *The Ideology of the Offensive: Military Decision Making and the Disasters of 1914.* Ithaca, N.Y.: Cornell University Press, 1984.

Sokolovskiy, V. D. *Soviet Military Strategy,* 3d ed. (Harriet F. Scott, ed.) New York: Crane, Russak, 1975.

Spielmann, Karl F. *Analyzing Soviet Strategic Arms Decisions.* Boulder, Colo.: Westview Press, 1978.

Sprout, Harold, and Margaret Sprout. *The Ecological Perspective on Human Affairs with Special Reference to International Politics.* Princeton, N.J.: Princeton University Press, 1965.

Spykman, Nicholas J. *The Geography of the Peace.* New York: Harcourt, Brace, 1944.

_____. *America's Strategy in World Politics: The United States and the Balance of Power.* Hamden, Conn.: Archon, 1970; first pub. 1942.

Steinberg, Jonathan. *Yesterday's Deterrent: Tirpitz and the Birth of the German Battle Fleet.* London: MacDonald, 1965.

Steinbruner, John. *The Cybernetic Theory of Decision: New Dimensions of Political Analysis.* Princeton, N.J.: Princeton University Press, 1974.

Steinbruner, John, and Leon V. Sigal, eds. *Alliance Security: NATO and the No-First-Use-Question.* Washington, D.C.: Brookings, 1983.

Stone, Norman. *The Eastern Front, 1914–1917.* London: Hodder and Stoughton, 1975.

Strachan, Hew. *European Armies and the Conduct of War.* London: Allen and Unwin, 1983.

Sullivan, David. *Soviet SALT Deception.* Boston, Va.: Coalition for Peace Through Strength, 1979.

Summers, Harry G., Jr. *On Strategy: A Critical Analysis of the Vietnam War.* Novato, Calif.: Presidio Press, 1982.

Sun Tzu. *The Art of War* (trans. by Samuel B. Griffith). Oxford: Clarendon Press, 1963.

Szamuely, Tibor. *The Russian Tradition.* New York: McGraw-Hill, 1974.

Talbott, Strobe. *Endgame: The Inside Story of SALT II.* New York: Harper & Row, 1979.

_____. *Deadly Gambits: The Reagan Administration and the Stalemate in Nuclear Arms Control.* New York: Knopf, 1984.

_____. *The Russians and Reagan.* New York: Vintage, 1984.

Thornton, A. P. *The Imperial Idea and Its Enemies.* London: Macmillan, 1963.

_____. *For the File on Empire: Essays and Reviews.* London: Macmillan, 1968.

Thucydides. *The Peloponnesian War*. London: Penguin, 1954.

Tuchman, Barbara. *The Guns of August—August 1914*. London: Constable, 1962.

Turner, L. C. F. *Origins of the First World War*. London: Arnold, 1976.

Union of Concerned Scientists. *Space-Based Missile Defense*. Cambridge, Mass.: Union of Concerned Scientists, March 1984.

Ury, William L. *Beyond the Hotline: How Crisis Control Can Prevent Nuclear War*. Boston: Houghton Mifflin, 1985.

Vigor, P. H. *The Soviet View of War, Peace, and Neutrality*. London: Routledge and Kegan Paul, 1975.

———. *Soviet Blitzkrieg Theory*. New York: St. Martin's, 1983.

Walzer, Michael. *Just and Unjust Wars: A Moral Argument with Historical Illustrations*. New York: Basic Books, 1977.

Weigley, Russell F. *The American Way of War*. New York: Macmillan, 1973.

———. *Eisenhower's Lieutenants: The Campaigns of France and Germany, 1944–1945*. Bloomington: Indiana University Press, 1981.

White, Stephen. *Political Culture and Soviet Politics*. London: Macmillan, 1979.

Wieseltier, Leon. *Nuclear War, Nuclear Peace*. New York: Holt, Rinehart, and Winston, 1983.

Wight, Martin. *Systems of States*. Leicester (U.K.): Leicester University Press, 1977.

———. *Power Politics*. New York: Holmes and Meier, 1978.

Williams, Phil. *Crisis Management: Confrontation and Diplomacy in the Nuclear Age*. London: Croom, Helm, 1976.

Wohl, Robert. *The Generation of 1914*. London: Weidenfeld and Nicolson, 1980.

Wolfe, Thomas W. *The SALT Experience*. Cambridge, Mass.: Ballinger, 1979.

Wolfers, Arnold. *Discord and Collaboration: Essays on International Politics*. Baltimore: Johns Hopkins University Press, 1962.

Wright, P. J., ed. *Theory and Practice of the Balance of Power, 1486–1914: Selected European Writings*. London: Dent, 1975.

Yergin, Daniel. *Shattered Peace: The Origins of the Cold War and the National Security State*. Boston: Houghton Mifflin, 1977.

York, Herbert. *Race to Oblivion: A Participant's View of the Arms Race*. New York: Simon and Schuster, 1971.

CHAPTERS IN BOOKS

Aspaturian, Vernon V. "The Anatomy of the Soviet Empire: Vulnerabilities and Strengths." In Keith A. Dunn and William O. Staudenmaier, eds., *Military Strategy in Transition: Defense and Deterrence in the 1980s*. Carlisle Barracks, Pa.: U.S. Army War College, 1984, pp. 97–146.

Bathurst, Robert. "Two Languages of War." In Derek Leebaert, ed., *Soviet Military Thinking*. London: Allen and Unwin, 1981, pp. 28–49.

Booth, Ken. "American Strategy: The Myths Revisited." In Ken Booth and Moorhead Wright, eds., *American Thinking About Peace and War*. Hassocks, Sussex (U.K.): Harvester, 1978, pp. 1–35.

Brennan, Donald G. "The Case for Population Defense." In Johan J. Holst and William Schneider, Jr., eds., *Why ABM? Policy Issues in the Missile Defense Controversy*. New York: Pergamon Press, 1969, pp. 91–117.

Cohen, Eliot. "Guessing Game: A Reappraisal of Systems Analysis." In Samuel P. Huntington, ed., *The Strategic Imperative: New Policies for American Security*. Cambridge, Mass.: Ballinger, 1982, pp. 163–91.

Crowe, Sir Eyre. "England's Foreign Policy." In Robert L. Pfaltzgraff, Jr., ed., *Politics and the International System*. Philadelphia: Lippincott, 1969, pp. 384–88.

Erickson, John. "Soviet Theater Warfare Capability: Doctrines, Deployments, and Capabilities," In Laurence L. Whetten, ed., *The Future of Soviet Military Power*. New York: Crane, Russak, 1976, pp. 117–56.

_____. "The Soviet Military System: Doctrine, Technology, and 'Style.' " In John Erickson and E. J. Feuchtwanger, eds., *Soviet Military Power and Performance*. Hamden, Conn.: Archon, 1979, pp. 24–35.

Fabyanic, Thomas A. "Triad Without Trilogy: Strategic Analysis, Strategy, and Strategic Programs in the Reagan Administration." In Stephen J. Cimbala, ed., *National Security Strategy: Choices and Limits*. New York: Praeger, 1984, pp. 237-65.

Gray, Colin S. "Mobilization for High-Level Conflict: Policy Issues." In Robert L. Pfaltzgraff, Jr., and Uri Ra'anan, eds., *The U.S. Defense Mobilization Infrastructure: Problems and Priorities*. Hamden, Conn.: Archon, 1983, pp. 33–49.

_____. "Arms Control: Problems." In R. James Woolsey, ed., *Nuclear Arms: Ethics, Strategy, Politics*. San Francisco: Institute for Contemporary Studies, 1984, pp. 153–69.

_____. "American Strategic Culture and Military Performance." In Asa A. Clark IV et al, eds., *Military Technology*. Baltimore: Johns Hopkins University Press, forthcoming.

Harris, William R. "Breaches of Arms Control Obligations and Their Implications." In Richard F. Staar, ed., *Arms Control: Myth Versus Reality*. Stanford, Calif.: Hoover Institution Press, 1984, pp. 134–53.

Holst, Johan J. "Strategic Arms Control and Stability: A Retrospective Look." In Johan J. Holst and William Schneider, Jr., eds., *Why ABM? Policy Issues in the Missile Defense Controversy*. New York: Pergamon Press, 1969, pp. 245–84.

_____. "Comparative U.S. and Soviet Deployments, Doctrines, and Arms Limitations." In Morton A. Kaplan, ed., *SALT: Problems and Prospects*. Morristown, N.Y.: General Learning Press, 1973, pp. 53-95.

Howard, Michael. "The British Way in Warfare: A Reappraisal." In Michael Howard, *The Causes of Wars and Other Essays*. London: Unwin, 1983, pp. 189–207.

Huntington, Samuel P. "The Renewal of Strategy." In Samuel P. Huntington, ed., *The Strategic Imperative: New Policies for American Security*. Cambridge, Mass.: Ballinger, 1982, pp. 1–52.

Kahn, Herman. "On Establishing a Context for Debate." In Frank E. Armbruster et al., *Can We Win in Vietnam? The American Dilemma*. London: Pall Mall, 1968, pp. 19–63.

Kaufmann, William. "The Requirements of Deterrence." In William Kaufmann, ed., *Military Power and National Security*. Princeton, N.J.: Princeton University Press, 1956, pp. 12–38.

Kennedy, Paul. "Japanese Strategic Decisions, 1939–1945." In Paul Kennedy, *Strategy and Diplomacy, 1870-1945: Eight Studies*. London: Allen and Unwin, 1983, pp. 181–95.

———. "Strategic Aspects of the Anglo-German Naval Race." In Paul Kennedy, ed., *Strategy and Diplomacy, 1870-1945: Eight Studies*. London: Allen and Unwin, 1983, pp. 127–60.

Kime, Steve F. "The Soviet View of War." In Graham D. Vernon, ed., *Soviet Perceptions of War and Peace*. Washington, D.C.: National Defense University Press, 1981, pp. 51–65.

Lambeth, Benjamin S. "The Sources of Soviet Military Doctrine." In Frank B. Horton III et al., eds., *Comparative Defense Policy*. Baltimore: Johns Hopkins University Press, 1974, pp. 200–16.

Legvold, Robert. "Military Power in International Politics: Soviet Doctrine on Its Centrality and Instrumentality." In Uwe Nerlich, ed., *Soviet Power and Western Negotiating Policies, Vol. I: The Soviet Asset: Military Power in the Competition over Europe*. Cambridge, Mass.: Ballinger, 1983, pp. 123–59.

Lind, William S. "The Case for Maneuver Doctrine." In Asa A. Clark IV et al., eds., *The Defense Reform Debate: Issues and Analysis*. Baltimore: Johns Hopkins University Press, 1984, pp. 88–100.

Luttwak, Edward N. "On the Meaning of Strategy . . . for the United States in the 1980s." In W. Scott Thompson, ed., *National Security in the 1980s: From Weakness to Strength*. San Francisco: Institute for Contemporary Studies, 1980, pp. 259–73.

McClelland, Charles A. "The Acute International Crisis." In Klaus Knorr and Sydney Verba, eds., *The International System: Theoretical Essays*. Princeton, N.J.: Princeton University Press, 1961, pp. 182–204.

Marshall, Andrew W. "Arms Competitions: The Status of Analysis." In Uwe Nerlich, ed., *Soviet Power and Western Negotiating Policies, Vol. 2: The Western Panacea, Constraining Soviet Power Through Negotiations*. Cambridge, Mass.: Ballinger, 1983, pp. 3–19.

Marshall, Charles Burton. "Arms Control: History and Theory." In Richard

Staar, ed., *Arms Control: Myth Versus Reality*. Stanford, Calif.: Hoover Institution Press, 1984, pp. 180–88.

Mayer, Arno J. "The Problems of Peacemaking." In Hans W. Gatzke, ed., *European Diplomacy Between Two World Wars, 1919–1939*. Chicago: Quadrangle, 1972, pp. 14–39.

Nuechterlein, Donald E. "National Interests and National Strategy: A Need for Priority." In Terry L. Heyns, ed., *Understanding U.S. Strategy: A Reader*. Washington, D.C.: National Defense University Press, 1983, pp. 35–63.

Osgood, Robert E. "The Post-War Strategy of Limited War: Before, During and After Vietnam." In Laurence Martin, ed., *Strategic Thought in the Nuclear Age*. Baltimore: Johns Hopkins University Press, 1979, pp. 93–130.

Pipes, Richard. "Soviet Political Dynamics." In *Soviet Dynamics—Political, Economic, Military*. Pittsburgh: World Affairs Council of Pittsburgh, 1978, pp. 19–29.

_____. "Diplomacy and Culture: Negotiation Styles." In Richard F. Staar, ed., *Arms Control: Myth Versus Reality*. Stanford, Calif.: Hoover Institution Press, 1984, pp. 153–62.

Rader, Ronald R. "Anglo-French Estimates of the Red Army, 1936–1937." In David R. Jones, ed., *Soviet Armed Forces Review Annual, Vol. 3, 1979*. Gulf Breeze, Fla.: Academic International Press, 1979, pp. 265–80.

Rakowska-Harmstone, Teresa. "The Soviet Army as an Instrument of National Integration." In John Erickson and E. J. Feuchtwanger, eds., *Soviet Military Power and Performance*. Hamden, Conn.: Archon, 1979, pp. 129-54.

Ropp, Theodore. "Strategic Thinking Since 1945." In Robert O'Neill and D. M. Horner, eds., *New Directions in Strategic Thinking*. London: Allen and Unwin, 1981, pp. 1–13.

Rosen, Stephen Peter. "Foreign Policy and Nuclear Weapons: The Case for Strategic Defense." In Samuel P. Huntington, ed., *The Strategic Imperative: New Policies for American Security*. Cambridge, Mass.: Ballinger, 1982, pp. 141–61.

Rowen, Henry S. "The Evolution of Strategic Nuclear Doctrine." In Laurence Martin, ed., *Strategic Thought in the Nuclear Age*. Baltimore: Johns Hopkins University Press, 1979, pp. 131–56.

Schelling, Thomas C. "Reciprocal Measures for Arms Stabilization." In Donald G. Brennan, ed., *Arms Control, Disarmament, and National Security*. New York: Braziller, 1961, pp. 167–86.

Sloss, Leon. "The Strategist's Perspective." In Ashton B. Carter and David N. Schwartz, eds., *Ballistic Missile Defense*. Washington, D.C.: Brookings, 1984, pp. 24–48.

Snyder, Glenn. "Deterrence by Denial and Punishment." In Davis Bobrow, ed., *Components of Defense Policy*. Chicago: Rand McNally, 1965, pp. 209–37.

Stone, Norman. "The Historical Background of the Red Army." In John Erickson and E. J. Feuchtwanger, eds., *Soviet Military Power and Performance.* Hamden, Conn.: Archon, 1979, pp. 3–17.

Turner, L. C. F. "The Russian Mobilization in 1914." In Paul M. Kennedy, ed., *The War Plans of the Great Powers, 1880–1914.* London: Allen and Unwin, 1979, pp. 252–68.

———. "The Significance of the Schlieffen Plan." In Paul M. Kennedy, ed., *The War Plans of the Great Powers, 1880–1914.* London: Allen and Unwin, 1979, pp. 199–221.

"U.S. Objectives with Respect to Russia, NSC 20/1, August 18, 1948 (Top Secret)." In Thomas H. Etzold and John L. Gaddis, eds., *Containment: Documents on American Policy and Strategy, 1945–1950.* New York: Columbia University Press, 1978, pp. 173–203.

Van Cleave, William R. "The Arms Control Record: Successes and Failures." In Richard F. Staar, ed., *Arms Control: Myth and Reality.* Stanford, Calif.: Hoover Institution Press, 1984, pp. 1–23.

Wolfe, Thomas W. "The Convergence Issue and Soviet Strategic Policy." In *RAND 25th Anniversary Volume.* Santa Monica, Calif.: RAND Corporation, 1973.

Zavizion, General-Lieutenant G. T., and Lieutenant Colonel Yu. Kirshin. "Soviet Military Science: Its Social Role and Functions." In *Selected Soviet Military Writings, 1970–1975 (A Soviet View).* Soviet Military Thought Series of the U.S. Air Force, No. 11. Washington, D.C.: USGPO, 1977, pp. 76–85.

JOURNAL ARTICLES AND SERIES PUBLICATIONS

Adams, Benson D. "In Defense of the Homeland." *U.S. Naval Institute Proceedings* 109, no. 6(June 1983): 44–49.

Alexander, Arthur J. *Decision-Making in Soviet Weapons Procurement.* Adelphi Papers Nos. 147–48. London: International Institute for Strategic Studies, Winter 1978–79.

Allison, Graham T., and Frederic A. Morris. "Armaments and Arms Control: Exploring the Determinants of Military Weapons." *Daedalus* 104, no. 3(Summer 1975): 99–129.

Arnett, Robert. "Soviet Attitudes Towards Nuclear War: Do They Really Think They Can Win?" *Journal of Strategic Studies* 2, no. 2(September 1979): 172–91.

Baldwin, David A. "The Power of Positive Sanctions." *World Politics* 24, no. 1(October 1974): 19–38.

Ball, Desmond. *Déja Vu: The Return to Counterforce in the Nixon Administration.* Santa Monica, Calif.: California Seminar on Arms Control and Foreign Policy, December 1974.

_____. *Developments in U.S. Strategic Nuclear Policy Under the Carter Administration.* ACIS Working Paper No. 21. Los Angeles: UCLA, Center for International and Strategic Affairs, February 1980.

_____. *Can Nuclear War Be Controlled?* Adelphi Papers No. 169. London: International Institute for Strategic Studies, Autumn 1981.

_____. *Targeting for Strategic Deterrence.* Adelphi Papers No. 185. London: International Institute for Strategic Studies, Summer 1983.

Ball, George W. "The Cosmic Bluff." *New York Review of Books* 30, no. 12(July 21, 1983): 37–41.

Betts, Richard. "Surprise Attack: NATO's Political Vulnerability." *International Security* 5, no. 4(Spring 1981): 117–49.

Blechman, Barry. "Do Negotiated Arms Limitations Have a Future?" *Foreign Affairs* 59, no. 1(Fall 1980): 102–25.

Bondarenko, V. M. "The Modern Revolution in Military Affairs and the Combat Readiness of the Armed Forces." *Communist of the Armed Forces,* December 1968, p. 29.

Bozeman, Adda. "Book review of Ken Booth's *Strategy and Ethnocentrism.*" *Survival* 22, no. 4(July/August 1980): 187–88.

Bracken, Paul. "Mobilization in the Nuclear Age." *International Security* 3, no. 3(Winter 1978–79): 74–93.

Brecher, Michael, and Jonathan Wilkenfeld. "Crises in World Politics." *World Politics* 34, no. 3(April 1982): 380–417.

Brennan, Donald G. "Soviet-American Communications in Crises." *Arms Control and National Security* 1(1969): 81–88.

_____. "The Case for Missile Defense," *Foreign Affairs* 43, no. 3(April 1969): 633–48.

Brodie, Bernard. "Strategy as a Science." *World Politics* 1, no. 4(July 1949): 476–88.

_____. "The McNamara Phenomenon." *World Politics* 17, no. 4(July 1965): 672–86.

_____. "The Development of Nuclear Strategy." *International Security* 2, No. 4(Spring 1978): 65–83.

Brown, Archie. "Gorbachev: New Man in the Kremlin," *Problems of Communism* 36, no. 3(May–June 1985): 1–23.

Buchan, Glenn. "The Anti-MAD Mythology." *Bulletin of the Atomic Scientists* 37, no. 4(April 1980): 13–17.

Bull, Hedley. "European Self-Reliance and the Reform of NATO." *Foreign Affairs* 61, no. 4(Spring 1983): 874–92.

Bundy, McGeorge. "To Cap the Volcano." *Foreign Affairs* 48, no. 1(October 1969): 1–20.

_____. "Maintaining Stable Deterrence." *International Security* 3, no. 3(Winter 1978–79): 5–16.

Bundy, McGeorge, George F. Kennan, Robert S. McNamara, and Gerard Smith. "The President's Choice: Star Wars or Arms Control." *Foreign Affairs* 63, no. 2(Winter 1984–85): 264–78.

Burt, Richard. "Arms Control and Soviet Strategic Forces: The Risks of Asking SALT to Do Too Much." *Washington Review* 1, no. 1(January 1978): 19–33.

———. "A Glass Half Empty." *Foreign Policy*, no. 36(Fall 1979): 33–48.

———. "Reassessing the Strategic Balance." *International Security* 5, no. 1(Summer 1980): 37–52.

———. "The Relevance of Arms Control in the 1980s." *Daedalus* 110, no. 1(Winter 1981): 159–77.

Buzzard, Anthony. "Massive Retaliation and Graduated Deterrence." *World Politics* 8, no. 2(January 1956): 228–37.

Carnesale, Albert. "Reviving the ABM Debate." *Arms Control Today* 11, no. 4(April 1981): 1–2, 6–8.

Carter, Ashton B. "The Command and Control of Nuclear War." *Scientific American* 252, no. 1(January 1985): 32–39.

Chayes, Abram. "Nuclear Arms Control After the Cold War." *Daedalus* 104, no. 3(Summer 1975): 15–33.

Cleveland, Harland. "Crisis Diplomacy." *Foreign Affairs* 41, no. 4(July 1963): 638–49.

Cohen, Eliot A. "The Long-term Crisis of the Alliance." *Foreign Affairs* 61, no. 2(Winter 1982–83): 325–43.

Cordesman, Anthony H. *Deterrence in the 1980s: Part I: American Strategic Forces and Extended Deterrence.* Adelphi Papers No. 175. London: International Institute for Strategic Studies, Summer 1982.

Creveld, Martin van. "Caesar's Ghost: Military History and the Wars of the Future." *Washington Quarterly* 3, no. 1(Winter 1980): 76–83.

Davis, Lynn Etheridge. *Limited Nuclear Options: Deterrence and the New American Doctrine.* Adelphi Papers No. 121. London: International Institute for Strategic Studies, Winter 1975–76.

Deane, Michael. "The Soviet Assessment of the 'Correlation of Forces': Implications for American Foreign Policy." *Orbis* 20, no. 3(Fall 1976): 625–36.

de Rose, Francois. "Inflexible Response." *Foreign Affairs* 61, no. 1(Fall 1982): 136–50.

Douglass, Joseph D., Jr. "Strategic Planning and Nuclear Inequality." *Orbis* 27, no. 3(Fall 1983): pp. 667–94.

———. "What Happens If Deterrence Fails?" *Defense Science 2001+* 2, no. 5(October 1983): 29–43.

Dunn, Keith A., and William O. Staudenmaier. *Strategic Implications of the Continental-Maritime Debate.* Washington Papers No. 107. New York: Praeger (with the Georgetown Center for Strategic and International Studies), 1984.

Erickson, John. "The Soviet View of Deterrence: A General Survey." *Survival* 24, no. 6(November–December 1982): 242–51.

———. "Toward 1984: Four Decades of Soviet Military Policy." *Air University Review* 35, no. 2(January–February 1984): 30–34.

Ermarth, Fritz. "Contrasts in American and Soviet Strategic Thought." *International Security* 3, no. 2(Fall 1978): 138–55.

Evangelista, Matthew A. "Why the Soviets Buy the Weapons They Do." *World Politics* 36, no. 4(July 1984): 597–618.

Evera, Stephen van. "The Cult of the Offensive and the Origins of the First World War." *International Security* 9, no. 1(Summer 1984): 58–107.

Feiverson, Harold A., and John Duffield. "Stopping the Sea-Based Counterforce Threat." *International Security* 9, no. 1(Summer 1984): 187–202.

Foster, Richard B., and Francis P. Hoeber. "Limited Mobilization: A Strategy for Preparedness and Deterrence." *Orbis* 24, no. 3(Fall 1980): 439–57.

Freedman, Lawrence. "Arms Control: No Hiding Place." *SAIS Review* 3, no. 1(Winter–Spring 1983): 3–11.

_____. "Weapons, Doctrines, and Arms Control." *Washington Quarterly* 7, no. 2(Spring 1984): 8–16.

Friedberg, Aaron L. "A History of the U.S. Strategic 'Doctrine'—1945–1980." *Journal of Strategic Studies* 3, no. 3(December 1980): 37–71.

Frye, Alton. "Strategic Build-Down: A Context for Restraint." *Foreign Affairs* 62, no. 2(Winter 1983–84): 293–317.

Gelb, Leslie H. "A Glass Half Full." *Foreign Policy*, no. 36(Fall 1979): 21–32.

Glaser, Charles L. "Why Even Good Defenses May Be Bad." *International Security* 9, no. 2(Fall 1984): 92–123.

Gormley, Dennis M., and Douglas M. Hart. "Soviet Views on Escalation." *Washington Quarterly* 7, no. 4(Fall 1984): 71–84.

Gouré, Daniel, and Jeffrey R. Cooper. "Conventional Deep Strike: A Critical Look." *Comparative Strategy* 4, no. 3(1984), pp. 215–48.

Gray, Colin S. "Foreign Policy and the Strategic Balance." *Orbis* 18, no. 3(Fall 1974): 706–27.

_____. "Across the Nuclear Divide: Strategic Studies, Past and Present." *International Security* 2, no. 1(Summer 1977): 24–46.

_____. "Nuclear Strategy: The Case for a Theory of Victory." *International Security* 4, no. 1(Summer 1979): 54–87.

_____. "SALT II: The Real Debate." *Policy Review*, no. 10(Fall 1979): 7–22.

_____. "Targeting Problems for Central War." *Naval War College Review* 33, no. 1(January–February 1980): 3–21.

_____. "The Most Dangerous Decade: Historic Mission, Legitimacy, and Dynamics of the Soviet Empire in the 1980s." *Orbis* 25, no. 1(Spring 1981): 13–28.

_____. "Presidential Directive 59: Flawed but Useful." *Parameters* 11, no. 1(March 1981): 29–37.

_____. "Nuclear Strategy: A Regrettable Necessity." *SAIS Review* 3, no. 1(Winter–Spring 1983): 13–28.

_____. "Abiding Realities and Strategic Needs." *Air Force Magazine* 66, no. 7(July 1983): 73–76.

————. "War-Fighting for Deterrence." *Journal of Strategic Studies* 7, no. 1(March 1984): 5–28.

————. "Why an ASAT Treaty Is a Bad Idea." *Aerospace America* 22, no. 4(April 1984): 70–74.

————. "Moscow Is Cheating." *Foreign Policy*, no. 56(Fall 1984): 141–52.

————. "Planning for U.S. Security Interests." *U.S. Naval Institute Proceedings* 110, no. 12(December 1984): 37–43.

————. "Strategic Defense, Deterrence, and the Prospects for Peace." *Ethics* 95, no. 3(April 1985): 659–72.

————. "The Nuclear Winter Thesis and U.S. Strategic Policy," *Washington Quarterly* 8, no. 3(Summer 1985), pp. 85–96.

Colin S. Gray and Keith B. Payne. "Victory Is Possible." *Foreign Policy*, no. 39(Summer 1980): 14-27.

Gray, Robert C. "The Reagan Nuclear Strategy." *Arms Control Today* 13, no. 2(March 1983): 1–3, 9–10.

Green, Philip. "Method and Substance in the Arms Debate." *World Politics* 16, no. 4(July 1964): 642–67.

————. "Science Government and the Case of RAND: A Singular Pluralism." *World Politics* 20, no. 2(January 1968): 301–26.

Griffiths, Franklyn. "The Sources of American Conduct: Soviet Perspectives and Their Policy Implications." *International Security* 9, no. 2(Fall 1984): 3–50.

Hanson, Donald W. "Is Soviet Strategic Doctrine Superior?" *International Security* 7, no. 3(Winter 1982–83): 61–83.

Hart, Douglas M. "The Hermeneutics of Soviet Military Doctrine." *Washington Quarterly* 7, no. 2(Spring 1984): 77–88.

Holloway, David. "Technology and Political Decision in Soviet Armaments Policy." *Journal of Peace Research* 4(1974): 257–79.

————. "Military Power and Political Purpose in Soviet Policy." *Daedalus* 109, no. 4(Fall 1980): 13–30.

Holsti, Ole R. "The 1914 Case." *American Political Science Review* 59, no. 2(June 1965): 365–78.

Howard, Michael. "The Forgotten Dimensions of Strategy." *Foreign Affairs* 57, no. 5(Summer 1979): 975–86.

————. "On Fighting a Nuclear War." *International Security* 5, no. 4(Spring 1981): 3–17.

————. "Reassurance and Deterrence: Western Defense in the 1980s." *Foreign Affairs* 61, no. 1(Winter 1982–83): 309–24.

————. "Men Against Fire: Expectations of War in 1914." *International Security* 9, no. 1(Summer 1984): 41–57.

Hunt, Kenneth. *The Alliance and Europe: Part II. Defence with Fewer Men.* Adelphi Papers No. 98. London: International Institute for Strategic Studies, Summer 1973.

Huth, Paul, and Bruce Russett. "What Makes Deterrence Work? Cases from 1900 to 1980." *World Politics* 36, no. 4(July 1984): 496–526.

Iklé, Fred C. "Can Nuclear Deterrence Last Out the Century?" *Foreign Affairs* 51, no. 2(January 1973): 267–85.

_____. "Nuclear Strategy: Can There Be a Happy Ending?" *Foreign Affairs* 63, no. 4(Spring 1985): 810–26.

Jervis, Robert. "Deterrence Theory Revisited." *World Politics* 31, no. 2(January 1979): 289–324.

_____. "Why Nuclear Superiority Doesn't Matter." *Political Science Quarterly* 94, no. 4(Fall 1979): 617–33.

Kaegi, Walter E. "The Crisis in Military Historiography." *Armed Forces and Society* 7, no. 2(Winter 1980): 299–316.

Kahler, Miles. "Rumors of War: The 1914 Analogy." *Foreign Affairs* 58, no. 2(Winter 1979–80): 374–96.

Kahn, Herman. "Issues of Thermonuclear War Termination." *Annals* 392(November 1970): 133–72.

Kass, Ilana, and Michael J. Deane. "The Role of Nuclear Weapons on the Modern Battlefield: The Current Soviet View." *Comparative Strategy* 4, no. 3(1984): 193–213.

Kelly, J. B. "Interview with Richard Quandt." *Near East Report* 25, no. 4(January 23, 1981): 15.

Kime, Steve F. "How the Soviet Union Is Ruled." *Air Force Magazine* 63, no. 3(March 1980): 54–59.

Kincade, William. "A Farewell to Arms Control?" *Arms Control Today* 10, no. 1(January 1980): 1–5.

King, James. "Nuclear Plenty and Limited War." *Foreign Affairs* 35, no. 2(January 1957): 238–56.

Kissinger, Henry A. "Military Policy and Defense of the 'Grey Areas.'" *Foreign Affairs* 33, no. 3(April 1955): 416–28.

_____. "The Future of NATO." *Washington Quarterly* 2, no. 4(Autumn 1979): 3–17.

Komer, Robert W. "The Neglect of Strategy." *Air Force Magazine* 67, no. 3(March 1984): 51–56.

Kortunov, V. "Socialism and International Relations." *International Affairs* (Moscow), no. 10(October 1979): 39–49.

Kugler, Jack, and A. F. K. Organski. "Deterrence and the Arms Race: The Impotence of Power." *International Security* 4, no. 4(Spring 1980): 105–31.

Lambeth, Benjamin S. "The Political Potential of Soviet Equivalence." *International Security* 4, no. 2(Fall 1979): 23–39.

_____. "Uncertainties for the Soviet War Planner." *International Security* 7, no. 3(Winter 1982–83): 139–66.

_____. "On Thresholds in Soviet Military Thought." *Washington Quarterly* 7, no. 2(Spring 1984): 69–76.

————, and Kevin N. Lewis. "Economic Targeting in Nuclear War: U.S. and Soviet Approaches." *Orbis* 27, no. 1(Spring 1983): 127–49.

Lebow, Richard Ned. "Misconceptions in American Strategic Assessment." *Political Science Quarterly* 97, no. 2(Summer 1982): 187–206.

————. "Windows of Opportunity: Do States Jump Through Them?" *International Security* 9, no. 1 (Summer 1984): 147–88.

Legvold, Robert. "Strategic 'Doctrine' and SALT: Soviet and American Views." *Survival* 21, no. 1(January–February 1979): 8–13.

Luttwak, Edward N. *Strategic Power: Military Capabilities and Political Utility*. Washington Papers, vol. IV, no. 38. Beverly Hills, Calif.: Sage, 1976.

————. "Perceptions of Military Force and U. S. Defence Policy." *Survival* 19, no. 1(January–February 1977): 2–8.

————. "A New Arms Race?" *Commentary* 70, no. 3(September 1980): 27–34.

————. "The Problems of Extending Deterrence." In *The Future of Strategic Deterrence, Part I*. Adelphi Papers No. 160. London: International Institute for Strategic Studies, Autumn 1980, pp. 31–37.

————. "The Operational Level of War." *International Security* 5, no. 3(Winter 1980–81): 61–79.

McNamara, Robert S. "Defense Arrangements of the North Atlantic Community." *Department of State Bulletin* 67(July 9, 1962): 67–68.

————. "The Military Role of Nuclear Weapons: Perceptions and Misperceptions." *Foreign Affairs* 62, no. 1(Fall 1983): 59–80.

Mack, John E. "Psychosocial Effects of the Nuclear Arms Race." *Bulletin of the Atomic Scientists* 37, no. 4(April 1981): 18–23.

Maxwell, Stephen. *Rationality in Deterrence*, Adelphi Papers No. 50. London: Institute for Strategic Studies, August 1968.

Metcalf, A. G. B. "The Minuteman Vulnerability Myth and the MX." *Strategic Review* 11, no. 2(Spring 1983): 7–9.

Moody, Peter R. "Clausewitz and the Fading Dialectic of War." *World Politics* 31, no. 3(April 1979): 417–33.

Nitze, Paul. "Deterring Our Deterrent." *Foreign Policy*, no. 25(Winter 1976–77): 195–210.

————. "Strategy in the Decade of the 1980s." *Foreign Affairs* 59, no. 1(Fall 1980): 82–101.

————. "The Objectives of Arms Control," *Survival* 27, no. 3(May/June 1985): 98–107.

"NSC-68: A Report to the National Security Council." *Naval War College Review* 27, no. 6(May–June 1975): 51–108.

Odom, William E. "Who Controls Whom In Moscow." *Foreign Policy*, no. 19(Summer 1975): 109–23.

————. "The 'Militarization' of Soviet Society." *Problems of Communism* 25, no. 5(September–October 1976): 34–51.

_____. "The Soviet Approach to Nuclear Weapons: A Historical Review." *Annals* 469(September 1983): 117–35.

"Ogarkov on Implications of Military Technology." *Survival* 26, no. 4(July–August 1984): 187–88.

Owens, Mackubin Thomas. "The Utility of Force." *Backgrounder* (Heritage Foundation), no. 370, August 1, 1984.

Panofsky, Wolfgang K. H. "The Mutual Hostage Relationship Between America and Russia." *Foreign Affairs* 52, no. 1(October 1973): 109–18.

Payne, Keith B. "Are They Interested in Stability: The Soviet View of Intervention." *Comparative Strategy* 3, no. 1(1981): 1–24.

_____. "Commentary on Robert Scheer's *With Enough Shovels.*" *Comparative Strategy* 4, no. 3(1984): 315–18.

Payne, Keith B. and Colin S. Gray. "Nuclear Policy and the Defensive Transition." *Foreign Affairs* 62, no. 4(Spring 1984): 820-42.

Peterson, Phillip A., and John G. Hines. "The Conventional Offensive in Soviet Theater Strategy." *Orbis* 27, no. 3(Fall 1983): 695–739.

Pierre, Andrew. "The Diplomacy of SALT." *International Security* 5, no. 1(Summer 1980): 178–97.

Pipes, Richard. "Why the Soviet Union Thinks It Could Fight and Win a Nuclear War." *Commentary* 64, no. 1(July 1977): 21–34.

_____. "A Reply" (to Wladislaw G. Krasnow, "Anti-Soviet or Anti-Russian"). *Encounter* 54, no. 4(Spring 1980): 72–75.

_____. "Soviet Global Strategy." *Commentary* 69, no. 4(April 1980): 31–39.

_____. "Militarism and the Soviet State." *Daedalus* 109, no. 4(Fall 1980): 1–12.

_____. "How to Cope with the Soviet Threat: A Long-Term Strategy for the West." *Commentary* 78, no. 2(August 1984): 13–30.

_____. "Can the Soviet Union Reform?" *Foreign Affairs* 63, no. 1(Fall 1984): 47–61.

Powers, Thomas. "What Is It About?" *Atlantic* 253, no. 1(January 1984): 35–55.

Ranger, Robin. "The Four 'Bibles' of Arms Control." *Book Forum* 6, no. 4(1984): 416–32.

Rathjens, George W. "The Dynamics of the Arms Race." *Scientific American* 220, no. 4(April 1969): 15–25.

Ravenal, Earl C. "Counterforce and Alliance: The Ultimate Connection." *International Security* 6, no. 4(Spring 1982): 26–43.

Richelson, Jeffrey. "The Dilemmas of Counterpower Targeting." *Comparative Strategy* 2, no. 3(1980): 223–37.

_____. "PD-59, NSDD-13 and the Reagan Strategic Modernization Program." *Journal of Strategic Studies* 6, no. 2(June 1983): 125–46.

Rogers, Bernard W. "Greater Flexibility for NATO's Flexible Response." *Strategic Review* 11, no. 2(Spring 1983): 11–19.

Rosecrance, Richard. *Strategic Deterrence Reconsidered.* Adelphi Papers

No. 116. London: International Institute for Strategic Studies, Spring 1975.

Rosen, Stephen Peter. "Vietnam and the American Theory of Limited War." *International Security* 7, no. 2(Fall 1982): 83–113.

———. "Systems Analysis and the Quest for Rational Defense." *Public Interest*, no. 76(Summer 1984): 3–16.

Rosenau, James. "Muddling, Meddling and Modelling: Alternative Approaches to the Study of World Politics in an Era of Rapid Change." *Millenium* 8, no. 2(Autumn 1979): 130–44.

Rosenberg, David Alan. "U.S. Nuclear Stockpile, 1945 to 1950." *Bulletin of the Atomic Scientists* 38, no. 5(May 1982): 25–30.

———. "The Origins of Overkill: Nuclear Weapons and American Strategy, 1945–1960." *International Security* 7, no. 4(Spring 1983): 3–71.

Sagan, Carl. "Nuclear War and Climatic Catastrophe." *Foreign Affairs* 62, no. 2(Winter 1983–84): 257–92.

Sagan, Scott. "Review of Robert Dallek's *The American Style of Foreign Policy: Cultural Politics and Foreign Affairs*." *Survival* 25, no. 4(July–August 1983): 191–92.

Schelling, Thomas. *Controlled Response and Strategic Warfare*. Adelphi Papers No. 19. London: Institute for Strategic Studies, June 1965.

Schilling, Warner R. "U.S. Strategic Nuclear Concepts in the 1970s: The Search for Sufficiently Equivalent Countervailing Parity." *International Security* 6, no. 2(Fall 1981): 48–79.

Schlesinger, James." The Eagle and the Bear: Ruminations on Forty Years of Superpower Relations," *Foreign Affairs* 63, no. 5(Summer 1985): 937–61.

Schmidt, Helmut. "Alastair Buchan Memorial Lecture." *Survival* 20, no. 1(January–February 1978): 2–10.

Schoenbaum, David. "The Wehrmacht and G.I. Joe: Learning *What* from History? A Review Essay." *International Security* 8, no. 1(Summer 1983): 201–7.

Schultz, James B. "En Route to End Game Strategic Missile Guidance," *Defense Electronics*, September 1984, pp. 57–63.

Shapley, Deborah. "Technology Creep and the Arms Race: A World of Absolute Accuracy." *Science* 19 (September 1978): 1192–1196.

———. "Arms Control as a Regulator of Military Technology." *Daedalus* 109, no. 1(Winter 1980): 145–57.

Shy, John. "The American Military Experience: History and Learning." *Journal of Interdisciplinary History* 1(Winter 1971): 205–28.

Sigal, Leon V. "Rethinking The Unthinkable." *Foreign Policy*, no. 34 (Spring 1979): 35–51.

Simes, Dimitri. "The Death of Detente?" *International Security* 5, no. 1(Summer 1980): 3–25.

———. "America's New Edge." *Foreign Policy*, no. 56(Fall 1984): 24–43.

Sloan, Stanley R., and Robert C. Gray. *Nuclear Strategy and Arms Control: Challenges for U.S. Policy.* Headline Series, No. 261. New York: Foreign Policy Association, 1982.

Slocombe, Walter B. *The Political Implications of Strategic Parity.* Adelphi Papers No. 77. London: International Institute for Strategic Studies, May 1971.

————. "Extended Deterrence." *Washington Quarterly* 7, no. 4(Fall 1984): 93-103.

Sloss, Leon, and Marc Dean Millot. "U.S. Nuclear Strategy in Evolution." *Strategic Review* 12, no. 1(Winter 1984): 19-28.

Smart, Ian. *Advanced Strategic Missiles: A Short Guide.* Adelphi Papers No. 63. London: Institute for Strategic Studies, December 1969.

Smith, Theresa C. "Arms Race Instability and War." *Journal of Conflict Resolution* 24, no. 2(June 1980): 253-84.

Snyder, Jack. "Civil-Military Relations and the Cult of the Offensive, 1914-1984." *International Security* 9, no. 1(Summer 1984): 108-46.

Solzhenitsyn, Aleksandr. "Misconceptions About Russia Are a Threat to America." *Foreign Affairs* 58, no. 4(Spring 1980): 797-834.

"Soviet Military Spending Increased." *Air Force Magazine* 67, no. 9(September 1984): 33, 35, 37.

Stead, William T. "The White Man's Burden." *Review of Reviews*, February 15, 1900.

Steinbruner, John. "Beyond Rational Deterrence: The Struggle for New Conceptions." *World Politics* 28, no. 2(January 1976): 223-45.

————. "National Security and the Concept of Strategic Stability." *Journal of Conflict Resolution* 22, no. 3(September 1978): 411-28.

————. "Nuclear Decapitation." *Foreign Policy*, no. 45(Winter 1981): 16-28.

Stewart, Blair. "Peacekeeper." *Defense Systems Review and Military Communications*, June 1984, pp. 46-52.

Strode, Dan L., and Rebecca V. Strode, "Diplomacy and Defense in Soviet National Security Policy." *International Security* 8, no. 2(Fall 1983): 91-116.

Strode, Rebecca V. "Soviet Strategic Style." *Comparative Strategy* 3, no. 4(1982): 31-39.

Toner, James H. "American Society and the American Way of War: Korea and Beyond." *Parameters* 11, no. 1(March 1981): 79-90.

Treverton, Gregory F. "Issues and Non-Issues." *Survival* 21, no. 5(September-October 1979): 194-97.

Trofimenko, Henry. *Changing Attitudes Towards Deterrence.* ACIS Working Paper No. 25. Los Angeles: UCLA, Center for International and Strategic Affairs, July 1980.

Tucker, Robert W. "The Nuclear Debate." *Foreign Affairs* 63, no. 1(Fall 1984): 1-32.

Turco, Richard, et al. "The Climatic Effects of Nuclear War." *Scientific American* 251, no. 2(August 1984): 33–43.

Tyushkevich, S. "The Methodology for the Correlation of Forces." *Voyennaya Mysl*, FPD 0008/70, no. 6(June 1969): 26–39.

Ulsamer, Edgar. "The Prospect of Superhard Silos." *Air Force Magazine* 67, no. 1(January 1984): 74–77.

Velikhov, E., and A. Kokoshin. "Iaderno oruzhie i dilemmy mezhdunarodnoi bezopasnosti" ["Nuclear Weapons and the Dilemmas of International Security"] *MEMO*, no. 4(April 1985): 33–43.

Vincent, R. J. *Military Power and Political Influence: The Soviet Union and Western Europe.* Adelphi Papers No. 119. London: International Institute for Strategic Studies, Autumn 1975.

Walker, Richard Lee. *Strategic Target Planning: Bridging the Gap Between Theory and Practice.* National Security Affairs Monograph Series 83–9. Washington, D.C.: National Defense University Press, 1983.

Wallop, Malcolm. "Opportunities and Imperatives of Ballistic Missile Defense." *Strategic Review* 6, no. 4(Fall 1979): 13–21.

Warnke, Paul. "Apes On A Treadmill." *Foreign Policy*, no. 18(Spring 1975): 12–29.

Weickhardt, George G. "The World According to Ogarkov." *International Security* 8, no. 4(Spring 1984): 182–85.

Wells, Samuel F. "Sounding the Tocsin: NSC 68 and the Soviet Threat." *International Security* 4, no. 2(Fall 1979): 116–58.

Wiesner, Jerome. "The Cold War Is Dead, but the Arms Race Rumbles On." *Bulletin of the Atomic Scientists* 23, no. 6(June 1967): 6–9.

Wit, Joel S. "American SLBM: Counterforce Options and Strategic Implications." *Survival* 24, no. 4(July–August 1982): 163–74.

Wohlstetter, Albert J. "The Delicate Balance of Terror." *Foreign Affairs* 37, no. 2(January 1959): 211–34.

———. "Illusions of Distance." *Foreign Affairs* 46, no. 2(January 1968): 242–55.

———. "Bishops, Statesmen, and Other Strategists on the Bombing of Innocents." *Commentary* 75, no. 6(June 1983): 15–35.

———. "Between an Unfree World and None: Increasing Our Options," *Foreign Affairs* 63, no. 5(Summer 1985): 962–94.

Woolsey, James R. "The Politics of Vulnerability: 1980–83." *Foreign Affairs* 62, no. 4(Spring 1984): 805–19.

Yost, David. "European Anxieties About Ballistic Missile Defense." *Washington Quarterly* 7, no. 4(Fall 1984): 112–29.

Zimmerman, Peter D. "Will MX Solve the Problem?" *Arms Control Today* 10, no. 1(January 1980): 7–9.

POPULAR MAGAZINE AND NEWSPAPER ARTICLES

Brower, Michael. "Controlled Thermonuclear War." *New Republic,* July 30, 1962, pp. 9–15.

Burt, Richard. "Soviet Nuclear Edge in Mid-80s Is Envisioned by U.S. Intelligence." *New York Times,* May 13, 1980, p. A12.

_____. "After Almost a Decade, the ABM Dispute Resumes." *New York Times,* August 30, 1980, p. 5.

Cohen, William S. "The Arms Build-Down Proposal: How We Got from There to Here." *Washington Post,* October 9, 1983, p. C8.

Conquest, Robert. "Worse to Come?" *New Republic,* January 17, 1980, pp. 29–33.

"Excerpts from Reagan Interview on Policies He Would Follow." *New York Times,* October 2, 1980, p. B13.

Halloran, Richard. "Pentagon Draws Up First Strategy for Fighting a Long Nuclear War." *New York Times,* May 30, 1982, pp. 1, 12.

Kissinger, Henry. "Kissinger's Critique." *Economist.* February 3, 1979, pp. 17–22.

_____. "Should We Try to Defend Against Russia's Missiles?" *Washington Post,* September 23, 1984, p. C8.

Pond, Elizabeth. "European Reflections on Reagan's 'Star Wars' Defense." *Christian Science Monitor,* April 11, 1983, p. 5.

"President's Speech on Military Spending and a New Defense." *New York Times,* March 24, 1983, p. 20.

Record, Jeffrey. "Why Our High-Priced Military Can't Win Battles." *Washington Post,* January 29, 1984, p. D1.

Scheer, Robert. "Pentagon Plan Aims at Victory in Nuclear War." *Los Angeles Times,* August 15, 1982, p. 1.

Van Cleave, William. "A Debate: Are U.S. Defenses Ready, Rusty, or Adequate?" *New York Times,* October 12, 1980, p. E5.

PUBLIC DOCUMENTS

Brown, Harold. *Department of Defense Annual Report, Fiscal Year 1979.* Washington, D.C.: USGPO, February 2, 1978.

_____. *Department of Defense Annual Report, Fiscal Year 1980.* Washington, D.C.: USGPO, January 25, 1979.

_____. *Department of Defense Annual Report, Fiscal Year 1981.* Washington, D.C.: USGPO, January 29, 1980.

_____. Speech at the U.S. Naval War College. Newport, R.I., August 20, 1980.

_____. *Department of Defense Annual Report, Fiscal Year 1982.* Washington, D.C.: USGPO, January 19, 1981.

Hoffman, Fred S. *Ballistic Missile Defenses and U.S. National Security.* Summary Report of the Future Security Strategy Study. Washington, D.C.: Department of Defense, October 1983.

Nixon, Richard. *U.S. Foreign Policy for the 1970s: A New Strategy for Peace.* Washington, D.C.: USGPO, February 1970.

President's Commission on Strategic Forces. *Report.* Washington, D.C.: The White House, April 1983.

_____. *Final Report* (Letter Report to the President), March 21, 1984.

Rowen, Henry. "Formulating Strategic Doctrine." In Commission on the Organization of the Government for the Conduct of Foreign Policy, Vol. 4, Appendix K, *Adequacy of Current Organization: Defense and Arms Control.* Washington, D.C.: USGPO, June 1975, pp. 219–34.

U.S. Congress, Joint Economic Committee, Subcommittee on International Trade, Finance, and Security Economics. *Soviet Defense Trends: A Staff Study,* 98th Cong., 1st sess. Washington, D.C.: USGPO, September 1983.

U.S. Congress, Office of Technology Assessment. *The Effects of Nuclear War.* Washington, D.C.: USGPO, 1980.

U.S. Congress, Senate, Committee on Armed Services. *Military Implications of the Treaty on Limitation of Anti-Ballistic Missile Systems and the Interim Agreement on Limitation of Strategic Offensive Arms, Hearings,* 92nd Cong., 2d sess. Washington, D.C.: USGPO, 1972.

_____. *Department of Defense Authorization for Appropriations for Fiscal Year 1985, the President's Strategic Defense Initiative, Hearings,* Part 6, 98th Cong., 2d sess. Washington: USGPO, March–April 1984.

U.S. Congress, Senate, Committee on Banking, Housing and Urban Affairs. *Civil Defense, Hearing,* 95th Cong., 2d sess. Washington, D.C.: USGPO, January 8, 1979.

U.S. Congress, Senate, Committee on Foreign Relations, *The SALT II Treaty, Hearings,* 96th Cong., 1st sess. Washington, D.C.: USGPO, 1979.

_____. *Nuclear War Strategy, Hearing,* 96th Cong., 2d sess. Washington, D.C.: USGPO, September 16, 1980.

_____. *U.S. Strategic Doctrine, Hearing,* 97th Cong., 2d sess. Washington, D.C.: USGPO, December 14, 1982.

U.S. Department of the Army, Historical Division. *United States Army in the World War, 1917–1919: Policy-Forming Documents, American Expeditionary Forces.* Washington, D.C.: USGPO, 1948.

U.S. Department of Defense. *Defense Against Ballistic Missiles: An Assessment of Technologies and Policy Implications.* Washington, D.C.: Department of Defense, March 6, 1984.

_____. *Report to the Congress on U.S. Policy on ASAT Arms Control,* March 31, 1984.

Weinberger, Caspar W. *Annual Report to the Congress, Fiscal Year 1984.* Washington, D.C.: USGPO, February 1, 1983.
_____. *Annual Report to the Congress, Fiscal Year 1985.* Washington, D.C.: USGPO, February 1, 1984.
_____. *Annual Report to the Congress, Fiscal Year 1986.* Washington, D.C.: USGPO, February 4, 1985.
_____. *Soviet Military Power, 1985.* Washington, D.C.: USGPO, April 1985.
Wildavsky, Aaron. "Rescuing Policy Analysis from PPBS." In U.S. Congress, Senate, Committee on Government Operations, Subcommittee on National Security and International Operations. *Planning—Programming—Budgeting,* 91st Cong., 2d sess. Washington, D.C.: USGPO, 1970, pp. 639–58.

OTHER SOURCES

Barnett, Frank. "Conflict Chess in a Global Mode." Speech at Pepperdine University, January 15, 1980.
Davis, Jacqueline K., et al. *The Soviet Union and Ballistic Missile Defense.* Special Report. Cambridge, Mass.: Institute for Foreign Policy Analysis, 1979.
Douglass, Joseph D., Jr. *A Soviet Selective Targeting Strategy Toward Europe.* Arlington, Va.: System Planning Corporation, August 1977.
Douglass, Joseph D., Jr., and Amoretta M. Hoeber, eds. *Selected Readings from Soviet Military Thought (1963–1973).* SPC Report 854. Arlington, Va.: System Planning Corporation, April 1980.
Erickson, John. "The Soviet View of Nuclear War." Transcript of broadcast on BBC Radio 3, June 19, 1980.
Foster, Richard B. *The Soviet Concept of National Entity Survival.* SSC-TN-7167-1. Arlington, Va.: Strategic Studies Center, SRI International, March 1978.
Gray, Colin S. *The Defense Policy of the Eisenhower Administrations, 1953–1961.* Unpublished doctoral dissertation, Oxford University, 1970.
_____. *Protracted War: The Lessons of History.* Fairfax, Va.: National Institute for Public Policy, 1984.
_____. *Towards Defense Dominance.* Fairfax, Va.: National Institute for Public Policy, September, 1984.
Guthe, Kurt R. *MARS: America's Strategic Retaliatory Doctrine and Its Implications for Force Posture.* Honors thesis, Harvard College, Department of Government, March 1978.
Kanzelberger, Michael W. *American Nuclear Strategy: A Selective Analytic Survey of Threat Concepts for Deterrence and Compellence.* R-1238-AF. Santa Monica, Calif.: RAND Corporation, 1979.
Keenan, Edward L. "Russian Political Culture." Unpublished manuscript.

Cambridge, Mass.: Harvard University, Russian Research Center, July 1976.

King, James. *The New Strategy.* Unpublished manuscript.

Lambeth, Benjamin S. *Selective Nuclear Options in American and Soviet Strategic Policy.* R-2034-DDRE. Santa Monica, Calif.: RAND Corporation, December 1976.

———. *How to Think About Soviet Military Doctrine.* P-5939. Santa Monica, Calif.: RAND Corporation, February 1978.

Luttwak, Edward N. *The Missing Dimension of U.S. Defense Policy: Force, Perceptions and Power.* Alexandria, Va.: Essex Corporation, February 1976.

Payne, Keith B. *Soviet and American Approaches to Escalation.* HI-3208-DP. Croton-on-Hudson, N.Y.: Hudson Institute, July 30, 1980.

Reagan, Ronald. "Strength: Restoring the Margin of Safety." Address to the American Legion National Convention, Boston, August 20, 1980.

Roche, John P. "Moscow and the 'Window of Opportunity': A Cautionary Brief." Unpublished manuscript, 1980.

Schlesinger, James R. *Selected Papers on National Security, 1964–1968.* P-5284. Santa Monica, Calif.: RAND Corporation, September 1974.

Snyder, Jack L. *The Soviet Strategic Culture: Implications for Limited Nuclear Operations.* R-2154-AF. Santa Monica, Calif.: RAND Corporation, September 1977.

Spielmann, Karl F. *The Political Utility of Strategic Superiority: A Preliminary Investigation into the Soviet View.* IDA Paper P-1349. Arlington, Va.: Institute for Defense Analysis, May 1979.

Wohlstetter, Albert, et al. *Protecting U.S. Power to Strike Back in the 1950s and 1960s.* R-290. Santa Monica, Calif.: RAND Corporation, April 1956.

———. *Legends of the Arms Race.* USSI Report 75-1. Washington, D.C.: United States Strategic Institute, 1975.

Index